MW00565136

DRAWN TO FREEDOM

DRAWN TO FREEDOM

Christian Faith Today in Conversation
with the Heidelberg Catechism

Eberhard Busch

Translated by

William H. Rader

WILLIAM B. EERDMANS PUBLISHING COMPANY

GRAND RAPIDS, MICHIGAN / CAMBRIDGE, U.K.

First published as *Der Freiheit Zugetan: Christliche Glaube heute —
im Gespräch mit dem Heidelberger Katechismus*

Published 2010 by
Wm. B. Eerdmans Publishing Co.
2140 Oak Industrial Drive N.E., Grand Rapids, Michigan 49505 /
P.O. Box 163, Cambridge CB3 9PU U.K.
www.eerdmans.com

Printed in the United States of America

15 14 13 12 11 10   7 6 5 4 3 2 1

Library of Congress Cataloging-in-Publication Data

Busch, Eberhard, 1937-
  [Der Freiheit zugetan. English]
  Drawn to freedom: Christian faith today in conversation with the
  Heidelberg catechism / Eberhard Busch; translated by William H. Rader.
       p.   cm.
    ISBN 978-0-8028-6378-2 (pbk.: alk. paper)
  1. Heidelberger Katechismus. 2. Theology, Doctrinal — Popular works.
  3. Liberty — Religious aspects — Reformed Church. 4. Reformed Church —
  Catechisms — History and criticism.   I. Title.

  BX9428.B87   2010
  230'.42 — dc22
                                                       2009050936

Excerpts from *The Heidelberg Catechism*, translated by Lee Barrett,
are reprinted by permission of The Pilgrim Press.

Contents

Translator's Preface

Linking freedom with a catechism may come as something of a surprise. The word "catechism" can suggest dry bones of doctrine, rather than free exploration of ideas. But this book has come to me as a free, fresh, carefully developed, wide-ranging exploration of what it means to answer the question "Why are you called a Christian?" and to see the relevance of the gospel for living in this tangled world. My desire to do the translation stems also from my friendship with the author, whom I have known since we were fellow graduate students in Basel under Karl Barth. The book reflects Eberhard Busch's conversations as a pastor in Switzerland, university professor in Germany, and participant in ecumenical working groups not only in Switzerland, Germany, and eastern Europe, but also in Japan, Canada, Great Britain, and the United States.

Among the issues in the world today that make it seem urgent to help give this book a wider reading, I lift up two. One is that in the country where I am a citizen, the United States, freedom is spoken of a great deal. However, many of its people, despite the nation's great wealth, feel isolated, fearful of terrorism, caught in powers and systems that seem overwhelming. As a result, many are searching, sometimes almost frantically, for meaning. Some find it in being an American. America wants to use its political and military power to defend freedom and to further it throughout the world, and the ventures this has involved us in become ever more costly for the world. Yet there often does not seem to be reflection about what the word "freedom" means. The rough and ready characterization of freedom one sometimes hears in America is: "My freedom ends where the other person's nose begins." While this view keeps freedom from being absolute willfulness, it pictures the other person as an obstacle to my freedom. Eberhard Busch proposes that freedom is really the opposite: freedom is found only in relationship. Here the deep connection with the Heidelberg Catechism becomes evident. For the catechism begins by talking, not about freedom in the sense usually thought of — independence — but about belonging. Professor Busch affirms gladly that freedom is not freedom from others, but freedom with others, in conversation with them, in walking with them. Above all, and before all, it is the freedom chosen by God in which Jesus Christ makes us free. And Jesus comes to us not apart from others. The others are by no means limited to those presently living on earth, but include those who have gone before us, such as the authors of the Heidelberg Catechism, as well as philosophers, musicians, poets, scientists, and theologians past and present, with whom the author converses in this work.

A second issue is the glaring chasm in the body of Christ, especially within the United States, between those members on the one hand who are anxious that faith be related to issues of individual and family morality, but tend not to question the morality of the directions their government is taking, and those on the other hand whose view is wider, and who look at these directions with a critical eye. Conversation between members of these two groups has become increasingly difficult. Because Eberhard Busch gives close attention to both individual and social concerns, linking the inward with the outward journey, I hope the reflection on the gospel he offers will encourage both sides to do critical rethinking of their stances and to engage in conversation with one another.

Among the chief requisites for fruitful conversation are that participants listen carefully to one another and that they are open about where they are coming from. In addition to listening to the Heidelberg Catechism and above all to the Bible, Professor Busch listens carefully to those who are of different convictions, who sometimes raise questions and objections, make counter-proposals and denials, and present alternative views. Also, from the outset, Professor Busch carefully explains where he is coming from and how he believes theology should go about its work. Following the example of the Heidelberg Catechism he uses very few technical theological terms.

The English translation of the Heidelberg Catechism used is by Lee Barrett III, *The Heidelberg Catechism: A New Translation for the 21st Century* (Cleveland: The Pilgrim Press, 2007). In isolated cases the translation authorized by the Christian Reformed Church (Grand Rapids, 1998) or the

400th Anniversary edition by Allen O. Miller and M. Eugene Osterhaven (Cleveland: United Church Press, 1962) is used, as indicated by asterisks. For quotations from the Bible I use the New Revised Standard Version except for a few quotations from the New International Version, Today's English Version, or the Jewish Study Bible, indicated by asterisks. Where English translations of works could be found, these are designated in the footnotes with the letters ET. Otherwise, translations of quotations, including those from hymns, are my own. For the frequently cited *Church Dogmatics* of Karl Barth, the abbreviation *KD* (for *Kirchliche Dogmatik*) is first used, followed by *CD*. For Martin Luther, *WA* (for the Weimar Edition) is followed by *LW* (for Luther's Works).

I express my thanks to Eberhard Busch for allowing this translation, and for giving encouragement and counsel; to Richard Berg, Director of Library Services in Lancaster Theological Seminary; to my family for support, in particular to our daughter-in-law Elke, fluent in both languages. Finally, I thank my wife, Clara, for constant encouragement, careful reading, and helpful suggestions, from the perspective of a college teacher of English composition.

WILLIAM RADER
Dauphin, Pennsylvania

Author's Preface

"Drawn to freedom" — the title picks up on a characteristic affirmation of the Reformer Ulrich Zwingli: "God favors freedom." And this is the good news: that God puts God's own freedom on the line in order to "demonstrate to humanity real favor." God is *so* committed to freedom that God wants to give humans their own freedom. Yet the humans to whom this good news is directed are not free. A person becomes free in being freed by God. One *becomes* free as did the man in the grave when Jesus called with a loud voice: "Lazarus, *come out!*" And the man bound hand and foot and robbed of the light of day *"came out"* (John 11:43f.). This is how a person becomes "drawn" to freedom and its right use. The title of this book intends to indicate the sum of the message with which the Christian movement is entrusted, and which it is the task of its theology to think through.

There is good reason to think it through. More than a hundred years ago the theologian D. F. Strauss put to himself and his contemporaries the question, "Are we still Christians?" and answered with a resounding No. He added the further question, "But do we still have religion?" and answered this with a definite Yes. Strauss was clear-sighted enough to understand that the Yes to the latter question in no way, not even tacitly, means a Yes to the first question, but can mean a No to it. One at times has the impression that our situation today is similar to the one then — perhaps with the difference that the awareness of what Strauss was so clear-sighted about seems to have dwindled. The difficulty this points to is not easily overcome, and surely not by shouting unreflectively Yes to the question about whether we are still Christians. But the task indeed remains, and the question "Why are you called a Christian?" (Heidelberg Catechism, Question 32) needs to be seen and tackled.

To answer this question is the task being undertaken here. This will be done in the comprehensive way in which it has always been done in the catechisms of the church: an attempt is made to understand the Apostles' Creed along with the Prayer of Jesus and the Ten Commandments. The following exposition will include both a theological and an ethical dimension. We cannot speak of what God does for us without also speaking of what God wants with us and from us. We cannot *believe* in God without *confessing* God with the action of our lives.

The intention here is to interpret the confession of faith in this way, to help people in our time think through and reflect on the great and inexhaustible treasure of the assurance and claim of the gospel, and to encourage them to do their own confessing of Christian faith in the challenges of our time.

Because church history does not begin with us, the book proceeds by giving its interpretation in ongoing conversation with one of the classic texts of the church's past: the Heidelberg Catechism of 1563. The primary purpose is not to understand the Heidelberg Catechism, but rather *through it* to understand what it means for us to believe in the merciful and just triune God. This is our God today, who always was our God, and will be our God tomorrow. The following text is understandable in itself, even if you do not have the catechism at hand. Of course it is preferable to have it at hand, and I hope that this book will whet your appetite to do this. As a rule, I follow the newly revised version of the text: Neukirchener Verlag, 1997. Where I refer to the original wording, this is indicated. The individual sections of the catechism, which are composed of a question and an answer, I designate with the term Article (abbreviated as Art. in parentheses). I follow the widespread usage that instead of "Heidelberg Catechism" speaks in a shorthand way of "Heidelberg."

I thank the Evangelical-Reformed Church, the Evangelical Church in the Rhineland, in the Palatinate, and in Hesse-Nassau for their friendly provision of subsidies for printing costs. In writing the book I had the students in the Theological Faculty of Göttingen in mind, but also a whole series of congregations with which I have come in contact.

I dedicate this book to the Theological Institute in Klausenburg, Romania, in thankfulness for their granting me an honorary doctorate.

EBERHARD BUSCH
Göttingen, June 1998

Sources Frequently Cited

Karl Barth, *Die Kirchliche Dogmatik* (abbreviated as *KD*), 13 vols. (Zurich, 1932-1967).

English translation: *Church Dogmatics* (abbreviated as *CD*), 13 vols. (Edinburgh: T. & T. Clark, 1936-1969).

John Calvin, *Institutes of the Christian Religion*, 2 vols., ed. John T. McNeill, trans. Ford Lewis Battles (Philadelphia: Westminster, 1960).

Martin Luther, *D. Martin Luthers Werke: Kritische Gesamtausgabe* (abbreviated as *WA*), 117 vols. (Weimar: Herman Böhlau, 1883-2002).

English Translation: *Luther's Works* (abbreviated as LW), 55 vols., ed. J. Pelikan and H. T. Lehman (Philadelphia: Fortress, 1955-1968).

1. Introductory Explanations

1.1. The Task

"The first step you take, my child, is the one on which the rest of your days depend" (Voltaire). At the beginning of our venture we need to come to a mutual understanding of what theology is and what it aims to achieve, for on this first step the rest of our journey depends. Admittedly, the answer to this question is in dispute. In our time (not for the first time), there are two essentially different conceptions of the meaning and task of Christian theology. Within each of the two conceptions there are of course many conceivable variations, yet each stands in flat contradiction to the other. Sometimes the difference is not easy to recognize. The two at times even merge into one another and are then both represented by the same person. This is no accident. While theology means "speech about God," where Christian theology is involved it must also speak about God *and* humans, and about the relationship between them. But one can speak about this relationship in vastly different ways.

We can make the difference clear by looking at the first question in the Heidelberg Catechism: "What is your only comfort in life and in death?" This can be taken in fundamentally different ways. Let the word "comfort" stand as a kind of summary of what is involved in the Christian confession of faith, which theology reflects on. The question can be formulated in this way: What is really decisive in Christian faith? Or with Paul Tillich: What is our ultimate concern?[1] Theology has to try to give an answer. But theology can take this question in contrasting ways.

1. P. Tillich, *Wesen und Wandel des Glaubens* (Berlin: Verlag Ullstein, 1961), p. 9. ET: *Dynamics of Faith* (New York: Harper, 1958), p. 2.

1

Possibility One: I understand this question as a common human one that wells up from my own head or heart. I thereby consider every person as someone who seeks and asks for comfort, for support, for security, for meaning. Theology is then the endeavor that answers this seeking and asking and says: what you are searching for, or something very much like it, really exists. The Christian tradition, or so-called revelation, or (what amounts to the same thing) religious creeds, have an answer ready for you. Now, a question such as the one thus described is never only a question. It already contains an "answer" within itself. Pascal recognized this in his sentence: "You [human being] would not seek me [God] if you had not found me."[2] This question expresses a particular expectation. In it a person formulates a need to be met and thereby gives the standard for what will satisfy the need. If theology gives an answer, it can basically give only what the questioner wants, according to that person's wishes and corresponding standards. If the answer does not satisfy, the pressure will be on to bend the answer so far, or to read so much into it, that it finally fits the pre-formulated expectation. In one way or another, the answer is basically always replaceable by some answer you like. Why not also by an answer other than Christian — by a Hindu or Buddhist answer, or by a mix of them all, if it satisfies the yearning just as well or better? Yes, consistent representatives of this position have always known that here the human subject not only has in advance the standard which the theological answer must meet, but actually already knows the answer itself. Theology in this vein would then have only the task of being a kind of midwife for the answer I am fully capable of bringing forth myself. This was the fundamental conviction of the philosophy of Socrates. Here theology would have as its object to serve as an activation of common human capabilities. Does not this conception in the final analysis lead to a monologue with oneself? The sinister suspicion of Ludwig Feuerbach will then be hard to dispel — that Christian theology in truth does not deal with God; it deals only with the reflections of its own wishes and yearnings projected into heaven.[3] Here we will not take the path of Possibility One.

Possibility Two: "What is your only comfort in life and in death?" It is also possible, after all, to think that the one who puts this question to us is

2. B. Pascal, *Pensées* (1670), Fragment 553; in *Pascal*, ed. R. Schneider (Frankfurt/Hamburg, 1954), p. 210. ET: *Pensées*, trans. A. J. Krailsheimer (New York: Penguin, 1995), p. 290.

3. L. Feuerbach, *Das Wesen des Christentums* (1841; Leipzig, 1957), e.g., pp. 45ff., 80-90, 270-71. ET: *The Essence of Christianity* (New York: Peter Lang, 1989), pp. 52ff., 93-94, 288-89.

first and last God, and not some human being. Here a human being does not ask, and then theology has to find or formulate a divine answer. On the contrary, God puts me before a question, one indeed that I would not have come to in this way on my own. So I am called on to try to answer. God is not accountable to me to deliver what I have figured out that I desire for myself. It is the other way around. God is the one by whom I am called to responsibility and to whom I am accountable. And theology in this context is a special human undertaking to listen to this question posed by God, and to try to answer it. But the answer is not to come off the top of my head in some arbitrary way. For in this context as well, there is not a question without an answer. God does not ask us what our only comfort in living and in dying is without saying and showing what our only comfort is.

Therefore we cannot begin to answer this question without recognizing that God has already made a beginning with us by preparing such a "comfort" for us. And if God asks what our only comfort in life and in death is, and if Christian theology is to answer this question, then this much is clear: theology does not have to invent the answer. Theology has to discern the answer already given along with the question God puts to us, to express this answer in its own words, and to reflect on the answer. Karl Barth was right when he said: Thinking in theology is thinking after.[4] This means that we do not have to deduce from an inborn human wish for comfort what our only comfort in living and in dying is, in order then to ask whether what we desire exists somewhere. We are to understand what our comfort is from God's own preparing it and presenting it to us, and only in this way.

Here too we cannot seek without already having found, or much rather, having been found by God. To be sure, we cannot be found without immediately having to turn around and seek — because *we are now asked:* What do you say to this? Do you discern it too? Here Paul's words apply (Phil. 3:12): "Not that I have already obtained this . . . but I press on to make it my own, because Jesus Christ has made me his own." In this second conception of theology we can with a good conscience look Feuerbach's suspicion straight in the eye — the suspicion that says Christian theology deals only with reflections of human wishes. Nevertheless, it is clear that in a certain way we are defenseless against this suspicion, because we cannot remove it; only God can remove it — and God has already

---

4. K. Barth, "Denken heisst: Nachdenken," *Zürcher Woche* 15, no. 24 (1963): 5.

removed it. We can and should only think in response to God's initiative. If Christian theology does not want to find itself without an object, it will work along the line of this second possibility, and not the first. Then it will be a meaningful and promising activity. This decision, which needs to be made at the starting point, is in keeping with the Heidelberg Catechism and generally with Reformed theology. When we make it, certain characteristics and structures present themselves for the task of theology on this second track.

1. The object of Christian theology is the gospel: that is, a message which is spoken to me, and which I cannot tell myself. After it has been shared with me, it is not like an instruction manual I do not need anymore once I have grasped how to operate the device it accompanies. This is a message that, once spoken to us, we become dependent on: we need to have it spoken to us again and again. This is the specific way in which the theological object is not at our disposal. It does not consist in the incomprehensibility or hiddenness of a highest being — a hiddenness that ceases or is considerably reduced when God is revealed to us. The God who opens God's own self to us is, and remains, beyond our ability to control. The gospel is the object of theology, and theology's task is to reflect on the gospel. This means that its object is not the abstract existence of some divine being. It is not a general idea or rule of life that can be known always and everywhere. Rather, the gospel is the event, or the history, in which God encounters us, speaks to us, and in this way sets the divine self in relation to us. And this is grace. Although we need God to do this for us, God is not forced to do so. Yes, although we have not deserved it, God nevertheless does it — overcoming the obstacle that we are not worthy.

Now we need to make more precise the thesis proposed earlier: that theology is about the relation between God and humanity. It is not we who set up this relation, as the old and ever-modern Christian mistake runs; God sets it up. It is not we who have to bring humanity into relationship with God. That is the kernel of the old and new clericalism. Instead, we must always proceed from the conviction that God has brought and continues to bring Godself into relationship with us. Because the gospel has this content, it is a joyful message that gladdens head and heart and all our senses. It says: Praise God, we are not alone; God is with us. Again, this gospel is not a general truth, not even a so-called Christian truth, let alone one that could warrant the inflated claim of a Christian absolute. This truth is inseparable from the history, from the person, from the name in which it has presented itself, and again and again presents itself. It is inseparable from the history witnessed to in the Bible then and there, inseparable from the name of Jesus Christ who has come in Israel to the world. The gospel that is the object of theology is the gospel of Jesus Christ. He is the content as well as the author of the gospel. It is right — and today we have renewed understanding of this — that his name is inseparable from the story of Israel and that of the New Testament community. But not to be forgotten is the fact that this twofold story is in turn not separable from his name as the shining light in it. Because theology has this gospel as its object to reflect on, it is above all a "joyful discipline." If it is carried on with a sad face, it has missed its calling.

2. It is indispensable for Christian theology that it is oriented to holy scripture and that it is formed through scripture's witness. While the first form of theology described will also use holy scripture, it will do so through the filter of human wishes. Consequently, such theology will not experience from scripture any good news, but only what it "rediscovers" with this filter — only what it in essence already knows. Therefore it will not be indispensable for this kind of theology to open holy scripture. It will one day find other holy scriptures, read them with devotion, and find just as much or even greater gain. It is true that the Bible always speaks to us in a certain selectivity. But it is one thing for the dilemma to exist that we read scripture again and again with blinders, and quite another that we make out of this dilemma a virtue and a hermeneutical rule. That this venture is a problem, and that we can do something to guard against this problem by at least loosening the blinders a little — this we know only when we recognize the indispensability of the Bible for our theological reflection. It is indispensable because it tells us something that no other book does: only the Bible witnesses to the gospel that took place then and there in a particular history. As the gospel is inseparable from the history that took place then and there, so theology is inseparable from the Bible as the primary, unsurpassed witness of this story.

The Bible gives this witness in various ways, and in doing theology we always have to struggle not to get rid of this variety by reading it with those blinders. (Breaking up scripture into ever more sources and layers can *not* come from joy in its great riches. Rather, it comes from a fierce doggedness to cut out everything that does not fit our "blinders perspective" as "not genuine," as "secondary," as "churchly addition.") Again, it is not Jeremiah or Paul, or any others who as such are binding for us. They are binding only insofar as they witness to and point to that gospel which is taking place. Only "what furthers Christ" is binding in the Bible

(Luther[5]). This is not to be understood as a criterion of selection, but as the reading guide in the use of scripture. In the church's reading of the Bible this guide has proved itself again and again. Since scripture itself suggests this guide, scripture is the primary witness of the gospel, not superseded by another witness. Theology needs to examine all churchly witnesses to see if they agree with this primary witness. Remember the saying of Jean Cocteau: "Most springs are not in agreement with the stream." To this extent theology is necessarily a listening discipline, listening to the witness of scripture. It cannot cease from listening again and again.

3. Christian theology is connected to the Christian church. This is not meant in the ridiculous sense that theology has to let regulations be made by church leadership. Rather, it means that we in Christian theology cannot ignore that we are members of the Christian church and therefore do not do theology as neutral observers. I do not say simply we should not ignore this; I say, we cannot ignore it. For as soon as we ignore it, we will no longer be doing Christian theology, but rather partly a special kind of literary criticism, partly a kind of history of religion. This certainly can take place under God's wide heavens. But it does not change the fact that theology and this other discipline are two different things. That theology as a churchly discipline is carried on in a secular university is surely a strange fact not to be sneezed at. But that dare not seduce us into letting theology give up its task as churchly discipline. That we cannot do Christian theology except as members of the Christian church tells us first of all simply that church history did not begin with us. We would not be where we are today if others had not gone before us. They have no doubt left behind for us all kinds of old burdens. But they have also left manifold witnesses of the gospel. And what is an old burden and what is a witness will be argued about again and again. At any rate, they have dealt with problems that present themselves to us anew, each in its own way. Our questions are never completely new. Others before us have concerned themselves with them and analyzed them. In their struggles, ideas have come that can be helpful to us today. We cannot do theology today without letting those who have gone before converse with us.

Furthermore, Christian theology's being a churchly discipline means something even more basic. H. Gollwitzer rightly declared: "Theology is a

5. M. Luther, *WA*, Die Deutsche Bibel, vol. 7, p. 384, lines 27 and 29. LW35, Preface to the Epistles of St. James and St. Jude, p. 396.

supplementary concern. As theory, it stands between practice and practice." It follows that theology is "neither the mother nor the ruler but the servant of Christian faith and life" in the church.[6] We can illustrate what this means by a remarkable fact. The Reformation broke the medieval rule that clergy did *not* have to study theology in order to enter their vocation. Why did the Reformation break this rule? For this reason: now the *proclamation* of the word of God — instead of the enactment of a mystery — was discovered as the central act of the worship service. The clergy were no longer priests, but preachers, *verbi divini ministri,* servants of the word of God! *Therefore* it was now clear that *for this* the study of theology was needed as a necessity for new church praxis. *Therefore* this study consisted decisively in the study of scripture and in getting ready for continuing this study throughout life. *Therefore* the division of the church into clergy and laity dissolved — which division dare not be repeated in a new division into theologians and non-theologians.

The practice of proclamation, which theology is to serve, does not put *one* (large) part of the congregation into the position of "mere" listeners (much less the kind who listen to experts talk about something the listeners have no understanding of). What would "mere" mean? Before the word, which is what matters, everyone, first of all the proclaimers themselves, are only *listeners.* But all are listeners who *through this word* are addressed as those who give attention to it, who understand, who are responsible, and who think with one another and walk with one another. In this act all are in a basic sense theologians, including the so-called "laity." Take care that this "better part . . . not be taken away" from them (Luke 10:38-42) when one denigrates the proclamation of the word as "too much head stuff"! Often enough those alleged lay people were indeed more theologically informed than the "wise and intelligent," for whom in all their skill God's mystery remained "hidden," according to Jesus' word in Matthew 11:25. This word expresses a real experience in the history of the church — and a limit to all academic theology that needs to be taken seriously. In its connection with the task of the church, theology, in spite of all its theoretical work, is still a practical science.

4. Theology is also an activity in which I myself am always called to *accountability.* I cannot do it without realizing: *tua res agitur* — this has to do with me. I have to take part by engaging all the powers of my understand-

---

6. H. Gollwitzer, *Befreiung zur Solidarität* (Munich, 1984[2]), p. 38. ET: *An Introduction to Protestant Theology* (Philadelphia: Westminster, 1982), p. 35.

ing, but hopefully also of my heart, with my ears, eyes, and mouth. Granted, I do not believe without the Bible, but I do not believe in the Bible; I believe as a member of the church, but I do not believe in the church. This means practically that all the binding of theology to scripture and church does not exclude using my own reason in mature responsibility. So I have to hold to Kant's famous call: *Sapere aude!*[7] Dare to think!

In theology I am ultimately responsible only to God. To be sure, it is the God of the gospel witnessed in the Bible and proclaimed by the church, but only to God. And God is a living God, as surely as Jesus Christ has not remained in death, but has been raised and lives. Because God is living, therefore I myself am to live with God and to hold myself open again and again to God, and God's claim and guidance. This is why in theology I cannot live off the interest from capital once gathered by the church or theology or by my own hard work. This is why in theology I do not one day gain a kind of master key I carry with me and only have to apply in the supposition that it fits all locks. This is why theological work is such a critical activity. In it I may now receive some light and yet in the next moment must ask and seek again, ashamed at the end of the day that I have made so little progress, and joyful the next day that I may begin again and that I may go on with faith, with learning, with hope and love. This vitality of God is not simply identical with the changing demands of the times, through political and social circumstances, through scientific knowledge and economic conditions. These challenges also exist. Today they are no longer the same as yesterday, and we should surely pay careful attention to them. But there is no general recipe that says whether in theology we should open ourselves to them or shut the door. It takes continual attention to the God who is living and speaking today in order to discern how to respond to these challenges. The hard questions are always before us. Should we enter into these challenges now or not? Do we need to join with others in confronting them? Must we perhaps swim against the stream of the majority? A theology that understands this will be a free discipline.

5. Finally, theology is an incomplete activity. Its knowing and reflecting take place within a certain limit we on earth and in time will not go beyond. It takes place, as the old Reformed tradition said of its confessions, and as the chief author of the Heidelberg said of his text, always unavoid-

---

7. I. Kant, *Werke in Zehn Bänden*, ed. W. Weischedel, vol. 9 (Darmstadt, 1968), p. 53. The call "Sapere aude!" can be found in *Kant: Political Writings*, ed. H. Reiss (Cambridge: Cambridge University Press, 1991²), p. 54.

ably under the proviso that we may be taught better through holy scripture.[8] Yes, joyful as this discipline is, even in its limits, it is at the same time like the way of Israel through the desert. We may have the exodus out of the house of slavery in Egypt behind us, but we are not yet in the promised land, toward which we are still wandering, sometimes going astray. John Calvin characterized theological instruction as a "school";[9] and when Friedrich Schleiermacher in advanced age used to add to his name the title "stud. theol."[10] he apparently knew that in this life we are not let out of school. Basically we always stay ABC-pupils, whose spelling skills are not yet up to what really matters. "For we know only in part. . . . For now we see in a mirror, dimly, but then we will see face to face. Now I know only in part; then I will know fully, even as I have been fully known" (1 Cor. 13:9, 12). How inadequate is all that we do — at best an attempt!

You can, despite the joyfulness of the gospel, stand before it in great confusion, because again and again it eludes your grasp, because it so rarely lets itself be hitched to our ideas and programs. It puts us *before* a mystery we cannot get *behind*. You can chafe terribly at the Bible, too, and at the knowledge of being bound to it. Your surveying the organized church, past and present, can get angry juices flowing. You can also really suffer under the burden of theology. And you can finally sigh heavily under your own insufficiency, in and despite all the hard work. Whoever does not know this has only seen theology from the outside. But blessed is the person who does not give up! This one hears the word, "No one who puts a hand to the plow and looks back is fit for the Kingdom of God" (Luke 9:62)! The promise of the kingdom of God is what gives us strength not to let our hand sink from the plow for at least the next step. We will have to ask God again and again not to let this hand become lame. The *"ora et labora,"* the "Pray and work!" are not to be separated in theology. So theology is necessarily also this: a praying discipline, praying for what it cannot give itself.

8. J. Rohls, *Theologie reformierter Bekenntnisschriften* (Göttingen: Vandenhoeck & Ruprecht, 1987), pp. 315ff. ET: *Reformed Confessions: Theology from Zurich to Barmen* (Louisville: Westminster/John Knox, 1998), pp. 265ff.

9. J. Calvin, *Institutes* III.21.3; IV.17.36.

10. K. Barth, *Einführung in die evangelische Theologie* (Zurich, 1962), p. 188. ET: *Evangelical Theology, an Introduction* (Grand Rapids: Eerdmans, 1979), p. 172.

1.2. The Companion Book

Theology has to answer the question put to it — briefly stated: "What is your only comfort?" Since everyone in the church must be able to give an answer to this, we in the church are all theologians. I myself have to answer — but not I alone. In theology I cannot be merely an individual who lets my thoughts run where they will. Therefore I do not answer in unguided fantasy. I can do theology only as a member of the church of Jesus Christ — namely as specific witnesses are set before me, first those of holy scripture and then those of the Christian church. Only as I connect myself with their witness, by taking up their witness and thinking it through again, can I do theology. I would not be a member of the church at all if others in the church before me had not given their answers to this question. It makes sense therefore that theology cannot avoid working with texts.

The book that will accompany the following reflection on the Christian confession of faith is the Heidelberg Catechism, which is among the most widely used and influential texts of the Reformation period. It is especially useful as a companion book for the task that lies before us. It undertakes to expound the whole truth of the gospel in concise outline. It does this in connection with texts from scripture and church history by explaining in free but not arbitrary paraphrase the Ten Commandments, the Prayer of Jesus, and the Apostles' Creed. And it does all this in such a way that across the centuries it is still inviting and stimulating enough to propel us to reflect anew today on the truth of the gospel. So what follows will not be a historical commentary on what the text probably said in the sixteenth century. Rather, the aim is with the help of this text to answer the question it answered in its time: "Why are you called a Christian?" (Art. 32). Our main text is the truth of the gospel itself. In the reading of it the Heidelberg is a companion text. The fact that the catechism wants to be understood this way is indicated by the presence of many biblical references in its articles. The Bible will lie open before us as we try to hear with the Heidelberg how that main text explains itself to us.

Why the Heidelberg commends itself especially as such a companion book may become clearer as we take note of a few historical circumstances of this text.

This catechism, published for the Palatinate in 1563, is a late fruit on the tree of the Reformation. It stands on the threshold of the transition from the age of Reformation to the age of Old Protestant Orthodoxy. It stands on the threshold on which the renewing of the church became a renewed church. What the church had to do now was to live with the under-standings won by the Reformers and to confirm them. The time in which the Heidelberg came into being was surely a dangerous time. (A similar judgment could also be made about the closure of the Lutheran confes-sional writings in the Formula of Concord.) It was dangerous because the impression could arise that the truths for which the first generation had fought could now be treated as a kind of possession. You could feel that you no longer had to wrestle and pray for this treasure. You could just hold fast to it and conserve it. You did not really have to discover it, but only re-fine it. Still, to conserve a hard-won truth is a different matter than living with it. You can say that the Heidelberg gives guidance for the latter. It does this while having features of a compilation. That is, with thoughtfulness and industry it pulls together an abundance of confessional statements al-ready at hand, and sorts, gathers, and arranges them.

The other danger on that threshold in which the catechism came to be was that the reforming revolution was on the verge of losing its energy by splintering. The situation in the Palatinate illustrates this. The Palatinate was late in opening itself to the Reformation, doing so under the influence of Melanchthon in 1546. It opened itself in such a way that soon strict confes-sional "Gnesio-Lutherans," mild Melanchthonians, Zwinglians, and Calvin-ists lived with one another, or rather in conflict against one another. When Frederick III took over the governing of the Palatinate in 1559 in Heidelberg, he tried to mediate in the conflict and to bring about unification. Frederick was an amazingly knowledgeable lay theologian, originally Catholic. His wife had convinced him that the Lutheran confession was right, but then through his own intensive study he became open to the correctness of Re-formed teaching about the Lord's Supper. The catechism that in 1562 he commissioned his Heidelberg theologians to create, and that he helped to write, was unquestionably supposed to serve the cause of conciliatory living together by the various factions in his land. Therefore the catechism has fea-tures of a compromise document. Aside from a few points, it stays away from extreme statements of the various camps and at the same time takes up in-sights from the differing sides, in order to make possible their coexistence.

When we say that the catechism has features of a compilation and of a compromise, we need to add that these features cannot explain the ex-traordinary significance this text has won. Its significance is explained only when one sees that it accomplishes both purposes aimed for: (a) an ar-rangement of Reformation understandings and (b) a settlement among diverging camps. But it does this in such a way that it succeeds in presenting its own well-thought-out, integrated new design. Yes, it is a real creative work, far from either derivative stolidness or spiritless cobbling. It is a work on a high theological level and at the same time in popular clarity, written in thoroughly beautiful, singing language and in formulations that often refer to one another. Here reflection comes before speaking. Matters are brought to a head in such a way that difficult issues are expressed simply and memorably without losing their depth. And everything aims toward the comforting, admonishing, and spiritual upbuilding of the congregation. The text simply spoke for itself when it impressed posterity, right up into the present. So this late fruit on the tree of the Reformation is a ripe fruit. It is understandable then that along with Luther's Catechism this Heidelberg Catechism, of the many catechisms that arose in the sixteenth century, remains the most widely used and most noteworthy. — Now a few more detailed pointers:

1. *Composition.* It is certain that the text had already been brought before a synod in Heidelberg in January 1563 and was subscribed to by the participants. In March and April slightly revised second and third editions appeared. In November a further revised fourth edition was published which is considered the "textus receptus." This edition appeared as part of the new Palatinate church order. When sending the text to Calvin and the Zurich Reformer Heinrich Bullinger in April 1563 the Heidelberg church councilman Olevianus wrote: "Here the thoughts of *many* are gathered together."[11] Perhaps in response to this, Calvin in July dedicated his commentary on Jeremiah to Prince Frederick and praised his extraordinary piety, his warm zeal to protect and spread true faith, and his calm moderation.[12] The fact that here the thoughts of many are gathered together has a twofold meaning.

For one, the catechism is the product of teamwork. Leading the team was the 28-year-old student of Melanchthon, Zachary Ursinus, who also had good connections with Zurich. A native of Breslau, he had been a theologian on the Heidelberg faculty since 1562. By that year Ursinus had already composed two catechisms, from which many formulations as well as the three-part organization came into our text.[13] Newer research considers the

---

11. Letter of Olevianus to Calvin, Apr. 3, 1563, in *Calvini Opera*, 19 (Braunschweig, 1879), col. 684; letter of Apr. 14, 1563, to Bullinger; cf. K. Sudhoff, *C. Olevianus und Z. Ursinus. Leben und ausgewählte Schriften* (Elberfeld: Friderichs Verlag, 1857), pp. 482-29.

12. *Calvins Lebenswerk in seinen Briefen,* trans. R. Schwarz (Neukirchen-Vluyn: Neukirchener Verlag, 1962), vol. 3, pp. 1239, 1242.

13. Cf. A. Lang, *Der Heidelberger Katechismus und vier verwandte Katechismen* (Leipzig: Deichert Verlag, 1907).

contribution of Caspar Olevianus, a 26-year-old from Trier who was a student of Calvin, to be minimal,[14] but not on absolutely convincing grounds. Perhaps behind this estimate of the part of Olevianus is an interest in minimizing the Calvinist influence. In addition to these two and Prince Frederick, others on the team were the theologically astute Heidelberg professor of medicine Thomas Erastus, the theology professors Boquinus and Tremellius, the pastor of the Frankenthal refugee congregation Datheus, and the secular councilmen Cirler and Eheim. It is certain that Olevianus, while the catechism was being refined, worked on another catechism, which apparently aimed to further explicate the first. Furthermore, chief credit for the Palatinate church order, in whose framework the text appeared in November and which in many ways meshes with the text, goes to Olevianus.[15]

Second, the "many" whose thoughts were gathered in the catechism include also the various prototypes used and interpreted in its composition. Granted, here we are dependent more on indications. We cannot say exactly what took place, because in the abundant literature of Reformation catechisms there are all kinds of connections. So thoughts mediated by the catechisms used as models could have flowed into the Heidelberg from the catechisms they in turn had used. Fairly certainly the Heidelberg used as models the "House Book" (German 1558) by Heinrich Bullinger, or a selection from it (1559), the catechisms by Leo Jud (1534, 1541), the Geneva Catechism of Calvin (1545, 1563 in German in Heidelberg), catechetical works by Melanchthon and probably Luther too, a Strasbourg catechism, and that of the German refugee congregation in London, written by a M. Micron. Further, it no doubt used the Emder catechism of the East Friesland reformer Laske and finally a "Short Confession" of the Genevan Theodore Beza, which appeared in Heidelberg in German in 1562. If you look at the large number of these models — and perhaps there were more — out of which the Heidelberg eclectically picked this and that, it is astounding that it came rather quickly to its resultant form. It is even more astounding that in the city of Heidelberg at this time there was a group of theologians capable of forming out of a colorful mix of the most varied stones a mosaic that gives us the impression of a convincing, unified, beautiful whole.

14. Many scholars agree with the negative judgment of W. Hollweg, *Neue Untersuchungen zur Geschichte und Lehre des H. Katechismus* (Neukirchen-Vluyn: Neukirchener Verlag, 1961), pp. 124ff.

15. K. Sudhoff, *C. Olevianus und Z. Ursinus,* p. 134; and E. Sehling, ed., *Die evangelischen Kirchenordnung des XVI Jahrhunderts,* vol. 14, Palatinate (Tübingen: Mohr, 1969), pp. 44-45.

2. *Character.* In view of its origin, we can understand the judgment of
E. F. K. Müller, that the catechism documents "the transition of Lutheran-
Melanchthonian churches to a moderate Calvinism."[16] This also means
that the catechism was close to the "Philippistic" direction set by Melanchthon, rather than to the other, strict confessional direction then developing
in Lutheranism, the Gnesio-Lutherans. In its central alignment on the
soteriological question of the "only comfort" it actually stood closer to
Melanchthon than to the theologians in Zurich and Geneva. And if it
opened itself to the Reformed position, especially in the understanding of
the Lord's Supper, we must add that the catechism in this matter also followed a piece of advice Melanchthon had given in 1560.[17] "Moderate Calvinism" means here then, openness and not exclusiveness toward the Lutheran tradition, at least toward the Lutheran tradition represented by
Melanchthon.

The Philippistic and the Calvinist directions coincided in the will to resist the splitting of the Protestant church into two confessions, despite existing differences in their understandings. The writers of the catechism were
imbued with this desire of their teacher. One could easily call their text a
union confession, formulated in view of the confessional age already ap-
proaching, as an attempt to work against Protestant division. Very typical
Calvinist elements are not mentioned, or their points are blunted. K. Barth
was right on the mark in saying "peculiarly Reformed doctrines play only a
small part in this catechism . . . it is a document which expresses a general
evangelical comprehension. . . . A reasonable Lutheranism should also be
able" — apart from a few points — "to stand on this ground."[18] This union
character of the text has always led people to combine with it the word
"mild," and to say it is a "mild" or "mildly-Reformed" catechism. Perhaps it
owes its wide dissemination throughout the church, and its notable historical influence, to this character. Still, the mildness does have its limit in one
respect: its strong rejection of Roman works-righteousness and eucharistic
doctrine. Its harshness in this direction is prompted by its authors' reaction
to the third and final session of the Counter-Reformation Council of Trent,

16. E. F. K. Müller, ed., *Die Bekenntnisschriften der reformierten Kirche* (Leipzig:
Deichert Verlag, 1903).

17. Philip Melanchthon, *Werke in Auswahl,* ed. R. Stupperich, vol. 6 (Gütersloh:
Bertelsmann, 1955), pp. 482-86.

18. K. Barth, *Die christliche Lehre nach dem Heidelberger Katechismus* (Zollikon, 1948),
pp. 18-19. ET: *The Heidelberg Catechism for Today* (Richmond, VA: John Knox Press, 1964),
pp. 24-25.

where even minor suggestions of reform by Emperor Ferdinand I, who was of Catholic conviction, were rejected.

3. *Function.* Its wide dissemination and influence, however, probably rest more on the fact that it succeeded in an impressive way in bringing its intended varied uses into harmony. It combines four functions:

(a) It was intended for *liturgical use* in the worship service. Its melodious oral style and its suffusion with biblical phrases made it more suitable than other comparable texts. One way its liturgical destination was made evident is its division in the textus receptus of November into nine sections. These were to be presented regularly and in order in the worship service as a reading before the sermon — a practice still customary in some Reformed congregations. Another is the fact that the text appeared in the church order of the Palatinate between the liturgies of baptism and Lord's Supper, and so was designated as itself a liturgical piece. This liturgical purpose means that the doctrine the text offers deliberately binds itself into the life of the worshiping congregation and intends to serve it. K. Barth observes: "More clearly than all other confessions of Lutheran or Reformed origin, it grew out of the immediate necessities of life of a *church*." So it is "not a piece of abstract theology, abstract polemics, or church politics; it is an element of the life of the church."[19]

(b) Naturally, its purpose is also *catechetical,* aimed at instruction in the elementary doctrines of faith. For this purpose, the text is presented in the form of questions and answers, in which the teacher asks and the pupil answers. Its numbering into 129 articles first appears in the Latin version of 1563, in German in the edition of 1570. The catechetical purpose is again shown in two ways. One is its placement between the orders for baptism and for the Lord's Supper. Those baptized, it states explicitly, shall be so instructed that they can confess their faith before the congregation. The other is that the church membership, since "it has been brought up in Papacy without a catechism"[20] and kept dependent, shall now be educated so that it will be articulate in questions of faith. For this purpose, the catechism, like the other Reformed catechisms, presents itself as an interpretation of the four classical "basic catechetical elements": the Apostles' Creed, the Ten Commandments, the Lord's Prayer, and the sacraments. In addition, it directs that the text be studied in schools and homes and ex-

---

19. K. Barth, *Die christliche Lehre,* p. 16. ET, p. 22.

20. W. Niesel, ed., *Bekenntnisschriften und Kirchenordnungen der nach Gottes Wort reformierten Kirche* (1938; Zurich: Theologischer Verlag, 1985), p. 148.

pounded in its own Sunday-afternoon worship service. For this last purpose the textus receptus is also divided into 52 sections, so that it can be gone through once each year.

(c) The catechism was also thought of as a *teaching norm* for pastors, yet in a differentiated way. According to the "Installation of Church Servants" of July 1564, pastors were bound to present the word of God according to scripture and in keeping with the three ancient church creeds. Only after these, and subordinate to them, is the catechism mentioned.[21] This subordination is related to the fact that the Reformed confessions are only relatively authoritative for the Reformed Church and its theology. For these all remain, as Ursinus put it, subject to testing by the church and its members, "in order, if some mistakes are found . . . to take account of and examine them, and if something is found needing improvement, that with the general agreement . . . of the church . . . it can be improved or cleared up."[22] Since the catechism was a norm for teaching in this sense, it is noteworthy that for pastors nothing other was binding than the same norm they had to expound to the congregation. And in turn, the clergy had to hold *themselves* to the same norm to which they were to hold the rest of the congregation. If the catechism for the church membership was at the same time teaching norm for the pastors, then their task was strictly service to and among the church membership. Clearly, this stance denies a basic difference between pastors and church people. Pastors and lay people were bound to the same thing. Would not then the assimilation of the catechism by the members of the congregation also count as a kind of "Installation for Service"?

(d) Finally, the catechism was intended for *home use* as a book for edification. This is why the arrangement of the text shows that the knowledge spread out here "helps you," "is useful for you," or "comforts you." This is why the church order of 1563 recommends that the first question be read to sick people.[23] This is why, as G. Locher observes, "One can pray almost the whole Heidelberg."[24] This is the reason for the remarkable fact that from the first edition on, the catechism gives a number of Bible passages for each article. This fact probably goes back to the wish and cooperation of

21. E. Sehling, ed., *Die evangelischen Kirchenordnung*, p. 425.

22. J. Rohls, *Theologie reformierter Bekenntnisschriften*, p. 318. ET, p. 267.

23. W. Niesel, ed., *Bekenntnisschriften und Kirchenordnungen*, p. 210.

24. G. Locher, "Das vornehmste Stück der Dankbarkeit. Das Gebet im Sinne der Reformation nach dem Heidelberger Katechismus," in *Handbuch zum Heidelberger Katechismus*, ed. L. Coenen (Neukirchen-Vluyn: Neukirchener Verlag, 1963), p. 173.

Prince Frederick. The purpose of supplying such Bible passages was not simply to claim that all the assertions of the catechism were backed by scripture. It was rather the converse, that the catechism should serve as a study help in order to lead its readers to the scripture and help them understand it better. Church members were thereby invited to look up these passages at home and, guided by the catechism, to reflect on them.

4. *Opposition.* Soon after its appearance, a somewhat distressing opposition began on the part of strict Lutheran theologians. They called the Heidelberg inflammatory, yes, even against God, or accused it of calling itself a "catechism" when Luther had already written one, and so on.[25] Still, the opposition focused mainly on its doctrine of the Lord's Supper, which indicates that the rest was acceptable to Lutherans. At that time this one point in the "second Lord's Supper conflict" between Calvin and the Gnesio-Lutherans had become so much a status confessionis that the opposition against this doctrine of the Lord's Supper meant: (a) the tough intra-Lutheran attack on the Philippistic wing, which could live with this doctrine; (b) the passing of the Palatinate into the Reformed camp; and (c) highly political consequences for the laws of the land. For since the Palatinate counted as Reformed (solely) because of its doctrine of the Lord's Supper, it was excluded from the protection of the Augsburg Religious Peace of 1555, which applied only to Roman Catholics and Lutherans.

The existence of Reformed regions was later felt as a problem in the Augsburg Imperial Council of 1566 and was first definitively recognized in the Peace of Westphalia in 1648. Before that, however, a dangerous situation had developed. Duke Christoph of Württemberg had threatened sanctions. It did not come to that, because Hesse and Saxony refused to go along. Still, the political threat from Duke Christoph was all the more critical because his Swabian theologians, in a week-long discussion in April 1564 with the Heidelberg theologians in Maulbronn, were not able to teach the latter better by the strength of their theological arguments.[26] On the other hand, the Lutheran Swabians refused to concede. In short, because of the Lutheran opposition and the suppression of the Philippistic wing in Lutheranism, the Heidelberg Catechism, against its intention, was from then on not regarded as a document of union, but as a purely Reformed text. There was also Catholic opposition to the catechism against question

---

25. M. Lauterburg, "Katechismus, Heidelberger," in *Realencyclopädie für protestantische Theologie und Kirche,* 3rd ed., vol. 10, p. 170. K. Sudhoff, *C. Olevianus und Z. Ursinus,* p. 142.

26. K. Sudhoff, *C. Olevianus und Z. Ursinus,* pp. 260-90.

80, included later, in which the mass is called a "cursed idolatry." As late as the nineteenth century in the Swiss canton of Aargau, the church's use of the text was forbidden by the Parliament — on the grounds of disturbing the peace between the confessions.[27]

5. *Dissemination.* After Frederick III came Ludwig VI, who in 1576 again introduced the Lutheran order of worship and catechism in the Palatinate. But his successor, Johann Casimir, once again prescribed the Heidelberg. Very quickly after its appearance, the catechism was spread into other areas outside the Palatinate. Gradually it was adopted in all German Reformed regions: in Nassau-Siegen, Wittgenstein, in Bremen, Lippe, Anhalt, Hesse-Cassel, and then in Brandenburg, then also in Holland, in Poland, Hungary, and Siebenbürgen, and hesitantly also in Switzerland. Although Reformed people in England, Scotland, and France valued it, they preferred to stick with their own catechisms. However, it was used intensively in North America. It was significant that the international delegated Reformed Synod of Dordrecht in 1619 recommended the catechism to all as an "unusually careful compendium of orthodox Christian teaching."[28] It should also be mentioned that the text in the course of the centuries has received a stately row of commentaries from outstanding theologians. This shows on the one hand the stimulating nature and vitality of this text, and on the other, that a piece of work like this stays alive only as people think through its message in their own times.

1.3. The Basic Theme

What is the real object, the basic theme of Christian theology? This will be clarified by looking at the carefully considered and artful construction of the Heidelberg. For an initial orientation, note two things. First, after a summary preface in Article 1, Article 2 names the "three parts" into which the catechism is divided: "The magnitude of my sin and wretchedness" (Art. 3-11), "How I am released from all my sins and misery" (Art. 12-85), and "How I am to be grateful to God for such redemption" (Art. 86-129).

---

27. J. Heiz, "Zur 400 jährigen Jubiläumsfeier der Berner Reformation an die Glieder der reformierten Kirche des Kt. Aargau," in E. Marti, *1528-1928 Menschenrat und Gottestat* (Bern: Kommissionsverlag von Büchler, 1928), p. 19.

28. Acc. to M. Lauterberg, "Katechismus, Heidelberger," p. 171.

Second, into the structure arranged in this way according to its content are integrated the classical "basic catechetical elements": the confession of faith (the Credo), the sacraments, the Ten Commandments (the Decalogue), and the prayer of Jesus (the Lord's Prayer). This is done in such a way that the first two elements are introduced and explained in the second section, and the latter two in the third section. Now the question is: How does the catechism arrive at such an arrangement of its material, and how is it to be understood?

Here we need to look first into the distinction Otto Weber introduced between a synthetic and an analytic catechism.[29] His thesis is that in the great flood of Reformation catechisms, the majority follow a synthetic form, with the main catechetical elements more or less arbitrarily put together and explained — as in the catechism of Luther. A minority of the catechisms — like the Heidelberg — follow the analytic method, not coincidentally developed in the Reformed sphere, which arose amidst humanist influence. Here the catechism is framed by an anthropological starting question (as a rule, What or who are you, human/Christian?). Consequently, the Credo is handled before the Decalogue. Weber's thesis surely needs to be questioned — generally, in view of the catechetical literature of the time, and specifically, in its application to the Heidelberg.

This thesis hardly explains why the analytical method is characteristic for the realm of Lutheran theology on the whole, and not for the Reformed — a fact Weber[30] himself points out. It is also not clear why the analytic method should result in beginning with the Credo. At any rate, the Strasbourg Catechism of 1536 and 1537, which proceeds analytically, puts the Decalogue before the Credo, as Luther did.[31] As a matter of fact, J. Marbach, who worked in the Palatinate in 1556 and following years, could spread Luther's catechism there by prefixing an anthropological starting question that effortlessly made the catechism analytic.[32] This was effortless because Luther's allegedly synthetic catechism was not at all unsystematically conceived. Rather, precisely in its deliberate placing of the Decalogue first, it answers the implicitly presupposed question, "How can

29. O. Weber, "Analytische Theologie," in *Warum wirst du ein Christ genannt? Vorträge und Aufsätze zum Heidelberger Katechismus*, ed. W. Herrenbrück and U. Smidt (Neukirchen-Vluyn: Neukirchener Verlag, 1965), pp. 24-39.

30. O. Weber, "Analytische Theologie," pp. 34-35.

31. J. M. Reu, *Quellen zur Geschichte des Katechismus-Unterrichts*, vol. 1, *Süddeutsche Katechismen* (Gütersloh: Bertelsmann, 1904), pp. 105ff., 123ff.

32. J. M. Reu, *Quellen zur Geschichte des Katechismus-Unterrichts*, pp. 149ff.

a human, who does not keep the law, still be saved?" These hints raise questions about the validity and fruitfulness of Weber's thesis.

In particular, it is questionable whether the Heidelberg, allegedly characteristic for the analytical type, really corresponds to the criteria for this type. This is questionable already in view of Article 1, which can only by some forcing be understood as an anthropological starting question. Here theology is not "analyzed" from linkage with a general human condition. Rather, at the beginning comes a tremendous statement that anticipates in a summary way all that follows, and basically says everything. Here you are not led from a general human inclination toward God, or from a felt need, to theological contents. The sum of the theological contents comes right out at the beginning. The Heidelberg has thereby understood the important fact that we cannot get to real theological substance if we do not begin from it with the first step. There is no *preambulum fidei*, as Roman theology says — that is, no general human entryway to faith, in which I can first look around in the world, apart from faith, to see if on our human side there is receiving equipment for, or interest in, such faith. As I can learn to swim only by beginning to swim, so I can come to faith only by beginning to believe.

The correctness of this interpretation of Article 1 — not as an anthropological starting question, but as a summary of the whole — is confirmed when we look at the organization of the entire catechism. You could indeed call the catechism "analytic" in *this* sense — that all which follows just develops and expounds what is already said in Article 1. If the only comfort is what Article 1 says it is, then three questions can be inferred from its statement (cf. Art. 2), which the catechism then in fact addresses one after the other. So it unfolds in detail what is said in Article 1: 1. Why do I need this comfort that is announced to me in advance? Answer: Because I am in *misery!* 2. Who gives me this comfort? Answer: The God who *redeems* me out of my misery! 3. What effect does this comfort bring about? Answer: That for this redemption I am *thankful* to this God! These are the three pieces into which the catechism is divided.

This threefold division of the material is no invention of the Heidelberg. It is already found in the Catechesis Minor of 1562 by Ursinus,[33] who quite surely took it from the catechism of the Regensburg Lutheran N. Gallus, printed in Heidelberg in 1558. This text presents three parts: of sin revealed by the law, of the gospel that forgives sin, and of the good works by

33. A. Lang, *Der Heidelberger Katechismus*, p. 200.

which we "show ourselves thankful for this."[34] Here these three steps appear to be understood as a description of the subjective process of salvation. Gallus, like Ursinus, was a student of Melanchthon, yet came to be opposed to Ursinus, and rejected the Reformed path. This indicates that this three-fold division, usually called typically Reformed, actually somehow had Lutheran origins. In fact, we can find in Melanchthon beginnings in this direction.[35] Moreover, Gallus remarks that behind his threefold division stands the doctrine of the threefold use of the law — a conception which goes back to Melanchthon:[36] as an outward rule of life for sinners, as a mirror for recognizing sin, which drives me to trust in the forgiveness of Christ, and as motivation to keep the commandments with the help of the Spirit. The hazard of this doctrine is that the whole matter is in danger of coming under the sign of the law. Consequently, it speaks of how I, who should keep the Law, but cannot keep it, nevertheless get to the place where I do keep it. In this way the gospel of the grace of Christ, instead of being the *middle* of the whole, would be the *medium* for our fulfillment of the law.

It is important to see clearly that the Heidelberg does not slavishly follow the previous threefold division of the material. Rather, much as it does connect with it, the Heidelberg thoroughly reworks it. Make note of several facts: not only does the text not treat the first use of the Law, but it conspicuously does not treat the Decalogue at all in its first part — it does this only in the third part. On this account alone, the danger that the Law's greatness will dominate is remote. The Heidelberg does not ask how the human lawbreaker is brought to keeping the law, but rather above all, how the miserable human is redeemed. It is no accident then, that the first catechetical element treated is the Credo, that is, faith in the gospel of redeeming grace. So it is clear that the grace of God is here understood neither as a means to an end, namely human fulfillment of the law, nor as being under the limiting condition of legal demands. Rather, discussion of the redeeming grace of God, the "only comfort," is the decisive word, and the placement of the Decalogue in the third part shows that keeping the law is understood as only the thankful response to grace, which has come first. This is all the more so since this thankfulness has its "most important form" (Art. 116) not in keeping the Decalogue, but in calling on God in

---

34. J. M. Reu, *Quellen zur Geschichte des Katechismus-Unterrichts*, pp. 447-48, 201-2.

35. Philip Melanchthon, *Werke*, vol. 2, part 1 (1953), p. 7; ET: *Loci Communes of 1521*, trans. C. L. Hill (Boston: Meador, 1944), p. 69; vol. 6, 1955, pp. 169-71.

36. J. M. Reu, *Quellen zur Geschichte des Katechismus-Unterrichts*, p. 742.

prayer. So it becomes unmistakably clear that the middle part of the catechism is its genuine center. Its theme is not how, by means of grace, pious people can keep the otherwise unfulfillable law. Rather, its theme is that God's grace redeems us miserable folk, and does this so thoroughly that it frees us "to live for him from now on" by grace (Art. 1).

This insight becomes even more pointed when we turn in particular to the problem of the first part of the Heidelberg. It is a noteworthy fact that its first part is strikingly short. This is because the Decalogue has been pushed into the third part — although it would have been expected in the first, according to Reformed tradition. While the second part fills much more than half of the text, the first part claims only 11 of the 129 questions, only a bare 7 percent of the whole text. This part is so short that you might say it does not have its center in itself, but rather in the text following. Yes, you can even say its testimony ("Humanity's Sin and Guilt") is already "drawn into the comfort" of which Article 1 and then the second part speak, and "therefore it must not be abstractly developed."[37] This assumption is all the more convincing since into the middle of the first part (from Art. 9) the Heidelberg seamlessly works a train of thought taken over from a "Short Confession" by Theodore Beza, which forms a transition into the beginning of the second part (to Art. 18). (Beza's work had been published in German in Heidelberg in 1562,[38] just a year before the Heidelberg's publication.) Because this material is inserted, the question that would otherwise naturally arise does not come up. The obvious question would have been, "What do we, who have been shown by God's law that our condition is miserable, need for our salvation?" But this question is displaced by the other question "How does God, who is merciful but also just, consider our sin?" The answer is that God can only justly condemn it. Thus Part I already deals thematically with God. God's good creation of the creature comes before sin (Art. 6), against which stands God's righteousness, without which God cannot be merciful (Art. 11). So the misery of humans *becomes* most definitely the *question* that calls for redemption.

At this point the thesis advanced by W. Herrenbrück can make sense to us. He claims that the Heidelberg's "famous threefold arrangement is itself conceived in a trinitarian way."[39] This thesis can be maintained be-

37. K. Barth, *Die christliche Lehre*, p. 30. ET, p. 35.

38. W. Hollweg, *Neue Untersuchungen*, pp. 111-12.

39. W. Herrenbrück, "Der trinitarische Ansatz des Heidelberger Katechismus," in W. Herrenbrück and U. Smidt, eds., *Warum wirst du ein Christ genannt?* (Neukirchen-Vluyn: Neukirchener Verlag, 1965), pp. 46-48.

cause of the way the Heidelberg treats the traditional threefold arrangement of catechetical material. If the thesis is correct, it has the weighty consequence that the three-part division of the catechism is not to be understood primarily as a description of the subjective process of salvation within a person, but rather as a designation of the work of the triune God on, for, and with a person. But does this hold?

To begin with, it is clear, and in the original text expressly stated, that the second part ("Humanity's Redemption and Freedom") is organized in trinitarian form. The fact that this part consists largely in the interpretation of the Apostles' Creed is a strong sign that this is so. Granted, the title of the second part shows that it is going to speak of the work of the second person of the Trinity, of the work of the Mediator, the work of Jesus Christ. But when the Heidelberg speaks of "our Lord Jesus Christ, who is freely given us for total redemption and righteousness" (Art. 18), and interprets and organizes this in a trinitarian way, it shows a fine feeling for the fact that the Christological doctrine is the root of the doctrine of the Trinity. For the doctrine of the Trinity is only the theo-logical consequence of the Christological confession that it is God who in Christ has bound God's own self with humanity and has brought about reconciliation.

From here it is only a short step to the conclusion that the work of sanctification, which belongs to the Holy Spirit (Art. 24), is interpreted mainly in Part III ("Our Thankfulness and Obedience"), without simply repeating what has already been said about it in Part II (Art. 53). According to Article 8, we are "unable to do any good . . . unless we are born again through God's Spirit"; Part III tells about how we become able. According to Article 6 we are created "in God's own image, that is, in genuine righteousness and holiness" in order that we love God, live with God, and praise God, but this destiny of ours is blocked by the Fall: the beginning of Part III states that Christ "through his Holy Spirit . . . renews us in his own image" (Art. 86) in order with our whole life to thank and praise God. All this shows that Part III in its entirety speaks of this renewal by the Holy Spirit. The Spirit "awakens" faith within us (Art. 65): this is the presupposition of the "good works" that "are motivated by true faith" (Art. 91) and are thematically treated in Part III. And in the exposition of the third article of the Apostles' Creed in Part II the topic is justification, which takes place without being earned by works, yet not without active "fruit of thankfulness" (Art. 63-64); Part III continues the treatment of these works in a way that makes good sense — in connection with the interpretation of the Ten Commandments (Art. 114-15). In short, Part III obviously deals with the sanctifying work of the Holy Spirit.

It can now be ascertained that the first part of the Heidelberg treats the work of the first "person" of the Trinity, the work particularly of God the Father and Creator, despite the fact that the title of this part ("Humanity's Sin and Guilt") does not sound like it. Certainly, as Part III does not repeat what has already been said in Part II about the article on the Holy Spirit, so Part I is not a doubling of what is said in Part II in the articles on God the Creator (Art. 26-28). To be sure, the text speaks here about the human misery uncovered by the law (Art. 3-5). This is in keeping with its "Melanchthonian" prototype. But as has been said, this prototype is immediately so submerged by the insight of Beza that the entire Part I is drawn into the light of a new perspective. In this perspective, Part I now proclaims above all that God "created human beings good and in God's image," in order that humanity could know "God our Creator," and love and praise and live with God (Art. 6), and have no occasion to sin. After the Fall this God has the right to be "merciful, but . . . also righteous" toward the creature (Art. 11) and so to forgive as well as to condemn human sin. So the thought of the work of God the Father and Creator stands at the very least as the background in forming Part I.

Hence one can defend the thesis that the Heidelberg has handled the traditional three-part catechetical material in such a way — by relating it to the work of the trinitarian God — that it receives a new character. Beyond this, it should be noted that the central part that forms the axis of the catechism lifts up the fact that the work of the "Son" is at the same time also the work of the "Father" and the "Spirit." Also, the work of God envisioned in Part I, although attributed to the Father and Creator, is so interpreted that it is at the same time also the work of the Son (Art. 4) and the Spirit (Art. 8). Correspondingly, the work of the Spirit treated in Part III is so understood, that with God the Spirit also God the Father and the Son are at work (cf. Art. 120). So here three great divine works are addressed: Creation, Redemption, and Sanctification, knowable as the works of God who as three is the *one* God.

From all these observations about the construction of the catechism we can now draw the conclusion that as a whole and in its three parts, the one basic theme of Christian doctrine is the action of the triune God on, with, and for humanity. Note well, the basic theme is not just knowledge of God abstractly. How could it be anything like that? It is not about a God who is lonely, but about the triune God. It is about *this* action of God toward humanity, in which a relationship with humanity is included. Of course, theological knowledge in this basic theme is focused not just on the effect of this action of God on the human person, not just on the subjective process of salvation on and within him or her. It is focused on an event whose all-decisive subject is God and not the human person. The human is the addressee of the divine action, to be sure. In fact, the human subsequently becomes a cooperating subject. But the human becomes this on the basis of action in which God is and remains the primary subject. So, according to the guidance of the Heidelberg, we can say that the basic theme of Christian theology is the action of the triune God on humanity, for us and with us.

Now the fact must be underscored that this basic theme is about knowledge of the triune God who in *Jesus Christ* has bound the divine self with us and has reconciled us and therein has revealed God's self to us. This makes the central position of Part II and the carefully crafted trinitarian organizing of this, the Christological part, understandable. For the knowledge that God has done all this in Christ is the root of the knowledge of God as three in one. In this root is lodged the Christological knowledge the ancient church summed up in the formula: Jesus Christ is both the Son of God and the Son of humanity, "true God and true human being." Only when we keep this root in view is it unmistakably clear that the action of the triune God is in fact God's action toward and with human beings. The Heidelberg was well aware of this when it made that formula of the ancient church its own with definite exposition. Although Christ — "personally united to" the divine nature (Art. 48) — is "true human being and true God," it is very important that these two "natures" are not mixed, but rather are held in their uniqueness. This is somewhat different from the Lutheran emphasis.

According to the Heidelberg, the assertion about these two "natures" is to be understood in this way: that Christ is called "true God" means that he does something *for* us ("by the power of his divinity," Art. 17) in our place and for our redemption — something which he alone accomplishes and which we could never do. That he is "true human being" means that he is really *like* his sisters and brothers in every way (except for sin) and *continues to be* like us (Art. 35). For only so is what he has done for our redemption effective for us, and only so do we take part in it. The affirmation of the enduring distinction between his two "natures" has two important consequences: on the one hand, it guarantees the enduring distinction between Christ's redemption and all human efforts at self-redemption; on the other hand, it guarantees the enduring togetherness of the man Jesus with his "sisters and brothers" (cf. Art. 49). Making effective what Christ has gained for us is the work of the Spirit. As the human nature of Jesus was "taken on by the true God" at his birth "through the Spirit" (Art. 35), so the Spirit is the power of God that binds us to Christ (Art. 49), and through this power what Christ has accomplished for us as "true God" becomes what he accomplishes in and with us.

The Christological doctrine of the Heidelberg is apparently the basis for a dual structuring that without harming its trinitarian organization — indeed, combining with it — shapes the catechism. According to Karl Barth[40] the thinking of the Heidelberg works in a scheme of two poles. The one is Christ's "objective action for us" and the other is "his subjective action on and in us." J. F. G. Goeters[41] sees a similar two-pole scheme in the theology of the catechism: it speaks "of two divine works . . . of the reconciling work of the Son become human, accomplished outside of and beyond us, and of this reconciliation's being made effective within the believer by the Ascended One through the Spirit." Behind the two-pole structure of the "for us" and "on, in and with us," the Heidelberg's exposition of the ancient church formula can easily be recognized.

From this vantage point, it is easy to see this two-pole structure expressed in the relation of Parts II and III, which make up the lion's share of the text. It now becomes very clear why Part I is so extraordinarily brief and goes imperceptibly over into Part II. Part II mainly clarifies the redemptive interceding of the mediator Jesus Christ *for* us and in our place. And when Part III deals with our thankful acting and praying, it stands on the presupposition that "Christ having redeemed us with his blood also renews us in his own image through his Holy Spirit," so that "we may show with our whole lives how grateful we are to God for God's goodness"(Art. 86). So this last part has to do on the whole with that "subjective work" of God in Christ through the Spirit on and in us, which makes possible, and brings about, such acting and praying.

Apparently this Christologically determined two-pole structure is reflected on the anthropological plane in a further characteristic thought-form of the Heidelberg. It sees human beings in a double relation — to

40. K. Barth, *Die christliche Lehre*, ET p. 31.

41. J. F. G. Goeters, "Christologie und Rechtfertigung nach dem Heidelberger Katechismus," in *Das Kreuz Jesu Christi als Grund des Heils,* ed. E. Bizer (Gütersloh: Mohn, 1967), p. 47.

God and to neighbor. Conspicuously, it sees the divine law in the law of *Christ* and therefore in the *double commandment of* love (Art. 4). What is special about Christ's law is apparently not so much its demanding character as its connecting the vertical and horizontal dimensions. Therefore, as sin is transgression in this double relation (Art. 5), so the renewal of the image of God by the Spirit takes place in the same double relationship (Art. 86). God's way for human life calls for praying and working, and therefore the two tables of the Decalogue (Art. 93) and then also the two parts of the Lord's Prayer are understood in light of this double aspect. The assumption lies close at hand that the Heidelberg sees in this double aspect a human correspondence to the Christological double aspect: as Christ is true God and as such acts *for* us and redeems us, so we live according to God's heart when we live in relationship to *God,* and love God as Creator and Savior. And as Christ is true human, "like his fellow human beings in all things," and as such acts *on* and *with* us, so we live according to God's will when we live in relation to our *neighbor,* and love our neighbor as the one who has come close to us in our common brother Jesus.

Since for the Heidelberg the basic theological word is "comfort," it makes sense — after all that has been said — to understand by this word the comprehensive event that fundamentally determines its text, both in content and form, and wherein, according to its guidance, we have to recognize its basic theological theme. It is the work of the trinitarian God, who in Jesus Christ has bound God's self to us and reconciled us — "objectively and subjectively" in action for us and with us. Because God is personally acting and revealing the divine self, this is the action of the God who is to be known as the triune God. This is our "only comfort in life and in death." Because *this* is our comfort, there is no real distance from the intention of the catechism when the theological path that follows here is unfolded, in content and form, under the name of another basic word: freedom. The basic theme, which is to be expounded from various viewpoints, is the free God and the free human being. The one comfort consists in the freedom of God to meet and to be together with humanity, and in the freedom thereby granted humanity to answer God and so live with God. This is not about an abstract, willful freedom of competing individuals. Instead, God's freedom is what God uses for coexistence with us. Correspondingly, our freedom is what God gives us so that we coexist with God and with those who are given us by God to be close as neighbors. In this sense the "synopsis" of Christian faith presented here deals with the free God and the free human being.

2. God's Deliverance of the Captive

2.1. God's Word of Assurance (Art. 1)

2.1.1. God's Belonging to Us

Article 1 is a preview and summary of the whole Heidelberg Catechism. Everything the catechism will say is an unfolding and variation of what is summed up here. So Article 1 is the substantive center of the catechism. Everything it considers and invites us to consider turns on what it presents here, like a wheel around its axle. At the same time, Article 1 sets us on a path where there will be many things to pay attention to. And after the path has gone through the 129 articles of this text, it will not yet be at an end. In fact, it will still be in the beginning stages. Yet it is a path with a clear goal, dependent on its clear beginning. It aligns itself toward the one "who is the Alpha and the Omega, the beginning and the end" (Rev. 1:8). In this alignment the catechism can take confident steps. It does not move about aimlessly, even when there are detours and sidetracks. Its beginning does not leave us hanging in an idyllic past which we must mourn for; rather, it lays our hand on a plow, so that we have to look forward and go forward (Luke 9:62). And yet even the most extreme openness of which we are capable still does not see the One who is the goal if that One is not, from the first step onward, the beginning. The catechism is exemplary in that it begins with the beginning. We follow its example when along with the catechism we let ourselves be asked: "What is your only comfort in life and in death?"

This question, as has been said, does not connect with an assumed general human need for comfort. Rather, it proceeds from the conviction that comfort is given us, that this comfort is the only one that can comfort us in life and in death, and that this comfort is the sum, center, and Alpha and Omega of the Christian confession of faith. It proceeds from the conviction that because this comfort holds for us from the beginning, what is left for us to do is respond by asking what this comfort is about. The basic word "comfort" had a much wider, stronger, and more objective ring in the sixteenth century than it has today. In German, it has its root in a concept that includes the meanings faithfulness, trust, and reliability (Gothic: *trausti* = covenant). The Latin *consolatio* means consoling words, encouragement. The Greek *paraklesis* means comfort, but also exhortation, and calling for help.

If, according to 2 Corinthians 1:4-7, God is the "God of all comfort," then God is the one who by the divine word of encouragement helpfully and effectively lifts up those who have been struck down. If according to 1 John 2:1, Jesus is now with the "Father" as the Paraclete for us sinners, then he is the one who steps in for us so that our sin is completely covered. When, according to John 14:16, 26; 15:26, Jesus promises his disciples the Spirit as the "Paraclete," he promises to stay with them so that they are not orphans, not deserted, but rather through his presence delighted, lifted up, and set straight. In the basic word "comfort" these older meanings resonate, so that we need to hear the beginning question in this way: What gives you courage? What gives it in such a way that it really lifts you up, so that you can rely on the one who is unfailingly faithful? Where does the support for your whole life come from, a support that holds rock-firm, capable of bearing heavy loads, sure and reliable — and what does it consist of? So the beginning question is already thought about in light of the answer that follows.

The main sentence of this answer goes: This is my comfort — not something, not a thing, and not any idea that I can "have," but a person, a subject, who is facing me, who steps toward me and meets me, who turns to me and speaks to me. My comfort is my *Comforter.* This is my comfort: "*Christ* wills to be our comfort."[1] Comfort, real comfort, the comfort we need, the comfort given us by God, is different from that meant by W. von Humboldt, who said comfort "can never be found in any other than in myself."[2] However, neither is comfort something outside me that I deem com-

1. From stanza 1 of the hymn "Christ ist erstanden" ("Christ Is Risen").
2. W. von Humboldt, "Briefe an eine Freundin" (May 26, 1823) (Leipzig, n.d.), p. 98.

forting on the basis of a criterion within myself. Comfort consists in someone's sticking with us and holding us fast so that we cannot be dropped. As
a rule, this comfort takes place in such a way that only afterwards, but then
more and more, do we begin to realize how much we need it. Nor is comfort something like a security blanket Christ simply offers. Rather, comfort
is Christ himself, who offers himself to us so reliably that we can totally
rely on it.

Comfort is not something that Christ hands to us, as if we could
keep in our hand a gift separated from its giver. Rather, it is Christ himself, who holds us in his hand and does not let us go. My comfort is that I
"both body and soul" (in all dimensions of space, not only spiritually-
inwardly-mentally, that too, but also publicly and bodily), "in life and in
death" (in all dimensions of time, in the splendid hours and in the
nights, in the middle and at the limits of existence) — in short, that I,
whether I realize it or not, in each and every dimension, am not fallen or
withdrawn from my faithful savior, but have fallen into his arms and
have been drawn to him. It is he who promises good to me, and for my
good says "I am with you!" What he says is comforting because he says it;
all comfort for body and soul, in living and in dying, lies in the fact that
he promises this to us. What he promises says something about the You
who is spoken to, but first something about the I who is speaking — the
divine I in the savior Jesus Christ. About the You it says: you will not be
alone, will not be without me. And about the I it says: It is my will not to
be alone, not to be without you. This section will take a closer look at the
latter statement.

1. The statement that I "belong" to Christ, and that this is my comfort,
is misunderstood so long as we do not understand that the statement presupposes this other statement: In Christ God comes to belong to *us* before
bringing us to belong to God. Granted, in self-giving to us, God also makes
a determination about us. But God makes this determination about us in
no other way than that in which God has already made a determination
about God's own self. Nothing forces God to do this. Doing it is the primal
act of freedom. In freedom God does something not only to us, but beforehand to God's own self. God's meeting us in a definite comforting assurance and claim presupposes the divine *self*-determination to be the God
who *is* "comforting" to us and who relates to us in this way. It presupposes
that God meets us as the one who commits God's own self, who is self-
binding. God is free to do this.

That God reveals Godself to us means in the first place that God *de-*

fines Godself. And this means that God commits to be this one and no other — therefore "your only comfort," because God wills to be for us the "God of all comfort" (2 Cor. 1:3). This is why God's being our only comfort does not mean authoritarian control over us which we would have to submit to apart from or against our will, or which we could, in trying to be tolerant, relax, or interpret as applying only to "us Christians" and not to others. No, this commitment affects first of all neither us nor others, but *God's own self.* In self-disclosure, God decides first of all about God's own self. Because God's self-commitment is based on God's freedom, it does not give any room for us to audaciously tie God down and take control of the Divine. God does not give away the divine freedom by tying Godself down. This does not mean that God could at any time repeal the divine self-definition. But it does mean that God always remains free to make clear and to decide what God's commitment means for us at any given time. At this point we understand the danger of all our definitions of God, though we may have looked them up in the Bible — for example "God = love." The danger is that in the place of God we put a concept already filled by our own experiences and wishes. God's self-definition does not go over into our definition of God. It always goes before it, so that ours can always only follow God's.

2. God's defining Godself means that God is limited to be this and no other. But God does not make this self-limitation in an exclusive way that stays within God's self. Rather, this definition takes place in an incomparable boundary crossing: God's self going across and away to the human being, in order to be bound with humanity and to reconcile humanity with God. We dare not understand God's revelation in Christ to mean simply that tidings are given us about a being previously unknown to us, and that in this way a conceptual formula is handed out, "God is . . . ." What is revealed to us is not a "something" behind God's gracious turning to us, in which case the turning would be a neutral, "correct" mediation of that something. No, the turning itself and as such *is* the definition of God. God is God in this gracious turning to us. God is not "more" than God is in this turning, let alone that this "more" is the really divine. God *is* in God's turning to us. This is why God's turning is God's full, valid, comprehensive, *definitive* definition: God is the God who turns to us, who is turned to us. In this definition, God limits Godself to exist in this boundary crossing as the God who does not exclude us from Godself, and above all does not exclude Godself from us. God does indeed exclude, but only what would separate God from us and us from God. In not excluding Godself from us, God will

definitely always reserve the right to fight for the exclusion of whatever is a deadly threat against God's turning to us, whatever aims to separate us from God.

God is defined in God's word of assurance to us, and in gracious turning to us as the One whose being consists in being for us. God is the One who belongs to us, the One dedicated to us, sharing with us and claiming to be ours, devoted and vulnerable. But there is still more. We would not be saying that God really turns to give attention to *us,* we would not be acknowledging our own deep involvement, if we did not say further that by graciously turning to us, God is the one who takes part in our being, just as we are, and in what we are up against. We matter to God, who is able to hold us in the divine heart, who as such is in the position to take what burdens and troubles us from ourselves onto Godself.

God is the "God of all comfort." Again, the uniqueness of the comfort lies in what is first of all binding for Godself — being *this* God. And again, God is defined this way in God's own freedom. God becomes our neighbor, to be sure, but not our possession. We can depend on, but not control God. God is with us as our comfort, but not as our furniture. God is ours, not on the basis of our limited knowing, by which *we* know things, not in themselves, but only in relation to us. If God were ours only on the basis of this limitation of ours, then we would have to do with God only as God appears to us, but not with God's own self. So God would actually be someone else. But if God is ours on the basis of God's own freedom, then in the God who is *ours,* we have to do with God's own self.

3. The self-definition of God cuts out the idea that God is a universal being, and all particular descriptions according to which God is this or that are only human conceptions of God, adaptations to suit ourselves, or ideas about God that are incidental, and could be lacking without God's ceasing to be God. Such conceptions or views could probably be explained as various "ways of salvation." The god of various ways of salvation is always the god of that undetermined, universal being. That god is the undecided, neutral god who lacks the capability to decide to be this one and only this one, this kind of God, and only this kind. It is that god, who does not want to be bound to being our god, with regard to whom we correspondingly need not and dare not bind ourselves to the way that kind of god is given us. Toward that god one *must* posit various ways of salvation. That god is not ours on the basis of God's own self-definition, but because we say so. Then much is possible without our having to tie it down in particulars. Along this line we can finally only say with Faust,

Name it what you will,
Name it Happiness! Heart! Love! God!
I have no name
For it! Feeling is everything; name is sound and smoke. . . .[3]

This notion may be insightful in its own way. Perhaps there is nothing else reasonably left than this, once we look away from God's self-definition in God's self-disclosure. But we cannot look away from God's self-definition once we have caught sight of it. It is not the case that we reject Faust's notion and then bind ourselves to another one. Rather, our being drawn to God's self-definition is the result of our meeting the God who has first made a decision that affects God's own self. This decision is to be the One who is known in graciously turning to us. By this decision God excludes the notion of existing as a universal being. *God* excludes it because God is actually the most special being — the God who alone wills to be God in this way:

Before you made me by your hand,
In your own heart you boldly planned
How *you* would now be *mine*.[4]

Never apart from this concrete and gracious turning to us, but only in it, is God truly God. So the god of universal being is not the god with whom we have to do, or more importantly, who has to do with us.

4. All this makes clear in what sense the talk of the "only comfort" is to be understood. It has to do with the reliable faithfulness in which God in Jesus Christ commits to be *this* God, the "God of all comfort." It has to do with the good reason for us to hold on to the conviction that God is always, even in the greatest adversity, our God, our "faithful savior." If we were to proceed from a need for comfort grounded in the human heart, in order then to search for how we could satisfy it in the most advantageous way, then we could not speak of an "only" comfort, or could do so only presumptuously. We could merely say that the "Christian comfort" is one possibility among others to satisfy this need. Even if persons in need of comfort choose the Christian possibility, or if living in Western culture

3. J. W. von Goethe, *Faust.* Marthens Garden.
4. From stanza 1 of the hymn "Ich steh an deiner Krippe hier" ("I Stand Here by Your Manger"), by P. Gerhardt.

suggests it, they would still always be circling around themselves as the center of their lives. Christ would be only the helping hand for these persons to obtain what they at times cannot obtain for themselves. Christ would have influence on them only on condition that Christ deliver to these I-centered persons what they ask for. Christ would then be the object of a human desire, which as such defines what a god has to provide. Christ would in principle always be replaceable by something else, or combinable with something else that satisfies just as well or better the alleged desire of these people for support. The Christ chosen by these selfish ones as their comfort can at any time be thrown away, and it is probably only the power of habit, or "tradition," or lack of knowledge and opportunity that keeps them from doing this. But they *can* always do it, because in this framework their desire is the constant, and what satisfies it is variable. Hidden in this framework lies a natural unfaithfulness toward all to whom these persons may turn in their yearning.

But this framework is broken where the promise of God in Jesus Christ meets us. This is the promise that God will in *any* case be our God and *no* other. Here we are moved to a trust that relies on this, and, what is decisive, relies *only* on this. For this trust is founded on the trustworthiness of God, which excludes the possibility that God could be other than who God is here shown to be. It would be foolhardy, actually unfaithful to the faithful God, to reckon in the same breath with even the possibility of other "revelations" of God. According to these revelations, the content of the will of God would be other than that which has here been made known. According to them, God could just as well not be the One who pledges to be our only comfort in living and in dying. What indifference would have to be in us if we once got this God in view and then did not believe God's word! And how much "tolerance" does such indifference attribute to *God!*

5. God's self-defining by crossing over the boundary to us is also the basis for our *knowledge* of God. In God's self-giving to us, God is also given to be known as our God. God's gracious turning to us meets us concretely as God's word of assurance to us. By coming in word, God wants to be known by us, to be taken seriously by us. In this way God wants us to "take every thought captive to obey Christ" (2 Cor. 10:5). But let us not talk thoughtlessly about the danger of "intellectualizing faith"! That way we could let a dark, mindless irrationalism have the floor. The word of God to us does not turn off our mind. It enlightens our mind. It does our mind good to think about God. But it is truly important that the word of God to

us is not directed only to our head, but to our whole heart. It is an ongoing event that embraces our life, body and soul. Because God's word to us is God's gracious turning to us, the grounding of all knowledge of God must be summarized in the sentence: God gives Godself to be known by us. This sentence has two meanings. For one, it says God grants to us that we know God. So our possibility of knowing God does not lie within ourselves, and we do not bring it from ourselves to God's disclosure. The only, but real, possibility of knowing God is given to us in that God gives God's self for us to know.

This does not create a sixth sense in us. But the way our senses know God is not that we begin with ourselves, and in particular with our reason, which seeks out this object to be known and then subsumes it under the principles of our reason. Rather, our knowledge of God takes place in the opposite way. This object to be known chooses us as the persons it addresses. Our reason and our senses need to adjust themselves to the structures that lie in the object of our knowing. In this sense God is known only through God. Second, that we know God in God's giving God's self to be known means that we are dependent on this giving-of-God's-self-to-be-known. This is not about the giving of a gift we previously did not have, and afterward possess. God is not at first merely hidden, in order then only to be revealed to us. Rather, the giving-of-God's-self-to-be-known remains in God's hands. We know nothing if God does not again and again give God's self to be known. So we must say that only when God becomes *revealed* do we know who the *hidden* God is. It is the God who, in giving Godself to us to be known, also withdraws. For in letting us know about Godself, God establishes a relationship in which we are constantly dependent on God's self-giving to be known by us anew.

6. God's defining Godself as our God, and giving Godself to be known in this way, is the description of something that has *happened*. We know that God has defined Godself, and done it this way, only by the fact that God has done it in a particular time and place, in the context of a particular history, in the bearer of a particular name. Everything that is to be said here, and that I have tried to say up to now, must stand under the clear sign of action that has happened (not, for example, that might happen or ought to happen). "It is finished" (John 19:30). If theological knowledge sways here even a little, it soon lands on slippery ground. "No other foundation can anyone lay than *has* been laid, which is Christ Jesus" (1 Cor. 3:11). In the context of the history of Israel, it is he "in whom lie hidden all the treasures of wisdom and understanding" (Col. 2:3). In him God has defined himself as our God. In him God

has shared our common lot and so is made known to us. Take away this time aspect of the verbs and you have set all of Christian faith on sand!

This time aspect is of a very special kind. It denotes an event that in having happened has not become just a dead, closed past. Such a past we could let rest, or reach back to, as we please. We then would need to make it alive again for today by all kinds of artifices, or continue it by new experiences. There could be no more fundamental denial of the resurrection of Christ than this! It is an event with which we have to do today, not just because it has historical consequences, like the appearance of a Goethe, or the First and Second World Wars. It is an event in which God has defined Godself at a *particular* time. But in this particular time, it is *God* who is doing the defining as our God: God, by offering Jesus into death, but then also into his exaltation to life, by which God did not leave him hemmed in by death. It is an event that indeed happened *once,* but once for *all time.* Hence in its time aspect it can neither become past nor be superseded by further time. It goes from itself beyond itself into every time, including ours, in order to present itself to us as that event which has to do with us directly, affecting us immediately. It is current, not because we actualize it. We try to understand it as current because it *is* current. Because this event that has taken place cannot become dead past, there is also no present and future empty of it, which we would then need to fill with it, or with some substitute. God would not have defined Godself as our God if this were not as valid today as then, if it were not as contemporary as it was for Peter and Paul and the others. The "ugly ditch"[5] between then and today only God can overcome. But God does overcome it. "God himself spoke to the fathers, prophets, apostles, and still speaks to us."[6] Therefore Article 1 rightly says that the One who in Christ has "liberated" you by action completed in the past, is in the present "your only comfort in life and in death."

7. The first thing we can know of God is the gospel that above all and before all, God has defined God's self as our God. We need to act in accord with this, both in theological work and in church proclamation, by always

---

5. G. E. Lessing, "Über den Beweis des Geistes und der Kraft" (1777), in Lessing, *Gesammelte Werke,* vol. 9 (Leipzig, 1856), p. 85. ET: "On the Proof of the Spirit and of Power," in *Lessing's Theological Writings* (London: A. & C. Black, 1956), p. 55.

6. *Zweites Helvetisches Bekenntnis* (1562) acc. to E. F. K. Müller, ed., *Die Bekenntnisschriften der reformierten Kirche* (Leipzig: Deichert Verlag, 1903), p. 170. ET: *The Second Helvetic Confession,* in *The Book of Confessions,* Part 1 of the Constitution of the Presbyterian Church (U.S.A.) (Louisville: Office of the General Assembly, Presbyterian Church [U.S.A.], 1994), p. 55.

beginning with the gospel. Since God has begun by first of all turning graciously to us, and has bound Godself to be the One who is graciously turned to us, there is nothing else we can do than begin here in our thinking, speaking, and acting. God's going ahead precludes the human going ahead of the divine. It excludes our reversing the order by having a preliminary knowledge of God that precedes the gospel. So we ought not declare what we know by ourselves, even though it be in religious matters, as preliminary knowledge. What "God has revealed to us through the Spirit . . . no eye has seen and no ear has heard, nor has it entered into the human heart" apart from this revelation (1 Cor. 2:10-11). A person knows nothing about it except it be given by a word addressed to him or her. And if the word comes to a person, then it is by all means a "story good and new."[7] When it tells us that God is our God, we do not need to worry that this will be incomprehensible to people. The gospel speaks concretely each time into the human situation. To be sure, even the most precise analysis of the human situation cannot anticipate what the good news is going to say to it. There is no sense, then, in attaching to the sharing of the gospel any sort of preambles that are not already oriented to the gospel. Such preambles would necessarily lift the person sharing the gospel into the role of a sort of mediator between God and humanity, in competition with Christ and the Holy Spirit. And such preambles would just as necessarily be based on some kind of knowledge prior to the gospel. One way this would work out is that you dissolve the gospel into mere clarification of what you basically already know and have. Another way is that you lose yourself in continual precaution against any inappropriate prior knowledge that might govern the course of one's thinking and speaking, with the result that you can articulate the gospel only in continual reaction against such knowledge. In one way or the other, you stay stuck in prefaces. In one way or the other you withhold the gospel from people. In one way or the other you go against the apostolic word, "I am not ashamed of the gospel of Jesus Christ" (Rom. 1:16). What an appalling view of the gospel must a person have to think that not only its misuse but also its right use would be an encumbrance and impertinence without such unevangelical preambles! It is as though the gospel would not be palatable for people without the admixture of syrup that actually works against the gospel! Since for God, self-determination to be our God is the beginning of God's way with us, how

---

7. From stanza 1 of the hymn "Vom Himmel hoch," by M. Luther. ET: "From Heaven on High" in *LW* 53:289.

far would we have to be from the gospel if taking this beginning seriously is not first and most urgent for us as well!

2.1.2. Our Belonging to God

"What is your only comfort in life and in death?" We said that God is this comfort, our Comforter, because of being our God in the "faithful savior" Jesus Christ. In light of this statement, the answer the catechism sees emphatically given to its question becomes more illuminating than ever: This is my only comfort, "that I belong . . . not to myself, but to my faithful Savior Jesus Christ" (I am his). The testimony that "I am not my own, but Christ's" cannot be detached from the testimony given at the same time, that this same Jesus Christ is "my faithful savior" (He is mine). Both testimonies belong so firmly together that they describe one and the same event in two phrases. The first phrase, that he is ours, includes the second, that we are his. If we say only the second (that we are his) without this being the immediate consequence of the first (that God has caused God's self to be our God) then we are saying what the principle of "natural theology" is: that persons on their own initiative are open for God. Then we fundamentally contest that belonging to God depends completely on God's grace alone. Then belonging to God is part of a person by nature (as "religion"). Then God resides in the extension of that toward which a person reaches out, ventures forth, asks about. This may be in the form of an intuition, a search for the satisfaction of a need, or the drive to create something new. In this conception, instead of your being close to God because God has come close, it is you who are already close to God and come closer on your own. In place of God who reveals God's self comes your openness for something other than God, which is interpreted as being ultimately open for "God."

What shows that this conception runs counter to God's revelation, rather than being simply its corresponding human side, is the fact that it has no room for God's revelation as God's self-definition. In this conception, God is actually that undefined being which receives its definition through what you attribute to it, put into it, imagine it having. You make these projections, believing they lead to the fulfillment and confirmation of your intuitions, or needs, or openness to what is new. If in this view God could be called "our God" it would not be because God *is* this according to self-definition in God's self-revelation. In this view God is actually considered more divine the more God is kept away from everything human. In this view God is actually not our God, because God does not choose at all and does not determine to be our God. Rather, I choose and decide that God will be my God. If God could still be called "our God," then it would be only because God appears so on the basis of my expectations directed toward God. God is thereby the symbol for the possible fulfillment of these expectations. In this way there comes, instead of God's self-revelation, a human impression or a number of varied human impressions of the divine, depending on the various expectations directed toward God. Then the protest would make sense that I cannot set up any one of these various impressions as absolute. But that is a protest that would make sense only on the assumption that we basically have to disregard God's self-revelation and self-definition as our God. The protest depends on the belief that we know nothing more of God than our own varied human impressions.

It is just as mistaken, however, to say the first phrase (that God is our God) without stating that the event this denotes includes the truth of the second phrase (that we are God's) as its immediate consequence. For if we speak only the first phrase, then we are giving expression to what the *result* of such "natural theology" is: that a person would like to have power over God. Then we contest that God is ours only in God's own freedom. Then I, who belong only to myself, understand God as one of the objects I include in the attempt to treat everything as my own, as being naturally available. This is the attempt of a person who generally measures, weighs, values, estimates, and orders everything by the question, "What does it do for me?" All this is to further my well-being, heighten my happiness, secure and increase my possessions, enhance my position. It is the attempt of persons who sometimes let themselves be served by others, and sometimes serve themselves at the expense of others. What is the outcome when I, according to the principle of "natural theology," possess a natural openness for God and when "God" has to correspond to the conditions of this human openness? How can this sort of theology avoid coming out at the point where I circle around myself, relate everything to myself, and now even cap it all off by trying to draw God into this circling around myself?

When it finally comes out at this point, the truth about this theology is uncovered. Even persons open to God, with whom this theology begins, do not get free from themselves, as it claims. Rather, these persons stand in the center of their efforts, and as such dictate the conditions for a relationship with God. So they finally besiege and exploit the Most High with their questions: What do I get from religion? What do I get from God? How do I get into heaven? How do I get a satisfying solution to my ultimate questions and needs? And how can that be fitted into what I already make my own? If these persons were already alone to begin with, then in the end they are all the more so, and receive through "religion" just a final protection of their being by themselves. If they can name God as their God, they can do so only by bracketing in the fact that they had already chosen God to be their God. They will then honor only the deity whom they have previously subjected themselves to. They will bow only to the deity whom they have previously fashioned to suit themselves and whom they are able to subsume in the framework of interests that results from their grasping for everything possible.

Christian theology can naturally only reject such "natural theology." For the god whom a person can have power over is not God at all; it is a scarecrow. Christian knowledge stands or falls with the insight that God chooses to be ours and thereby chooses us to be God's. Yes, God cannot become ours without our ceasing to be our own, entitled to ourselves. And we cannot be God's except through the One who is beforehand self-defined as ours. "Natural theology" militates against this, as Christian theology must militate against "natural theology." Although the same words can apparently be used on both sides, they mean different things, which differ more fundamentally than fire and water. Everything depends on clarity about the fact that we have to choose between these two theologies. For Christian theology there can be no lack of clarity about how it has to choose.

Not a word would need to be spent on this if Christian theology were not again and again tempted to make "natural theology" an even greater problem by combining instead of choosing. It is drawn to this by an enticing argument: in order to make Christian convictions persuasive we have to connect with views already familiar to people, otherwise the convictions will not be understandable. This is indeed true. "All speaking means connecting." This was the assertion of Karl Barth, known for his "No" to natural theology.[8] But the decisive question is: How does this connecting take place? It takes place rightly only when the two alternative gods are not brought down to any common denominator. On the one hand is that false god whom we choose as ours, and set ourselves as belonging to. On the other hand is the true God of the gospel who chooses to be our God, and chooses us to belong to God. The connecting takes place rightly only when from the beginning we handle that first alternative in accordance with the

---

8. K. Barth, *KD* IV/3, p. 569. *CD* IV/3, p. 495.

gospel, and by no means vice versa. If we work in the opposite direction, then the message of the gospel will unavoidably be integrated into the framework of human possibilities for setting oneself in relation to an Ultimate and belonging to it. But the gospel goes beyond the scope of this framework. If we stay in this framework, then concern that the gospel be understood will inevitably find the criterion for the goodness and usefulness of the gospel in human intuitions, needs, and preconceptions. To be sure, the gospel speaks of God's goodness toward us, and of the comfort granted us. But no one can tell on one's own, and before actually encountering the gospel, that it is good for us. Here the saying applies, "Appetite comes with eating." The fact that "the need does not come before its satisfaction"[9] is characteristic of believing in the gospel.

This is the way to speak if it is true that by defining God's self as ours, God also leads us to know who we really are, and that therefore a person is not to be viewed otherwise than in the light of this decision. Let us inquire further about the meaning of the testimony made about us this way.

1. Our belonging to God definitely does not mean that we are by nature beings so open to God that the more we are in touch with ourselves, the more we are in touch with God. It also has the critical meaning that we do not belong to ourselves. That "I belong to my faithful Savior Jesus Christ" excludes belonging to myself. The Yes spoken to us unconditionally is not to be had without an equally unconditional No spoken to us at the same time. It is the No to those who believe they belong to themselves and who conceive of themselves as their own property. They are thus schooled to see and deal with everything by means of the question "What is mine?" They sometimes try to secure their "I" from the grasp of others, and sometimes attack others to enrich themselves, making life insecure for others. For those who make themselves the midpoint of all things, meeting God means the shaking, the denial, yes, the annulment of their circling around themselves. Meeting God will set a definite limit to their drive to exclude and to acquire, to their measuring everything by "what I get from it." Their life then receives a new center. And this center will without fail no longer lie in themselves. It now lies in God — not in an empty, strange God, but in the One who is our God. Therefore not only the Yes of God is beneficial and comforting to them but also the No. Therefore this No is just the reverse side of the Yes. Therefore a person is not submerged under

---

9. E. Jüngel, *Anfechtung und Gewissheit des Glaubens* (Munich: Kaiser Verlag, 1976), p. 59.

this No. For by it you truly gain yourself, in a new way, so that you lose your previous isolated central position. The *question* in Article 1 may give the appearance that I am looking for ultimate security for my central position. But the *answer* dispels this appearance: This is my whole comfort in living and in dying, that I with body and soul "do not belong to myself." Because God in Christ belongs to me, in God I am a person who belongs to God and not to myself. Jesus says: "Those who would save their lives will lose them; but those who lose their lives for my sake will keep them" (Mark 8:35). In no other way than by being graciously drawn out of the central position will a person be saved. This is my salvation and my comfort, that I do not belong to myself, but am one who belongs to Jesus Christ.

2. The truly comforting nature of this assurance becomes clear when we deal with an objection that lies close at hand. The word "belong" is often threatening to people. "That I belong to him" arouses fears that we wind up under the alien rule of an authoritarian, subjecting, enslaving tyrant. These are fears of the selfish person who circles around self and distrustfully suspects that all others are just as selfish. Yet all the distrust does not prevent a sad result, but provokes it. What happens is like what happens when a person in great fear tries to get out of the way of a dog. The result is that the dog now really becomes eager to attack. Again and again tyrants show up who circle around and get people twisted and turned. These tyrants do not let go until they have sucked their victims dry; then, they let them fall. "That I belong . . . to my faithful savior Jesus Christ" does not mean that we selfish persons are subjected to another selfish person. It does not throw us from one comfortless situation into another. "That I belong to my faithful savior" says that through him and in him, who as ours is surely not selfish, I am graciously drawn out of this being who circles around itself, who lurks in me, and also meets me from outside in the form of selfish tyrants. It says that through him and in him I am freed — from abandonment to such alien rulers, but also from the "tyrant in my own breast."[10] If I belong to the one who frees me, then I am really free; free not for myself alone, but free through him, so also with him and for him. I am free from my egoistic loneliness, in which all those alien rulers try to attack me, or in which I may try to defend myself by asserting my will against them, resulting in a still more tenacious circling around my self.

That I "belong to my faithful savior" tells me: You are not alone, and not for yourself only, as you vainly think and accordingly act, and as, to

10. K. Barth, *KD* I/2, p. 749; *CD* I/2, p. 668.

your sorrow, you also experience from outside. You are not deserted by God. In Christ, God is truly and inseparably with you. Because God belongs to you completely, you also belong completely to God. As God has invested the divine freedom in being our God, so our being destined for freedom depends on God's choosing us as God's own. As our God takes part in our existence, just as it is, with all we are up against, so we are God's in that God grants us to take part in the life of God, in the divine peace, righteousness, and mercy. The Bible passage which the Heidelberg has its eye on here, and which really says all that is needed, is Romans 14:7ff.: "We do not live to ourselves, and we do not die to ourselves. If we live, we live to the Lord, and if we die, we die to the Lord; so then, whether we live or whether we die, we are the Lord's."

3. How comforting this is, and how little it can be used to support the allegation of an authoritarian power over us, becomes even more obvious when we make the following facts clear: The question of whether an alien rule is set up over us by our belonging to Christ can really be asked only when we forget that something burdensome and alien is expected of Christ, not of us. The question is not: "What do we get out of it?" The question is: "What does he get out of it, if we are his?" Advantages? Uses? Increase of his possessions? Rather, this is what he gets from it: giving, and giving himself away; costs upon costs; cares and burdens! Who are we for him? — Lost ones, like that lost son of Luke 15:11ff.; besmirched like that son, who "squander" our gifts in dissolute living; who, in a literal or figurative sense wind up with the pigs; people about the best of whom it is said in the decisive hour "Then all deserted him" (Mark 14:50). Could he not, would he not have to say to us, "Depart from me, all of you" (Matt. 7:23; 25:41)? Would he not have every right to say, "I do not want to be yours"?! If there is something like a Hell, then we should not picture it by means of all kinds of childish ideas, or as the place portrayed by the old painters, which really appears much more interesting than a heaven inhabited by palm-waving young men and women. No, we have to envisage, simply and terribly, an existence under that divine judgment because he justly does not want to have anything more to do with us.

But now this is "my comfort," that he does not deal with us this way. "He does not deal with us according to our sins" (Ps. 103:10). He deals with us like that father with his lost son. The father neither demands improvement as a condition for being accepted, nor extracts a confession of penitence, nor otherwise gives a moral lecture on guilt before he accepts him. Rather, this is how he acts: "But while the son was still far off, his father saw him and was filled with compassion; he ran and put his arms around him and kissed him" (Luke 15:20). "That I belong . . . to my faithful savior" is comfort because it is the very opposite of "Depart from me!" Instead, it is identical with the consoling word "Come to me, all you that are weary and are carrying heavy burdens" (Matt. 11:28). This word is directed not only to those who feel this way, but to all, because without him we are all in this shape. The church is where this call of the savior is spoken and heard as refreshing, liberating good news — and not where the church makes it a claim for domination: "Come to Christianity!" Likewise, the good news is not where this comforting word is watered down to a matter of private opinion. Then, in tolerance, no one can seriously be required to believe it, because a person could in good conscience hold another opinion. (To be sure, it is good if such weak stuff is not required of anyone!) But the good news, and the church, are where persons who live under the burden and malice of all the claims to domination, and under the hardship of trying to lessen these by themselves, receive the savior's call to their comfort, refreshment, and revival.

4. In light of what has been said, what we are now going to add should not be misunderstood as an authoritarian disposition over us. That "I belong . . . not to myself, but to my faithful savior," that we are related to him and do not exist just for ourselves — all this is not the result of our own decision. This does not, however, exclude our decision, and thus is not intended to have validity without our reflecting on it, and giving our assent. But our decision cannot create the validity; it can only acknowledge it. Our decision can only haltingly follow what has already been decided before we are even in a position to make a decision in this matter. The decision was made "while we were still weak" (Rom. 5:6). It has been decided in advance, going before our decisions, because it is included in God's decision to be our God. If this is our God, and no other, we are therefore and thereby not without God. So we are those who belong to God. This is so not because of who we are in ourselves, or because of what we have done. The possibility for it is not realizable by us; it is granted us by God. God's love for us alone creates those loved by God, who as such belong to God. God's belonging to us and our belonging to God can never be separated from each other:

> When I was not yet born, *you* were born for *me*,
> And before I ever knew you, chose *me* to be *your* own.[11]

11. From stanza 2 of the hymn "Ich steh an deiner Krippe hier" ("I Stand Here by Your Manger"), by P. Gerhardt.

We would put in question our entire comfort in living and dying if we wanted to make it depend on the condition that it holds only if we ourselves make God ours. Our entire comfort depends on the fact that the relationship in which I am no longer alone is brought about and sustained by an event in which Jesus Christ is the creative subject, not we. It is brought about not because we reach out to him and want to come to terms with him. It comes about only by his coming into our midst and binding himself with us and us with him.

At issue here, after all, is overcoming the selfishness of persons who always circle around themselves and thus end up being alone and for themselves. Selfish people can do a lot: they can become pairs, and can even conceive the principle that there has always been a relationship among all things. But this does not make them partners with God. Whatever they do on their own, they are not able to overcome their selfish nature. They must be "ransomed," "redeemed," made free. Only by God's *making* them God's own in Christ are they actually God's own. Only because God does not leave us alone, and because God persists in not leaving us alone, are we in fact not alone. The two-sided relation between God and ourselves, which is the aim of God's action in Jesus Christ, is and remains one-sidedly grounded in the grace of God. This is why I cannot reverse the sentence and make it say that my comfort is that Christ "belongs to me" — as though Christ should be glad that we do not leave him alone, when actually everything depends on his not leaving us alone.

5. What has just been said puts a question mark behind the endeavor into which so much zeal, energy, and imagination have been invested in our times. It is the endeavor to devise *ways* and *methods* by which we or others can *become* the kind of persons who "belong to Christ." Handled as an isolated task, this is trying to go down a blind alley. It starts from "outside," independently from belonging to Christ — and this independence is seriously taken for granted from the outset. Then it constructs stairs and bridges on which by our skill (if possible, unnoted) we can get beyond this "outside." But the starting point is false. So all the labor is in vain. If we start from such an "outside," then we will, at every conceivable end of our way, always still be "outside" of belonging to Christ. Finally we may imagine, on the basis of our movement from A to B in the blind alley, that we are no longer in it. Or we may satisfy ourselves with the clever theory that walking in place in that blind alley is also something meaningful. In any case there is no way — outside of the one who says "I am the Way" (John 14:6). No method, no way, can take his place. All methods are only worth

anything as they serve him. And in practice, that means this: they are of worth when they clearly and unswervingly move from the *starting point* that it is not first *we* who need to search for a way, to find it, to travel it, and to lead others on it. For he who is *the* Way wants to and will search for and find us all. Yes, he *has* already found us. I can only in response secondarily ask how we *become* those who recognize and understand what we already *are* in and through Christ. I certainly cannot and may not think about this by trying to bring it out of my own self-awareness. I can only discover that we *are* Christ's (before we "become" so from our side) if I do not say "I" and "we," but rather speak of *Jesus Christ*. If I talk about him, then I may truly sing and say:

> Now I will cling forever to Christ, my Savior true,
> My Lord will leave me never, whate'er He passes through.
> He rends Death's iron chain, he breaks through sin and pain,
> He shatters hell's dark thrall, I follow him through all.[12]

6. From all this, we draw the following conclusion: God, by defining Godself as the one who belongs to us, also *defines us humans* as those who belong to God. The revelation of God is at the same time the revelation of humankind. This seriously contests the idea that we already know by our own insight who we are. Just as it is important to understand that the self-definition of God is not something secondary that we might do without — when God *defines* God's self as ours then God *is* ours — so the corresponding truth holds for us. We *are* not really or essentially what we make ourselves out to be when we look at ourselves: a being intellectually superior to animals, or conversely a form of life to be subsumed biologically in the animal world; an incomplete being driven by unfulfilled desires; or a person always creating something new, with a view now more toward individuality, now more toward sociability, now conceived more from the head ("I think, therefore I am"[13]), now more from the stomach ("One is what one eats"[14]).

These kinds of discussions theology should treat like the apocrypha: "not to be held equal to holy scripture, and yet useful and good to read."

12. Stanza 6 of the hymn "Auf, auf mein Herz mit Freuden," by Paul Gerhardt. ET: "Awake My Heart with Gladness," by J. Kelly.

13. R. Descartes, *Discourse on Method* (1637), part 4, par. 3.

14. L. Feuerbach, cf. K. Barth, *Die Theologie und die Kirche* (Munich, 1928), p. 218. ET: *Theology and Church* (New York: Harper & Row, 1962), p. 221.

Theology will no doubt join the conversation, may take sides, and perhaps also have something to contribute. But if theology were to do any more than get involved secondarily, then one of these definitions would necessarily become so important that the definition of humankind given by God would become a side issue. Then we would have to say: human nature is this and this — and already so defined, can then also, among other things, be destined by God. But this is then such an incidental predicate of our otherwise determined nature that it could also be lacking without our essence being affected. Or do we think we can avoid such a definition of human nature, formulated without considering God — a God-less definition — by saying that our being destined by God, in the form of an inclination toward spirituality, *alongside* its being destined, for example, by its stomach or intellect, is part of our basic human equipment? But then we could only say that it is part of being human to have religion, among other things. We could never say that it is the essence of being human to belong to God.

In contrast, Christian theology cannot insist strongly enough that humanity is defined by God in the encounter with God, and that humanity essentially and truly *is* what this definition says. Just as we do not think rightly about God if we do not think of God as the one who according to God's own self-definition is the God who comes to belong to us, so we can say nothing truer about ourselves than this: in Jesus Christ and because of him we belong to God. We are God's humanity. We are humans not of ourselves, but of God. Though we are not placed on a level with God in the sense of being equal to, or within God, still we are placed *through* God's own being into being *with* God. If we set aside this truth in Christian theology, even if we do so in order to take humanity with utmost seriousness, we talk right past humanity and do not really take it seriously. We do not understand human nature when we view the human being who sets itself as the center of all things as the true, real human, instead of as the lost human who has forgotten its own self (which even then is not lost, but only because God has not let it be lost).

Furthermore, we will misunderstand and misuse the self-definition of God as our God — interpreting it in the framework of our selfish drive to possess — if it does not include the definition of ourselves as belonging to God. The word of God's becoming flesh (John 1:14), which involves God's self-determination to be our God, includes within it that God comes "to what is his own" (John 1:11), and so to those who are thereby declared to belong to God. This is why someone who deliberately "in and of oneself" lives outside of what God has destined us to be is not only alienated from God, but also from one's own self, and is a lost son or lost daughter. This is also why, when I recognize that my comfort is that I do not belong to myself but to my "faithful savior," I am not put under an authoritarian foreign power. On the contrary, I am brought home out of my alienation from God and from myself.

The fact that *Jesus Christ* is the subject of the main clause in the answer of Article 1 holds together the double assertion we have been talking about and makes it into an assurance of faith that can be expressed this way: because God is the one who belongs to us, we are the ones who belong to God. Jesus Christ is also the subject of the entire following statement, which is just an explanatory subordinate clause to the main clause. This subordinate clause shows very clearly that God's comfort is no delayed promise, no mere sympathizing, no comfort of the sort that E. von Feuchtersleben rejected: "For a real person, comfort is not healthy, because it makes one weak."[15] Nor is it the sort of comfort lamented about in Shakespeare: "Comfort's in heaven, and we are on the earth."[16] This subordinate clause underscores in three respects the main clause: I belong to Christ and belong together with him, so I am not alone — either in my sin, or in my creatureliness, or in my earthly end.

To the first point: Christ's not leaving me alone in my sin does not mean that he takes up company with sin. Rather, it means that he draws us out of our company with sin, tears us loose from the imprisonment in which it will not let us loose, takes on himself the cost of our liberation, and provides for our release. Behind this stands the Hebrew word *ga'al,* which means ransom, redeem. He draws us out of a false bond, which we enter as we are enticed by the prospect of having many things, whereas the outcome is that many things "have" us. Christ draws us out of the kind of bond in which these many things devote themselves to getting something from us, until they cannot get any more, until we are empty, burnt out, and ready to be thrown away. Out of this false bond — "all the power of the devil" — he draws us with his "blood," which means he does it in such a way that he commits nothing less than his own self for us. As he draws us out, that false bond is reversed in his bond with us. He expends what he is and what belongs to him so that we will have "some-

---

15. E. von Feuchtersleben, *Zur Diätetik der Seele* (1838). ET: *The Dietetics of the Soul* (London: John Churchill, 1852), p. 166.

16. W. Shakespeare, *King Richard the Second,* Act II, Scene 2.

thing" from him, namely that instead of being throwaways, we become saved and kept in him.

In drawing us out of the false bond, Christ does not take something that does not belong to him. No, that kind of action characterizes "the power of the devil," which grabs what it is not entitled to. In pulling us loose from this foreign rule and taking us to his side, Christ does something he has the right to do, and does it to what is his own. But he does not simply take control. He does to us what is in our own best interest. For he adopts us "body and soul," and heals the unholy split between body and soul into which sin throws us, and from which we try in vain to save ourselves. We try in various ways: idealistically — while despising the body, wanting to present the soul as something divine, hoping for salvation by cutting the soul loose from the body; or materialistically — while suppressing the spiritual, letting the Tempter inform us that humans live "by bread alone" (Matt. 4:3-4) and so can liberate themselves by solving this problem. However, since by the power of Christ's redemption we belong to him body and soul, nothing can separate us from him. Therefore we can no longer separate body and soul from one another. In our being drawn into belonging to Christ we also have our own selves given to us as bodily-spiritual beings. He does not leave us alone in our sin. Drawn away from the siren song of sin, we now listen to him to whom we belong.

To the second point: I am not left alone in my bodily-spiritual creatureliness, but in it belong to Christ. Not only the soul, but also the body needs comfort and is promised it by God. "Whoever comforts the soul, should also comfort the body."[17] So I belong to Christ not only at death, but already in life. I will not belong to him on the other side if I do not already belong to him on this side. But I do belong to him on this side, because by redeeming me from my sin he has shown that creaturely existence as such belongs to him and is not foreign to him. He redeems us from our sins, and precisely because of this does not redeem us from our creaturehood. In fact he "takes care" of it — to the smallest details — so "that not a hair can fall from my head without the will of my Father in heaven" (cf. Matt. 10:29-31). Now here many examples of suffering and evil come to mind in which God apparently has not guarded us or others in our creaturely life. True, this divine guarding takes place in such a hidden way that we often think it does not take place at all. But by speaking of it in second place, the Catechism gives us a pointer: Only when we believe the

17. H. Urner, "Paracelsus als Christ," *Evangelische Theologie* 9 (1949): 300.

first — that our sins do not cut us off from God — will we believe the second — that neither can anything else separate us from God. However hidden it may be to us, God says yes, and not no, to our creaturely life. We can only believe, largely against appearances, but yet believe, that the same God who loves us sinners gives no creature up for lost. And this same One sees to it that "everything must work together for my salvation." They must not drive me away from God. Rather, because first and last God stands hidden behind them all, they always draw me closer to God, and as I encounter them my trust in God deepens.

Finally, to the third point: Christ does not leave me alone in the future either, including at the place where I must die, where my body and soul will have an end, and I will have no more time. In view of this I cannot simply console myself by saying that this is just the way of all flesh. For this my end poses a problem. At my end does my belonging to him as he belongs to me also come to an end? Does not his giving himself to redeem me from all sins and "from the power of the devil" cease, so that this holds for me only temporarily, and then one day, when my days end, does not hold any more? Does not the love of God in Christ for us cease, because through our departure it loses its object? No, no one and nothing will tear us out of his hand (John 10:28). It will not be our "I," to which we cling so tenaciously, that will bear up eternally. But his love for us will do so. "Because I belong to him, Christ, by his Holy Spirit, assures me of eternal life." Eternal life is not the unending continuation of our life; it is the everlastingness of God's love for us. Though our temporal life is used up at our end, yet it remains *lifted up* in God's eternal love. This "love never ends" (1 Cor. 13:8). "God's steadfast love endures forever" (Ps. 100:5). Those whom God has loved in time can never be lost eternally. And this is what — because we cannot escape it — will finally move us to give up the resistance in which we try to live without or against God.

This is what will make us "wholeheartedly willing and ready to live for him from now on" — in our own affirmation with body and soul, in living and in dying, to live, to think, to feel, to act, to sigh, as those who belong to God. We are not left alone by God, including when we sleep, and even when we die. But God's not being alone, and our not being without God — this would all be up in the air if we did not thankfully accede to God, in readiness "to live for him from now on."

2.1.3. God's Claim on Our Assent

We have to consider this last matter more closely. In the Heidelberg at this point, the work of the Holy Spirit is mentioned with just a few words. What is involved here is a third step that needs to be taken in reflecting on the one comfort in living and dying. If God is so free as to become ours, and if our freedom can lie only in our being destined to be God's, it follows that we are really *free* in the following way: as we are moved by God, we on our part *assent* to what God has done. We will try to outline this third statement in more detail.

1. As those who *belong* to the faithful Savior Jesus Christ we stand under his *claim* — we could also say it with the old word: under his Lordship. For as the savior he is also *Kyrios*, "the Lord," holder of counterpower against all that arrogates power to itself and rules violently. He is in the position to set us free "from the power of the devil," to expropriate us from the grasp of the power of evil, or evil power, and to make us his own. We cannot emphasize enough that his power is not a special case in the framework of what is otherwise called power. On the contrary, it falls outside of this framework and smashes it. It is not simply an escalation, a higher level of earthly, human power. If it were, it could not really overcome earthly power and power blocs. It would then be at any time subject to being surpassed, because it would be only a variation in the general scheme. His power is of another, new kind — and therefore cannot be overthrown (Heb. 12:28; Dan. 2:44). His "kingdom is not from this world" (John 18:36). He is the Lord as the *Savior*. The lordship which lies on his shoulders and in virtue of which the titles "wonderful, counselor, mighty God, Father, prince of peace" apply to him, is that of a child (Isa. 9:6). He rules as "the Lamb that was slaughtered," and who *as such* is on the throne (Rev. 5:8-14). So he can put in question any other powers.

Therefore, under Christ's rule you do not go from the frying pan into the fire, not from one power holder to another, but from an oppressing to a freeing lordship. And so the claim he makes on those "weary and carrying heavy burdens" whom he calls to himself is an "easy yoke" and a "light burden" (Matt. 11:30). But — "'So you are a king?' Jesus answered, 'You say that I am a king. For this I was born . . . to testify to the truth. Everyone who belongs to the truth listens to my voice'" (John 18:37). His word to us is not without his claim on us. In acting for us and in us, he expects something from us and with us. Those for whom he gives himself, he wants to gather for himself. To be sure, he sets them free and does not subsequently restrict this freedom. But this freedom is by its very nature not abstract, not detached from him, but bound. It is freedom bound to him. In his word to us he does not leave us to ourselves and our willfulness. Rather, by his word to us he takes away our willfulness and binds us to himself. Our freedom is that of those who listen to him, who hear his voice and follow it. This is what is meant in the best sense by the beautiful word *obedience,* which is misused so often through lack of understanding. This is what his lordship aims at: our obedience. He does not lay claim to something he has no right to, but to obedience from us, who stand with him, who belong to him. Others do not have the right to make an ultimate claim on us, and it is an evil fairy tale that obeying *him* means obeying *all* who are powerful. Obeying him makes us critical toward other claims. There is another problem besides that of "blind obedience," which is rightly condemned: obedience to a *false* power.

2. What shows that the appealing and exacting power of Jesus is the power of his *love* is the fact that what he does in and for us does not demand our mute subjection. What about the saying, "The word is free, obedience is blind"?[18] It is true that according to conventional wisdom a power is all the greater, the blinder the obedience it can gain from its subjects — the more it is "zombie obedience." If the power of Jesus is different from the power of earthly kingdoms, not only quantitatively, but also qualitatively, then it breaks this rule. Then the words "freedom" and "obedience," which are otherwise incompatible, move closely and inseparably together. Then blind obedience is just as impossible as free disobedience. Then freedom is obedient freedom and free obedience, as Calvin loved to say: "freewill obedience."[19] Then the power of Jesus cannot be acknowledged in mute subjection, but only in our being *"wholeheartedly willing and ready* to live for him from now on." What God in Christ has done in us and for us does indeed intervene mightily in our life. God therein not only makes a determination about Godself — namely, to be our God. God also makes a determination about us — namely, that we are God's. This latter also is not at our "free" disposal, and is not the result of our decision or the product of our achievement. Rather, God determines it. God's doing this for us and in us is the divine power God exercises toward us. But what shows that God does it for *us* and in *us,* and that it is a completely good de-

---

18. F. Schiller, *Wallensteins Lager,* Sz. 6. ET: *The Robbers and Wallenstein* (Harmondsworth: Penguin, 1979), Scene 6, Wallenstein's Camp.

19. Cf. e.g., J. Calvin, *Institutes* III.20.43.

termination, is the fact that it does not come over us like fate. It comes to us as an invitation to welcome, to consent, to verify, and to affirm the decision God has made about us. This decision is not intended to get to us in any other way — indeed it cannot.

God in Christ basically makes no other claim on us — not the fulfilling of a smaller or bigger catalog of all kinds of light or heavy requirements, but rather simply our freely obedient and obediently free affirmation that because God is ours, we are God's. God lays claim only to our willingness and readiness, "wholeheartedly" granted and manifested, "to live for God from now on." But this too God does not leave to our discretion, because God does not leave us alone anymore at all. God is not indifferent to what happens to God's gift to us. God makes us responsible for it. This is why God makes a claim on us: that at every turn we think and act as God's people, who belong to God and therefore are not "subjected" to any other power, or to ourselves. What we then are to think and do specifically, we do not have to worry about in advance. That will be made clear. God will make it clear, and instruct us thereby.

3. The Heidelberg speaks of God's claim on our assent in connection with the work of the *Holy Spirit*. The Holy Spirit is once again God's own self and nothing less than God, but God acting and working in a definite way on us and in us. God's effectively asserted claim on our assent is the Holy Spirit. If we reckon with the Spirit, we make a threefold acknowledgment.

First: We do not achieve by our own effort the fulfillment of the divine claim for acknowledgment and affirmation of our belonging to God and our "wholeheartedly" consenting to it, so that we are "willing and ready to live for him from now on." This fulfillment does not happen automatically, either. It comes by the Holy Spirit's coming to us. By the Spirit we are *made* willing and ready. Again, it is God's own self who provides for this.

Second: God provides for this as a result of the work of Jesus Christ. Because Christ chooses us as his own, we are brought through the Holy Spirit to assent to what has been imparted to us through Christ. This is implied in the last section of Article 1: Besides choosing us as his own, which is involved in God's defining God's self as our God, Christ also gives us through the Spirit assurance and power to live as his own. This is why the Holy Spirit is called "his," that is, Christ's. The Spirit is called the Spirit of Christ in Articles 53 and 86 as well.

Third: Therefore our saying yes to the fact that through him we are his is a result of the work of Christ. Saying yes is not superfluous. Nor is it something excluded because the work of Christ is a work of grace. On the contrary, our yes is something God desires. And God not only desires it. God works so that it is really we who not only are told that we belong to Christ, but who also say yes to this belonging. If we would not and could not ever affirm that we "belong to Jesus Christ," it would only be something foreign to us, not something we had earnestly made our own.

These three explanations make it clear that this work of the Holy Spirit is the final, the fulfilling work of God. With it "eternal life" dawns. The Holy Spirit makes true in our lives what is true in Christ, and "assures" us of our belonging to Christ. With this, all adverse delusions must yield, according to which we are and must stay in seductive, strangling grips of powers that want to tear us out of his hand. With this, he assures us of "eternal life." Yes, eternal life is the endlessness of the love of God, but the love of God that does not lose us, which enfolds us eternally. In the work of the Holy Spirit the work of God is fulfilled, because in eternal life God's love enfolds us in such a way that it at the same time unfolds our potential. In the unfolding security and the enfolding opening of ourselves that takes place in the love of God we are no longer different from what we really are. Then there is nothing else for us to do than give pure assent to being who we are: those who belong to God. And there is nothing other than to concur fully with who God is as our God, and thus to rise up as God's people "to praise God forever" (Art. 58). As John 17:3 says, "This is eternal life, that they may *know* you, the only true God, and Jesus Christ whom you have sent."

We sum up the sense of all that has been said with a concept that in the Heidelberg does not stand in the foreground: the concept of the kingdom of God. Yet what has been said really has to do with this concept. The kingdom of God is first of all the rightful claim that God makes. More than this, it is the claim that establishes what is right — the "lordship" which God carries out over all whom God has redeemed at great cost in Christ. According to Jesus' word, this kingdom "has come near" in him (Mark 1:15). This does not mean that it will come soon, or even sometime or other, with great delay. Rather, it means that in him the kingdom is right in our face, so to speak. By bringing all for whom he has "totally paid" into belonging to him, he has really come close and has laid claim to them. So he is not like that king "John without a country." Christ has a realm over which he rules. He also sets up a way of life in which those who belong to him can live according to his intention, in peace, freedom, and justice. *He* sets up this kingdom; they do not build it. As it has come near in him, so they can only pray, and live according to their prayer, that it *come* (Matt. 6:10).

There is urgent cause for this plea. For although it has already come close in him, although he is already ours and we his, still it is not yet fulfilled. According to Jesus' word, it is like a feast already prepared, for which the host now sends out his invitation to all sorts of people: "Come, for everything is ready now" (Luke 14:15-17). Because "everything is ready," it in no way needs to be actualized by them. But it needs to be fulfilled. And it will be fulfilled if they accept the invitation to take their place at the table spread for them. This fulfillment is the work of the Holy Spirit — so that those manuscripts make sense that have the petition for the coming of the kingdom in Luke 11:2 read "Your Holy Spirit come upon us." This is why this is "the full coming of your kingdom" (Art. 123) — the *eschaton*, the "end": what God has prepared wins our consent, and our life comes into accord with this, and so God is "all in all." So we can also say that the *eschaton*, the fulfillment, is the new human being. For the new human being is the one who assents to what God has prepared, and lives in agreement with it, and corresponding to it. *This is the one* who is enabled to do what "no eye has seen, nor ear heard, nor the human heart conceived" (1 Cor. 2:9): "praise God forever" (Art. 58).

This eschatological fulfillment of the kingdom of God is beyond our history, that is, beyond all possibilities given in *our* human history. But already this side of the *eschaton* it presses on our history and stands in conflict and battle with all the situations and actions on our side that do not correspond with it, but contradict it. For although the kingdom of Christ is not "from this world," it aims to get a foothold in this world. It does so, not in contempt of this world, but in contesting its wrongness. It cannot leave this world to itself in its opposition and contradictions. As a sign of this, the kingdom of Christ already breaks into this world here and there in the Holy Spirit. The kingdom already arouses in this and that person a transformation that makes them "wholeheartedly willing and ready to live for him from now on." So it awakens "now" in the "heart the beginning of eternal joy" (Art. 58). The Spirit does this not by setting forth an ideal we would have to actualize, but by confronting us with a new reality by which we have to orient ourselves.

An objection that could be raised is this: Is not the kingdom of God more than that? Is it only the new human being who in the power of the Holy Spirit consents to and lives in accord with the reality prepared for us, of belonging to the God who has come to us? Is not instead a completely new creation promised us by the kingdom of God? Is it not a kingdom in which "the blind receive their sight, the lame walk, the lepers are cleansed, the deaf hear, the dead are raised, and the poor have good news brought to them" (Matt. 11:5) — all this so that they will all experience full justice? Jesus speaks these words in the context of a question that he indirectly, yet clearly, answers in the affirmative: "Are you the one who is to come, or are we to wait for another?" And he adds the words "And blessed is anyone who takes no offense at me" (Matt. 11:3, 6). One can apparently take offense at how the kingdom of God becomes reality in him, for it takes place in contradiction not only to our contradictions, but also to our ideas about how our contradictions would have to be overcome. For the kingdom becomes reality in this way: the redemption of persons from their great wretchedness and many miseries is fully *included* when Jesus' "lordship" is realized in the creation of our assent to and correspondence with the reality that we are his, as he is ours.

> His salvation and grace . . .
> Heal within hearts' inner reaches (and because into the innermost,
>   also unto the outermost)
> Pains' sharp, death-dealing breaches,
> And make us whole in time and eternity.[20]

"Strive first for the kingdom of God and its righteousness, and all these things will be given to you as well" — all "that you need" (Matt. 6:32-33).

In the fulfillment of the promise that "God will dwell with them and be their God; they will be his people" — which takes place in Christ, who is the one who is "making all things new" — are included the wiping away of all tears and the assuaging of all suffering and pain (Rev. 21:3-6). Since the work of the Holy Spirit aims to bring us into harmony with the reality prepared for us in Christ, so that "God will be all *in* all," the Spirit's work may be seen as a kind of divine surpassing of the work of Christ (1 Cor. 15:28) — but never as an abrogation, devaluation, or superseding of it by something entirely different.

Here a question could be put in return to the foregoing objection: Does the objection not have in mind an entirely different kingdom? Is it not waiting for another? Does not its talk about the kingdom of God aim at abro-

---

20. From stanza 8 of the hymn "Die goldne Sonne" ("Evening and Morning, Sunset and Dawning"), by P. Gerhardt.

gating Christ? Is not this talk born of the fact that it takes offense at him and is disappointed in him because he does not bring what we consider to be the kingdom of God? Its talk about the kingdom of God could also have arisen by first setting up a catalog of what one considers in need of improvement or change in the world, or in one's surroundings — depending on the time or the state of one's information — in order then to call the realization of these wishes "the kingdom of God." If *this* kingdom is denoted by the beautiful term "new creation," then God is expected to share our judgment that God should make the divine work better than before, or even make something good that God has not yet made. This contradicts Genesis 1:31 and also 2 Corinthians 5:17. The achievement of this goal will then in time be seen in one of two ways. Either it will be recognized in advance as unattainable, and people will probably nevertheless be incited to sacrifice for a future glory within history which unfortunately they will never experience. Or it will be claimed that this goal is reachable by us, and appeals will be made to our good intentions. We will be called on to make good finally what humanity till now has done wrong, or even what God was not able to make good — and where possible to redeem God from this inability — and so to "build" and to "actualize" the kingdom of God. Do not many conceptions of the kingdom of God imply such an appeal to humans, so that of all people, those who in our time have instigated such unspeakable evil are now expected suddenly to do everything for the good? This "kingdom of God" will then tacitly be like a kingdom without God. Even if you call on God for this undertaking, you will hardly know why you do so rather than simply omit God. In place of the sovereign I in which Jesus says "*I* make all things new" you then secretly or openly smuggle our own individual or collective I. What is decisive for the biblical promise of the kingdom of God is that all our life comes into harmony with the gracious, saving reality, prepared for us in Christ, with our belonging to the God who belongs to us, and that in this all that we need is provided. But in that other view of the kingdom of God, this decisive character comes only at the margin, at best, and in the end not at all. We cannot join this view.

Now you could also make the objection against the Heidelberg that it suffers from a questionable narrowing of horizon. It concentrates so much on the personal promise of salvation, on comfort for the believing "I," that it is not able to get the wide, corporate horizon of the kingdom of God in view. It is right that the outlook toward this kingdom widens our sights to a more comprehensive reality than is now before our eyes in the shape of Christian life in the church. It stretches our vision out toward the fulfillment of the promise "that at the name of Jesus *every* knee should bend in heaven and on earth and *every* tongue should confess that Jesus Christ is Lord, to the glory of God the Father" (Phil. 2:10). The outlook has to do with something more than just increasing the number of believing individuals in the church by the addition of other such individuals. In this case the kingdom of God would consist in the fact that in it a few more would become as I already am in my faith. The "many" or "all" to which the Bible refers is no quantitative term. It is rather a qualitative, specific, structured term. The "many" or "all" will not really touch the "I" whose gaze is fixed on itself.

But the outlook to the rightly understood kingdom of God means a constantly critical disturbing of precisely this believing "I." For it is always inclined to calm itself and thereby to make secure its conviction that it is already a sure candidate for the kingdom of God, while the candidacy of others is an open question. Forgotten is the fact that according to Jesus' word it is the other way around. It is no question whether "the poor, the crippled, the blind, and the lame" and those on the streets and the lanes "will eat bread in the kingdom of God." It is a serious question, however, whether the first aspirants to it will ever find a place there (Luke 14:15-24). Forgotten is the troubling point of the parable of the sheep and the goats (Matt. 25:31-46), that the problem is not the salvation of the prisoners, the hungry, and the strangers. The big problem is whether we, the believers, the church members, will ever have part in it when we have not greeted Christ as the brother of those others in them. Forgotten is the word of Jesus that the first will be last and the last first (Luke 13:30; Matt. 19:30). In view of this, one can ask whether the Heidelberg does not stand in danger of salvation egoism, if its predominant way of thinking concentrates on how "not only others, but I too" share in what God has prepared (Art. 21).

Still, this "I too" probably did not have the narrowing tone at that time which it may have for us today. Think about what it meant that, according to the wish of the writers, the following message should be announced in every last house: all that is so promising holds not only for the inwardly or outwardly, financially, intellectually, religiously privileged. "I too" am included — the "little people," the ones so often overlooked, forgotten, and disadvantaged, who at that time were almost serfs. Even the Reformers called these people "riffraff" and said all kinds of unfriendly things about them. There is, however, some truth to the claim that these "little people," so long as they were not considered mature, and were not taken as complete adults, did behave as "riffraff." At the same time, those who looked down on them were therefore all the more inclined to act as stiff-necked masters and mistresses. But according to the directives of the catechism, the "little people" were not to be spoken to any longer as immature, or treated that way. Looked at this way, the Heidelberg itself compels us to turn its perspective around, thus avoiding the danger of salvation egoism a reader today might suspect. All that is so full of promise holds not only for me, not by a long shot, but also holds very definitely for others.

To see these others we need to look out beyond the margins of the believers and church members. For Christ is "the head of his church," to be sure, but the head through whom "the Father governs all things" (Art. 50). His kingdom reaches farther than the church can ever reach, and ever dare reach. It is oriented to "the great multitude that no one could count, from every nation, from all tribes and peoples and languages" (Rev. 7:9). It therefore already finds not only those who have been made "willing and ready to live for him from now on." It finds also a crowd of those who unknowingly and unintentionally serve him. Who knows whether in all their unknowing and unintentionality they may not serve better than those who think they are excellent in being "willing and ready"? Those concerned may themselves not know it. But for the church, it is important to know that the breadth of Christ's realm is much more comprehensive than that of the church. A church that knows this, and discerns signs of it in the world, will rejoice in it. It will thereupon put its trust all the more in the Lord instead of in itself. And it will remember self-critically the word of Jesus, that "the children of this age are more shrewd in dealing with their own generation than are the children of light" (Luke 16:8).

From here we can venture a look at something hardly in view for the catechism:[21] the relation of *church and state*. The church is not the kingdom of God; the state is not either. The fact that neither is the kingdom is

21. In a certain way, the Catechism no doubt did have this in view: The text, which for reading in the worship service was divided into nine sections, provided as a tenth reading a collection of Bible verses about living as citizens of various stations. Cf. W. Niesel, ed., *Bekenntnisschriften und Kirchenordnungen der nach Gottes Wort reformierten Kirche* (1938) (Zurich: Theologischer Verlag, 1985), chap. 1, n. 20, pp. 63ff. This last reading was indebted to the "household code," which Luther appended to his Small Catechism. The way in which the Bible verses were put together, and their direct transfer into the social situation of the time, inculcated almost entirely obedience by the subordinates in a hierarchically arranged society. The problematic of this does not need to be pointed out here. But after all, the Catechism, by the addition of this tenth reading, had at least seen the *question* to be discussed here.

connected with the fact that they are two different entities. Only in the fulfillment of the kingdom of God will both be one. There will be no temple there (Rev. 21:22), only "city," *polis,* but the city completely ruled and enlightened by God and the "Lamb on the throne" — the "holy city" (Rev. 21:2), the "city of the living God" (Heb. 12:22). When the church tries to take over the state, or the state the church, it is always an arbitrary anticipation of the kingdom of God, and therefore in reality a dangerously warped kingdom of humans. Where the church on its side thinks it is realizing the kingdom of God, it stands in danger of undermining the task of the state. This may happen by its dreaming up a clerical state, or in the opposite way, by seeing itself as an "island of the blessed," isolated from the state, which is seen as the kingdom of darkness.

Or on the other side, when the state does not leave room for the church to do its own task, it threatens to become a self-absolutizing, demonic counter-image of the kingdom of God, and to make the church into a conforming "state church." The fact that church and state exist side by side shows that the state finds itself "in the as yet unredeemed world in which the church also exists."[22] Yes, the fact of the state alongside the church reminds the church that it too is not yet the kingdom of God. In this as yet unredeemed world, which still awaits the fulfillment of the kingdom of God, the state has its own positive task. It has to provide for the most tolerable life possible, and that for believers and unbelievers alike. Therefore it is not to govern by articles of faith, but "according to the measure of human judgment and human ability" — and if necessary, also "by means of the threat and exercise of force."[23] The state needs to provide for all in a ("national") living space with more or less random boundaries, but defined by a common legal order. Yet it dare not ("nationalistically") absolutize itself over against other living spaces, or seal itself off from them. Since the church likewise stands in the as yet unredeemed world, it has another task, its own task. For it knows the Redeemer of this as yet unredeemed world. It listens to his word of assurance and his claim. It believes in him, loves him, and hopes in him. It prays for the coming and the fulfillment of his kingdom. It looks forward to this and journeys toward it, rejoices in it and sighs for it.

---

22. *Theologische Erklärung von Barmen,* May 1934, Thesis 5. ET: "The Theological Declaration of Barmen," in *The Book of Confessions,* Presbyterian Church USA (Louisville, 1994), p. 258.

23. *The Book of Confessions,* p. 258. Cf. *Heidelberg Catechism,* Article 105.

The existence of church and state side by side dare never mean for Christians that they stand under two kinds of equally binding claims: here within the church or inwardly, the voice of Jesus Christ — there beyond the church doors or outwardly, some other sort of authority. Jesus says unmistakably: "No one can [not merely dare not or should not — can not!] serve two masters; for a slave will either hate the one and love the other, or be devoted to the one and despise the other" (Matt. 6:24). In some circumstances, especially when the state becomes a counter-image of the kingdom of God, this can involve conflict with its authority; and when the church engages in this conflict, it shows that it has not become a "state church" (which it can become even as a "free church"!). However, the church's independence from the state does not necessarily involve the church in constant conflict with the state authorities. For the church can recognize the state, even though the state is so obviously a "worldly" establishment in the framework of the as yet unredeemed world. The church can do so without thereby becoming untrue to the claim of its Lord, which alone is binding for it. Why? Once again: because its Lord Jesus Christ is "the head of his church through whom the Father governs all things" (Art. 50). The church relates to Christ differently in the domain of the state, but not to anyone else but him.

Therefore, when the church acknowledges the state and its authority, it does not necessarily go into territory foreign to the claim that is decisive for the church. It can also recognize in the secular state some similarity to the kingdom of God. Specifically, it can recognize the state's provision for a tolerable life for individuals and for living together as a sign that the kingdom of God is a healing promise for life *this side* of the *eschaton.* And the church can see in the state's assignment to provide for all, regardless of their faith, a sign that the kingdom of God, which justifies the godless, promises something more comprehensive than the church and the band of the pious. Therefore the church does not do something foreign to its mission when it takes part honestly in the task of the state, critically, but also constructively. How could the church omit this, when it is called to pray for the state (1 Tim. 2:1-2), and thereby makes itself responsible for it? Therefore the church does not require anything strange of state governance when the church becomes involved in it and stands up for human counterparts to the hoped-for kingdom of God: for *freedom,* specifically for the greatest possible informed participation of all citizens in the state's task; for *justice,* specifically according to the rule that help is offered to creatures who are disadvantaged, and to truths that are suppressed; and for *peace,* specifically that the power of the powerful be limited, and so war be prevented by the creation of peaceful conditions. Even with every effort for these things, the kingdom of God will certainly not be "realized." Yet this is how, in all weakness, the way is prepared. The state reminds the church that state and church stand in the as yet unredeemed world. The church, when it is true to its mission, reminds us that redemption in the fulfillment of the kingdom of God is promised to this very world.

2.2. God's Judgment

2.2.1. Our Lack of Insight (Art. 3-4)

Now we turn to talk about our *sin.* We desperately need the comfort Article 1 speaks of, as God knows. Yes, God knows (as we so often do not know) how much we stand in need of it. By making Godself ours, God reaches out to humans who in and of themselves are in no way God's, or still worse, live as God's in a warped way. We believe we belong to ourselves, and even if we call on a "God," this only confirms our belief in belonging to ourselves. By deciding for coexistence with us, God relates to a people who in no way correspond to this divine action. They exist in contradiction to it. They are unfree, "firmly bound," in need of liberation. In giving us comfort, in giving *Godself* to us and so being our comfort, God also pronounces *judgment* on us: we are in a comfortless condition; for we do not have this comfort, and have not deserved it, and yet need it "in life and in death."

In the title of its first part, the Heidelberg does not use the word "sin." It speaks of our *"misery."* Misery is the opposite of comfort. Misery is comfortlessness, as comfort is the removal of misery. In the Latin manuscript of Ursinus the word *miseria* stands for misery. *Miseria* is the opposite of the basic concept of the gospel — *misericordia,* mercy. In light of the mercy of God, in which our misery goes to God's heart *(cor),* this misery that God wants to have mercy on, and already has mercy on, is revealed. This is why the Reformation, in discovering anew the greatness of God's mercy, also saw once again the depth of human misery. And it was not the other way around: not because the Reformation thought so pessimistically, or because some of its representatives had such depressing experiences, did it then excessively underscore the grace of God. Optimists need the mercy of

God too, much more than they suspect. And pessimists usually do not hold on to God's mercy, but instead, even when they give up, hold on to themselves in despairing self-love. Whoever does not know the greatness of the mercy of God, in which God alone saves us, also does not know the depth of the misery that we cannot help ourselves out of in any way. When the word "sin" is explained by "misery," this must be understood in a three-fold sense.

1. I have gotten into this misery — in distinction from some other situations called misery — *through my own fault,* and not regrettably and tragically through a dark fate, and also not simply through the fault of someone else. When I recognize this, I can only accuse myself, and do so as someone who is not worthy to be called God's child (Luke 15:19).

2. I am however so entangled and trapped in this misery that in my own strength and with every good intention, I cannot free myself from it. Indeed, good intentions do not lead me even a little way out, but actually further into it than ever. And all human help, however much it is elsewhere indicated, cannot help me in this case. For the rest of my contemporaries are also in this common misery, from which they cannot find a way out by themselves.

3. This misery, even if one makes oneself comfortable in it like a prisoner in his cell, is *not a good existence.* A bad person not only does wrong; the wrong does no good to this person. This person is not simply someone to be condemned, but also someone to be pitied. The person's evil is not simply deplorable, but is also misery, a crippling, under which one suffers objectively and in some way also subjectively. When sin is considered only moralistically, it is easily understood as forbidden desire and so as something fun after all. But it is not fun; it is a "sickness unto death."[24] It is something unbearable, and not mere incompleteness, which a person can bear in dignity. — A Christian doctrine of sin dare not let any of these three senses fall by the wayside.

The word for misery in German, *Elend,* is connected with the word *Ausland,* foreign land. Sin means alienation. Sin means living far away from the place where I really belong, far from home, far from relationships without which I cannot really be myself — so far that I cannot find the way out of the foreign land by myself, so far that I finally may no longer even want to get out. But let us be clear about this: "far" here means decisively far from *God,* in alienation from *God.* Wanting to be independent does not

24. Title of a work by S. Kierkegaard, 1849.

have to be bad. But wanting to be independent from God, to live detached from God, this is what is bad: *this* is the guilt we incur; *this* is the imprisonment we cannot get out of by ourselves, and *this* is what does us no good. If there is a misery, then it is precisely this: our life, instead of being lived from God and with God, circles around ourselves, pulsates within ourselves, makes us the midpoint of all things — a life in which we belong to ourselves and want to make as much as possible belong to us.

If the root of our misery is our wanting to live detached from God, then in this root is also the drive to blot out of our consciousness the misery into which it has brought us. This occurs when we reason in a way like this: to be independent can in itself seem advantageous. Why then should it be a misery in relation to God and not much rather, and all the more, advantageous? Let us work down through the three senses of sin to see how this plays out.

1. To distance ourselves from God and make ourselves independent is our *guilt*, which God can only condemn. We withdraw thereby from what God intends for us: to give our assent to God's will, in which God determines to be our God and chooses us to be God's people. Still, the person who does not assent does not have to be irreligious. One may be thoroughly religious at certain significant times, though not always. One may perhaps work out a theory that God is not needed for much of life, and then act *etsi deus non daretur,* as though there is no God. It is not for nothing that you want to be an independent person. But at times you need God after all for ceremonial self-confirmation and especially when troubles arise in your independent life. You need God then for the support of a selfish life. But this god does not help you out of your guilt. This god hardens guilt in you. This god confirms only the Yes you already give yourself. This god is not needed. This god does not exist, but is only a mirror image of you, your better I. Yet insofar as you believe in this god, insofar as you give credit to this god for a life that in practice is detached from God, you do not *notice* that with the attempt at such a life you are — a *sinner.*

2. Our detachment from God is our *imprisonment.* It consists concretely in our being incapable of taking up anew the relationship with God that we broke off. If we get ourselves out of relationship with God, we cannot get ourselves out of this misery. But the argument Erasmus raised against Luther is this: We have "free will." With this we can do a lot, and can choose between A, B, and C. Why should we not also be *able* to choose between good and bad, between God and no God, and so set ourselves in

relation to God? When Luther and Calvin, against Erasmus, speak instead of our "unfree" and "enslaved" will,[25] we dare not hear this either as though we are marionettes, without a will of our own; or as though we are unfree only in relation to God, but otherwise free; or as though we only become unfree when we freely decide for something perverse. Rather, the "enslaved will" has its seat precisely in what Erasmus considered the "free will." *Within the will itself* is a false presupposition and a perverseness that the will puts into effect in *each* act of choosing, so that in no act of the will's choosing can it be set aside. For the person with this free will is the one cut off, the independent one, who as such necessarily faces everything and everyone, good and bad, God and anti-God, as *neutral,* and who can control all possibilities at hand in willful freedom. Precisely this freedom is *in itself,* and not just in one of its results, perverse. It is the bondage of one who circles around oneself, the egotistical person who is twisted inward, and cannot get loose. "Everyone who commits sin is a slave to sin" (John 8:34); you activate your bondage, and not your freedom. But in considering ourselves free, we do not *notice* our bondage. And "no one is more a slave, than the one who considers himself free without being free."[26]

3. Cutting oneself off from God puts a person in *need* of the comforting help of God. In cutting ourselves loose from God, we remain needy, but we figure this means that what we need "in life and in death" we are to get *for ourselves* (perhaps also with the use of a deity — this is not excluded). But it is the self-centered person, who shifts for oneself, who as such can only "use" God for goals set without God! In place of the good which God gives, and only God can give, steps *the better,* which we look for and promise to provide for ourselves. This now puts us into a restless hunt for progress, with only occasional pause to leisurely enjoy the better we believe we have found. But "the better is the *enemy* of the good." We provide for ourselves the better, which we look for and find, but not the good that we need. Indeed, by this yearning for the better we stand in the way of our ever receiving the good. Our improvements are always only corrections in a false system that do not correct the false system itself. They only activate anew the twisted root out of which our miseries come. This is why every improvement has its flip side. The false root consists in our alienation

25. M. Luther, *De servo arbitrio,* 1525. ET: *The Bondage of the Will* (Grand Rapids: Eerdmans, 1931); J. Calvin, *Institutes* II.2.

26. J. W. von Goethe, *Maximen und Reflexionen,* 1116/43. ET: *Goethe's World View Presented in His Reflections and Maxims* (New York: F. Unger, 1993), p. 139.

from God. This is our misery. But on account of the better that we try to provide for ourselves — we do not *notice* this misery.

Three times it has been said now that we do not *notice* our misery. *Are* we perhaps really not in such misery after all? If we look over the history of ideas in modern times, we can ascertain with amazement that what the church used to call "sin" has been rationalized away, step by step. G. W. F. Hegel nullified it by saying that it is a necessary moment of passage on the way from what is given to what is better[27] — and F. Schiller cancelled sin out by going so far as to explain that the Fall is an act of freedom that puts the human being on its own two feet.[28] K. Marx understood "sin" as the expression of unjust economic conditions, which would stop by itself with the abolishment of private property.[29] S. Freud located it in the denial of drives that a person lets the superego impose — a denial that in its undesirable entanglements can be treated.[30] F. Nietzsche put it down as an idea totally objectionable to the lordly human being, a Jewish invention to humble humans before the alleged grace of an "honour-craving Oriental" in heaven.[31] K. Lorenz interpreted "so-called evil" as the aggression needed to survive in the fight for existence[32] . . . and so on. These kinds of ideas seem to have become conventional wisdom today, so that we hardly ever meet people anymore who consider themselves sinners. Rather, they are confident of being good people. This sounds absurd, to be sure, in a period in which there have been such orgies of brutality as never before — and without this having brought back a strengthened consciousness of sin. "The murderer with the white shirt" has become a symbol of our time. But are not these connected: the atrophy of consciousness of sin and the sea of wickedness — and both to our alienation from God?

27. G. W. F. Hegel, *Vorlesungen über die Philosophie der Religion,* ed. Lasson (1927), part III, p. 105. ET: *Lectures on the Philosophy of Religion* (Berkeley: University of California Press, 1988), part III, p. 133.

28. F. Schiller, "Etwas über die erste Menschengesellschaft," in *Sämmtliche Werke,* vol. 10 (Stuttgart/Tübingen: J. G. Cotta, 1836), p. 446.

29. K. Marx, *Pariser Manuskripte* (1844) (Hamburg, 1966), pp. 59ff. ET: *Economic and Philosophic Manuscripts of 1844* (Amherst, NY: Prometheus Books, 1988), pp. 132ff.

30. S. Freud, *Das Unbehagen in der Kultur* (1930), chap. 7. ET: *Civilization and Its Discontents* (New York: W. W. Norton, 1989).

31. F. Nietzsche, *Die fröhliche Wissenschaft,* in *Werke,* ed. K. Schlechta (Munich, 1960²), vol. 2, pp. 131-32. ET: *The Gay Science* (Cambridge: Cambridge University Press, 2001), pp. 125f.

32. K. Lorenz, *Das sogenannte Böse* (Vienna, 1965). ET: *On Aggression* (New York: Harcourt, Brace & World, 1966).

At the same time, the church today in its talk about sin is fairly embarrassed — and we mistrust, not without reason, those fundamentalists who want to heat up talk about it in an artificial way. Do we not also sense that the once-favored method linking the message of grace to a presumed universally present consciousness of sin does not work? But then how shall we proceed? Shall we say that human beings are not bad, but that it is always just the "environment"? There is truth in this position. For example, a person seldom becomes a criminal without previously having been the victim of some offense. But when we look only at this aspect, have we really seen what sin is? Do we actually understand sin if we see it more like a sickness for us to heal than a guilt for God to cleanse? Or shall we say that sin is only this or that individual mistake for which a person can pardon herself, or which a person can atone for or make good himself? There is some truth in this, too. Though we are fallible creatures, we still cannot be released from responsibility for our actions. But have we seen what sin is if we do not see that in it only God's grace can help, and not our earnest efforts? Or shall we substitute for the concept of sin that of human need? To be sure, legitimate needs are involved. But if we take this route, how can we say what teaching about sin must say: that we have not deserved God's help? It is remarkable that even when we inquire about it like this, sin apparently slips away from us in a new way.

This should make us hesitate to confront the modern fading of the consciousness of sin with moral indignation. Rather, we have to reckon with the fact that this fading is a variation of a process that has always been going on, though differently in other times. It is a process which, when we think theologically, cannot surprise us. For Article 3 asks, "How do you learn of your misery?" The question itself shows that it is by no means to be taken for granted that sinners realize they are sinners. Nor is it obvious to us that even when we do not notice our sin, we are still sinners. The answer to Question 3 gives no room for assuming that I can recognize my sin on my own. Rather, in accord with Romans 3:10, it says that I learn of it "from the law of God." It takes a special word from God, and confrontation with the divine claim on us in order to come to the awareness that we are sinners. Only when the One from whom we have distanced ourselves comes close does it dawn on us that we have distanced ourselves from God, and how far we have distanced ourselves. Only in God's meeting with us do we gain insight into that which we apparently do not see otherwise. We are sinners who do not deserve — and cannot give ourselves — what we nevertheless urgently need in order not to fall apart: that God accepts us, enfolds us, and draws us out of our misery.

The fact that we have to be told this entails the following assertion: it is part of our sin that we do not know anything true about our sin. Yes, our lack of insight into our sin belongs to the essence of our sin. It is part of sin's essence that we hide it from ourselves. As best we can, and as long as it is in any way possible, we deny, dispute, suppress, and justify it, until it does not look half so bad, or even seems advantageous. Finally we do not know it anymore. Of course, we see some shortcomings ("Who does not have some faults?") under which we may sigh. In the face of them we sometimes do not know for the moment how to go on. Yet we know how to appeal for understanding for them. Ultimately we know how to live with them. To be sure, we see some things that in our view are not in order. But then we can either minimize them ("No harm was intended"), or cover them up ("With time the grass will grow over it"). Yes, now we call evil what is not evil at all, but only a breach of "good" custom, and call good what is not good at all, but which serves our advantage or prejudice. So long as we ourselves hold the measure for sin in our hand and test ourselves with it, so long will we as a rule absolve ourselves (and if sensitive persons do not succeed in this, we can support them until they can do it too).

Sinners do not know real sin so long as they know it only as that which they *themselves* must cope with — *and can.* Indeed they can as a rule cope with what they might call sin: they may by means of "self-help" provide easing and unburdening through their own efforts or with the advice of another. But for this they need *no grace of God.* This will lead to fatal consequences. Because they think they need no grace for themselves, they will also show no grace toward other people. Equipped with the criteria for judging what is not good, they will look all the more sharply at others for the sin they do not find in themselves. When they see it, they will accuse the others without mercy and be outraged about them (Matt. 7:3-4). In this way they will try to hinder any closer look at themselves. By not keeping their eyes on God in determining sin, they do not see the sin in themselves. And as soon as there is a glance toward God and even a thought of guilt shows up, sinners will hold themselves blameless by shoving the guilt onto others. So it was in the Fall, which reached its depth when Adam, confronted by God about his disobedience, answered: I am not to blame, but "the *woman* whom *you* gave me" is the one (Gen. 3:12)! In this way, sinners deny their sin. They deny it also when they want to be humane and overlook the sin in others that they overlook in themselves. So the other person, in a new way, still does not need any grace.

Our inability to free ourselves from our sin is reflected in the fact that we are not able to let ourselves know about it. Yes, here sin reaches its high point, its unique pinnacle. For we who have cut ourselves loose from God now shut ourselves up all the more within ourselves. In our sin, we also contest our dependence on God and God's grace. Thereby we deny that in our misery — beyond the relief we ourselves may achieve (and for which we may even call upon a god) — we need actual liberation by God. Are we who in this way have lost God (even in and with the aforementioned calling on the divine), for our part lost to God? No. God does not let us go. God takes our sin seriously, and wants to liberate us from it, because this is the only way we can be liberated. God goes after us. God speaks to us who have closed ourselves off from God, and does so because what we do in our sin is not good, cannot lead to good, and does us no good. God makes a claim on us in "the law." Whatever else remains to be said about the law, it also means this for us: that by it we *recognize* "our misery." It brings us out of our blindness to insight. Recognizing our misery sets us on the way to salvation. But this way involves recognizing the *agonizing truth,* which we tried to *hide* with all our might. The "law" *reveals* our misery and so *enables* us to recognize a threefold truth: 1. You — not first the others with whom you associate — but you *yourself* are a sinner. 2. Further, you are this *totally,* so that you cannot liberate yourself even with the greatest effort. 3. What you as such a sinner do not rightly deserve, this is just what you *need* in every area of your life: forgiveness, grace, help, comfort, redemption.

What is this "law of God"? Here a note about the understanding of the law in the Heidelberg is needed. Common opinion is that it simply takes over Melanchthon's teaching on the threefold use of the law. According to Luther, God gave the law for a double purpose: to guide the authorities in punishing and inhibiting the *outward* eruptions of evil; and to shock us *inwardly* by the fact that the law cannot be fulfilled, thus making us receptive for grace. To this Melanchthon added a third "use of the law": those who have been *born again* by God's grace can fulfill it. Perhaps he wanted in this way to remind us that the Bible says other things besides what Paul says in Galatians about the penal role of the law. But Melanchthon did not carry through well on this concern. For if it is the case that the law is given for us to do righteous works, and thus to stand uncondemned before the authorities, but inwardly to fail, then this third use of the law threatens to offer a new works-righteousness. And then it becomes involved in a questionable doctrine of grace. Grace appears to be a substantive power in the service of the law, on the basis of which we are able to do what we formerly could not do.

But apart from Melanchthon's idea, other dangers lurk in this conception of the law. Some that have surfaced in our time are: (a) When the law is seen only as demand, what is decisive about the law of *God* may come to be not *what*, but only *that* it demands. If this is so, could not, for example, *everything* that a so-called authority demands look like a command of God? (b) Further, the claim of God's law may be seen as answered in *works-righteousness* — which was supposed to have failed inwardly — so that works-righteousness will be considered to depend on God's ordinance rather than on misuse of the law by sinners. But dare the Ten Commandments or the Sermon on the Mount be understood in this sense? (c) Still further, God's law may slip into such an *opposition* to divine grace that the law is seen as all the more divine the more mercilessly it is handled. (d) And then grace in turn may come to be considered so undemanding, expecting so little from us, that it can pardon us for the actions we take under that merciless law. And finally, (e) God's grace itself may become a divine renunciation of carrying out the law that has been ordained by God and is therefore just.

The Heidelberg probably has some awareness of this problem when it sets the accents *differently* in its talk about the law of God. It takes the Ten Commandments out of the context of recognition of sin, in which they belong according to Lutheran teaching, and takes the confession of faith, rather than the Ten Commandments, as the *first* main section of the catechism. Furthermore, the first "use of the law" — hindrance by the authorities of the outbreak of sin — is dropped, so that a threefold "use of the law" does not arise. Lacking also is the view that God gives us the law for righteousness by works in order to let us fail with them, or to reach the goal after all by means of a grace understood as a capability piped into us. So Article 4 does not ask, "How does the law *work?*" in order to answer that it shatters us inwardly by its demand. Rather, Article 4 asks "What does the law of God require of us?" By no means everything demanded of us is commanded by *God* (Art. 91!). We have to do with *God's* law only when what is commanded is determined by *this* content: Love God and your neighbor (Matt. 22:37ff.)!

This law probably expects too much from us who are bent on our own independence. This is not because it is a merciless law, but because we sojourn in a world lacking in grace, and even feel comfortable in this world. God's law points to another world, from which we have alienated ourselves, to our distress and disharmony. Yet this is the world in which we belong for our wholeness and peace. It is a world not of the isolated individual, but a world of relationships to God and other people, a world of coexistence, not of various people who want to be independent, competing against one another. It is a world of freedom in being with one another, not the kind of freedom that means being without and against one another. The law of God points graciously to this grace-filled world and thereby also exposes the lack of grace, the misery of the world in which we find ourselves. But even in showing the misery of the world, the law shows us the love of God. It is true that when we independent people hear this law, we misconceive it to mean that we have to lift ourselves out of our misery by our own efforts and put ourselves into this divine world. Thereby we cut the law of God loose from the grace of God. Then we deal with the law mercilessly. Then all our efforts wind up as counterproductive. The well-meaning attempt to keep the divine law in our own strength and by ourselves is even worse than breaking it. For doing so means more than ever the hardening of our perverse perspective, in which we who are estranged from God want to achieve and be something *by ourselves alone* — to our own misery. Well-meaning people become more stubbornly caught in their misery than obvious lawbreakers. We begin to surmise why Jesus called out woes over the Pharisees (Matt. 23:13ff.), who were all good people, while he loved to keep company with the most obvious sinners (Matt. 11:19; Luke 15:2).

But this kind of separation of the law from the love of God is fundamentally impossible and superfluous for us. Article 4 indicates this with its answer to the question about what the law of God requires: "Christ teaches us this." The law of God is not to be recognized apart from Jesus Christ. Jesus Christ however is the one who (also for the Heidelberg) not only *teaches* us but is the one in whom God *accepts* us and *has mercy* on us. He "teaches" us to love God in that he lets us know that God is self-revealed beforehand as *our God,* the one who loves us with a whole heart, soul, and mind. And he "teaches" us to love our neighbor in that he chooses us beforehand as *his people,* those who belong to God, and thus has loved *us,* not only "me," but also my neighbor. We cannot and do not have to overcome our alienation from God, because in Jesus Christ God has come close to us. We cannot and do not have to put ourselves into that good, Godly world; God does it by giving the divine self as ours and accepting us as God's. This was no light thing for God to do. It meant God's own self-giving stepping into the misery of our alienation in order to carry through God's good will with us. This is the gospel of Jesus Christ.

And this gospel includes the divine law that "Christ teaches us." It is

Christ's claim on us, on our assent to the relationships into which he has put us, his claim on us to love the One who has given the divine self to be ours, and to love those whom he has chosen to be his. This assent includes the recognition of our *misery* in and of ourselves, which God wanted to have mercy on, the recognition of how far we on our part are from true love for God and neighbor. As those loved by God, we do not have to fear the exposure we open ourselves to with the admission that we are such miserable figures, whom God accepts. As those loved by God, we are free to be satisfied with the judgment of God, that God devotes love to *those completely lost.* So we can lay aside our blindness and become insightful. In view of the great cost to God of overcoming our alienation, we now see rightly what previously we had denied. And shaken, we must *confess:* 1. Yes, I am a sinner and have not deserved God's grace. 2. Yes, I cannot free myself from my misery. 3. Yes, I need nothing more urgently than that which God gives me: the "only comfort in life and in death."

2.2.2. Our Perverseness (Art. 5-9)

In talking about the recognition of sin, we need to rule out a common misconception: the notion that sin is only a lack of understanding, an error of thought, insufficient self-knowledge. This is what Socrates thought, and many after him. Sin, according to this view, is always basically only a false appearance, and we ourselves can get rid of it, perhaps with a little help from others, or by learning from our own mistakes. However, when we began by talking about the "recognition of sin," it was because of the immensity of sin. It is so great that sinners cannot even give a true accounting of its reality to themselves. The One who does give us an account of it is not an abstract god, and not an abstract "Thou shalt." It is the one God, besides whom there is no other, the God who loves us in Jesus Christ. God loves not only me, but also my neighbor in just the same way as me. This is the One who acts toward us as our God and treats us as those who belong to God. This is the God who therefore has every right to lay claim on us to live in such love and so also to love ourselves. Through this God, who loves us graciously, and graciously commands, we receive a true accounting of our sins. But it is an accounting of what we *are,* and not merely what we *appear* to be!

The fact that we cannot give an accounting of sin for ourselves is only a particular aspect of the fact that we cannot free ourselves from it. The fact that it takes nothing less than the love of God to free us from sin is proof that we cannot help ourselves out of it. But if we cannot do this, then our sin is *real* misery, *real* alienation, and *real* lack of freedom, not simply a mistake in our thinking that we can set right. It is a distortedness that is determinative and pervasive for our existence, and that we cannot repair. Measured by the good life God has prepared for us, it is nothing but contradiction to and opposition against the love of God for us and our neighbor, and so against the fact that God is ours and we are God's.

As such contradiction and opposition, our sin therefore has a twofold form. According to Article 5, it is lack of love for God and our neighbor — yes, in both directions it is hate. For if we do not love, then everything else that might be felt instead toward God and neighbor, be it apathy, neutrality, or disinterest, is in truth hate. Actually, apathy is the worst form of hate. For hate in its usual sense, with all its wrong and evil, nevertheless still sees the others, and even in its brutality nevertheless turns toward the others; however, for the apathetic the others are so far away that the apathetic do not even rise up against them. But we say now that sin is hate, in its uprising against others and in its keeping distance from them; hate that poisons us through and through and hurts others through and through.

The question in Article 5 begins in a rather harmless way: Can you "do . . . perfectly" the law taught by Christ in Matthew 22? A conceivable answer would be the one we sinners so gladly come up with: surely not fully; in some ways and at some times I act contrary to the law. But no, the answer goes: "No, for I am by nature prone to hate God and my neighbor." The words "by nature" could be misunderstood to mean that God has created us with such a perverse nature that we are forced to act this way. But to this misunderstanding Article 6 will say a further "No." No, we do not *have* to act this way. We in fact do so, without force and necessity. But since we do it, we cannot act as though it only takes place on our surface, while underneath the rough shell we have a good core that is intact. We cannot act this way unless there is something radically wrong that has first infested and poisoned our whole "nature," a nature created good by God. This poison penetrates to our core, into heart and mind. It is hate — that is, our contradiction against the love of God for us and our neighbor, and so our contradiction against the love we are thereby commanded to have toward God and our neighbor. This hate, this contradiction, is inseparably twofold: it turns against God and against the neighbor.

It is on the one hand the sin of Adam and Eve, whose perversity consists at its core in their wanting to be like God (Gen. 3:5). In short, we can say that their sin is godlessness. But it takes place in such a subtle way that their godlessness is not obvious. It does not appear to be an irreligious act. Indeed, is not what these humans do here even a peak achievement of human religiosity? They do not appear at all to want to topple God from the throne. Rather, they want to identify with God, find themselves in God, be absorbed in God. The sin of godlessness takes place in the most crass way in the midst of human piety — in the midst of the church. We can say further, their sin is that of human pride. But watch out! This is what the church has said for centuries, but in a way so disconnected from the biblical witness that the church thereby actually engendered a mentality of subservience. The church forgot that there is also a very healthy and much-needed Christian pride, namely that which is against all unduly claimed power.

We must look at the sin of godless pride, or prideful godlessness, more closely. This sin is the behavior of humans who imagine that they are on their own, either because they distrust God, whom they see as a competitor, and wish were gone, or because they fancy that they are left alone by God. Feeling either arrogant or helpless and anxious, they imagine they have to fend for themselves. Then they fall into the nightmare that they have to be more than, better than, other than what God has created them to be, and what they are in relationship *with* God. They think instead that they have to be "*like* God" (Gen. 3:5): independent, free, an absolute being. In other words, they think they have to be detached beings who can exist by themselves and for themselves. What is bad about this is not that they overreach to claim for themselves the authoritarian, all-powerful absoluteness that a deity jealously wants to have and keep for itself. What is bad is that they think up *such* a god and then to validate themselves want this god confirmed. They think of a god who does not exist — and now we can understand that here godlessness takes place.

What is bad is that in wanting to be "*like* God" they are actually without God. They talk about a "God," even bow down before, or rise up against this deity, but are always really speaking of *themselves,* and so do not get free from themselves. But the image of an independent being existing for itself, which is considered the highest being, is not God. It is a product of pure fantasy, a picture of an anti-God, a devilishly distorted picture of God. The production of this image of God and equating it with God is sin. It is sin, because it denies and controverts the "true God" — the God of the gospel, the God who is self-defined as our God. This God uses sovereignty in order to be bound to humanity, to have mercy on them, to love them. In bypassing and opposing this God and setting themselves as absolute, in exalting themselves into a deity that does not exist, but is only the mirror image of their own setting of themselves as absolute, in making themselves like this alleged god, they instead *lose* God and in truth go "to the devil" and let "hell loose."[33] Not the contesting of this alleged "god," but the contesting of the real God, the God of the gospel, is in fact hellishly dangerous for us.

On the other hand, our sin is the sin of Cain against his brother Abel, according to Genesis 4. It is so because it is sin against God's love, which is also for our neighbor. Cain's sin is that of inhumanity. This sin is likewise not visible immediately and without further reflection. Long before it comes to murder, this sin lies at the door, the door of our hearts, and covets us. Until it is visible, it is also hidden under a religious veil. Before it comes out plainly as inhumanity, it grows, of all places, in offering and sacrifice, in an act of worship, during the carrying out of a pious exercise. But while the sin of godlessness probably hides itself more under a religious cloak, under "wanting to be like God," the sin of inhumanity hides more under a cloak of moralism. The cynical reply, "Should I be my brother's keeper?" has something moral about it, with the implication that those who do not watch out for themselves, who do not take care of themselves, are themselves at fault if something happens to them. "Take care of yourself!" "Be careful" — this is one of the ground rules of human morality. But both forms of sin hang together, that of godlessness and that of inhumanity. "Those who say 'I love God,' and hate their brothers or sisters, are liars; for those who do not love a brother or a sister whom they have seen, cannot love God whom they have not seen" (1 John 4:20). So hatred of neighbor is also denial of God — godlessness. The sin of Cain flows out of that of his parents. Inhumanity flows out of godlessness.

So, godlessness is not simply the theoretical denial of an abstract god. It is bypassing the God who is bound to us and loves us, in order to think up the existence of an absolute being existing for itself, and wanting to be like it. In fact, this is atheism, and the result is this: human beings set themselves up as absolute beings who exist for themselves, unattached from all that is not themselves, a human I without a real You, a human without fellow humans. "The human who is not a fellow human, is inhuman."[34] For when humans become humans in, of, and for themselves, other humans

---

33. K. Barth, *KD* IV/1, pp. 469, 500. *CD* IV/1, pp. 422, 450.
34. K. Barth, *KD* IV/2, p. 474. *CD* IV/2, p. 421.

are a constant source of unrest that they seek to overcome and turn off in order to secure tranquility. They attempt this either by taking them over, taking advantage of them, humiliating them, oppressing them, exploiting them, or by getting them off their own necks by breaking the others' necks. In one way or another, a human being becomes *homo homini lupus* — a person who is a wolf.[35] In one way or another, a person begins to feel, think, and act as J.-P. Sartre formulated it: "Hell — that is other people."[36]

The image which humans make of God, and which they try to imitate, the image of a being existing for itself, corresponds to the image of humanity in which a human is a human without other humans. As the sin of godlessness stands in contradiction to the gospel of the God bound to us in love, so the sin of inhumanity stands in contradiction to the truth that we are children of this God. Thus it contradicts the gracious command of God, who also loves our neighbors, and so is bound to them. For in wanting to be what they are not — God, they are not doing what they are supposed to do: they are not acting as humans. By substituting themselves for their neighbors, they always love only themselves instead of others.

This twofold sin is the misery, the comfortlessness, the bondage of humans. It is bondage in the sense (a) that here a damaged and damaging freedom rules — one in which humans are free and unrelated and isolated *from* God and fellow humans. These are godless and inhumane humans, in essence mere egos, humans curved back into themselves.[37] They are stunted, imprisoned humans, closed in, bound to self, sometimes rather inhibited, then again uninhibited, sometimes proudly content with self, sometimes despairing in tears, but always only these egoistic humans, without God and neighbor. For these humans see themselves as divine and as neighbors to themselves. The bottom line is that these humans need neither God nor neighbor, except to use them for themselves. In this framework they can appear religious, with ethical principles. They can use God and neighbor as assistant, as bellhop, as supporter of their interests. But only in this way and only for themselves can they use them, and this is why they basically do not even need them — not as You, not as partner. And this is why in certain moments it seems clear that they can do without them.

35. Thomas Hobbes, *Opera philosophica* (1839; repr. Aalen, 1961), p. 135. ET: *De Cive, or The Citizen* (New York: Appleton-Century-Crofts, 1949), p. 1.

36. J.-P. Sartre, *Bei geschlossenen Türen*, in *Dramen* (Hamburg, 1957), p. 95. *No Exit* (Hollywood, CA: Samuel French, 1958), p. 52.

37. M. Luther, *WA* 56:365 and 3:183. ET: *LW* 25:245.

Bondage means also (b) that these humans cannot free themselves from being bound to themselves, or heal themselves from being curved into themselves, or get loose from their being separated from God and neighbor. They cannot get out of their not being free for God and neighbor. It is eerily true: "This is the curse of the evil deed, that it must give birth to ongoing evil."[38] To be sure, in the chain of guilt this deed sets and keeps in motion there will be brighter and more acceptable links. But it will still be debatable what is bright and acceptable and what is not. It will often be the case that the link that seems bright to me will mean darkness to others, or bring darkness to them — as Brecht's verse pictures it:

Some stand in darkness, others in light,
Those in the light for the others lack sight.[39]

In short, it is an illusion that these brighter links are more than just links in the same chain. They do not help anyone get out of the chain. It takes nothing less than the mercy of *God*, in which God in Christ came into this chain of guilt in order to break it; this is the convincing demonstration that *we* cannot break it and cannot escape it.

Bondage means finally (c) that the godless and inhuman humans, because as such they know no real partner, are surrounded with, and surround themselves with objects. Partly these objects are raw materials they believe they can use at will; partly they are products that have arisen out of this willful use. Because they do not have any real partner with whom to relate, they know no limits: they prescribe in their production a growth without end. They transform themselves into the image they ascribe to God — that of one who can do everything. And in fact they can do more and more, but do not ask whether they should do what they are able to do. What they can do, they do, and they maintain that what they can do, they should do. Although growth without limits means the damages of growth are increasingly limitless, they assure themselves that they already have a grip on these damages as an "unavoidable remnant of risk," or that they will get a grip on them. But in this way humans make it ever more difficult to reverse their wrong path. So they overlook the fact that in the midst of this development a reversal of another kind is taking place: the relation be-

38. F. Schiller, *Die Piccolomini*, 5,1.

39. B. Brecht, in the concluding stanza of the film *Die Dreigroschenoper (The Threepenny Opera)*.

tween them and their objects and products is reversed. Having these objects and products at their disposal they set a process in motion that overwhelms them. The result is that they no longer rule over these objects, but the objects rule over them! They in turn now become products of their own products, marionettes in the hand of the process they have set in motion! This is the end station of their bondage.

Where does the dismal misery of evil come from then, and from where is this bondage of humans? From God? Article 6: "No, on the contrary, God created human beings good and in God's own image, that is, in genuine righteousness and holiness, so that we might truly know God our creator, love God wholeheartedly, and live with God in eternal blessedness in order to praise and glorify God." So God is not guilty when there is guilt. God is not evil when there is evil. And this is not because God is, as it were, a moral individual who, like Pilate, washes his hands in blamelessness: I have nothing to do with this; I am blameless. Look to it yourselves! Instead, God works so that evil may not happen, so that humans may not sin.

The chronological notion of an original blameless condition of humans — first God created the world and the humans in it good, and then after a while humans twisted it all to evil — is not appropriate, but not because it is primitive. (Let us never despise the primitive!) It is inappropriate because it is theologically insupportable. For it would mean that humans have the power to make the world created good by God into another, evil world, and the divine Creator simply has to accept it. From this it would follow that it remains in the hands of these same humans to transform the world they have ruined into a wholesome creation again. This is all theologically insupportable. For what God has created good *remains* good, and cannot be canceled by humans, any more than they can cancel the image of God in which they are created. And its irrevocability is validated by the fact that humans can only *try* to live as godless and inhumane. The attempt is a very bad thing, so bad that humans themselves cannot remedy it. But the attempt can never succeed. Humans may deny God and concoct a new image of God, bypassing the God of the gospel, and so want to be godless. But even this way they do not get away from God. And they may have a lot of fellow humans on their conscience. But they *have* them on their conscience. They can hate God and neighbor. But bad as that is, even in hate they cannot get away from God and neighbor. Humans must, even in the contrary way of hate, bear witness that they belong to God and that other humans are their neighbors. And therein they must actually witness to their being created good. They can sin outrageously in many ways against their being created good. Even so, they cannot eliminate it, but must actually thereby testify that it is not God's fault when they sin.

Then where does "this corrupt human nature come from?" Article 7: "From the fall and disobedience of our first parents." I paraphrase the meaning of this answer in the following way: Sin comes from sin. This sentence explains as little as does the tautology of Uncle Braesig: "Poverty comes from destitution." However, just as it is, this statement is the most profound that can be spoken about the origin of evil. In short, there is no basis for evil. It is not only what is forbidden. It is the absolutely unauthorized, unfounded, inexplicable, the completely brute fact. If one were able to *explain* its origin, then its coming into being would be understood as unavoidable. And if it were unavoidable, then we would have understanding for its presence and could become reconciled with it, or at least resigned to it, and thereby treat it as harmless.

You can see this clearly in the theses of idealistic philosophy, according to which the origin of sin is human freedom. From this one deduces not only that sin must therefore be conquerable by humans themselves, but also that sin itself, despite its negative appearance, must be a positive act of freedom. So G. W. F. Hegel could name the Fall the eternal myth of the way humans become human,[40] and Friedrich Schiller designated it as "the first venture" of humans to make use of their own understanding.[41] And even if you look for the origin of sin in the anxiety of humans, as Kierkegaard did,[42] sin likewise gets the appearance of something unavoidably included in the nature of humans. It is then more than ever rendered harmless, as something you can sympathize with, and needs no forgiveness. Every "explanation" for the existence of evil cannot escape the necessity that it thereby ascribes to sin a legitimacy. Against this the assertion must be made: as evil has no basis in God, so also it has no basis in God's creature. So it is just there without any basis. It is just groundlessly there. Sin comes from sin. This statement does not dispute its reality. The statement does say, however, that it is never there other than as disorder that God from the beginning has not called good.

The statement "Sin comes from sin" also means that each sin that occurs presupposes sin. This is so not merely in the sense that bad conditions

40. Hegel, *Philosophie der Religion*, p. 123. ET: p. 153.
41. Cf. note 28.
42. S. Kierkegaard, *Der Begriff Angst* (1844) (Jena, 1923). ET: *The Concept of Anxiety* (Princeton: Princeton University Press, 1980). Especially on pp. 42ff. and 58-59 he tries to respond to the above objection.

ruin people. It is so above all in the sense that each sinful *deed* presupposes that we *are* sinners. We would not show ourselves as sinners in this and that way if we were not always already sinners, as Article 7 drastically says: "conceived and born in sin." This alludes to the old, admittedly questionable concept of inherited sin. This concept is questionable not only because it casts a mistaken shadow on the whole process of reproduction and birth, and not only because the nonsensical thought lies close at hand that we have inherited sin like a genetic disposition (which one could even exclude by gene manipulation!). It is questionable because it brings about the exact opposite of what it wants to achieve. It strengthens and hardens the sheer ineradicably wicked way in which sinful humans divert attention from their own sins to the sins of others.

Instead of speaking of inherited sin, let us use the term basic sin. Each individual sinful deed points back to a root within us, which can bring forth such things. As Jesus says: "The bad tree bears bad fruit" (Matt. 7:18). This tree is what is meant here by basic sin. Basic sin does not mean simply "All humans are sinners." This is correct, but also endlessly boring. Basic sin means that even the one whom I very much want to see as an exception, whom I would always like to see excused, whose being accused I continually answer with counteraccusations — namely, *I myself* am a sinner. As an example, picture one of the appalling concentration camp murderers, who waded in the blood of his fellow humans, and when possible used words like those of Himmler, who said, "To have coped with this and in it to have preserved our decency is what has made us strong."[43] If I were to see such an unspeakable type before me, I would say as a moral person: What a villain — that one there! But if I know what basic sin is, I will say, in a shaking voice: the roots that in him have borne such terrible fruit lie *also in me.* And this drives me neither into an understatement of sin nor into a moralistic indignation at others; it drives me into the solidarity of sinners, in which I honestly and earnestly know that *I, I without God's radical mercy, am just as lost as he. Then without focusing on the sins of others I can beat my own breast: "God, be merciful to me, a sinner" (Luke 18:13). Whoever acts and speaks this way has understood what basic sin is.*

If we have understood this, then Articles 8 and 9 are also self-explanatory. Article 8 says that sin is a devilish *power* we cannot escape, except through God's helpful intervention. And Article 9 says that this power

43. L. Davidowicz, "Die Massenvernichtung als historisches Dokument," in *Gott nach Auschwitz,* ed. E. Kogon and J. B. Metz (Freiburg: Herder, 1979), p. 52.

is not, however, blind fate; rather, under the power of sin we are *responsible* for our sin and not to be excused (cf. Rom. 1:20-21).

2.2.3. The Judge (Art. 10-11)

We have made a case that sinners themselves cannot give a right account of their sin. But God can give us a right account. For God knows it perfectly well. Our sin, which in its unbearable depth is hidden from us, is open before God. God knows each sin, even the most hidden, and knows it in such a way that for God sin is unambiguously sin. Therefore God can bring it to our attention. Furthermore, as we have heard, our sin consists in opposition undertaken by us, that cannot be averted by us, against the One who is our God and to whom we belong. It is against the God who loves us and our neighbor. But it is not as if God simply accepts this opposition or delays taking any stand against it until St. Never Ever Day. Our opposition, our sin, cannot take place without God's setting against it immediately, yes in advance, God's opposition. The reality of sin can only be thought about theologically in such a way that it stands, from beginning to end, and in every connection, under the No of God. It is not tolerated by God, but accused and condemned. Because of the fact that God acts as our judge and gives divine judgment and condemnation, our sin is absolutely rejected. It is rejected because it rejects. This is why our sin is essentially something that will in no case be approved, hushed up, or minimized — whatever God will do with us. So the fact that God's love holds wonderfully for us sinners can never mean a minimizing of the reality of our sinful opposition against God. God's loving us cannot mean that God thereby ceases to be our judge. Yes, precisely for the sake of love, God must also be our judge.

It is not we who are our judge; God is. As such, God gives us an account of our sins. If we were able ourselves to give an account, it would mean that we have the measuring rod for judging in our own hands. In that case we would unavoidably fashion this measuring rod according to our likes. We would perhaps look for it in a dominant moral code, or perhaps in a new counter-morality, pitted against the dominant one. In one way or another, we would fashion this measuring rod until it suits us. How well it suits us will be shown in the fact that as soon as the measuring rod for judging sin is an instrument in our hands, we are no longer merely sinners, but at the same time also judges in our own behalf. As soon as we think we are even somewhat such judges, it will invariably go like this: we will become our own lawyers and defenders, who more or less, and in essence, absolve ourselves. These defenders will explain that they basically have no accusation to bring. They will then even so manipulate the measuring rod that it can show nothing against them. We then become literally *self*-righteous. You can usually recognize self-righteous persons by the fact that they take that measuring rod, whose particulars they interpret as loosely as possible with regard to themselves, and apply it all the more stringently to others they seek out. They do so because they always find people who deviate from the norms they themselves have set up! Their deviation from us can be ground enough for their being objectionable. So the minimizing of our sin and hardness against the sins of others are at bottom close together, and it is often a small step for one or the other to come to the forefront. For those are the two possibilities where humans have the measuring rod in their hands: laxity, or indignation toward sin. Both of these possibilities are without grace in the breast of the self-righteous. By virtue of the measuring rod in their hands they can, as the self-righteous who always appear very moral, avoid looking at their own failures and feast on the failures of others.

This is why self-righteous persons are very sensitive to criticism coming to them from outside. If they cannot answer right away with a counter-attack, they feel themselves badly misunderstood, are totally aggrieved in their guiltlessness, melt in self-pity: "See how wickedly I am being treated!" They cannot even consider the idea that the others may perhaps be witnesses of the divine judge and could — even though perhaps with mixed and impure motives and expressions — get them on the right track. If they would consider this, they would not be self-righteous anymore. And if they were not, they would bow before the judgment of God and recognize God as their one true judge (which these others are not, neither when they castigate a person nor when they give eulogies at one's coffin). Then they would get serious about the confession: "With *your* judgment, almighty God, we stand and fall."[44] Then they would be free with regard to criticism from people around them. Perhaps they would simply accept the criticism, but would be just as free not to let it get under their skin. They would be assured that the criticism cannot rob them of their honor, and confident that

44. K. Barth, *Gebete* (Munich, 1963), p. 85. ET: *Selected Prayers* (Richmond, VA: John Knox Press, 1965), p. 68.

No judgment dire can cause alarm;
What evil foe could do me harm?[45]

Then they would also be free to think somewhat more kindly of their difficult neighbor. "The self-righteous church speaks in indignation, the true church speaks in intercession."[46] For "there are two kinds of people: the righteous, who consider themselves sinners, and the sinners, who consider themselves righteous."[47]

Still, it is sometimes the case that when persons want to become the judge themselves, they pronounce themselves guilty instead of others. This can happen, too — and we should never name this "repentance." Repentance is the readiness to accept God's judgment on us as right. But there is no such repentance when persons, setting themselves in the place of the divine judge, condemn themselves, continually stand in their own way, hate themselves, despair of themselves, even want to ruin themselves. Do not say that these persons have thereby put themselves in the favorable position of candidates for God's grace. Self-hatred is a variant of self-love, of self-righteousness. The contempt of self-righteous persons for others is only altered, and not overcome, when they "judge" against themselves. This is why their self-contempt can at any time switch into contempt for others. These persons can only be healed (how this can be done psychologically needs special consideration) by having their indignant, as well as their despairing, arrogance in being the decisive judge contradicted. Only when this despairing arrogance is contradicted will we once more become glad that we are not our judge. "Judge not!" (Matt. 7:1). This holds with reference to all our own judging of sin, even that apparently most justified. This game, the game of the self-righteous person, is over when God brings to bear the just, divine contradiction against our contradiction of God's love. When God does this, God makes clear that in the matter of our sin God alone is the judge, and that we are nothing other than God's people, accused by God. In this way, God makes clear that we have no ground for self-righteousness, but all the more grounds for beating our own breasts: "All our righteous deeds are like a filthy cloth" (Isa. 64:6). So it is not the persons whom everyone already condemns, not the

45. Stanzas 1 and 3 of the hymn "Ist Gott für mich, so trete" ("If God Be for Me"), by P. Gerhardt.

46. H. Gollwitzer et al., *Predigten* (Neukirchen-Vluyn: Neukirchener Verlag, 1967), p. 87.

47. Blaise Pascal, *Pensées*, Frag. 760. ET: *Pensées* (Kila, MT: Kessinger, 2004), p. 127.

unrighteous, but the *self-righteous*, who are really the burning problem of the doctrine of sin.

The self-righteous are the problem because they hold the measuring rod for good and evil in their hands. "How do you come to know your misery?" It is not enough to answer that in place of a measuring rod we create, we get a different measuring rod created by God for the assessment of our sins. It is not even enough to say that the measuring rod lies in God's hands rather than in ours. It is true that our sin is discerned, not by measuring ourselves, but only by ourselves *being* measured. But this happens irrefutably because the measuring rod that measures us is not merely a code composed in such and such a way. It is no work of paragraphs. Instead, it is a "person," a particular one, facing us from beyond ourselves — our judge who meets us. The entrance of our judge, the judgment on us that follows, the No spoken to our sins — this is the measuring rod for the objectionable nature of our sins. As long as the measuring rod for determining sin is a code, we cannot understand why it should not be handed over to us for our own self-condemnation. We will then keep on protesting that it is arbitrary not to hand it over, and we will try to overcome the fact that we are deprived of it, because we want to make out of our condemnation a self-condemnation. Whereas, we cannot override someone who encounters us as our final judge. By encountering us, relations are established which are clear: this One is the judging person, and we are the ones who are being judged. This One says No to our sins, and we are the ones to whom the No is spoken. This judgment is by no means an arbitrary one, to which we have to submit blindly. This judgment is just. This does not mean that we set the conditions for determining to what extent it is just. But it does mean that as we look at this judgment we can understand that it is just. Sin is really recognized when we understand the justice of the divine judgment on it, and with insight affirm it in confession of sin and repentance.

The Heidelberg speaks about this same theme in Articles 10 and 11. It does so by taking over a train of thought, almost copying it word for word, that stands in a "Short Confession" stemming from the Genevan student of Calvin, Theodore Beza. This confession appeared in German in Heidelberg shortly before the publication of the Heidelberg Catechism.[48] By taking over this train of thought, the first part of the Heidelberg gets an accent

---

48. Cf. W. Hollweg, *Neue Untersuchungen zur Geschichte und Lehre des H. Katechismus* (Neukirchen-Vluyn: Neukirchener Verlag, 1961), chap. 1, n. 14, pp. 87ff.

that goes beyond the scope of the Lutheran doctrine of the law. For the Lutheran doctrine is decidedly interested that we become convicted of being sinners by the second use of the law. The Heidelberg speaks of this also, in its own way. But by taking over Beza's view, it gains a new perspective. What is important is not simply how *humans* stand over against God — namely as sinners. Most important now is how *God* relates to the fact of sin and being sinners — namely: *God* says No to it, *God* opposes it, *God* in the function of judge prosecutes the sin and judges the sinner. Thus a new horizon of inquiry opens up. The question is no longer simply subjective-anthropological: How does the sinner come to forgiveness of sins? The question is now also, and in fact primarily, a question of the doctrine of God: How can God love us sinners without loving the sin? How can God say Yes to us, when as doers of sin God can only say No to us? Would not God's love, were it separated from God's condemnation of sin, come to be complicity with evil? But how can God say No to our sin without our being destroyed by this No? How can God condemn us as sinners and yet love us? How can God be our righteous judge and still be our merciful advocate and intercessor? If these questions were not cleared up, there would be danger that the love of God would be thought of either as the minimizing of our sin or as powerlessness toward our sin. Or it could be that a split within God would be postulated, whereby God arbitrarily sometimes accuses and other times pardons.

The train of thought the Heidelberg takes over from Beza and develops from Article 10 to Article 18 was not invented by Beza. It goes back to a formulation of the doctrine of reconciliation, completely new in contrast to the tradition, that is the work of Anselm of Canterbury, who lived at the turn from the eleventh to the twelfth century. This doctrine, which the Heidelberg latches onto, has been disputed in many ways. One aspect must concern us here: the so-called Anselmic penal theory.[49] What is meant, we read in Article 10: "Will God allow such disobedience and rebellion to go unpunished? Certainly not, for God is terribly angry with our inborn sinfulness as well as our actual sins and will punish them according to God's righteous judgment in time and eternity." We read something similar in Article 11: God's righteousness requires "that sin committed against the

---

49. Cf. G. Plasger, *Die Not-Wendigkeit der Gerechtigkeit. Eine Interpretation zu "Cur Deus homo" von Anselm von Canterbury* (Münster, 1993); further: W. Metz, *Necessitas satisfactionis? Eine systematische Studie zu den Fragen 12-18 des Heidelberger Katechismus and zur Theologie des Zacharias Ursinus* (Zürich/Stuttgart: Zwingli-Verlag, 1970).

most high majesty of God must be punished with extreme, that is, with eternal punishment of both body and soul." The catechism seems to want to say: not because humans are sinners do *they* need the love which reconciles them to God, but because God has been offended by sin, *God* needs the reconciliation, the change of attitude, in order to again become mild and loving. But this can only happen *after* God has carried out a penalty for the human crime.

About this punishment theory, understood this way, Adolf von Harnack remarked critically:[50] "The worst" in it is "the mythological concept of God as the powerful private man, who because of his offended honor is angry and will not give up his anger until he has received satisfaction at least as great," that is, until he has carried out his punishment somehow on someone. This, however, portrays God as subject to being hurt like a human, and reacting to hurt like humans, who can be satisfied only when their anger has vented itself. And that, said Harnack, is a sub-Christian concept. Instead, God is love, and must be thought of as a reconciling being. Does the Heidelberg actually represent the view that Harnack attacks here? But first, let us ask about the view revealed in Harnack's criticism. His criticism follows from a position that has been put forward again and again from the time of the Enlightenment into the present. According to it, God is so much the "dear God" that any conception of God's anger, and that means any serious rejection and "punishing" of sin, must be kept far away as a sub-Christian view. The idea of anger in God would give God the visage of a Grobian, an oppressive despot. Or it would impart the features of a sadist who forages on the victims of his wrath — features that simply do not jibe with the concept of the love of God. What can be said to this portrayal of God?

So that we do not fall into Christian arrogance about the statement on the sub-Christian nature of the "anger of God," let us remember the Jewish tale about the meeting between a rabbi and a pastor. The pastor asks: "Do you Jews still believe in the God of wrath, in contrast to us Christians, who believe in the God of love?" Answers the rabbi: "Yes, we still believe in the God of wrath. But while we leave the wrath to God in order to practice kindness on earth, you Christians have done it the other way around!" There is profound meaning in this answer: if God is reduced to the function of being kind, then on earth hardness and malice spread like weeds. This is a dangerous statement, to be sure. For it could be understood in the

50. According to Plasger, *Die Not-Wendigkeit der Gerechtigkeit*, pp. 13f.

sense of the miserable teaching that has tainted whole generations: "Love alone doesn't work! Whoever doesn't listen, must feel" — the rod or even the lash. "It hurts me to do this. But it is only for your own good." The peak achievement of this teaching consisted in interpreting this loveless, "hard righteousness," yes even the rod and the whip, as pure love. So we were supposed to welcome this rod or lash thankfully and without a whimper. This teaching, whether practiced by humans or ascribed to God, only made people hard and cruel. The talk about God's being only love is perhaps to be valued as a protest against such miserable teaching.

But the question is whether this protest is enough, and whether it achieves what it intends. For the profundity in the protest of the rabbi against reducing God to the function of being kind needs to be looked for in another place, rather than in such bad teaching. This reduction is to be seen in light of the effort undertaken in modern times to make God as weak as possible and humans as strong as possible. God is presented in such a way as to have as little as possible to say, and to hinder humans as little as possible from doing what they have in mind to do anyway. Humans are presented in such a way that they basically need nothing from God except agreement with the self-affirmation of humans, which is going on anyway. And this is then "the dear God." Limiting God to this figure smells strongly like narrowing God's task to a confirmation of human self-affirmation. If this self-affirmation of humans meets its limits in the experience of suffering and problems, then the God long since made weak in human conception cannot help any more. Then humans get no answer to their question: Why do you let this happen? Then humans may still console themselves with the thought that now God also suffers (if it is comfort to know in your suffering that God is also powerless). Or then people alleviate the pain emotionally by saying that they may accuse God (and think thereby that God has overlooked the complaint, or is taking time to answer — until no time is left, which is the *eschaton*). Or people may find comfort in the idea that they are needed to redeem, and thereby substitute for, the God who in the face of problems is convicted of being incapable, while they at least deal better with the issue, and are kind. This line of thought, though winding this way and that, finally comes out to just this: because "dear God" in the face of human sin cannot angrily say No to it, humans can now take over the business of battling sin themselves. In order to do this, since they have made God as weak as possible, they must also make their sin as small as possible — so small that on God's side there is nothing to get angry about. They make sin so small that it cannot really harm our feeling of self-worth, so small that either we can make it good ourselves, or have this disturbance taken away by therapy, or manage to live with it, as we would hay fever. In short, the modern reduction of God to the function of love only, to the exclusion of that which the Heidelberg, in keeping with biblical usage, calls the anger of God, by all appearances hangs together with the effort to think of God as being as weak as possible and of sin as being as small as possible.

The Reformation, and the Heidelberg in particular, did not go along with this reduction. They did not take part in the minimizing of God, or of sin. Among them, speech about the anger of God against sin and those committing it was not swept under the carpet. Do they then think of God as a lord whose honor is aggrieved, as though God could be hurt like a human? In a way, Harnack was right about this. But we must stay far away from letting indignant, mindless thoughts of a human lusting for revenge be reflected onto God. Instead, we cannot make it clear enough that this is all about the God who has turned to us humans, the God who is free for coexistence with us, who — far from any honor of a "private man" — sets God's honor on being ours and living together with us. It is about the God who does indeed love us and who in love for us does not rest until we as partners answer this love in love to God and to the creatures loved by God. The honor aggrieved by sin is not the honor of a lofty private man, but the honor that God in gracious purpose has placed within us. Because sin thwarts this will, because it contradicts the love of God for us and its aim for our love in return, we harm first ourselves and at the same time God, because God loves us.

It would be a powerless and helpless love — which such a limited love of God necessarily is — if God took this thwarting of loving will toward us, and our self-inflicted damage by sin with a mild smile; if God did not become "angry." In such a reductionist love, God would become the accomplice of injustice. And in such a love God would be indifferent about us people of sin, even if we cause God pain. In getting angry with us, God is not indifferent toward us. It is sometimes the case among us humans, and is at any rate the case with God, that God would not get angry if God did not love. Because God is not indifferent to any human, because God loves each one, for this reason, and only for this reason, God does become *angry*, "terribly angry with our inborn sinfulness as well as our actual sins," about the basic sin and its symptoms. God gets angry and punishes, not because God's love secretly has sadistic features, but because God would not really love without negating whatever threatens to negate and annul this love.

God's anger is only this: the entirely *just* No to that which contradicts God's love to humans, and its awakening of human love in return; God's No to sin and the doers of sin. Anger is the side of God's love for us humans that does not condone contradiction and those who do the contradicting, but judges it as sin and condemns it to death, to an end, with all its disaster.

According to Articles 10 and 11, God will "punish" sin and those who commit it, in time and eternity, in body and soul, that is, now and always and in every respect. This does not correspond to the hell that people can prepare for one another in their lovelessness. Rather, we need to understand it as the effectiveness and strength of the divine No to sin and those who commit it. God's No is effective and strong in that humans in their sin and as sinners would really be lost and left to themselves in time and eternity, in body and soul, if God would not say Yes *and* No, if God were not their savior *and* their judge. We would really be completely lost if God did not have mercy on us to whom God must say No, *and* if God did not condemn that which contradicts God's love and mercy. God's love includes both this Yes and this No, both unmixed and inseparable. God's love would not be love if in the face of the sin that contradicts it, it did not thwart, condemn, negate this sin. For love "does not rejoice in wrongdoing" (1 Cor. 13:6). But in rejoicing over righteousness, it loves us. What has been said is even more grounded and brought to light by the statement in Article 11 (which definitively dismantles Harnack's objection): "God is indeed merciful, but God is also righteous." About this statement we must understand four points:

1. "Merciful and righteous" are not two ideal concepts whose meaning we already know before we ascribe them to God as divine qualities, in order then to balance them out theoretically to see how both of them can be harmonized in God. Rather, the train of thought that begins with Article 10 moves so strongly toward Article 18 that it is conceived from its goal, that is, from *Jesus Christ*, "who was given us to set us completely free and to make us right with God" (Art. 18). That God is "merciful, but . . . also righteous" is defined in God's *acting* toward us in Jesus Christ mercifully and justly. This is where the explaining of God's justice and mercy needs to begin.

2. These two concepts must not be separated, as though one followed the other in time. God does not let angry righteousness rage until the fury has cooled off in order afterward to be only merciful. God is *both* in divine action, and both *at the same time:* "merciful, but also righteous." Both be-

long together. A mercy of God without righteousness would be secret complicity with evil. And a righteousness of God without mercy would be just eerie mercilessness. Rather, God is righteous in being merciful, and merciful in being righteous. God is our judge and our savior, and as our savior, God is our judge. God is merciful in the form of righteousness and righteous on the basis of mercy.

3. What does merciful mean, and what does righteous mean? We have said that God is self-defined as our God, and we as God's people. God's completed decision for this "covenant," and God's will to let this have its way, whatever the cost, no matter what stance humans take toward it, is God's *mercy*. This mercy contains for God, as for us, God's claim to live according to this covenant. This is God's *righteousness*. So from the beginning it notes something positive. God is true to this claim in that God loves us and our neighbor. But are we true to God's command to love God and our neighbor? We are from the start not God's people, and live again and again like those who are not. Under these circumstances, God is our merciful God in that the divine righteousness fights against us, who *are* God's, but do *not live* as God's people. So God is "merciful, but . . . also righteous" toward us.

4. Once again: this is about the measuring rod for the judging of our sins. God is our judge. As such, God has this measuring rod in hand. The measuring rod with which God judges us, like the verdict God pronounces upon us, is recognizable in the way God acts toward us in Christ. In him God wields that measuring rod and pronounces the verdict, which is "merciful but . . . also righteous." God does this in such a way as to make valid our taking comfort in God's mercy, which we in no way deserve. God does it by exercising mercy in the form of righteousness, and righteousness full of mercy. God does it by completely affirming and completely denying us, namely denying the "old human" of sin, crucified with Christ (Rom. 6:6; Gal. 2:19), and in merciful righteousness making an end of this old human in order to open up for us a new life in righteous mercy which lives from God's love. This is our judge: "God is *just,* a *helper* worthy, whose scepter bright is *mercy*."[51]

---

51. From stanza 2 of the hymn, "Macht hoch die Tür" ("Fling Wide the Door, Unbar the Gate"), by G. Weissel.

2.3. God's Acquittal

2.3.1. The Liberator (Art. 12-18)

Article 1 says *what,* or more exactly, *who* our only comfort is. Articles 3-11 say that we have *no rightful claim* on this comfort, but that we urgently *need* it. Articles 12-18 now say that despite our sin, God nevertheless actually does give us this comfort. God's comfort is much *more* than any mere thing. It is God's *giving* us the great assurance of loving us. It is fundamentally and comprehensively God's *Yes* to us in our misery: "*Yes,* I will carry *you*" (Isa. 46:4). God does *not* abandon the work of God's hands, does not abandon us either to the sin that we do and has power over us, *or* to the misery in which we find ourselves far from God, whether we groan under it or resign ourselves to it. Yes, God is actually much more ready to abandon God's *own self* to all this misery than to abandon *us.* "You have burdened me with your sins, you have wearied me with your iniquities," says God, but also promises to be the One "who blots out your transgression for my own sake, and I will not remember your sins" (Isa. 43:25). This is how God says Yes to us.

In this Yes to us, God does not tie us down to our misery, but instead draws us out of it. By the Yes, God does not affirm that we are miserable people. God says yes to us *in defiance* of our misery and our sin, but does not say yes to us without also saying *no.* This is why earlier we could not speak about God's No without speaking of God's Yes to us. Both belong together. Hence the passage Articles 9-18 (or 3-20) describes a context in which the beginning of the second part of the catechism, introduced in the midst of the passage, does not constitute a break in it. What follows will only be an explanation of what has already been said. To be sure, the train of thought from Article 12 forward has a new accent. Now it comes to light that our judge *actually* is our savior. In a hidden way, it was already a boon that as our judge God did not accept our miserable opposition to God's good will without opposing it. But the fact that this is really a boon becomes clear in that God as our savior says yes — to the very same people to whom God also says no. The movement from No to Yes is unambiguous and irreversible. God says No for the sake of God's Yes. "For the Lord does not reject forever, but first afflicts, then pardons in his abundant kindness. For He does not willingly bring grief or affliction to man, crushing under his feet all the prisoners of the earth" (Lam. 3:31-33, Jewish Study Bible). And yet God's Yes is not without God's No. It is not as though God says one or the other partly or alternately! God's No belongs *within* God's Yes. God says No *because* God says Yes. God says no because God says yes to those in *misery*, to "all the *prisoners*." God says No because God's Yes is not a *transfiguration* of their imprisonment, but *liberation* out of it.

In this way the Yes of God differs from the self-affirmation of miserable humans. Not that self-affirmation is always objectionable! Those affirmed by *God* may also joyfully affirm *themselves*. But God's Yes contradicts the Yes that humans trying to be independent from God have made it their life task to speak. These people can no longer hear God's Yes to them — unless it be as an expression of their own attempt at self-affirmation (in a religious moment, which is possible for them). *These* persons, because in their separation from God they no longer recognize themselves as affirmed, must ask what then gives them worth. *These* persons now have to answer this way: I have worth insofar as I can make myself worthy and therefore affirm myself. This throws them into endless — and ultimately always futile — effort. It is all the same whether they experience moments of self-satisfaction, or are continually dissatisfied with themselves. One way or another they must look out for affirmation *themselves*, because they do not otherwise feel affirmed. They must continually overexert themselves or foster all kinds of illusions about themselves (without getting free from themselves when these illusions sometimes burst). And *to this* striving to make ourselves worthy, God says No — in saying yes to us. In choosing us, God rejects this striving. By affirming us, God says No to the entire cave in which those independent of God are enclosed, and with all their self-affirmation close themselves in even tighter. By saying this No along with the Yes, God gives the Yes power to free people from their cave. It negates their cave existence by putting them in relation to God: in this relation they are from the start continuously affirmed and worthy. So they are free from the hopeless business of having to create their own worth.

The comfort God *gives* us, the great Yes, is therefore no *mere* word. It is the word in an *action* that is healing beyond all measure. The comfort God gives us is this: "God takes on what is ours in order to bring us what is God's."[52] It is God's becoming our God in order to make us God's people. The entire work in which God says Yes to us has this point, this meaning, this goal: the togetherness, the interaction of the *free* God and the *free* human being. The fact that God gives this comfort means that it cannot otherwise be had in any other way, that humans are not able to give it to them-

52. M. Luther, *WA* 1:28, 52.

selves. Humans who could come into consideration as free partners of God do not exist — unless God *makes* them free for this. They are not in themselves free — this is the extent of their sin, not the result of fate. Their comfort has only this enduring basis: the liberation of humans from bondage. In giving us what we need so much and yet cannot give ourselves, God liberates us for it.

In our ears this is no doubt a provocation, since we consider ourselves already thoroughly free. The enslaved will of humans turned in on themselves plays out in the framework of their arbitrary and independent freedom. In its name they will vigorously protest against the claim that they have to *be set free.* They will assert that this freedom of theirs already makes them capable of relating to God — *as much* as *they* want to! Latin-American liberation theology reflects some of this provocation when it tells us that the poor are not simply under*developed* people who need to be developed *by us* to our standard of living. They are oppressed people who need to be liberated. And this liberation is not in order that they may follow the example of the freedom of our "free world." Instead, it is in order that *at the same time we too,* who with our corrupt freedom have done the oppressing, may be set free.[53] Above all, and prior to anything else, it is in relation to *God* that we are prisoners in our corrupt freedom. In each act of our independent freedom we at the same time activate our alienation, even if within it we reach for the highest. With all *our* freedom, we always confirm our imprisonment in our "misery," our having set ourselves loose from God. If we supposedly free persons must first of all be *set free* in order to be free for the togetherness of the free God and free human beings, then this is clear: *this* freedom is no mere application of an independent freedom that we have at our disposal. *This* freedom we do not *have.* It must be *given* to us. We cannot *take* it, as is the case with that arbitrary freedom. For *this* freedom we must *be* set free. This freedom comes out of the process of liberation. We are free in it always thanks only to the liberation that *has taken place* for us who are bound. Jesus says it this way: "So if the Son makes you free, you will be free indeed" (John 8:36). Our liberation consists not in acquiring a *concept* of freedom; it consists in real liberation *coming* to us.

The title of the second part of the Heidelberg, "Humanity's Redemption and Freedom," is *"De hominis liberatione"* in the Latin original of Ursinus:[54]

---

53. G. Gutiérrez, *A Theology of Liberation* (Maryknoll, NY: Orbis, 1973), pp. 81ff.

54. *The Heidelberg Catechism in German, Latin and English* (New York: Charles Scribner, 1863), p. 144.

"On the Deliverance" of humans by God. This is what the *whole* second part is about, and especially the passage Articles 12-18, which is like an advance summary. Deliverance is liberation. And liberation is deliverance: not of the soul from the body, not of an immortal seed from its grubby time-bound shell, and also not of a single, better individual out of a "lost mass." Deliverance is unbinding of the bound who cannot unbind themselves from their entanglement. Liberation is "buying the freedom" of humans with "hard cash," out of the hand of powers to which they do not belong, so that they will come into the good hand of the One to whom they do belong. This is done so validly that every right of that foreign hand to them is annulled. Deliverance is their redemption from their sin, from their misery, from the whole system of their separation from God. In this separation they strive to be free from God, and in this very striving become bound. For they exist in contradiction to the truth that God is ours and we are God's. Deliverance is redemption in that God stands firm and bears up against this opposition, professing to be our God and affirming that we are God's people.

This is what Articles 12-18 are about. But they speak about it in such a unique way that this passage is widely challenged: "It doubtless belongs to the weakest material in the Heidelberg"; for it has a "badly construed and purely theologizing character about it."[55] Two main objections are raised. The *first* objection relates to the conception of how this liberation takes place. It latches onto the reproach against the Anselmic punishment theory and bears on the "doctrine of satisfaction" associated with it. Although the Latin word *satisfactio* is usually translated "satisfaction," in the sixteenth century it was also translated "payment." Both concepts appear, for example, in Article 12 ("God wills that the divine justice must be satisfied; therefore full payment must be made to God's justice. . . ."). The doctrine of satisfaction is conceived in the following way by this objection: It presupposes someone who in his honor or sense of justice is offended (as happens often enough among *humans* — perhaps even in their relationship to *God*!). The offended person can only become calmed down if he *beforehand* reestablishes his honor, if he *beforehand* gets compensation, "satisfaction" for his aggrieved sense of justice, if he *beforehand* "pays back" the wrongdoer. It is rather like what happens in the terrible custom of dueling. An aggrieved man demands "satisfaction" for himself. The other man or he himself may in the process be finished off, but only in this way can the

---

55. A. Lang, *Der Heidelberger Katechismus und vier verwandte Katechismen* (Leipzig: Deichert Verlag, 1967), p. lxxxix.

aggrieved get satisfaction. Only *after* taking care of his bloody business will he again be at peace, but at peace only *with himself* — though it be the peace in which he has gentle rest in the grave. The outcome of the restoration of aggrieved honor, peace with himself, shows that the duel is a stupid fruit on the tree of a person turned in on himself. According to the interpretation of the doctrine of satisfaction in the above objection, this is how God is supposed to behave. The doctrine would project the mentality of an aggrieved person onto God. Then it would understand God as one who gets satisfaction for *God's self,* with the goal of peace with *God's own self.* And this would be at the price of a sacrifice on the way. God would then really only say yes to God's own self and not at all to us who are in misery. And God would then not free us from our misery, but free God's self from the blemish of offended honor. A doctrine of satisfaction understood in this way would indeed be a horror.

The Heidelberg did not understand it this way. The lead question of the whole passage is this: "How may *we* . . . be reconciled to God, being received with favor?" (Art. 12). It is not that *God* must clear things up with God's own self. *We* have to be cleared up. And this takes place not in *our* achieving it: it will be "given" us by God (Art. 18). We attain God's "favor" because God practices favor toward us who are in misery, in order to set us free from our misery. Yet the whole answer to how we are set free is already given in the statement: "God is indeed merciful, but God is also righteous" (Art. 11). "Gracious is the Lord, and righteous" (Ps. 116:5). Once again, both belong indissolubly together: God's *mercy,* the undeserved friendliness in which God turns toward us and so determines to be our God and us to be God's, *and* God's *righteousness,* the rightful claim God makes on God's own self and likewise on us, to live in such community. But what happens if God's claim reaches out — and is threatened by emptiness? What if people do not give a "just" response to this claim? What if people do not live as God's, but in "misery," sin, and distance from God? Then we are "received with favor" only by God's being *more than ever* merciful *and* just. God keeps relationship with us only by turning in mercy more than ever to people who now exist in contradiction to God's merciful and righteous will. God does this, however, by first, and now more than ever, exercising righteousness. And under these circumstances, this will consist in judgment, in which God withdraws every right to exist from *the very people* on whom God has mercy, who exist in contradiction to God's good will. *This* is how God is "merciful, but . . . also righteous."

Let it not be said, as people have said in opposition to that misunderstood doctrine of satisfaction, that God exercises grace *instead of* justice. In this view, a grace is in charge that makes light of human wrong, and allows it to continue. A grace is in charge that, by not also looking out for righteousness, gets into an "unholy alliance" with injustice. Or it is a grace that lets justice and righteousness go to the devil, with the hidden thought that grace will shine all the brighter against this dark background. One way or another, this grace would in truth be powerless against injustice. From this angle it would always be open to challenge. But actually, grace cannot be separated from God's righteousness. How can God be gracious to humans in any other way than that in which God *is:* in grace, God exercises *righteousness.* God's righteousness does not contradict God's grace. But reconciliation with injustice does. It would be *unmerciful* if God were not at the same time just, if God did not totally negate the injustice of those whom God has mercy on. But God *is* merciful and therefore merciful in *righteousness.*

Therefore Article 12 answers the question of how we can return to God's *favor* in the following way: this takes place in that God achieves justice, or literally, that "God wills that the divine justice must be satisfied," "full payment must be made," an open account settled, a debt erased. It is not that a selfish God gets satisfaction for the divine *self* that allows God *afterward* to have a mild attitude. Rather, the merciful One lets grace rule for us by *at the same time* letting full and sufficient righteousness toward us rule. Certainly God condemns our injustice. But thereby God upholds justice and so makes grace for us powerfully right and unchallengeable. This way God does not let injustice persist. This way God distances it from God and from us. By virtue of being tied to righteousness, God's mercy is no easy "love," no mere sympathy, no putting up with "misery"; it is action for liberation from misery. Thus, by virtue of being tied to mercy, God's righteousness is no mere destructive, hard "penal justice," but condemning injustice and humans as its doers, it is a positive upholding of righteousness.

This is important to consider, because the misery of humans consists not only in that they do injustice, but also that they so often *suffer* injustice. If God's grace toward the doers of injustice did not proceed completely justly, the insoluble problem would arise as to whether God is somehow indifferent or unjust toward those who suffer injustice. Then we would have to push this problem off blindly to the Final Day. Surely suffering from injustice (as evil in the world generally!) puts us before a dark enigma. But in this enigma there is still a light for us: to believe that God is "merciful and just." It is true that in view of those who suffer injustice a question arises that goes beyond the question of the justice of *humans.* This is the question of whether *God* is just. But the same question arises, as we have seen, in view of doers of injustice. For the Bible, however, the question of God's righteousness does not arise so differently in view of each of these as modern people would often like to think. Humankind is not divided into two groups, those who do injustice and those who suffer injustice. There are not separate answers for each of these groups to the question of whether God is just. And this is not because for God doing injustice and suffering injustice are the same. Rather, it is because God does not separate the question about *God's* justice from that about *humans.* In tackling the problem of how *humans* are to be justified, God also justifies *God's own self.* Certainly "the most high majesty of God" is aggrieved (Art. 11) by both the doing of injustice and the suffering of injustice. For both threaten to annul God's good will for the creature. Yet God, in defiance of the worst opposition, does not sacrifice the work of God's hands. God shows that this is the case by being merciful in no other way than by ensuring that God's righteousness is satisfied, by not being gracious in any other way than by justly renouncing injustice and humans as its perpetrators. God asserts good will for humans, against that which negates this good will. In this way God "saves" not only the honor of God's creature, but also God's own honor. This honor has been based on letting nothing abolish God's relation with the creature. If nothing separates even the doers of injustice from God's love, though according to divine righteousness God parts from them and their injustice, then what would be able to cause separation from God? Should not this be the light for us in the problem of suffering caused by injustice, that the truth shines out more clearly than ever, that injustice cannot separate us from the love of the merciful and righteous God?

The *second* objection to Articles 12-18 relates to the presentation of the one *who* sets humans free. The answer is: God does this in the *"mediator"* Jesus Christ (Art. 18). The second objection focuses on this answer, calling it an "a priori construction." That is, out of general presuppositions the postulate is raised: there must necessarily be something like a divine-human redeemer, in order then to assert that what has been postulated truly exists. The objection seems to be well founded. Article 12: We sinners have deserved punishment, for the sake of justice. Articles 13-14: No creature is capable of paying the debt. Articles 15-17: Therefore the only one capable would be one who *would* be both God and human. Article 18: This figure postulated in thought *exists!*

Let those who protest against a postulated construction watch out that they not proceed in a similar way! For what is bad about it? This is what is bad: you think something out and consider it desirable or logically necessary and *thereupon* assert the reality of what you have thought out. By this procedure the reality of liberation and of the liberator must be formed and transformed according to the specification of what has been thought out. The result is that what is asserted to be real can no longer get beyond seeming to be only a thought-out wish. Such an a priori construction is a theological hoax.

Does the Heidelberg carry out such a construction here? It can be shown on the contrary that here too it thinks *a posteriori.* That is, it reflects *subsequently,* under the condition made by *God* and not by us, on the *reality* of the liberator given and revealed to us. It meditates on why this reality is good, meaningful, desirable, and yes, logical. Not because it must be so according to our way of thinking is it really so. Conversely: because it *is* so, it *must* manifestly be so. It is like the Resurrected One's saying in Luke 24:26: "Was it not necessary that the Christ should suffer these things?" This does not mean in the execution of a necessity set by fate! But after he has actually suffered, it becomes discernible in the light of Easter that this had to be, and was no lamentable accident.

Three reasons for holding that the Heidelberg thinks this way stand out. 1. Everything it says stands in the light of Article 1, and aims only to be an unfolding of what is already given: that the liberator is already here without first being thought of, wished for, or postulated. 2. The train of thought in Articles 12ff. would be far too venturesome — reason by itself could really not arrive at it, even in a dream! — if it were not that the train of thought is drawn by its goal, from the knowledge of the "mediator" who has been given us (Art. 18). Article 19 underscores this: "From where do you know this?" Answer: "From the holy gospel"! 3. The catechism gives Bible references for every article in this passage, as if to show that it is not free fantasy here making constructions; here too the witness of scripture is followed. For example, on Article 12 Romans 8:3-4 is cited: "For God has done what the law . . . could not do: by sending his own Son . . . so that the just requirement of the law might be fulfilled in us. . . ." And *therefore* the Heidelberg declares: "God wills that the divine justice must be satisfied." Or on Article 13 Matthew 6:12 is cited: "Forgive us our debts" — and therefore the Heidelberg answers the question "Can we make this payment ourselves?" with a resounding "By no means." Many similar examples could be given. In short, what is done here is not postulating. Here thinking follows after and reflects upon what has already been given, as is fitting in Christian theology. So the second objection is not founded.

But we need to take this matter even more *seriously* and to say that as we really come to recognize our sins in our encounter with the judge, so in our encounter with our liberator we come to know what our liberation is, why we need liberation, and what it frees us from and to. For as we recognize our sins where our judge condemns them, so we recognize our liberation only where our liberator redeems us. For this reason we cannot approach the biblical witness with a preformed conception of liberation and with a need for it. Therefore when we Christians talk about *liberation,* we must *first* talk about our *liberator,* and only in connection with him also about our liberation. For Christians, deliverance is neither an idea nor a program nor a Utopia, to which Jesus Christ is related only afterward in order to present him as a kind of representative or protagonist or prophet of it. Our liberation cannot be separated from our liberator the way an inventor can be separated from the invention. Only because "Christ the *Savior* is here" is *salvation* also here for us. What has happened in him has happened *for all time.* It intends to be repeated in every time, but always on the strength of what happened *once,* always in the name and in the power of *Jesus Christ.*

To connect this with the previous train of thought, let us review briefly. To the question of *what* sets us free, we heard: the merciful justice God exercises toward us! But this answer was given with a view toward the other question, about *who* sets us free. Its answer is: "Our Lord Jesus Christ!" (Art. 18). Christian theology cannot separate these questions about the what and the who — as in saying that the first interests Judaism and the second the church.[56] It is also not the case that you can be confident of clear knowledge about the what, but be unsure about *who* could carry through what is meant, if it is even a "someone" at all. Then again, when you look around at the world you can start to doubt whether God is actually "merciful, but also just." As a matter of fact, we cannot see in events around us that God is merciful and just. But we can see it in him who is sent as our deliverer. In him God's mercy and justice are defined. They are defined in him by the way God in him deals with us mercifully and justly. And in his acting toward us in this way, he is our liberating deliverer.

---

56. Cf. P. Lapide and J. Moltmann, *Jüdischer Monotheismus — Christliche Trinitätslehre. Ein Gespräch* (Munich, 1979), pp. 73, 78. ET: *Jewish Monotheism and Christian Trinitarian Doctrine* (Philadelphia: Fortress Press, 1981), pp. 73, 79.

It is a justified fear that if our liberation is separated from our liberator, liberation turns into an idea. It makes no difference whether we have thought out this idea, or can trace it back to divine intervention. It comes out to the same result: that *we* would first have to actualize our liberation, perhaps with divine support, but basically we alone. A self-liberation would then be assigned to the egotistical person, turned in on self, which could only result in an ever new asserting of this all-important I. But this way humans could never be set free from the root of their misery. They could only reach an apparent liberation — like the action of Moses, who struck out for the liberation of his people on his own, and who achieved only something that led to the intensifying of his captivity, not to liberation from it. Presumably *both* objections to the line of thought in Articles 12-18 have as their goal the same assertion: the misery of humans is after all not so abysmal that humans cannot free *themselves* from it, when strengthened a little with the thought of a "dear God." Yes, would those who object perhaps even *like to replace* the understanding of our liberation by the divine liberator alone with the idea of human self-liberation?

Certainly our liberation by God aims at our activation as free people. Certainly there are some things from which we can free ourselves. In the very answer of faith to the liberation given us by God, which we cannot accomplish, we are encouraged and propelled to liberations we ourselves may and should accomplish. But right in the answer of faith it also becomes clear to us that such liberations are only *relative* liberations. They are relative because they bring only provisional relief without having escaped the threat of new captivities. They are relative because as a rule we can never be completely sure whether we really need and get liberation at *the* point and in *the* way and for *the* purpose we intend. They are relative above all because they are borne by the knowledge that they can never replace *the* liberation God grants us. They are relative because they are also free from the illusion that in all of this we do not need another liberation, a healing of our misery at its *root* — or that the divine liberation is only a symbol of our own self-liberation.

With this, the point of the statement about the inseparability of our liberation from our liberator should be clear. The point is that this statement calls our attention to something outside ourselves, across from us, facing us, which can do and does what we cannot do for ourselves, and which our fellow humans cannot do for us. We need a liberation that only *God* can bring about for us. We do not merely assert such a liberation. God *brings it about* for us in the liberator, our "Lord Jesus Christ." In this way we learn that God alone gives it to us in the liberator and that we absolutely need it and that we cannot get it in any of *our own* liberations. We can witness to it in our relative liberations. But in contrast to such relative liberations, it is *radical* liberation.

Divine liberation is *radical* because it attacks our misery at its root. It attacks it where *God* sees our misery, where God actually mercifully accepts wretched humanity, with just rejection of its misery. God sets us free *fundamentally* from our *remoteness from God,* and not from this or that predicament from which we think we could stand to be liberated. While we can bear with "this or that" if no liberation is given us, what God frees us from is *unbearable* misery. This can express itself in all kinds of adverse symptoms, but it is also there when we do not feel any symptoms. It is a misery in the *root* of our existence. If our belonging to God constitutes the essence of our being human, and if our remoteness from God is a contesting of our belonging to God, then it is a distortion in the *core* of our being as humans. Then humans, distorted to the core, would have to be able to destroy themselves in order to set themselves free from the root of their misery. But this they cannot do. In themselves they always deliver only new drapings of the possibilities of the "old Adam" (and the "old Eve"). *Only God* can set them free from the root of their misery, which is what God does. God frees us radically from the root of our misery — not only by seeing it, and not only by condemning it, but also by dismantling it.

How does God do this? In our answer we have to guard against a separation of our liberator from the liberation we experience in him. The person of the liberator dare not be seen apart from the event in which this person deals with us. Who this person is becomes clear to us in this event: it is the "mediator who is simultaneously true God and a true and righteous human being" (Art. 18). This is not describing some kind of in-between being twixt God and humanity, half divine, half human, put together out of two "substances." Such a being would have nothing to do with *us*. It would so hover over us that it could not set us free. When the ancient church spoke of the one who is "true God" and "true human being," they did not mean such an in-between being. And such a being is not what the catechism means when it designates him with the term "mediator" (after 1 Tim. 2:5: "mediator between God and humankind" in that "God desires everyone to be saved"). The Middle High German word *mitteln* means to help someone gain something. Here it means that in a situation which has no way out for us, he steps "into the middle" in order to help us out of this distress (cf. Art. 15: mediator = deliverer).

By the concepts "true God" and "true human being" we need to think of the *event* that is inseparably linked with the name Jesus Christ. It is the event in which God is both active and self-revealing as our God and thereby enables us to step forward as God's people. It is the event in which *God* comes to us: to *us* who in one way or another are lost, who have run away from God, who have opposed God. It is the event in which God does not turn away from people such as us, but instead becomes involved in our misery. It is the event in which God does not call this misery good, but rejects it. It is the event in which God also draws us out of our misery and turns to us who have turned away from God. It is the event in which God victoriously and with healing affirms our community with God and with all who are loved by God, against all our contradiction. This event is inseparably bound with the name Jesus Christ. And in this event God shows what "true God" and "true human being" deserve to be called. When we speak of this event we speak of him who is "true God and true human being." Let us try, in a few steps, to talk about this.

1. *This* is what happens here:

> But God had seen my wretched state before the world's foundation,
> And, mindful of his mercies great, planned well for my salvation.
> He turned to me a father's heart, and did not choose the easy part,
> But gave his dearest treasure.
>
> He said to his beloved Son: "'Tis time to have compassion.
> Then go, bright jewel of my crown, and bring to all salvation;
> From sin and sorrow set them free; slay bitter death for them that they
> May live with you forever."[57]

God is the decisive subject in this event. If you look away from God, you get mixed up in one darkness after the other. But let us not look away from God, because through it all God is acting. Even when God gives the divine self to the uttermost, this is not an end to being *God,* to willing and doing what *God* wills and does. Here the "true God" in the "Son" identifies with *humankind* in order to stand in *mercy* at the side of us wretched ones. God does this in order *not* to be separated from those who have separated themselves from God. God has mercy on the very same wretched ones who

---

57. Stanzas 4 and 5 of the hymn "Nun freut euch, lieben Christen gmein" by M. Luther. ET: "Dear Christians, One and All," by R. Massie (1800-1887).

"according to the righteous judgment of God . . . have deserved temporal and eternal punishment" (Art. 12). God's verdict is just, because according to the justice of God, these folk are not "just": they do not live in covenant as God's people. On the very *same* ones whom God rightly condemns, God has mercy.

2. God identifies with them in such a way that the Word, which is God's own self, becomes flesh (John 1:1, 14). This means that the Son of God becomes *one* of us in order to embrace in him the *whole* of humankind. This one whom he becomes (not someone isolated from him) is the "true and righteous human being" (Art. 15, 18). "Truly human" means also that he is in body and soul a person, just as we are. But being a body-soul person does not yet mean being truly human. He is "*truly* human" in that he is "as we are, yet without sin" (Heb. 4:15; Art. 16). Our perverseness does not belong so necessarily to our humanity, created good by God, that Jesus' likeness to us ceases because he is "yet without sin." In fact, our dissimilarity to Jesus, who is without sin, means that we, who are distorted by sin, are not "truly human." Only by the removal of the distortion that removes them from God are humans — *human* (and not divine). Only the human "without sin" is "truly human." Jesus' sinlessness is not a virtuousness to be measured abstractly. It consists first of all in that he is the human who is chosen by God and included in unity with God. So he is the true and just human, that is, the one who is according to God's will.

3. God wants in this one to accept the *whole* of humankind. The fact that God takes this *one* in order to accept the *whole* of humankind exposes a terrible disparity between the "truly righteous" human and the humans we are in ourselves. That one is "as we are," but we are unlike him, because we are *not* "without sin," *not* "truly human and truly righteous." We do *not* live as those who belong to God. The merciful God wants to accept us. But according to divine righteousness, God cannot accept us without *not* accepting us as those who live outside our belonging to God. God never wanted those who live this way and will never call them good. God can only condemn them in order to *remove* them. God's justice does not conflict with God's mercy, but with our unacceptable perverseness. In mercy, God rightly wants to be gracious to the people of sin only by annulling the ground on which they stand. In its place God inserts the sinlessness of the *human,* Jesus. In sinlessness this human calls God's just rejection of the sinful human a just verdict. As "truly human and truly righteous" he affirms it as a just verdict "that human nature, which has sinned, must pay for its sin" (Art. 16). So he corresponds humanly to the divine No to human perverseness.

4. Yet how can God accept sinful *people* if God cannot accept the *sin* of the people — and if these people are not able to make themselves acceptable? God can do this the way God does it: *for us* and for our good God *takes over* doing what we cannot do. Without seeing this *for us* we will not understand a single Christological statement. The righteous God is our God, who is *merciful* in righteousness. God's divinity does not stand uninvolved with the negation justly performed on the people of sin. The negation strikes God's own self. The "true God" is the one who — in order to "give us everything" — "did not withhold his own Son (and in him God's own self) but gave him up for us all" (Rom. 8:32), into the deepest *humiliation,* into the night of the cross. In this, God is shown as the "true God," that the Son of God, given to us in love "by the power of his divinity," bore "in his humanity the burden of God's wrath" (Art. 17). As the "true God" he comes in among us in order to make our totally lost cause, to which he can only say no, his own cause. Our misery, which he condemns, wounds him. The merciful love of the "true God" goes so far that it is in complete solidarity with humans, whose perverseness God must condemn. In righteousness, God does not become guilty of this perverseness. But in mercy, God makes the just No to it a concern that strikes God's own self. Because of this, God's No rightly does not strike us. This is why we cannot be lost under the angry No to our remoteness from God. This is why it no longer separates us from God. In this way God separates us from our sin. For as it involves God, it no longer involves us. In taking the righteous No to the perverseness in the root of our being human into God's own self, what is imparted to us as our righteousness is this: our liberation out of the cave where humans are turned in on themselves, a cave locked from the inside, and our release into a life as those who belong to God.

5. God accepts us humans, and does so by taking over the task of healing the present damage on the part of humans. But the damage is to be healed in the way in which it is done in the one who is given up for us: at *the very place* where the damage is present, where *we* find ourselves. This is how Jesus is the *one* human in whom God accepts the *whole* of humankind: that he arrives just at this place. He is "truly, righteously" human, "as we are, yet without sin" because at this place he gives himself up to the just verdict of God on the people of sin, which verdict he affirms. At this place he is brother to all humans. And as "true, righteous human being" he is — in contrast to Cain — his "brother's keeper" and takes on himself the cause of his brothers and sisters with the burden of their misery so much that he takes on "that human nature, which has sinned" (Art. 16). Jesus' sinlessness

is evidenced in that he does not — as "holy ones" otherwise do — seclude himself from sinners, but shares their common lot. He does not allow himself to be alienated by their sin, which is alien to him. He takes them to his heart, and without the wickedness of others, takes it as his responsibility and confesses it as his own. This is how he is "*obedient* to the point of death — even death on a cross" (Phil. 2:8). In this way does he "bear *in his humanity* the burden of God's wrath" (Art. 17). In this way the just verdict of God on people of sin falls on *himself*. In this way he does "make payment for others" (Art. 16) and does it by *taking* the place where we find ourselves and in which all the damage is present. This is the place where our belonging to God is put in question, where we are no longer worthy of it, where God must "forsake" those situated there (Matt. 27:46).

Jesus' standing in this place has a twofold meaning: on the one hand we stand in the place where he is. In him, what befalls him befalls *us*. In him the old person of sin, which we are, and to whom God must say a just No, is done away with. And on the other hand: we are *not* any longer in the place where the No is already spoken to our perverseness, where the No is already accomplished, already accepted and suffered by him. Then he stands in the way of our falling back into this old person. At the same place stands another, who we are not in ourselves, but in him. The "true, righteous human" stands there in that he *obediently* affirms the just verdict of God. This obedience of Jesus is already the beginning of *our* obedience, the new birth of our life in belonging to him. *This* is God's mercy in this just event: for the sake of the one who in *our* place suffered God's No to us, at this very place nothing but Yes is said to *us*. For his sake I am pronounced righteous in him, "as if I had never committed any sin or had ever had sinfulness in me" (Art. 60): in a *gifted* righteousness corresponding to the *merciful* righteousness (Art. 18). In him we are pronounced free and made free for exit out of the cave of humans who are captives in themselves. From here there is only one way for us — the way into freedom, in relationship with the one who has set us free.

2.3.2. Witness to the Liberator (Art. 19)

That there is a liberator, that we need him, that as the mediator between the just and merciful God and us unjust and wretched humans, he frees us. "How do you come to know this? The holy gospel tells me!" This answer has three implications.

1. We cannot know about this, cannot believe in it, cannot live according to it, if it is not shared with us from outside ourselves. Just as we cannot give ourselves a true account of our sin, so we cannot give ourselves an account of the deliverer. Both have the same reason. We humans are too much I-people, turned in on ourselves, to be able to give a true account of either. Certainly we may seek out and think up all kinds of illustrious figures, strong or bright examples, who stand by us in our work of self-affirming our egotistical being. Through these figures with whom we identify we feel pardoned for much that we have done wrong. But they cannot free us from this our being, since they are only of the same being with us. Correspondingly, we cannot give ourselves the news that we cannot free ourselves, and that our liberation comes from outside ourselves through the liberator. We cannot surmise the news of this liberator, not even in our deepest and best religious and moral tendencies. It is inherent in the news of the liberator that it is witnessed to us from the *outside*. At first this surely takes place through people around us.

But if it is the news of *this* liberator, then these people will in turn rely on the news that has been witnessed to them. This is finally and decisively holy scripture. In it we come more surely than ever to the reason why we do not know this liberator unless he is *witnessed* to us. Because our liberation is inseparable from our liberator, and because this liberator has come forth in a particular story then and there, we are dependent on the primary witness about him. We are dependent on the Bible, which is decisive for all further witness about him. Because this story happened once and *for all,* we open the Bible still today in the expectation that it *speaks to us.* Because this history took place *once* and for all, we open precisely *this* book again and again, and it is the book of books.

2. But Article 19 does not say: holy scripture, although this is what it means. Rather "From where do you know this? From the holy *gospel.*" This gives us an important pointer. The Bible is not automatically such a witness. It is this only when we hear the *gospel* in it. This does not mean to say that the Bible is only partially such a witness, only in the favorite verses we seek out, and otherwise not. Our favorite verses could even be our wishes conveyed into them, so that we hear there only what we already know and want. Then it would no longer be the gospel witness for us at all, which tells us that even in our using the Bible, it can be for us a book with seven seals. Then you could examine it like a dead ladybug, analyzing it from all sides: its authors, its social environment, its spiritual psyche. But you will not see the forest (the gospel) for the trees. People search and examine —

and always find more or less congenial human words from humans who have long since faded away. People finally come away so empty-handed that they reproach the texts for withholding from us some much better human word. As compensation for what has escaped them in the biblical texts, people presume that this better human word is actually behind the texts. And — what a coincidence! — it is always identical with what *our* wishful conceptions are at the time.

Over against that kind of procedure, it is always something special when *in the act of reading* we have an experience like that of the disciples on the Mount of Transfiguration (Matt. 17:1ff.). At first they saw Moses and Elijah, and then finally: "They saw no one except Jesus himself alone." When this happens, scripture has done its service of being a *witness* for us. In reading *scripture* this can and does happen: that the gospel imposes itself on us and speaks to us. Not in looking around in the air, but in reading! When the church declares scripture to be canon, that is, the guide of faith, it tells us: we have had the experience that while reading scripture it has witnessed the gospel to us; try it, and see if you have the same experience! In response, we will read scripture with the expectation that this experience will be repeated in us. Then we will read with eager anticipation beyond our favorite passages. We will also go around for days with one single verse and knock on its door again and again, until it opens from inside. Then we will surely understand that what is witnessed here is a *holy* gospel which it is not appropriate to manipulate with unwashed fingers. We will do as Zwingli did. Each morning before he read scripture with the other Zurich pastors, he prayed this prayer: "Almighty, eternal and gracious God, whose word is a lamp to my feet and a light on my path, open and enlighten our understanding, so that we understand your words purely and in a holy way . . . through Jesus Christ, our Lord."[58] Such a prayer does not have the goal of bypassing glasses for reading. Its goal is having the glasses we are accustomed to bringing with us in this matter graciously lifted a little so that scripture becomes for us in the reading of it a witness to the gospel.

3. The gospel of our liberator becomes known to us through the sole witness of the Bible, but not *only* through its text. Because it is a *living* gospel, the biblical witness itself calls for its being received and witnessed to again and again in the *proclamation* of the church. But because there is always only one gospel, the gospel of Jesus Christ, the church's proclamation

---

58. *H. Zwingli, Eine Auswahl aus seinen Schriften,* ed. G. Finsler et al. (Zurich: Schulthess, 1918), p. 615.

always has to be measured by the biblical witness. Therefore the church's proclamation, like the biblical text itself, only becomes a witness when in its reception something takes place that is related to what scripture describes: "And we have seen his glory, glory as of a Father's only son, full of grace and truth" (John 1:14). The biblically witnessed gospel is living for us, not in that we — aping the divine power of creation — awaken a word, dead in itself, to life by trying to make it current. What is current will then hardly be of the gospel. We never have to invent the actuality of the gospel, but only to discover it. Then again, the gospel witnessed to by the church does not become the one gospel of *Jesus Christ* simply by insisting on certain biblical statements. The living gospel could die in our hands this way. The church's witness always stands in the double jeopardy of proclaiming "another gospel." Either we forget that we need to witness in ever new ways to *the same thing,* and not always something different, or we neglect to witness to the same thing in *ever new* ways, instead of always in the same way.

In its confession, the church provides itself a guard against this double jeopardy. On the one hand, the confession binds the church to scripture — against willfulness that always threatens — and holds the scriptural witness before the church as a measuring rod for the church's witness. On the other hand, it pushes the church — against sitting still on an alleged possession of truth — to confess the actuality of the gospel that is always to be discovered anew. The fact that the confession does its guard duty on both these sides makes it *binding,* and also keeps it from being *unconditionally* binding. According to Reformed understanding, the church's confession, including the Heidelberg itself, stands under the "proviso of learning better from scripture,"[59] and this means it is subordinated to scripture and looks toward the confessing which is always needed anew.

In Article 19 it is astonishing that the catechism talks in large part about the *Old Testament.* It is still more astonishing that it understands the Old Testament exclusively as witness to the *gospel,* and specifically witness to the gospel of the deliverer Jesus Christ. So the Old Testament is not, as E. Hirsch asserted in 1936, the "eternal picture of the religion of law which is negated in the gospel."[60] According to the Heidelberg, it is the witness affirmed in the gospel, because it reveals and proclaims the gospel. We need to go into

59. Cf. J. Rohls, *Theologie reformierter Bekenntnisschriften* (Göttingen: Vandenhoeck & Ruprecht, 1987), chap. 1, n. 8, pp. 317-18. ET: *Reformed Confessions,* pp. 267-68.

60. E. Hirsch, *Das Alte Testament und die Predigt des Evangeliums* (Tübingen: Mohr, 1936), p. 83.

this all the more because it has to do with more than the relation of two books to one another, not to mention the relation of two ages: of one preliminary story and one main story. The question about the relation of the Old and New Testaments always has to do also with the relation between the people of Israel, who read the Old Testament without the New Testament confession of Christ, and the church comprised of Jews and Gentiles, for whom the Bible consists of both testaments inseparably. At issue here is the relation between Jews and Christians, as conversely, in the relation between these two the question of the relation between the two testaments is up for discussion. We cannot enter carefully enough into the question of the relation between the testaments. Christian guilt, by which our relationship with Judaism is deeply shadowed, consists first of all in theological distortions and only after these, also in morally wrong behavior.

There are two statements to be made about this matter. They run counter to one another, and yet belong together.

1. The Old Testament, in Christian understanding, is not to be read without the Jesus Christ witnessed to in the New Testament. Just as we cannot get back behind Easter morning to an abstract consideration of the cross, as though Christ were not risen from the dead, so we cannot get back behind the New Testament witness to Christ to an Old Testament read in abstraction from him, as though Christ had not yet appeared, as though what is witnessed to in the Old Testament were not yet "fulfilled" (Art. 19). Let us not make use of this insight carelessly! It poses weighty problems: With what right does the church, whose members are largely Gentiles, count the Old Testament as part of the Christian Bible? Is it not misappropriating a Jewish book? Apparently only this "fulfillment" gives it that right. By what right is the Old Testament then not enough? Why does the church add on as holy scripture the New Testament, which most Jews dispense with? Surely because the Old Testament in itself does not speak of that "fulfillment." The Old Testament, read by itself, apparently leaves open the way to two conclusions: one to the Talmud, and one to the New Testament. This is what the Jewish theologian Martin Buber taught.[61] Christian agreement with this would mean viewing as two equally valid possibilities holding Christ as the fulfillment and as the non-fulfillment of the Old Testament. On the Christian side, even to consider seriously two such possibilities would mean not to depend on Christ's fulfillment, and

61. M. Buber, *Zwei Glaubensweisen*, in *Werke*, vol. 1 (Munich/Heidelberg, 1962), pp. 653-782. ET: *Two Types of Faith* (London: Routledge & Kegan Paul, 1951).

thus not to depend on what binds us to the Jews. But the New Testament does depend on it. Many times it says: "This took place that it might be fulfilled, . . ." as the Old Testament says. However convincing this may be in individual cases, it has to do with the realization about which Jesus in John 5:39 speaks to "Jews": "You search the scriptures . . . and it is they that testify on my behalf."

But what does fulfillment mean? Surely it does not mean tossing away a mere husk that has now become superfluous. Nor does it mean piling up the church's possessions, in contrast to the poor Jewish have-nots — not to mention the fulfillment of a general yearning of all people, for which the Old Testament would then be only *one* example among others. It is the fulfillment of the promise and pledge given to Israel. In it God is first engaged only with the people of the covenant. In this fulfillment God does not impose on them something new, something not already presaged in the Old Testament. According to Article 19, God "revealed" to God's people "in the beginning in the Garden of Eden" the *just* rejection of the poisonous snake (Gen. 3:15), the overwhelming power of evil. For this people, God's *merciful* forgiveness was "foreshadowed through the sacrifices" of the priests. And to this people the *revelation* of the hidden name and will of God was "proclaimed through the holy patriarchs and prophets" in the divine action of royal righteousness and priestly justice. So the promise given to Israel is from the beginning no empty promise, and therefore no one can maintain that because it has been "finally fulfilled through God's own well-beloved Son," it is null and void.

But this is what is new in the New Testament: the threefold activity of God recounted in Article 19 becomes visible as a *pointer* to the event in which the threefold activity takes place in *one* action in *one* person. In this event what has been promised to Israel receives radical validity and importance. God is shown here at the same time as merciful and just, in taking onto God's own self the No to those who have separated themselves from God, thus taking away all separation from God's people. At the same time God's holy name is revealed in the words spoken to the one in whom this takes place: "This is my Son, the Beloved; with him I am well pleased; listen to him!" (Matt. 17:5). This is the fulfillment, "the confirmation of the promises" in the Mediator Jesus Christ. In *this fulfillment* he is "a servant of the circumcised" (Rom. 15:8), for in it he answers the question that is murmured again and again in the Old Testament, from the plagues of Job to the suffering in Exile, from the laments of the Psalms to the fearful accusations of the prophets against the renegade and faithless people: Does God stand by the divine pledge? Or is it not annulled by the wretched situations and persistent ways of Israel, this wrestler with God in its "conflict with the true God"?[62] The answer in this fulfillment is: Yes, God *does stand* by the divine pledge! For Jesus Christ is the grace in the covenant of grace. Hence it *remains* in effect: God speaks the liberating Yes to those who are miserable. Israel *remains* eternally chosen.

Does it remain chosen even if a majority in Israel says No to the fulfillment of the pledge given to this very people? While it is true that Israel's No is a fundamentally bewildering fact for the New Testament, we should not call the response "New Testament anti-Judaism." And we should not overlook the fact that in the bewilderment this nevertheless remains clear: "God has *not* rejected his people" — *for* "God has imprisoned all in disobedience so that he might be merciful to all" (Rom. 11:2, 32). Even with its No to the fulfillment of its promise in Christ, this people confirms the irrevocable validity of the fulfillment — and its effect. For if God says Yes in such a radical and definitive way to this people, on what miserable people will God then not have mercy? Precisely *because* God fulfills the divine pledge to Israel so justly and mercifully in Christ, and *because* he *hence* remains true to the divine Yes to Israel, therefore the door opens in this fulfillment to us, so many miserable Gentiles, who actually are not chosen at all. And yet we are now chosen together with Israel, because God in the Mediator and Deliverer says yes to us miserable ones also. Therefore we may now also count the Old Testament as part of the Christian Bible, and can do this only because for us the New Testament is added to it. We would have no right to read the Old Testament as our Bible too without the Christ witnessed to in the New Testament.

But if the fulfillment in Christ is to be understood in this way, then we have to say conversely:

2. The fulfillment by Christ witnessed to in the New Testament is not to be understood without the Old Testament witness. With this statement we part ways with the modern tradition according to which the New Testament leaves the Old behind as a butterfly leaves its cocoon. In this tradition Friedrich Schleiermacher declared that the Old Testament, because it is an un-Christian book, is not binding for Christians.[63] In this tradition Adolf

---

62. K. Barth, *Die Kirche Jesu Christi,* Theologische Existenz Heute, vol. 5 (Munich: Kaiser Verlag, 1933), p. 17.

63. F. Schleiermacher, *Kurze Darstellung des theologischen Studiums* (Leipzig, 1910³), par. 115. ET: *Brief Outline of the Study of Theology* (Richmond, VA: John Knox Press, 1966), p. 57.

von Harnack in 1921 urged the church "to clear the table" of this book.[64] In this tradition Rudolf Bultmann in 1933 expressed the opinion: "to the Christian faith the Old Testament is a closed chapter."[65] What does the church lose with the jettisoning of the Old Testament? The answer must be radical: It loses everything. It loses ultimately the New Testament too. The German Christians were consistent when in their supposed cleansing of the New Testament of all Judaic elements they had to cut out a good portion of the New Testament, and then had to fill it out with Germanic myths so that it would not come out too thin.[66] And that was not yet consistent enough, because the authors of the Old and also of the New Testament were Israelites. And again, so much of the Old Testament is enfolded in the New Testament that by abandoning this support the latter would always have to defend itself against the result that the New Testament is to be thrown out with the Old.

But what threatens to happen here? It is this: the original addressee of the gospel made definitive in Christ's fulfillment is dropped. This addressee is the people of Israel elected by God. God separates them from all the "Gentiles" and their religions in protest against identifying our way to God with God's way to us. Therefore Israel dare not be absorbed into the Gentile world (nor into the Gentile church!). And for this purpose God elects it to be God's partner. That God is self-determined to be our God and that we are destined to be God's people means first of all *only* that God is self-determined to be the God of *Israel* and that *Israel* is to be God's people. "I will be *your* God, and *you* shall be my people" (Lev. 26:12). Although the fulfillment of the promise to Israel is scarcely strange to them, the promise given to them is totally foreign to us from the start. Only through its fulfillment do we go from being "aliens," shut out from God's covenant, to becoming "members of the household of God" (Eph. 2:19). But this can only mean that it is *doubly* grace when we who were originally not elected become co-elected, and in this way God is actually *our God* and we *God's people*.

If the church suppresses the Old Testament and the addressee whom it

---

64. A. von Harnack, *Marcion: Das Evangelium vom fremden Gott* (Leipzig, 1924), pp. 222-23. ET: *Marcion: The Gospel of the Alien God* (Durham, NC: Labyrinth, 1990), pp. 137-38.

65. R. Bultmann, *Glauben und Verstehen*, vol. 1 (Tübingen: Mohr, 1958), p. 333. ET: "The Significance of the Old Testament for Christian Faith" in *The Old Testament and Christian Faith*, ed. B. Anderson (New York: Harper & Row, 1969), p. 31.

66. Cf. W. Niemöller, *Kampf und Zeugnis der bekennenden Kirche* (Bielefeld: L. Bechauf Verlag, 1948), pp. 419-20.

speaks to and who replies, then it will set itself up arbitrarily as the true addressee and claim that our way is God's way. It will then no longer be what it is by God's grace alone. This willfulness will then overshadow whatever it may say about this grace. Furthermore, the church will then no longer *know* that it lives only by God's word of assurance — even more so than the people of the Old Testament. It will then understand Christ's fulfillment as a possession it can administer. It will even understand it as the power for its own self-assertion. The church will no longer grasp the gospel as God's Yes to *those in misery,* but as the Yes to those who have much. It will then go in one of two directions: it will become a triumphal church of power, which by forced baptism or other means subjects peoples and merges them into itself. Or, if this leads to too much confusion, it will take the reality of the gospel so far back into the inner life that people in their outward lives can without inhibition do business with the powers of Mammon and Mars — as though Christ had not set them free from these! This is more or less the way part of church history has run, and it must run this way when the Old Testament is abandoned. And the church does not even comprehend why it obscures in this way the very gospel that its mouth professes.

For its own sake the church dare not throw away the Old Testament. If the church listens to it, the church knows that the Old is not the *old-fashioned,* but the *older* Testament. The situation resembles that of the parable in which the prodigal son also had an older brother at home, who also caused God heartache, and for whom finally there was no other grace left than that which saved the younger brother. So the church knows that the Gentiles are only *subsequently* addressees of the gospel and that it is just pure grace that God says yes to Gentiles also. Then it knows that the Gentiles more than ever are miserable, and dependent on God's Yes. They dare neither puff themselves up into a church of power, nor steal away inwardly into heaven while on earth the power of other gods rampages unchallenged. Listening to the Old Testament can guard the church against this. The "older" testament, as the word involving the original addressees of the gospel, witnesses to us as its subsequent addressees. Therefore we desperately need its witness. If we did not want to listen to its witness any more, we would be on the point of not hearing the gospel ourselves, or not hearing it rightly.

It is clear that in the question of the relation of the testaments, the relation of Jews and Christians also comes to the fore. We will not come to any right clarity at all in relation to the Jews if we first look in other books or merely settle on conversations with individuals, instead of recognizing that here first of all and decisively Holy Scripture stands as the measuring rod. This is why the attempt of so many Christians in 1933 and the years following to evaluate or to devalue the Jews under "racial" perspectives was, aside from other issues, a theological horror. Our understanding of the relationship of the testaments is linked with our understanding of our relationship with Jews. It is no accident that Schleiermacher, who wanted to cut the Old Testament out of the canon, declared: Christianity relates "to heathenism and Judaism the same way"; for us it is *one* foreign religion among others.[67] It is no accident that after the abandonment of the Old Testament, he understood Christianity as a "religion." That is, he understood it as the activation and expression of a general human tendency and capacity to set itself in relation to a higher being. But the gospel cannot be understood as a possibility within such a natural human tendency. In the framework of understanding Judaism and Christianity as two different religions, a great deal is possible: polemic, tolerance, dialogue, mission — but these are all just variations in *the same* framework. In this framework only one thing is absolutely impossible: recognizing that in the relation of Israel and the church there is a completely unique, indissoluble bond, the like of which is otherwise not possible between two religions. For when the testaments are so intimately and interdependently bound together, and when the New Testament proclaims the fulfillment of the Old Testament covenant promise and the Old Testament documents the covenant promise as fulfilled in the New Testament, then consequently the people of the Old Testament and the New Testament community, non-Christian Israel and the church comprised of Jews and Gentiles, are one people of God. Sadly, this people is divided. Yet it is joined together by the "gospel," by the Yes of God to those in misery, promised from Israel's beginnings on, and fulfilled in Christ. The same "arch of the covenant"[68] spans both. Here are a few elucidations of this.

1. A positive relation of Christians to Jews is impossible for Christians if they look away from Jesus Christ. This is precisely because if they look away they cannot see this special solidarity with the Jews. In relation to the Jews, Christians have an endless amount to be ashamed of, including their imperious way of talking about Christ. But they do not need to be

---

67. F. Schleiermacher, *Der christliche Glaube* (Berlin, 1835), vol. 1, p. 78. ET: *The Christian Faith* (Philadelphia: Fortress Press, 1976), p. 60.

68. K. Barth, *KD* II/2, p. 318; *CD* II/2, p. 289.

ashamed of the gospel of Jesus Christ (Rom. 1:16). Against current Christian attempts to make as little of the meaning of Jesus Christ as possible, for the benefit of a less tense relationship, the Jewish theologian Ginzel warned: "I belong to those Jews who have anxiety about a softening of the Christological confession. For what is left for Christians who want to suppress Christ? The deepest essential . . . of Christianity is in fact Christology, which at the same time separates us."[69] But does it really separate us? For:

2. We need to understand that it is no historic irrelevance "that Jesus Christ is a born Jew" as Luther said in 1523,[70] or as the Heidelberg in Article 35 says, that he is "the genuine seed of David." The Father of Jesus Christ is the same God who is the God of Abraham and David. That God's Word, which is God's own self, became flesh in Israel was not coincidentally, but necessarily so. This places him in the history of Israel. That God elected Israel as God's people and possession is confirmed by the fact that God in the divine Word elected Jewish flesh in order to become human and come into the world. Therefore we comprehend the uniqueness of Israel only if we do not observe and judge its members in themselves, apart from the God who elects them. Nothing we impute to this people by means of various impressions distinguishes it from the other peoples of the earth except this — that God has elected it.

3. But can this election not be taken away from Israel? The New Testament does not conceal the fact that by not acknowledging Jesus Christ, Israel obscures its belonging to God. For the New Testament proclaims Jesus as the Christ, that is, as the "Messiah of Israel"[71] sent first of all to make the Yes of God to Israel unshakable through the sacrifice of Jesus Christ for atoning its sins. But because this atonement takes place anyway, even a Jewish rejection of Jesus as the Christ cannot cross out Israel's election. "Even the unfaithfulness of Israel cannot invalidate the divine election. God remains faithful and does not let God's people go."[72] The assurance of this in Christ is for Christians the ground for confessing that the election of Israel holds. The greatest difficulty in Christians' relation to Jews is that Jews cannot acknowledge this ground on which the church must confess

69. G. B. Ginzel, ed., *Die Bergpredigt: Jüdisches und christliches Glaubensdokument* (Heidelberg: Lambert Schneider, 1985), pp. 16-17.

70. M. Luther, *WA* 11.314-36. "Dass Jesus ein geborener Jude sei," 1523.

71. Cf. B. Klappert/H. Starck, eds., *Umkehr und Erneuerung. Erläuterungen zum Synodalbeschluss der Rheinischen Landessynode 1980* (Neukirchen-Vluyn: Neukirchener Verlag, 1980), p. 265.

72. W. Vischer, "Zur Judenfrage," *Monatschrift für Pastoraltheologie* 29 (1933): 187.

the unconditional faithfulness of God to the Jews. But when *we* acknowledge this, then the church does not take the place of Israel and become the elect people of God in its place, which would be Christian anti-Judaism. So then there is only *one* people of God, in which Israel is inside and not outside, in which Israel is first chosen, and to which those from the Gentiles are to be called. The latter are not sole heirs; they are "fellow heirs" (Eph. 3:6) of the promise given to Israel.

4. The enduring election of Israel rests on God's free, severe, just grace alone, as it has been made definitive in Christ. If this "alone" is valid, then it holds that "God has imprisoned all in disobedience so that he may be merciful to all" (Rom. 11:32). If the covenant with Israel remains upheld on *this* foundation, who should *then* remain shut out of the covenant? This is why it is opened in Christ to the "Gentiles." This is why their original non-election does not hinder their being called into the one community of God. This is why their calling confirms the fulfillment of the covenant with Israel by the Reconciler. In the same grace that holds for the older son — and only *because* it holds for him — the younger son, the lost one, yes, for God the dead one, is welcomed into the father's house: the younger more than ever out of pure grace and in faith in Jesus Christ. This is the Christian church, which according to Paul is essentially church out of Jews and Gentiles. It is made up of Jews also, namely such as *recognize* in the grace of God in Christ the ground of their enduring election. This too is part of what is difficult in relation to the Jews, that the church must see in the Jews who believe in Christ those who remain true to their people of God, which was first elected. And yet when they are at the same time in the church, they document for the Gentile Christians the promised overcoming of the separation still existing in the one people of God, which is already *one.*

5. Even if Jews and Christians are only *one* people of the same God, they are not this in actuality. They will not be this, even if Christians finally turn back from their evil behavior toward the Jews, and even if they finally learn to know something of Jewish life. For even then, in the same Christ who binds us with the Jews, they are at the same time separated. In view of this division, how shall we relate with them? In mission to them? But if mission means proclamation of a different God, unknown to them, then this does not fit here. Or shall we look for the invention of a new theological theory? This does not fit either. For what God has joined together in grace, only God can join together, and not we by thinking about togetherness. Or shall we aim for a form of dialogue? Talking with one another is better than warring with one another. But if dialogue means tolerating one

another on the ground that there are various ways to God, then that does not fit here either. For Jews, like Christians, contrary to that view, live only from God's way to us. Rather, we must say: what is decisive is that they both discover themselves as witnesses of the same God, although in fact they do not yet live as the one people of God.

6. Jews, as the people of the Old Testament, are such witnesses for us. They remind us of our tenaciously clinging Gentile origin and of our resultant embarrassing tendency toward "peace with the false gods";[73] and so they remind us of our task to again and again convert the "heathen in the Christian."[74] They are such witnesses for us in their aligning their faith to the land of Israel, promised to them without their doing anything to earn it (Deut. 9:4). This entails a reminder we need, that God's love is not just an idea, but has bound itself to a concrete then and there. They witness to us that the God of the promises calls us at the same time to set out from the Gentile motherland in which we are only too rooted, as our tendency to be conformed to all kinds of profanity shows. They are witnesses also in their No to Christ, in that with it they impress upon us that we are saved and belong to God's people by God's grace alone. Only when we take them seriously as the witnesses appointed for us, can we also be witnesses for them. We are this by standing fast on the conviction that the Christ in whom they do not believe binds us inseparably with them through faith in him. We are this, by actually *being* Christians, by critically testing ourselves as to whether we do already seriously believe in Christ — so that "if you think you are standing, watch out that you do not fall" (1 Cor. 10:12). Where Jews and Christians are such witnesses to one another and so meet one another, then they are at least on the way to life as the one people of God to which Christ has called us.

2.3.3. Faith in the Liberator (Art. 20-22)

According to Article 21 this is true faith: "not only a sure knowledge by which I affirm as true everything that God has revealed to us in God's Word, but also a wholehearted trust that the Holy Spirit brings about in me through the Gospel. It is an assurance that not only to others but also

73. Cf. note 62.

74. F. Rosenzweig, *Der Stern der Erlösung* (Frankfurt, 1921, 1993), p. 317. ET: *The Star of Redemption* (New York: Holt, Rinehart & Winston, 1971), p. 285.

to me God has freely given the forgiveness of sins, eternal righteousness, and salvation, by grace alone solely for the sake of Christ's worth."

So faith is both knowledge and assurance. This explanation integrates well with our context. We talked about the fact that we come out of captivity and into freedom only by the divine liberation that takes place in the deliverer Jesus Christ. We also talked of the fact that we learn about this only when the news about it is given to us, first through the witness of the holy scriptures of the Old and New Testaments. This liberation, not made by us but for us, is intended to get through to us. And human testimony to it aims to be heard by us. This getting through and hearing, the Heidelberg calls "true faith." Again, it makes sense that this faith contains these two elements, without which it would not be faith. This faith is neither a general conviction that something is right, nor a merely private opinion, nor partial knowledge ("What you do not know exactly, you believe"). This faith cannot be explained by observing what goes on inside humans who have faith. Rather, I need to look at what is given to them, what takes place for them, and what happens to them. This faith is essentially both knowledge of what is shared with them, and trust in what is shared.

Faith is first knowledge, reception of that witness, observing of the truth that is shared with us in it. Witness goes ahead of faith, as Israel goes ahead of the church. Faith is the result of witness. We can even say: faith is listening — to that witness, or rather to the one who wants to get through to us in that witness. "Faith comes from what is heard" (Rom. 10:17) — but not as though the hearing were a mere prelude to faith which we in faith would then have behind us. Nor as though we could, after listening, consider at leisure whether we want to believe this witness or another. Real hearing of what is shared with us is itself already faith. So faith itself will always be a listening faith and will at no point stop listening. "My sheep hear my voice," says the good shepherd (John 10:27), and this hearing is only another word for believing.

Faith as such discerning or hearing includes two aspects. On the one hand, it is acknowledgment. For faith is not, as is usually the case, about an object which I have sought to know or to hear, but about a person who gives himself for us to know and to hear, whom we would not know and hear if he had not sought us out so that we would know and hear him. Insofar as faith includes acknowledgment, the question needs to be posed, as Article 22 formulates it: "What, then, is it necessary for a Christian to believe?" And the answer to this is not a legalistic one that an official prescribes: "You must believe all this, otherwise you do not believe!" Rather it has the sense of self-examination: I believe only when I believe, and thus acknowledge, "everything that is promised to us in the Gospel." On the other hand, faith is not blind subjection to a bill of goods served up, for example, by the church: "This you must blindly trust." We do not believe without having at least a little insight into what we believe. This will happen as a rule in a very tentative way, often contested, often so that "all our knowledge, sense and sight lie in deepest darkness shrouded."[75] And yet we would not believe if we did not in an initial way understand what and why we believe.

Faith is also *trust*. The fact that trust is named second makes logical sense. But this should by no means be understood as though knowledge and trust are factually separated. This must not happen, neither by rating knowing and hearing as mere prelude to trustful faith itself, nor conversely by thinking that faith can do without trust, whereby faith would become a merely theoretical business, a mere holding something as true intellectually. Faith does not simply receive "something" imparted to it. Its knowledge and hearing are linked with and awakened by the gospel witnessed to it by God's mercy and righteousness, by our deliverance in Jesus Christ. We are not able to do this knowing, this hearing, without experiencing a matchless boon, and without being overjoyed by it into our bone and marrow, without putting all our trust in this which awakens trust and is worthy of trust. Knowing and trusting are here one and the same. These two elements of faith do not allow themselves to be separated at all factually, and yes, not psychologically either. As knowledge is the form of faith, so trust is the substance of faith. Trust, no less than knowledge, is linked completely to its object, to the truth of the gospel that meets trust and allows it to take the gospel in. As the knowledge of faith is knowledge of Jesus Christ, and its hearing is listening to him, so the trust of faith is just as essentially trust in Christ, and this means instead of trust in our own ability, trust in God's wonderful action for us.

In trust we no longer have our center in ourselves. We have it eccentrically outside ourselves in the trust-awakening and trustworthy God of the gospel. We entrust ourselves now literally to God. In the trust of faith, persons bent inward on themselves now on their part step out of their cave and no longer have their lives in themselves, but in God. They are now in a pleasant freedom, in a freedom from false attachment to themselves and from false concern for earthly powers that surround and entangle us. They

75. From stanza 2 of the hymn "Liebster Jesus, wir sind hier," by T. Clausnitzer.

are free from these things, because they are free for letting the following be said to them, and for holding fast to it: "Cast all your anxiety on him, for he cares for you" (1 Peter 5:7). According to Psalm 118:8, "It is better to take refuge in the Lord than to trust in mortals" (Jewish Study Bible). So faith is also trustful: confident, undismayed, hopeful, courageous — to be sure, all this is only in beginning stages, just as knowledge is. On our side there is always a lack. But because there is no lack on the other side, "I lack nothing" (Ps. 23:1, Jewish Study Bible).

In summary: If the gospel is the truth about our liberation by God and about our liberator, and if this gospel is imparted by the witness to it, then faith is our appropriate answer to this. Faith is our answer in that we hear and take to heart, ponder and take seriously, know and trust the gospel and its witness. The fact that faith is the appropriate answer means that it is no arbitrary answer. It is also no meritorious accomplishment to be brought by us. It is the answer laid on our lips and hearts with the gospel and its witness, as the obvious response to it. Faith follows it as naturally as thunder follows lightning, as naturally as it played out with that tax collector to whom Jesus said: "'Follow me!' And he got up and followed him" (Matt. 9:9). So this faith is both in one: God's work on us and yet our own answer to this, our doing and yet our actual entrusting ourselves to that which not we, but God in Christ does for us. In this way, faith is our appropriate answer to the gospel and its witness.

Martin Buber saw a difference, yes a cleft, between Jewish trusting faith — which, according to Buber, Jesus himself shared — and the kind of faith newly formed by Paul — faith as acknowledgment.[76] The first believes God, trusts in God. The second believes in God, subjects itself to God. For Buber, this distinction is linked with an important insight into a genuine difference between membership in the Jewish people and membership in the Christian community. The difference can be described with the old statement: "A Jew is born, a Christian made."[77] That is, persons *are* Jews, as a rule, through their birth; persons *become* Christians through the special step out of unfaith into faith. A Gentile Christian is born as a heathen, so to speak, or as a non-member of the people of God, and becomes a Christian only by this special act.

This Jewish perspective on Gentile Christianity is insightful, because it

---

76. Cf. note 61.

77. Cf. H. Gollwitzer, *Befreiung zur Solidarität* (Munich, 1984²), chap. 1, n. 6, p. 129. ET: *An Introduction to Protestant Theology* (Philadelphia: Westminster Press, 1982), p. 128.

makes us aware that becoming a Christian is a matchless turn in human life — or rather would have to be. For this Jewish view makes us aware that the great danger of our Gentile Christianity is that we make this turn as small and cheap as possible, that we shift it as much as possible to a little-noticed place. And then we even make a theory out of it: the greatness of the grace of God is that it makes us into Christians without our noticing that we are Christians. This is why the sociologist Max Weber could declare that it is an essential mark of our mainline churches that their members are "born into" them by an "attributed membership."[78] The danger is that because the turn is almost submerged into imperceptibility, a lot of unconverted and unbaptized heathenism flows into Christianity. The result is an absurd "amalgamation" with the ideas and tendencies of *this* age, which was said from the beginning to be put into the past once and for all in the cross of Christ.[79] In such an amalgamation, paganism slips into Christianity unnoticed, as people become Christians without noticing it. This is why the continual danger of this Christianity is "peace with the false gods"[80] — and no doubt generally the facileness in which we, in contrast to Judaism, deal with the first table of the Decalogue: with the forbidding of images, with the misuse of the holy name of God, with keeping the Sabbath. Buber's thesis reminds us that for us, coming to faith is a passage, under the sign of a change of master. We do not accomplish this change. It is accomplished in the cross of Christ. But in faith we acknowledge it — and faith begins to be present when we acknowledge this change with all the consequences it will have for us.

This thesis, at the same time, makes us aware of the reason why the *Jew* Buber insists that faith is pure trust. If persons are actually *born* members of the elect people of God, what is basically left for them to do but to live in trust on the ground that has already been laid for them, on which they have always been standing? The danger here is a different one: not to trust, not to stay with the God of Israel, to make a "change of masters" away from God — yet without really leaving God! The danger here is not so much that of the Gentile peace with the false gods as the conflict against the well-known, true God — as the name Israel indicates: struggler with God (Gen.

78. M. Weber, *Wirtschaft und Gesellschaft. Grundriss der verstehenden Soziologie* (Tübingen, 1976⁵), pp. 692ff. ET: *Economy and Society* (Berkeley: University of California Press, 1978), pp. 1164ff.

79. K. Barth, *Das Evangelium in der Gegenwart*, Theologische Existenz Heute, 25 (Munich: Kaiser Verlag, 1935), pp. 31-32.

80. Cf. note 62.

32:28). This implies a unique difference between Israel and Gentile Christianity. — But can an *opposition* between faith as trust and faith as knowledge be derived from this, even from the Old Testament itself? This is what Buber thinks. In contrast to Jewish faith-as-trust, he sees in the Pauline faith-as-acknowledgment yet another danger than the one already named. Because this kind of faith is involved in the framework of a change of masters from the false gods to God, it tends to think dualistically. That is, a person would have to see the divinities previously worshiped, and not only the pagan gods, but also the God of Israel (from faith in whom the first witnesses to Christ themselves had come) as a ghastly enemy. The danger here lies, according to Buber, that such faith as acknowledgment brings itself onto the treacherous ground of having to create its certainty through continual *mis*trust against, and dissociation from, others. Along this line Theodore Adorno saw the source of Christian anti-Semitism in a self-understanding of Christians who "with a bad conscience convinced themselves of Christianity as a secure possession" by having to "confirm their eternal salvation by the worldly ruin of those" who could not understand revelation as such a possession.[81]

This critique needs to be taken seriously. But one may first ask whether what is criticized here can be overcome by playing off faith-as-trust against faith-as-acknowledgment. Is there really an alternative here where we must choose? Acknowledgment relates here to a fact not set by ourselves, and indeed not to some fact or other, but to this: the good news shared with us of God's liberating Yes to us. We cannot acknowledge this without *having knowledge* of what we acknowledge. And we cannot really take note of this merely intellectually, instead of at the same time putting our trust in it. We do this not in naïvely trustful bliss, because we *understand* where our trust is being put. True faith obviously excludes that alleged alternative. Acknowledgment means here entrusting oneself, and entrusting oneself means acknowledgment. It is this way already in the Old Testament. Already here trust is essentially trust *in* . . . and indeed trust in the One who in clear distinction to others gives self to be known, to whom all trust is owed. Trust is in the God of the covenant, who is to be distinguished from all other powers, and who has chosen to be in communion with Israel. Psalm 118:8: "It is *better* to take refuge in the *Lord* than to trust

---

81. T. Adorno, *Gesammelte Schriften,* vol. 3, *Dialektik der Aufklärung* (Frankfurt: Suhrkamp, 1981), p. 203. ET: *Dialectic of Enlightenment* (Stanford, CA: Stanford University Press, 2002), p. 147.

in mortals." Israel's faith is not marked simply by its trusting, but by its trusting in *God*. Faith distinguishes between where it can trust and where it dare not. And to distinguish means to acknowledge and understand this Lord in distinction from the other powers whom it could trust. The battle of the prophets was about their discernment that Israel trusted, even trusted in the covenant of God (cf. Isa. 8:12), but in blindness to its one, living God. It was zealous, but without understanding (as Paul says in Rom. 10:2). In this battle there is very likely also an ongoing demarcation — not against others, but against the *false* trust that threatens Israel itself, that is, trust in something other than the familiar God of Israel. Faith in the God of Israel has two elements in it, which are not to be separated from each other, let alone be played off against each other: knowing and trusting, acknowledging and entrusting.

Only where these are separated does that enter which we must above all guard against critically: that faith becomes a requirement. That is, faith is understood as our acknowledgment of what is believed, an acknowledgment to be accomplished by us, which is thus seen as the condition for the effectiveness of what is believed. So whoever does not fulfill this condition is without salvation. According to Helmut Gollwitzer,[82] a deep ambiguity pervades Luther's conception of faith. On the one hand, faith for him is the encounter with our liberation by the liberator Jesus Christ, who sets us free from our captivity within ourselves and free toward God and our world — an encounter shared with us, witnessed to us, and joyfully beheld by us. On the other hand, faith is a condition to be fulfilled on our side: only under the prerequisite that you believe is all this blessing valid for you. If you fulfill this prerequisite, then you are well off — in stark contrast to those who do not believe. This faith-as-condition (which may be what Buber had in mind with the label "faith-as-acknowledgment) is no longer a celebration, but a "ticket to the celebration."[83] This faith now steps into the place of the meritorious works of Roman teaching. You no longer have to present these, but this kind of faith, in order to come into the heaven of blessedness. And this faith now solidifies a deep cleft and dissociation — no longer between good and evil, but similarly and even more deeply, between believers and unbelievers. The result is that ultimately the heaven of grace is for Luther quite thinly populated: the Romans, the Enthusiasts, the Bap-

82. H. Gollwitzer, "Von Glauben und Unglauben bei M. Luther," *Evangelische Theologie* 44 (1984): 360-79.

83. Gollwitzer, "Von Glauben und Unglauben bei M. Luther," p. 377.

tists, the Zwinglians, the Jews, the Muslims, are all shut out of it. One shivers at the thought of such a heaven of grace, and asks oneself how gracious this grace really is.

It is a real question whether we do not come upon such an ambiguity in the conception of faith of the Heidelberg — in Article 20 (in the language of Rom. 5): "Will all people, then, be saved through Christ, just as they became lost through Adam?" Of the Reformers, it was probably only Zwingli who was inclined to answer this question with Yes. He could not think that the ruinous sphere of influence of Adam, the old human of sin, could be greater than the saving, reconciling sphere of influence of Jesus Christ. To the displeasure of Luther and Calvin, Zwingli even named names of thoroughly problematic pagans who he yet believed were saved by the grace of Christ.[84] It is in fact something to insist on: if where sin increased, grace in Christ abounded all the more (Rom. 5:20), how should the Fall have a greater range than salvation by him? In Christ, God loved the *world* — *so that* we may believe (John 3:16). But God loved not just some in the world *because* they believe. In Christ God reconciled the world to God's own self (2 Cor. 5:18-20) — which is to be proclaimed to the world so that it will let itself be reconciled. But this does not limit the reconciliation subsequently to *that* part of the world that "accepts" the proclamation. And God has shown the divine love for us in that Christ died for us while we were yet his enemies, and therefore before we believed (Rom. 5:6-10), which is just what is recognized and affirmed in faith. This is believed because it *is* true. It does not first *become* true by being believed. This does not mean that human unfaith is to be considered good. But the power to disempower what God in Christ has enacted is never to be conceded to this lack of faith. The presence of human unfaith does not make grace unimportant. But grace does not need to have its value enhanced by that dualistic confrontation between believers and unbelievers.

"Will all people, then, be saved through Christ just as they became lost through Adam?" The Heidelberg answers this question categorically: "No," not all are saved by Christ, "only those who are grafted into him by true faith and accept all his benefits." It looks very much as though this is meant in the sense of faith as a condition and a separating off from others. This appearance is so great because the statement, as it comes across, can be read in this way: Christ can have done what he wants, and grace, to which

---

84. E.g., H. Zwingli, *Schriften,* ed. Th. Brunnschweiler (Zurich: Theologischer Verlag, 1995), vol. 3, p. 114; vol. 4, p. 108.

God is self-determined in Christ, may be as great as it wants — but "no!" we are not blessed by this. First, an additional condition must be fulfilled. All that is only an offer, not yet valid in itself. It is first validated when we fulfill this condition and can present our faith. Where faith is understood in this way, the danger threatens that the creative power for effecting human salvation is displaced from the action of God for humans into the human process of faith. How then shall the further step be avoided that the human being rates in this matter also as the author of one's own fortune, that one's salvation is understood as the product of one's own religious energy? And how should it not one day make sense to ease the threat which unfaith poses to faith the way this was done in the Enlightenment: that in human faith it is not at all so important *what* faith believes in as *that* it believes — something or other? And something or other, ultimately everyone believes . . .

At any rate, the answer of the Heidelberg can also be read in a different way.

1. Even if we, with good reasons, resist faith-as-condition, the alternative to it dare not be that it is therefore all the same whether I believe or do not believe, whether I believe in the God of Israel and the Father of Jesus Christ, or in a field-, forest-, meadow-god. Hopping or jumping, the race goes to the same finish line. The "No" of the Heidelberg intends to protect us from such lightheaded talk about faith. If faith is about being incorporated into the body of Christ, that is, coming into the most intimate relationship with him; if we therein receive a share in all his blessings; if faith relates to Yes to the miserable and to God's liberation from the cave of the I-person bent in on self; then it would indeed be unpardonable lightheadedness to say that it is all the same whether this blessing reaches us, whether we notice and hear the news of it, whether we trust in it and "acknowledge" it, or not. It would contradict the blessing of God if it were only true in itself and did not aim to be attended to and made use of by us. And whoever believes even just a little, cannot possibly say: I could just as well do without that, or believe and trust something else completely.

2. We dare not read Article 20 apart from the definition of faith in Article 21, in which faith is understood as an act of convinced knowledge and deep trust. We dare not abstract this knowledge and trust from that which it knows and in which it trusts, any more than we dare abstract the biblical and corresponding churchly witness from that which is witnessed to us through it. But we must also draw a clear distinction here. Neither this witness nor such faith is itself the event of salvation. To be sure, this witness is

the instrument in God's hand to bring the news of the salvation event close to us; and yes, such faith is God's doing and our response to this bringing near. But neither is therefore identical with the truth and reality of the gospel as the definitive Yes of God to miserable people. This salvation event is no mere offer, but rather a reality, valid in itself. It is valid before it is witnessed to us and believed by us.

> God, who watched me from above,
> when I first began to be,
> enfolded me most graciously,
> before I knew of his great love.[85]

By this we can realize that the reality of the reconciliation of the grace and love of God always reaches much farther than the witness to it and faith in it. Quite certainly, God loves the *world* and reconciles *it* with God's own self. This means an objective change of the situation of this world, even if the world is far from being aware of it. But whoever does become aware of it in faith, sees this world differently and understands (turning Art. 21 around), that not only to me — but also to others — forgiveness, righteousness, and salvation are bestowed by God.

3. But not nearly all believe, as Article 20 points out. According to 2 Thessalonians 3:2, "Not all have faith." There is disparity between the love of God for the world and the few who believe — a disparity whose seriousness John 3:16 expresses as it continues. It was no naïve narrowing of the horizon, but rather deep relevance, when the Reformers, in thinking about unbelievers or those who believed something else, thought decidedly about persons in the church and not people outside. Calvin thought: "If the same sermon is preached, say, to a hundred people, twenty receive it with the ready obedience of faith, while the rest hold it valueless, or laugh, or hiss, or loathe it."[86] Still more skeptical was Luther's argument when he rejected a crusade against the Turks, because "in such an army there are perhaps five Christians, and perhaps worse people before God than the Turks, and yet they all want to take the name of Christ, which is the greatest sin of all, such as no Turk commits."[87] Unrest, not over the unbelief of

---

85. Stanza 2 of the hymn "Sollt ich meinem Gott nicht singen?" ("Should I Not Sing to My God?"), by P. Gerhardt (according to the hymnal of the Evangelical-Reformed Church of German-speaking Switzerland).

86. J. Calvin, *Institutes* III.24.12.

87. Acc. to Gollwitzer, "Von Glauben und Unglauben bei M. Luther," p. 364.

others, but over the disparity of faith and unfaith of Christians and merely nominal Christians *in* the church, has probably become strange to us in our churchliness, in which all count as Christians because they are members of the church. Perhaps because we no longer see the problem in the church, we must get exercised about it only in relation to those who do not believe, or have a different faith, outside the church. But because we no longer see the first problem, it is to be feared that we get exercised about the second in the wrong way. Perhaps today we are not so concerned about zeal for crusades, but rather in mildly treating as a matter of indifference whether people are in some way or other "believing." In the unrest about unfaith in the church, it became clear to the Reformers that for the removal of this disparity there is only one Christian instrument: the patient and clear proclamation of the gospel. With this proclamation, the attitude grows in us that according to Calvin is the appropriate one: "We ought to be so minded as to wish that all men be saved."[88] Again, you cannot make a general theory out of this attitude. Rather, it drives us all the more to witness to the gospel to all we possibly can.

4. Saying that only witness to the gospel is left to us in the face of that disparity, because no other instrument and no pushing can help, is not an expression of helpless resignation. Rather, it has a deep theological basis. No person can make another into a believer. People have already remarked that behind Article 20 stands the doctrine of election. It must in fact be discussed here. The word of Jesus about faith holds: "You did not choose me but I choose you" (John 15:16). No one chooses for himself or herself to have faith, in somewhat the way you can decide to hold particular principles as right. Rather, faith is "created in me by the Holy Spirit through the gospel" (Art. 21). What the Spirit creates in us is faith as our own answer to God's gospel. But no one has answered meaningfully to the gospel who has understood the answer as his or her own achievement. Rather, those who answer understand it as a gift made for them, laid on their lips and in their hearts. And there is no one whose answer has not become a renewed plea for faith: "I believe; help my unbelief" (Mark 9:24). Of such a faith no one will then boast over against other people.

Understood along these four lines, the conception of faith of the Heidelberg would stand in correspondence to the gospel and its witness.

88. J. Calvin, *Institutes* III.23.14.

3. The Free God

3.1. The Self-Disclosing God Who Is Our Beginning

3.1.1. The Triune God (Art. 23-25)

The whole work of God aims at the togetherness and interaction of the free God and the free human being. But who are we to enter into such togetherness? On our part we are not free for initiating this kind of togetherness and interaction — especially not in our freedom-as-independence. We have to be liberated for it. But we do not receive this liberation as something we can one day consider to be fortunately over and done with. Only by the gift and power of the ongoing liberation we experience through God do we become and remain partners of God who as such freely live and interact with God. Therefore the form of this togetherness will be determined by the fact that it takes place as a history in which God takes and keeps the initiative. In this history we do not make a beginning with God; God makes a beginning with us. God goes ahead of us, and we follow. God opens the interaction of these two partners and we, on the basis of this divine opening, subsequently become free partners of God.

Emphasizing the initiative of God in this process is not done to argue for an abstract preeminence of God. It is done because of the knowledge that, without divine beginning and intervening, this kind of togetherness would never have come about and endured. For humans on their own initiative cannot become partners of God. The divine preeminence, which God surely demonstrates in this way of acting, does not mean that God defensively and in an authoritarian way reserves the privilege of being "more" than humans are. It consists in the use of divine freedom for the sake of creating a reality different from God, and for the sake of the coexistence of God with this reality. The preeminence of God is the ability to give everything, in order not to be alone, but to be God together with human beings. Only because of the initiative of divine freedom are we moved, as God moves us, to become on our part free humans who coexist with God and with all with whom God coexists.

This divine initiative is what is referred to by calling God the self-disclosing God who is our beginning. It implies that the God of the biblical witness is not one of the presuppositions we make. God is not something we posit, or even set as the beginning of our thinking, in light of which we may ask what we can do with it, and how we can integrate it and evaluate it in the framework and horizon of the human being, who is circling around self. We cannot know the biblical God unless God sets God's own self before us. We know God only because God knows how to begin something with us, because God makes *this kind* of beginning so that we on our side can begin, and follow. God has the freedom to make such a self-disclosing beginning with us. God has the power to set and keep in motion the history of this togetherness in which God goes before us and we follow. This is the meaning of the ancient doctrine of the Trinity.

Trinity means the three-in-oneness of God. The "Apostles' Creed," which to this day is used in worship (cited in Art. 23), says that to believe in one God means to believe in "three" — in the Father, in the Son, and in the Spirit. The doctrine of the Trinity affirms that God in this threeness is still one God. This teaching was of course formulated in the first centuries of the church. But the proponents of this teaching set great store by the conviction that it has the backing of the Bible. It has this above all in a basic outline of God's acts that the Bible witnesses to, and not so much in individual biblical texts. However, when the church baptizes in the name of the Father, the Son, and the Holy Spirit, it is using a quotation from Matthew 28:19. Other passages the old theologians invoked are 2 Corinthians 13:14, 1 Corinthians 12:4-7, 1 Peter 1:2, etc. The grounding of the teaching in scripture persuaded the Reformers, after brief hesitation, to affirm this teaching wholeheartedly. So the Heidelberg writes in Article 25: "Since there is but one God, why do you speak of three: Father, Son, and Holy Spirit? Because that is how God has revealed himself in his Word; these three distinct persons are one, true, eternal God." Note that Article 24 attributes each of the three great works of God to one of these persons: to the Father our creation, to the Son our redemption, and to the Spirit our sanctification.

While it is clear that this is the tradition of the church, we may have some trouble with it. We are not the first. In the early church the teaching developed only gradually, and with many kinds of contradictions and false steps. In the sixteenth century there arose alongside the Reformation a movement which wrote on its banner the rejection of the Trinity, and which then led to the founding of its own church, the Unitarian Church. "*Uni*tarian" means that God is no trinitarian God, but only one in number. In the Enlightenment of the eighteenth century people made the fabulous mathematical discovery that three cannot be one and one cannot be three. Besides, people thought that this teaching was an idle mental game that produced only conflict and puzzlement and contributed nothing to the more important question of how we can live well and healthily.

But there are more serious grounds for having reservations here. Did not the Reformers, and especially the Reformed theologians among them, emphasize the oneness of God? Calvin, for example, does this in the first article of the Huguenot Confession of 1559: "We believe and confess that there is only one God."[1] And were they not right to emphasize this? In the Bible they treasured so much stand the words of Deuteronomy 6:4, repeated in Mark 12:29 and 1 Corinthians 8:4: "Hear O Israel, the Lord is our God, the Lord alone." And the first of the Ten Commandments says: "You shall have no other gods before me" (Exod. 20:2-3). Does not this commandment exclude anything like the acceptance of three-in-oneness? All the more so since the doctrine, with its talk of "three persons," even comes close to faith in three gods!

Indeed, all Christian churches acknowledge this commandment. This excludes for them faith in three gods. Christianity is therefore customarily counted with Judaism and Islam among the "monotheistic religions," for which the highest being is one single God. Sometimes the monotheistic religions are lauded as a spiritual advance beyond "primitive" polytheism, according to which heaven, and then probably the earth too, and all nature, are populated with numerous gods. Questions can be raised about monotheism's claim to spiritual superiority. In any case, the first commandment realistically does not dispute the existence of "other gods." Rather, it commands us not to worship them "alongside" the God who deals with and elects Israel. Now a new misgiving could raise its head. Does not Christianity with its doctrine of the Trinity upset pure, monotheistic

1. E. F. K. Müller, ed., *Die Bekenntnisschriften der reformierten Kirche* (Leipzig: Deichert Verlag, 1903), p. 221.

faith in one God? And does it not thereby also disturb compatibility among the monotheistic religions?

Islam does in fact take considerable offense at this Christian teaching, and above all at its root: the teaching of the divinity of the One who has become human. The Koran lets Jesus count as a prophet, but calls the Christians idol-worshipers because they say "Allah is Christ":[2] they are idol-worshipers because alongside the one God they also worship a Christ and so consider a creature to be divine. But Jews also take offense similarly at the teaching. Martin Buber summarized the criticism this way: according to Jewish faith, God is "superior to any of his manifestations." Therefore each of them can only temporarily, and never sufficiently, express God.[3] So faith in Jesus, like faith in God "the Father" — and also in the tri-unity of God — is unthinkable. This is why Chief Rabbi Steinsaltz of Jerusalem declared: "We as Jews could exchange most of our articles of faith with those of the Moslems without many people noticing; with the church, on the contrary, that is not possible."[4] In sum, should we not, especially for the sake of peace with the Jews, sacrifice the doctrine of the Trinity? And could we not do this with an easy conscience, since today many Christians' views on this are similar to Buber's dictum anyway?

In the face of so many questions, let us try to push ahead to some clarity. However, it will become clearer only if we understand one thing above all: the doctrine of the Trinity is the unfolding of the statement that "God has revealed God's own self in God's Word" (Art. 25). The decisive question behind the formulating of this doctrine is this: Who is Jesus Christ? How we answer this question will determine whether we affirm or reject this doctrine. And for whoever rejects this teaching, Christ can be nothing other than what the Koran or Buber sees in him: a prophet, or an impressive human brother.[5] The answer the church gave in lengthy wrestling with the question of who Jesus is, is the one essentially already given in the New Testament: he is *the* one. He is not just one person among others, though perhaps most extraordinary, whom Christians, because they think so highly of him, have made divine, as someone might call his beloved queen, although that is naturally not to be taken literally. Instead, in him it is *God's own self who* "came to what was his own" (John 1:11). Jesus does not

2. Koran, Sura 4:171-72; Sura 5:17, 72-73, 75; Sura 9:30-31.

3. *Versuche des Verstehens*, ed. R. R. Geis and H.-J. Kraus (Munich: Kaiser, 1966), p. 159.

4. *Der Spiegel*, November 4, 1994, pp. 215-16.

5. Cf. also Schalom Ben-Chorin, *Bruder Jesus. Mensch — nicht Messias* (Munich, 1967). ET: *Brother Jesus* (Athens: University of Georgia Press, 2001).

stand at the pinnacle of humanity, which points into heaven or forward into a better edition of humanity. He is, as it were, the opening edge that God projects into humanity, yes, takes up residence in it (John 1:14).

We should not call this unreflectively the "absolutistic claim of Christianity." That concept is unsuited for describing what is at stake here. It is not a matter of people raising some sort of claim over against others, a claim they could then modify for the sake of peace. It is not about our raising ourselves, but about God's lowering Godself. It is about holding fast what the New Testament witnesses to as the core of the gospel: "For God so loved the world that he gave his only Son" (John 3:16). What does this mean? It means that God gave not only *something*, but in the "Son" gave nothing less than *God's own self*. It means that God did not give temporarily, in order, if circumstances required, to take the gift back again and perhaps then to give us another. No, God gave us *definitively* what God wants to give us; we can therefore rely on this unconditionally. It means that God really *gave* the whole gift of pure love — not just a little of it. God has thereby made an unconditional decision. This decision applies first of all not to us, but to God's own self — that God always and everywhere wills to be none other than who God is in the gift of the Son: the God who in free grace embraces the world with love.

The church father Athanasius summed up this core of the gospel in the basic statement: "For this cause God [the Son of the Father, God by nature!] became human so that we humans would become divine [that is, belong to God]."[6] See John 1:12-14. This is the statement that informs Luther's Christmas hymn:

In him the eternal light breaks through,
Gives the world a glory new;
A great light shines amid the night,
And makes us children of the light.[7]

This same Athanasius was, not coincidentally, involved decisively in formulating the doctrine of the Trinity — *and* he showed thereby that the testimony about God's tri-unity is contained in this one basic statement. The doctrine of the Trinity is accordingly to be understood as an explica-

---

6. Athanasius, *The Incarnation of the Word*, par. 54.

7. Stanza 4 of the hymn "Gelobet seist du, Jesu Christ," by M. Luther. ET: "All Praise to Thee, O Jesus Christ," in *LW* 53:241.

tion of the gospel of Jesus Christ, as Luther has indicated in the stanza quoted. How is this so?

If God in Christ "becomes human," if God by taking on the life of one human takes on humanity *itself,* then in this form *God's own self* is here — God in another way, but not just something from God, not "something" that would be less than God. According to John 3:16, God gives the Son into the world as a complete demonstration of love. This means that a distinction is made between giver and gift; but you must not distinguish between the two in such a way as to make the gift be less than the giver, as though in this gift God's heart were not fully open and given to us: the gift is God's own self again. If the gift were less than God, then God would be giving us "something," but would be withholding God's own *self.* Then in this gift it would not be God's own self, and completely God, loving us. And then with the gift, God would leave us to ourselves. Then the gift could not bind us to its giver and make us really God's own. The same line of thought comes in the language of the ancient church: the "Son" is indeed distinguished from the heavenly "Father." But he is not separate from God; he is "one" with God (as John 10:30 says), not less than God, but "of one Being" with the "Father." So the Son is "true God," "Light from Light,"[8] and as such is not the opening wedge of the human attempt to get into heaven, but the opening wedge of the movement in which God comes into the world.

If a distinction is to be made between the divine giver and the gift, between the One who loves us and the One in whom we are loved, and yet these are not two, but one, then a further conviction follows. And this becomes fully evident for the first time: if the divine gift is not less than its giver, then in what God gives *us* in love, God's own self is at work. Then it is once again, in another way, *God's own self* at work, and not something less than God who brings it about that we become "God's own," God's children, the ones loved by God and thus bound together with God. The Bible calls this work of God the work of the Holy Spirit. Through the Spirit, the love of God comes into our hearts (Rom. 5:5). Through the Spirit, we therefore become God's children (Rom. 8:14-16). But if it is the Spirit of God who brings this about in and with us, then this Spirit is once again *God's own self.* This is God again in another way, but not something less than God. The Spirit is to be distinguished from the "Father" and the "Son," and yet not separated

8. Thus in the Nicene-Constantinopolitan Creed, doubtless to be understood in combination with James 1:17 ("Father of Light") and John 8:12; 12:46 (Christ is the "Light of the world") — that is, the Light of the world, which Christ is, is ignited by the Father.

from them, but is one with the "Father" and the "Son." Moreover, in the Spirit, the "Father" and the "Son" are one. The Spirit binds them together, and therefore can bind us together with them, and can make them be combined for us so that they are not, as it were, two addresses, but one.

This is basically what the doctrine of the Trinity says: the giver and the gift, and what they accomplish with us, is God. The one who loves us, and the one in whom God loves us, and the one through whom God makes us the beloved is one and the same God; God in three ways, but the one God. This is what the traditional way of speaking means: God is the Father, the Son, and the Spirit. God is not thereby three, but thrice the same *one* God. Again, God is no monotonous one, but the one God in these *three* forms. It remains true that "We all believe in *one* God." However, this God is no lonely individual, but rather "this bounteous God."[9] "God is love" (1 John 4:16). God does not become love by first needing to "have" *us* in order to be able to love. God *is* love, in eternal relationship, and is this before we exist. And if God then wants to love us too, this is out of overflowing, unindebted love. Yes, God's love does not presuppose our existence. Instead, our existence presupposes God's love.

This insight about God can be deepened still more by considering how it fits with the concept of grace. Karl Barth said clear-sightedly: "The God of all synergistic systems is always the Absolute, the general, the digit 1."[10] Synergism says that human salvation does not depend on God's grace alone, but depends on the help of humans. Such synergism is in fact unavoidable in an abstract monotheism, which is where the unity of God is thought of in the sense of the "number 1." For God in the sense of the "number 1" can actually not share and turn toward us unless we deliver the means and possibilities for it. Without our coming toward God with our natural, religious, or moral capacity, God would have to stay eternally lonesome across from us as mere "number 1." But if we hold fast to the truth that we live by God's grace alone, then we live by God's communicating the divine self with us and turning toward us attentively. We live by the love of God (the "Father") who loves us so much as to come to meet us with love (the "Son") and come into us (the "Spirit"). The fact that God, to demonstrate love, gives the Son, and in the Spirit makes us beloved children, is all God's work for us. All this is the work of grace alone on us. This

9. From stanza 2 of the hymn "Nun danket alle Gott," by M. Rinkart. ET: "Now Thank We All Our God," by C. Winkworth.

10. K. Barth, *KD* III/3, p. 157. *CD* III/3, p. 139.

inseparable connection of the doctrine of the Trinity with the gospel of grace is probably what moved the Reformers to acknowledge the doctrine of the Trinity. And conversely, disputing the doctrine of the Trinity has as a rule resulted in disputing the confession of the grace of God that alone brings us to salvation.

So the way to oppose understanding God as the "number 1," is to oppose synergism, the contesting of God's pure grace in devoted attending to us. The mistake of synergism is not corrected simply by thinking of God as the "number 3." The church has erred on this side as often as it has on the other. This further danger lies in not being serious about the fact that the grounding of our salvation in God's grace alone is *identical* with the event of revelation and reconciliation in Jesus Christ (the one who has necessarily been born, has died, and has risen in the elect people Israel). This danger lies in the fact that a conception of God takes over in which, although knowledge of God in Jesus Christ is taken into consideration, to be sure, it is only subsequently, only parenthetically in him, and not in an essential, paramount bond with the fact tied to a particular then and there: "The word became flesh" (John 1:14). A conception of God takes over in which God is first known apart from and elsewhere than in this event — perhaps directly from experiences of the created world, or spiritual experiences, or even from a combination of both. A conception of God rules here in which God can just as well be an other than the one revealed to us in Christ. And this conception of God is now supposed to provide the framework into which the knowledge of God in Christ is fit. What is fit into this framework can only be a variant of the conception of God that has already been gained apart from Christ. Knowledge of God in Christ can fit into this framework only by vigorous reinterpretation and devaluation. This cannot go well. The understanding of God as the "number 3" is the breeding ground for dissolving our bond to the revelation in Christ into a religious syncretism, into a "mix of religions."

From the demarcation against an understanding of God in the sense of the "number 1," we can understand why the ancient confession of faith (cf. Art. 23) and also the Heidelberg (Art. 24) see the creation as especially the work of the "Father," reconciliation especially as the work of the "Son," and sanctification (the working out of belonging to God) especially as the work of the "Spirit." It is readily apparent that in reconciliation it is especially the Son who is at work, and in sanctification, the Spirit. But how is it that the creation is especially connected with the Father? Well, the doctrine of creation deals with the basic precondition for God's demonstrating love for us: there needs to be a created counterpart. The human being does not provide this precondition for God's love. God takes care of this precondition. God creates it. This is the biblical meaning of the creation. Because the gift (the Son) in which God demonstrates love, presupposes the giver (the Father), therefore it makes sense that it is especially the work of the "Father" to prepare the created precondition for the demonstration of love to us.

Three times it has been said: this or that is especially the work of the Father, the Son, and the Spirit. "Especially" dare not mean that this or that is the work of one of the three alone. That would split up the tri-unity of God into three gods. This is why there must always be a counter to the statement about the special allocation of the three great works to the Father, Son, and Spirit. Room must be given for a clear line against an understanding of God in the sense of the "number 3." No, it is always the triune God who is the creator, reconciler, and sanctifier. In all three works we always have to do with the undivided and selfsame God. As the Creator, God is none other than the Savior of humankind, and the power that moves us to become children of God. And so the work of reconciliation and sanctification is always at the same time the work of the Father, the Son, and the Spirit. So always and in every way we have to do only with the one God who so loved our world as to give the Son so that all may believe in him and become children of God.

Here is a further observation about the concepts involved in the doctrine of the Trinity. The church has always emphasized, especially at this point, the inadequacy of all our concepts. This has to do with the description of a *mystery*. It is not a mystery completely hidden from us, otherwise there would be only silence at this point. However, it is a mystery we ultimately can only worship and praise, but never get into our grasp conceptually. Therefore, in this matter all concepts are only very makeshift. For example, calling the three "persons" is misleading and almost unusable today, since in contrast to earlier times, we understand "person" to mean an individual living on its own. In this meaning the tri-unity would become the collective of three individuals. Perhaps it is better for us to say that these three are three forms or three ways in which God lives and deals with us. Only it must be completely clear that God is the one God, not beyond these three forms, but *in* them.

Lately, offense has been taken at the designation of the three as "Father, Son, and Spirit." The charge is that a masculine worldview is projected into God. It is bad news if this suspicion fits! It would be a serious mistake, but it would not be corrected by further mistakes. We should not make images of God in any way. We should not in any way project into God things that seem valuable to us, in order then to retrieve them from God to confirm our views. The subject is really the God who turns to us attentively, not a god to whom we attribute something. Only when this is clear can it nevertheless be said that it is possible, and does not change the argument in the least, to describe the three with feminine terms. Such terms have often been interchanged with others in church tradition anyway, for example, Source, Wisdom, Power.[11] Or, as was attempted above, God is the giver who loves us, and the gift in which God loves us, and the process by which God makes us into the beloved. Again, all our concepts are makeshift in view of the mystery that encounters us here. All can only serve to signify the central matter.

Let us describe the matter in a summary way with words from the Preachers' Confession of East Friesland in 1528: "We believe in God alone, Father, Son, and Holy Spirit, which means: We confess and receive forgiveness of our sins, eternal justification and salvation solely through God the Father, the creator of heaven and earth, solely through the Son, our mediator Jesus Christ, solely through the assurance of the Holy Spirit, our Comforter. In this connection we reject everything which is not God's own self and does not do God's work, and consider other things not necessary for our salvation."[12] *This* God is the self-disclosing God who is our beginning, and is this by making God's own self the precondition for our believing, living, and thinking. *This* God wills to do this and can do it. God has done it, and will keep on doing it.

3.1.2. The Creator (Art. 26)

Who could ever come up with the idea of answering the question about the meaning of creation the way Article 26 does in its main declaration? It says that what is at stake is faith "that the eternal Father of our Lord Jesus Christ, who made heaven and earth, . . . is for the sake of Christ his Son also my God and my Father"! In this answer lies such deep, discerning theological awareness that we have to see if we can even come near to the level set for us. Let us risk an attempt.

---

11. So J. Calvin, *Institutes* I.13.18.
12. Müller, *Bekenntnisschriften,* p. 934.

1. The article about the creation, just like all the others, has to do with knowledge that comes through *faith*. In particular, it is an answer to the question, "What do you *believe* when you say, 'I believe in God, the Father, Almighty, Maker of heaven and earth'?" With this approach we differ at the outset from the common opinion that this article is not hard to believe, indeed that it does not really call for believing. Here, it is commonly assumed, we could perhaps better say "I know" or "I see" instead of "I believe." With "I believe," we separate ourselves from the old, seemingly logical procedure of reasoning back from all created causes to an original cause, in order then to call this cause "Creator." So farewell to the popular argument that reasons, "All this must come from somewhere." This "somewhere" will probably be a rather gaunt form, at best a vastly distant "big bang." At any rate, the faith meant here is never directed to such a being.

In a way, we are taking a *modest stance* when we say that the article on creation is about knowledge that comes through faith, although theology must be immodest enough to say something at this point that pertains directly to heaven and earth. Still, it does not say a great deal that many people might expect under the heading "creation." Theology is not, for example, covertly doing natural science. It does not necessarily need to contradict the theses or hypotheses of this science. There are no compelling theological reasons to say yes or no to Darwin's theory of evolution or to Einstein's theory of relativity. Theology will have to contradict natural science only where it becomes an ideology itself, as for example, where it wants to prove or disprove God. By trying to do this, natural science will also be doing violence to natural phenomena. And theology, on its part, must be thankful for contradiction by natural science when theology becomes an ideology itself, as was or is the case in its contradiction against Galileo, or in the fundamentalist zeal against Darwin. This mutuality shows a certain relation between natural science and theology: both must not bind themselves to a particular worldview, because both, when carried on rightly, think in ways that are a posteriori and not a priori. Neither must set up speculative assertions; both have, let us say, particular phenomena to explore. When theology proceeds in this way, it can no more see its statements refuted by natural science than a poem about the beauty of a sunset can be refuted by physical proof that the sun does not go down at all. Moreover, theology must remember that natural science also deals with evidence of interest to theology. Yes, it has to reckon with the fact that natural science, in its own way, may observe this evidence more carefully than theology. So theology has reason to accompany the research of natural science thoughtfully.

Knowledge that comes through faith, which is what is involved in theology, does not mean that something is blindly believed. A process of knowing does take place that is accomplished, to be sure, under particular conditions and within particular limits. But it is done in such a way that there is accountability, so that others, under the same conditions, can also comprehend it. The phenomenon, or manifestation, to which its knowing relates is the word of God. For the Word of God is also a phenomenon; looked at according to its content it is indeed the one original manifestation, because in it God appears to us, is revealed to us, opens up, and makes Godself perceptible. In this Word, we believe, God gives us knowledge about God and about ourselves and about God's relation to us — knowledge also that God is our creator. Note carefully that knowledge coming through faith relates only secondarily to a "something," to the creation, but primarily to God, the Creator, and God's action. I do not believe in the creation, but in the Creator. Because God in the divine Word lets us know that God is our Creator, therefore faith in God also includes this knowledge of God. In contrast, a theological doctrine of creation would be speculative, or be suspected of ideology to the extent that it lets imagination have free rein and does not hold fast to what God says in the Word of God witnessed in holy scripture. However, by holding fast to the Word, it is knowledge that comes through faith.

2. What does it mean to say: God is the Creator? It means this: God is and acts as the precondition of our creaturely existence. God was not only once, at some time or other, such a precondition, in order then like a clockmaker, the work having been completed, to let the product run its course. God was and is and remains the precondition of our being. The consequence for me, as for every living being, is that whether I wake or sleep, whether I know it or not, I stand and live under this precondition, under this sign, that God is my Alpha and also my Omega. I do not originate with myself, and I do not have my source only in my earthly ancestors, in the soil, in my social milieu. Preceding all of these, and relativizing them all, is this:

What are we and what have we in your world so broad and fair,
That does not come, O Father, from your freely given care?[13]

---

13. Stanza 3 of the hymn "Ich singe dir mit Herz und Mund" ("I Sing to You with Heart and Mouth"), by P. Gerhardt.

We know that God is our great Lord, above all else to be adored;
Our life is not achieved by us, but by God's grace most glorious.[14]

God, by taking the initiative as the self-giving and self-disclosing precondition, consequently puts us in the picture too. But we dare not say that by the fact that God is, we are also. That would have as a consequence the idea of an eternal creation, which would be a contradiction in itself. The creation would then be an emanation, in the way that a sunbeam is an emanation of the sun that exists as long as the sun exists, and does not exist without it. The creation then would not be created, but rather endless, divine.

Instead, the creation owes its existence to a decision expressly made by God. In this sense it has a beginning. Because God has started something with us, God is able to make a real beginning, a totally new beginning, which God does. The answer to be given to the question of what there was before the beginning is that of Augustine:[15] the question is meaningless because time is a created structure and was first created with Creation. Prior to that there is no chronological "before," just as there is no chronological "afterward" following it. Before and afterward there is only the eternal God. In this context, eternal is to be understood neither as endless time nor as timelessness, which actually go together. Whoever has endless time has no time at all. But the eternal God can take time for God's creature. God is eternal in that for God, time does not fall into the divisions of before, now, and after. Rather, God encompasses all before, now, and after. Thus God is able to be present to all, yet without being swallowed up by time. God is the Lord of time. As such God is from the outset God, but in such a way that beginning is not foreign to God. In eternal love, God can begin with Godself, before anything else exists. And as Creator, God, who is *before* all else, makes a beginning *with* everything else. In the act of self-giving as the precondition for our being, God also brings into existence those for whom God is the precondition: God's creatures.

Here we come to the aspect of biblical creation faith that is astonishingly critical of religion — its critique of idol worship. The critique does not consist in the foolish statement that the God of our tribe happens to be the one true God, and the others are idols. Nor does the critique cast doubt on the devotion in which people bow before their idols, as if to say that

14. Stanza 2 of the hymn "Nun jauchzt dem Herren, alle Welt" ("Now Rejoice in the Lord, All Who Live in the World"), Hannover, 1646.
15. Augustine, *Confessions*, bk. 11, chap. 12.

they should do this much more devotedly, as we do. Instead, this is what it is about: where *we* presuppose God, there this god is always a postulate *made* by us. It is literally a fictive god, an image made and conceived by us, a product of the "perpetual factory of idols"[16] we always keep busily running. These are the idols, the nothings, the non-gods, as Isaiah 44:9ff. so derisively calls them. We first learn that these are idols when the word of God lets us know that God, and God alone, is our Creator, the presupposition who gives the divine self as the advance condition for our being, and who thereby brings us into being. This tells us that God is not a creation of the creative human being, but we are creatures of the creative God. Blurring this knowledge is probably the chief danger of the modern trend of dissolving the doctrine of creation into the doctrine of providence — that is, into the doctrine of God's accompanying the creature. In this case, the creature is thought of as always present, and therefore in the strict sense is no longer a creature of the creative God, but covertly or openly is co-creator. And then how could the opinion be contradicted that biblical creation faith absolutely excludes: that God is a creation of the religiously creative human being?

3. God as the Creator has "made heaven and earth with everything in them out of nothing." This means that in creating, God sets up a reality different from God. However, it is not a reality foreign to God! The statement by Paul Tillich that the actualized creation is identical with the Fall,[17] and that being means existing in alienation from God, is not a valid consequence. God sets up this different reality in order to live with it. Whatever humans may undertake, they will not cancel the fact that God holds fast to the work of the divine hands and does not abandon it. This reality, willed by God, and affirmed, and so created, remains God's possession. It will stay this way, and this will remain true: "The earth is the Lord's and all that is in it" (Ps. 24:1). For this reason the incarnation of the Word of God will also mean: "He came to what is his own" (John 1:11). The creation is no reality foreign to God, but a reality different from God. It is an earthly creature. And being a creature means that it does not live eternally, and is not omnipresent. Rather, it is bound by time and place as a being that does not set itself up, but is created by God "out of nothing," that is, without any previ-

16. J. Calvin, *Institutes* I.11.8.

17. P. Tillich, *Systematische Theologie,* vol. 2 (Stuttgart: Evangelisches Verlagswerk, 1964³), pp. 51-52. ET: *Systematic Theology,* vol. 2 (Chicago: University of Chicago Press, 1957), pp. 44-45.

ous influence and aid from the creature. In recent decades, you can read about the "vision" of conceiving of the Creator as one who gives birth.[18] The idea is not new, as for example you can read in handbooks on the history of religion that the religious environment of Israel was filled with myths that presented the creation as the work of fertility goddesses. Israel renounced the use of such myths, apparently with complete deliberation. And this was not because they thought in a doggedly masculine way. Rather, it was on good theological grounds. For if the creature is the child of such fertility goddesses, then this child is similar to them. Then it is itself divine as well. Then all the love between these goddesses and the creature takes place according to the proverb, "Birds of a feather flock together." This is exactly what Israel dare not say. According to the knowledge of God given to Israel, the love of God is a love toward something unlike God. It relates to a reality *really* different from God, not divine, but not therefore by any means contrary to God.

In this way, Israel lays down a principle opposing the logic of the proverb quoted above. Being different is not a defect; it is not sin. And sin is not being different, which would have to mean that there is something devilish about being different. Then overcoming difference would be an obligation. But because God's love is love toward what is unlike God, being different is divinely valued, as a kind of distance from "me" that does not have to mean separation from "me." Being different is honored as something that conforms to God's will. It also becomes clear then that if God is "the totally other" in relation to us, this does not have to mean remoteness. It can also mean great closeness. Because God loves what is unlike God, the greatness and genuineness of God's love become all the more visible. For it includes the knowledge that God does not need to stay, as it were, "with God's kind." God does not have to look at something as different as we are in relation to God as a threat, a competitor. God wants so much to be together with a being who is different that God affirms and cherishes our existence. This is what those myths cannot say. But just this is what Israel must say in its faith in the Creator. God shows Godhood by earnestly cherishing the existence of, allowing space for, giving light to, providing food and drink for what is different.

---

18. U. Winter, *Frau und Göttin. Exegetische und ikonographische Studien zum weiblichen Gottesbild im Alten Israel und in dessen Umwelt* (Freiburg/Göttingen: Vandenhoeck & Ruprecht, 1983); and G. Weiler, *Das Matriarchat im Alten Israel* (Stuttgart: Kohlhammer, 1989).

What is different from God is the human being in the context of a world of manifold differences. The human being is spoken of in the Heidelberg as living in the world together "with everything in it." Humankind does not stand in the center of the world, with the assignment to be "master and possessor of Nature,"[19] as has been thought since the Enlightenment, first in praise of, and today in accusation of humankind. Rather, the human being is a creature like the others, and with them. If something distinguishes human beings, it is that they, in being directly aware of themselves, are the special partners to whom God speaks in the history of God with humans witnessed to in the Bible. Somehow the other living creatures are also partners to whom God speaks, and may even be much more attentive than humans. But we only have surmises about this. At any rate, we have in these creatures signs that they, like us, are not abandoned by God. This admonishes us not to overestimate ourselves in relation to our fellow creatures.

The creed, like Genesis 1:1, does not even mention humans. God creates "heaven and earth." Usually we understand by this that God has made the totality, or everything. So God has willed and made *each* creature. But "heaven and earth" means still more: heaven is that which is in principle inaccessible to us, and earth is the realm that is in principle accessible. Both belong to the creation: the freedom to live in what is accessible to us, and the limitation of the creature and its freedom by what is inaccessible. The freedom to affirm this side, which we do have access to, cannot become an idolizing of this side so long as we keep in mind the other side set for us. The mutual surveillance of natural science and theology, looked at from this vantage point, could be described in the following way: natural science reminds theology that it should not become neglectful of the earth, and theology reminds natural science that it should not trespass against the creaturely limits. What comes out of such trespassing in one way or another is shown in Genesis 11 by the tower whose top was supposed to reach "to heaven." The creatures who disregarded limits, prescribing limitless growth, achieved thereby only the disruption of the community. "Those who stride ahead in progress must stride across quite a few people" (Heinrich Böll). Again, this helps us understand more fully what it means to address God as "our Father in heaven." What is inaccessible to us is God's throne, or dwelling place. Yet heaven, like earth, is of a created nature. Though heaven means for *us* a boundary, and because of this boundary

19. R. Descartes, *Discourse on Method* (1637), 6, 3.

God is inaccessible to us from our side, yet the same heaven, because it is created, does not mean a boundary for *God*. This boundary does not hinder God from coming to us on the earth, so that God's "will be done on earth as it is in heaven" (Matt. 6:10). The reality of this side, while so different, is in fact not foreign to God; it is close to God.

4. Another condition of being a creature is "everything necessary for body and soul" (Art. 26). This reminds us of the twofold creaturely determinateness that the Catechism fixes its eye on again and again from its first lines onward. To the essence of being a creature, and being human, belong "living and dying" *and* having our being as "body and soul" (cf. Art. 1). In the article on creation, the Heidelberg speaks of this only in passing, but otherwise it talks about it again and again, mainly in light of what God does to help us in the face of perversion of this double aspect of our creatureliness. But we can only pervert both of these; we cannot suspend them. Therefore God opposes our perversion of both, but does not deny the fact of the limited duration and body-soul structure of our creaturely existence. God confirms this all the more, and anew. So we really understand what "living and dying" and "body and soul" mean when we look at this divine confirmation, and not at the human perversion of both.

The time limitation of our being, the fact that "living and dying" belong to it, does not in itself mean a hardship. To be sure, it is characterized by "urgent need" [old version of the Heidelberg], by the fact that we always need the basic necessities in order to live and die rightly. (When we do not need anything anymore, then our earthly life is at an end.) But no creature must be ashamed of its urgent need. This belongs to its creatureliness: its being dependent — on God, but in many ways also on other creatures. It only becomes a hardship when humans who want to be independent of God follow through and want to make themselves as independent as possible from their fellow creatures (Art. 5!), when they become ashamed of their "neediness." Then they will try as hard as they can to pile up possessions, and in order to do this, will exploit their fellow creatures. They will aim to be able to say: "Soul, you have ample goods laid up for many years; relax . . ." (Luke 12:19). The goal will be to reach the point where they no longer feel any urgent need. Yes, their secret dream and delusion is to make themselves immortal. But they will then have sustained the most serious damage to their souls, even "if they gain the whole world" (Matt. 16:26). In this way they will have won exactly nothing. By losing the sense for what is needed for living and dying, they will have to create ever new needs artificially. They will have to persuade themselves that they always need new things (which they actually do not need), before they can hope to "relax." And yet they will never find rest, because they have unlearned what is most simple, which is to be a human being, and thus *not* to be ashamed of one's "urgent need." The dying that is coming anyway can now be for them only either a catastrophe with which they have "never reckoned in life," or will be so gilded over with transfigurations that it appears as though it has never happened. In view of such lack of ability to die rightly, the truth about how distorted living must have been comes out. Yet Christ has died and risen for us in order to redeem us from such distortion, in order to let the "old self" which is determined by it, die, and to enable us to rise to a new life (cf. Art. 88), a life in which I no longer belong to myself, but "to my faithful savior Jesus Christ" (Art. 1). But he does not set us free from our creatureliness, and therefore not from our mortality (cf. Art. 42). He frees us from the distortion of these, and therefore frees us to affirm the fact that as God's creatures we live a while and then die. Dying belongs to my life too. I dare not be robbed by others of my living, or of my dying. But my dying, as my living, does not belong to me otherwise than that I belong not to myself, but "to my faithful Savior." As I do not have the freedom to end the life of another at will, so I do not have the freedom to put an end to my own life before its ending. But we have the freedom to affirm our dying just as we do our living, because whether we live or die, we are affirmed by *God*.

To our creatureliness belongs also our being *body and soul*. Actually, we do not *have* body and soul (as though we were put together out of two parts); we *are* body and soul — soul of our body and body of our soul. The Heidelberg, while speaking often about these concepts in order to describe the *wholeness* of the creaturely human being, seems to get along without definitions of them. Rather, it directs its interest to confessing that Christ suffered for us "in body and soul" in order to "redeem our body and soul" (Art. 37; cf. 34, 44, 69, 75-76) in order to make us belong to him "body and soul," and be "temples of the Holy Spirit" (Art. 1, 109). As with our life as a whole, so with regard to our body-soul structure, although we do not suspend our creatureliness, we distort it. Separated from God, we think that now we can and must take care of the pressing needs of body and soul (Art. 26) ourselves. Now we *are* no longer body and soul; now we *have* body and soul, as two parts that fight against each other and struggle to pull apart. We suppress and forget the needs of our soul in concern for those of the body, or vice versa. We get into either contempt, neglect, despoilment, and violation of our soul in favor of satisfying what we think are the needs of stomach, drives, and desires — or into contempt, neglect, dissipation, and antagonism of our body in favor of the cultivation of what we think are the only noble spiritual powers — those of mind, will, and emotions. Each of these can merge into the other. A culture of the body won while the soul is despised can in practice include a contempt of the body — namely of handicapped or old persons. And a culture of the soul achieved while the body is despised can actually bring with it contempt of the soul — for example, of the practical wisdom of the so-called little people. The statement that a beautiful soul cannot exist in an ugly body is right only if it also says that an ever-so-well-proportioned body is ugly if a beautiful soul does not dwell in it. "When a man thinks much and cleverly, not only his face, but also his body takes on a clever look."[20] Since Christ has given himself for the redemption of our body and soul, he makes us new as bodily-spiritual creatures. Since he regards them as so valuable that he committed his body and soul for them, how then should he not also redeem us from having contempt for them, and from splitting them off from each other? And how then should we not value and care for our bodies, keep them healthy, and adorn them — the body and also the soul ("Adorn thyself, O my soul!"[21])? However, it is essential to care for the one without neglecting the other, but joyfully affirming the wholeness that includes body and soul.

5. The chief affirmation of Article 26 has guided this conversation about the Creator all along. Article 26 states that to believe in the Creator means to believe "that the eternal Father of our Lord Jesus Christ . . . is for the sake of Christ his Son also my God and Father." This maintains the identity of the Creator and Redeemer God as is witnessed for example in Isaiah 43:1 and John 1:3, 14. Furthermore, it takes the doctrine of the Trinity seriously. The Creator is none other than the One who in the "Son" loves us and in whom the Spirit makes us children of God. But what does this mean? Let us start by noting that the Old Testament story of creation was a relatively late development in the literature of Israel. First, Israel came to recognize the God who chose it, rescued it from slavery, and covenanted with it. Only afterwards did it come to confess that this same God had also created us in the first place. The same development took place in the New Testament, which does not add anything to the Old Testament creation

20. F. Nietzsche, *Menschliches, Allzumenschliches*, in *Werke*, ed. K. Schlechta (Munich, 1960 [2]), chap. 2, n. 31, vol. 1, p. 702. ET: *Human, All Too Human* (Lincoln: University of Nebraska Press, 1996), p. 242.
21. The beginning of a hymn by J. Franck.

faith except the name of Jesus Christ. First, believers recognized Christ as the Savior; afterwards they came to say that "in him all things in heaven and earth were created" (Col. 1:16-17; Heb. 1:2). This process, common to both Testaments, is linked in an essential way with the content that is learned. More is involved than simply making clear a way of knowing, although it certainly is also important to grasp that we come to know God as the divine heart is opened to us. We come to know God in this divine mercy on the creature, and then recognize God also as the Creator of this very creature, who is God's possession. "It is vain for any to reason as philosophers on the workmanship of the world . . . until Christ shall have instructed us in his own school."[22]

But the truth of all this really dawns on us when we understand that in this matter we dare not think chronologically. We should not think that God first put the creation in place and then afterwards deliberated whether to love and affirm it. Instead of thinking chronologically, we must think logically, yes theo-logically. God's love for the creature, demonstrated in the covenant with Israel and reconciliation in Christ, does in fact come before the existence of God's creature. God's unconditional Yes to us creatures comes before our creaturely existence, so that I or any other creature cannot see the light of the world at all without already being so affirmed that no fall into sin can shake this Yes. Once again, "When I was not yet born, you were born for me." Ephesians 1:4 sets this forth, giving the best sense of the Christian doctrine of election: through him who has provided redemption, forgiveness, grace here on earth, "God has chosen us . . . before the foundation of the world." This Yes of God, spoken to God's creature in the one who has become human, Jesus Christ, is God's *first* word to us. It is precisely the precondition of our creaturely existence. It also throws a determining light on our creaturely existence. For now we understand that God's cherishing of the existence of a reality that differs from God reflects God's Yes to the creature. This cherishing gives witness that God is not alone, but wants to be together with God's creatures — and that therefore this creature is also not alone, not abandoned by God. Article 26 emphasizes all this by putting the word "Father" before the word "made." The order is exceedingly important. With the concept of father, do not think of all that earthly fathers may do, and of the images their deeds call

22. J. Calvin, *Auslegung der Genesis*, in *Auslegung de Heiligen Schrift*, vol. 1 (Neukirchen-Vluyn: Neukirchener Verlag, 1956), p. 8. ET: *Commentary on the First Book of Moses, Called Genesis* (Edinburgh: Calvin Translation Society, 1847), vol. 1, p. 63.

up in us! Think rather of the way this concept is used in Psalm 103:13 to designate the source of all mercy. God is first of all not "our" Father, but the Father of Jesus Christ — the Father who loved the world so much as to give this Son in order to make us in him into children of God. The love of the "Father" who is understood in this way goes before the act of creation, and so before the existence of the creatures.

With this proclamation, Article 26 stands in opposition to "natural theology" as it has flowed into Protestantism since the seventeenth century. On this subject, natural theology has the habit of thinking in reverse order from the way followed in the preceding paragraph; that is, it thinks chronologically. First the creation is here, and afterwards God may attend to it in grace.

This kind of natural theology comes in two forms. One says: we want to consider the creation without the revelation of grace, without the Yes of God, as the work of a generalized God. And people did this, with the result that they soon looked at creation apart from any God at all, as "Nature," as material for processing, for mastering, for exploiting by humans. Activities can be carried on in a depressingly merciless way when people look at the world so decisively apart from the grace of God. Can it really become less merciless when humans, sensing this mercilessness, want to simply turn things around and instead of understanding and claiming that Nature is part of humanity, claim that humans are part of Nature? And will it really help if this takes place under the heading of "vitality" and still not under the sign of divine grace?

The other form of natural theology puts it in somewhat the following way: we want to consider humans in and of themselves, apart from God's love. Humans "in and of themselves" are the precondition for God's loving them and for these humans being able to discern that they need this love. Against this it must be said that the doctrine of creation, rightly understood, implies the exact opposite. No human is the precondition for God's loving him or her. If this were so, such humans could exist "in and of themselves" without the love of God. But really, the love of God for humans is the precondition for their being here at all. Of course they have to be here eventually so that God can keep on loving them. But humans do not generate of themselves this provision for the love of God. This is the wisdom of the claim that God, according to Romans 4:17, calls forth the creation out of *nothing*. Because God loves the creatures already, before they exist, God provides this precondition for God's ongoing love for the creatures. God *creates* it.

6. Since God can do this, and actually does it, God is the "almighty Creator." The modern German of the Heidelberg alters the original to "the Almighty," a substantive, instead of an explanatory adjective defining the word "Maker." This makes a significant difference. We should not consider God to be generally a powerful, or all-powerful being. We dare believe that in the work of creation the Creator is all-powerful. But the thought of sheer omnipotence is nonsensical, even logically. One way of showing this is the sophism that if God is all-powerful, God must be able to make a stone so big that God cannot carry it. If God is that powerful, then God is not all-powerful after all, because God cannot carry the stone. And if God cannot make this stone, then God is likewise not all-powerful. But above all, the idea of sheer omnipotence points to a real devilishness. For it connotes pure arbitrariness, a terrible, meaningless, and limitless misuse of power in which someone is capable of anything, of every whim of whatever kind. Now instead of humans having this independent freedom, God would have it. God also would be caught within self, a being who does not need the other, or does so only as an object of arbitrary use. Jacob Burkhardt rightly said, "Power in itself is evil."[23]

God's power is not this kind of sheer "power in itself." It consists concretely in God's being *able* to do everything that God *wills*. And God wills to love the creature, and therefore also wills that it be here and that it live. But God does not will this in order simply to be well intentioned, without being able to do what is willed. Rather, what God wills, God can do. This is God's omnipotence. Concretely, it is the power of God's love. God creates what God wills. "God is able to do it, being almighty, and God is also willing to do it, being a faithful Father" (Art. 26). Because both belong here inseparably together, God does not simply place the creature into world history and then remain unaware that there are things like "need," "evil," and "burdens." God does not abandon the works of the divine hand, but "sustains and governs them" (Art. 26, 27). God is so powerful that in order not to abandon the creature, God can give God's own self, and actually does so. God is able to become weak and small. Because God, in such power, the power of *love* — but the *power* of love — creates the creature and will not let it go, God's work is good, and even "very good" (Gen. 1:31). And therefore it is good for us "to take refuge in the Lord" — our Creator (Ps. 118:8).

23. J. Burkhardt, *Weltgeschichtliche Betrachtungen* (Frankfurt/Berlin, 1963), p. 46. ET: *Force and Freedom* (Boston: Beacon Press, 1943), p. 115.

3.1.3. The Preserver (Art. 26-28)

The self-disclosing God who is our beginning is free to create us unique and different from God. There is no compulsion for God to be Creator. God does not become God by being our Creator. That would mean God would cease being God if we were not here. That would mean that not only is our existence owed to God, but also that God's existence is owed to us. This is the way the mystic Angelus Silesius thought: "I know that without me God cannot live a moment."[24] This idea rests on a confusion of Creator and creature, which Paul in Romans 1:25 views as a manifestation of sin. This idea would lead to either the notion that creation is eternal, or the notion that God is transient. Both are however excluded by faith in the Creator. This faith confesses that God is *free* to be our Creator.

But now God uses this freedom in order to provide for a created entity different from God. Just as we must understand that in the freedom of acting as Creator, God stands under no compulsion, so we may and must understand that God's freedom is not arbitrariness. If God is so free as to want us as creatures, this freedom is by no means to be understood as reserving the right, in other circumstances perhaps, not to want us, and to take back the divine Yes to the existence of the creature. The story of the Flood is, to be sure, a dark reminder that God, even after having let the divine Yes to the existence of the creature have its way, still stands under no compulsion. God *could,* instead of saying Yes, say No, because the inclination of the thoughts of the human heart is evil continually (Gen. 6:5). But the point of this very story is that God in fact lets the unconditional Yes to the creature have its way, despite the fact that the inclination of the thoughts of the human heart is evil from youth (Gen. 8:21!). If God is free to want the creature, then God is also free not to take back the divine Yes to the creature. God is free to stand by this Yes, remaining true to the creature, true even when the creature is untrue to God. God is not only free to *create* the creature, but also free to enable it to *be,* to keep it in existence "as if by God's own hand" (Art. 27). In setting up this existence of ours, God, as the precondition for our creaturely existence, takes responsibility for the creature, for its being and sustenance.

The working out of this responsibility for the creature, and so the preserving of faithfulness toward it, is the subject of the doctrine of divine providence, sometimes called predestination. The words may be rather in-

---

24. Angelus Silesius, *Cherubinische Wandersmann,* I, 8.

adequate, because they can evoke the idea of a weak God who only sees in advance what the creature will do, or the picture of a God of fate, who blindly and automatically lets a plan made in advance run its course. But the Latin word *providentia* means literally *care*. The doctrine of providence deals with God's care for the creature. This care of God is carried on in a way that comprises two aspects, as Articles 26 and 27 say: God "sustains and governs" what is created. To sustain means to stand by the Yes God has spoken to the creature. God does not take back this Yes. And to govern means to keep the work in hand. God does not leave what is created to itself and its own course, as a manufacturer, after the completion of the product, leaves it to the access of the consumers. God destines the course of what is created again and again, as the God who is faithful to it. We will now consider in more detail this caring work of God for what is created.

1. It goes without saying — and yet it needs to be said — that *God* is the real and decisive subject in providence.

What God hath wrought to show his power
He evermore sustaineth.[25]

This is the theme of this doctrine. *God* is the preserver of creation. There is much talk today in environmental ethics about preserving creation, and rightly so. But usually this term is used — by Christians too, sad to say — to mean the following: "What our God has created, that *we* now want to uphold and preserve." In contrast, the Christian contribution to an environmental ethic would have to start unshakably with the basic principle that God is the preserver of creation, and not we first of all. If this conviction is not nailed down tight, everything else will soon go. Then we will wander in our thinking and action into the wrong train. While sitting in this train, we may perhaps want to go in the opposite direction, because the present direction does not suit us. But we are unable to change the wrong direction of the train. Then faith in the Creator will start to waver, and we will want to portray ourselves as at least co-creators. But isn't that merely a hesitant concession to the triumphant spirit in which, at the beginning of modern times, the announcement was made that humans have the right of a master to use every lesser creature for the upholding and comfort of their life?[26]

---

25. From stanza 3 of "Sei Lob und Ehr dem höchsten Gut," by J. J. Schütz. ET: "Give Praise and Glory unto God," by A. Farlander and C. Douglas.

26. J. Locke, *Essay Concerning Human Understanding* (1690), 1.1.92.

What has resulted from the activation of humanity as lord of nature has been called a second creation. It would be impossible for us to ascribe this creation to God. "For this we alone are responsible."[27] "To recognize something unconditional which lies outside (of humanity) is not the passion of this thinking, which is always out for its own possibilities, and thus for construction (that is, for continual further development of that second, human creation)."[28] In this framework, in which humanity understands itself as creator or co-creator, when humanity becomes aware of the damage it has caused with its products and the producing of them, preservation can mean one of two things. It can mean that what we have created for ourselves we want to keep, and that we can lessen the damages by further products or technical advances. Or it can mean that whatever we have done wrong which has somehow tended to annul the good creation of God, we want to make good ourselves by not destroying nature, but protecting and preserving it. We could discuss at length whether the former or the latter statement is preferable. But it would be a discussion in the same framework, precisely in that framework of human thinking which is "always out for its own possibilities, and thus for construction — for further or new activation of humanity as the creator."

It is precisely this framework that is impacted and called into question when we believe and confess God as the Creator and ourselves as God's creatures. Whatever we humans may do in good or less good ways will always be action by the creature, and never such that we can set ourselves in place of the Creator and seriously bring about a second creation. We're beginning to suspect how dangerous the illusion is that humans think they are able to do this. But it is only an illusion, and it begins to fade at least somewhat when we believe in God the Creator. "To recognize something unconditional that lies outside of humanity" — the God who is unconditional in love — is the desire of thoughtful faith. Then it really becomes clear to us that "what our *God* has created, *God* will also preserve." God is the preserver of creation, but not God alone. For in contrast to the act of creation, which God brought about alone, in the preserving of creation we also have something to do. However, it is not the action of lords and co-creators, but rather action in service of the Preserver of creation. It may be obedient or rebellious service; it may be faithful or faithless answering to

27. Acc. to H. Schelsky, "Auf der Suche nach Wirklichkeit," *Gesammelte Aufsätze* (Düsseldorf/Köln: Diederichs, 1965), p. 446.

28. Schelsky, "Auf der Suche nach Wirklichkeit," p. 448.

God's preserving of the creation. One way or another, we can no longer reckon without the host.

2. If it is God who upholds and rules creation, then we have to do with a truth we cannot directly see in the course of nature and history. Instead, it looks as if God is not in control, which puts this truth in question. Article 26 says clearly that this truth is believed in combination with faith in God and in the Creator; we can really only believe it, and it is truly to be believed no less than, for example, the resurrection of the dead. That God is indeed in charge today, and is leading everything for the good, but is not mocked, seldom coincides with our view of the events of the day. In our zeal for interpreting history, and our own personal histories as well, we want to identify our interpretation with God's providence, equating our interpretation with God's way[29] in history. We think we can see the blessing hand of God in the history of the victors, of the successful in their well-being or their domination. And then we think we should interpret the history of the have-nots, their failure and their suffering, their being overlooked or passed over as a judgment of God, as God's absence from them. Be cautious about such identifications! Their questionableness is not removed when we simply turn that interpretation of history upside down, so that we then, for example, automatically understand something unhappy as sent to us from God.

In providence God leads all things in a good direction, seeing to it that God is not mocked, sometimes raising up movements, and sometimes putting them down. But the article about providence remains an article of faith. This raises a warning against putting our view of the course of events, in small or large matters, on a par with what God has ordained. The fundamental conviction applies here: "For my thoughts are not your thoughts, nor are your ways my ways, says the Lord. For as the heavens are higher than the earth, so are my ways higher than your ways" (Isa. 55:8-9). So with respect to divine providence it is also true that we walk by faith and not yet by sight. Not until God's future will what Christian Friedrich Gellert penned come to pass:

> There will I know in heaven's brightness
> what here was hidden without end;
> deem completion, holy rightness,
> what here I could not comprehend;

29. Cf. A. Meyer, *Bismarcks Glaube* (Munich: C. H. Beck, 1933[9]), p. 7.

there opens to my thankful soul
how all leads to a blessed whole.[30]

Still, there are foreshadowings of this future. Faith itself is such a foreshadowing. And faith, as we have said, is not simply blind. It knows and sees beginnings of this kind of future. In faith's knowledge we may now and then glimpse signs of divine providence — signs which for the moment comfort us by confirming that God is in charge and leads all things well, as well as signs which for the moment give shocking confirmation that God is not mocked. But these can only be pointers, not proofs. These pointers do not enable Christians to decipher events, whether they seem especially illuminating, or banal, or filled with profound meaning in so satisfying a way that they can no longer cause wonder or pain. The fact that the hand of *God* is at work in these pointers is what is surprising about them, making them astonishing or disconcerting discoveries. So a Christian will

of all people . . . always be the most surprised, the most affected, the most apprehensive and the most joyful in the face of events. He will not be like an ant which has foreseen everything, but like a child in a forest . . . one who is always rightly astonished by events.[31]

This is how the knowledge of God's providence is knowledge through faith.

3. Although this faith knows and sees always only in a very tentative way, not without being surrounded by much darkness, many questions, and doubts, yet it is still in one respect sure, and has good ground to trust and not to doubt (Art. 26). It may know only dimly by various signs, by conjecture, and sometimes not at all, *to what extent* God's hand is at work in earthly, creaturely developments. Still, faith knows *that* God's hand is at work. To put it more precisely, faith knows in any case *who* this God is. As

---

30. C. F. Gellert, *Sämmtliche Schriften*, Part 2 (Vienna: Frank Haas, 1789²), p. 229.

Da werd' ich das im Licht erkennen
was ich auf Erden dunkel sah;
das wunderbar und heilig nennen
was unerforschlich hier geschah;
da schaut mein Geist im Preis und Dank
die Schickung im Zusammenhang.

31. K. Barth, *KD* III/3, p. 275. *CD* III/3, pp. 242-43.

it looks at these developments, there is a great deal that faith is in the dark about. Faith does not understand these developments any better than others do. But about one thing faith is not in the dark. It is the same conviction that holds about creation: the Father of Jesus Christ, the God of the elect people Israel, "is for the sake of Christ his Son also my God and my Father" (Art. 26). This is the God who intends good for the creatures, and not only intends it, but being almighty as explained above, is able to bring it about. God not only intends good, but in all circumstances also does good. Yes, God also intends and does good when not allowing Godself to be mocked. God really says Yes, even where visibly having to say No.

Admittedly, even discerning faith itself cannot directly see in earthly events and developments themselves that God's hand is at work, intending and doing good. This is why the idea, recently advanced again, that even the non-human creation is endowed with vitality and spirit on a par with the Spirit of God, with what is called in Article 27 the "everywhere present power of God," is a short-circuited one. The discovery that non-human creatures are not, as Descartes formulated it,[32] machines and automatons, but living beings with spirit, is certainly beautiful and instructive. We may and should also believe that God's present strength gives them vitality and spirit. But this is something we *believe!* We cannot see this in them; neither can we claim that their creaturely spirit is directly, as such, the Spirit of God. Otherwise the statement "life = spirit" becomes a tautology, in which the latter word adds nothing to the former. Yes, otherwise the creature is made divine; or conversely, God's Spirit is made an earthly, creaturely entity. May the experience of the vital spirit of other creatures encourage us to handle them gently. Still, it is *we,* and always only we, who handle other creatures. This experience as such does not yet tell us that *God* handles us in a way that intends and does good. But we believe that God does this. We do not merely guess and claim this. We may be sure of it and trust in it as we look elsewhere than to events and experiences in the world. We look instead first of all, again and again, to that event in which God offered up the Son. By becoming a brother with the human creature through the Holy Spirit, God has demonstrated to the world the love that embraces the totality of the "world," so that we all may believe and none be lost.

"I so completely trust in God that I have no doubt that God will provide me with everything necessary for body and soul" (Art. 26). I must again and again look first in faith to the place where the one comfort is

32. R. Descartes, *Discourse on Method,* 5, 16.

shown, "that I belong, both body and soul and in life and in death, not to myself, but to my faithful savior, Jesus Christ," in order from there to be able to believe what follows: that with the others I too, in my life of body and soul, and in the burdens and tangles of creaturely events, do not fall out of God's hands, nor am I abandoned to other powers, nor to myself alone. When I have heard this good news, then, although I cannot see it, I can nevertheless believe without a doubt that the God of the good news has the course of the world in hand, with its great and small developments. God is so much in charge that creatures "cannot even move without God's will" (Art. 28). Then I cannot believe there is a kind of higher double bookkeeping: here a realm in which I belong to this God, and other realms in which I belong to others. And I cannot believe that in the general course of the world some other power rules, such as fate or chance or the bare battle for life or the simple principle of life for life's sake.

But on the contrary, I will believe this: because God does not will the death of *sinners*, but that they live (Ezek. 33:11), therefore God wills that we live *in every respect* — and not only we, but we in the midst of much other life which God also wills to live. God is no doubt present in this other realm in a way different from the presence in the revelation of grace. However, God is not present as a different god, but as the one revealed in Christ. This same God is, in this realm, hidden, but not absent, and not in contradiction to the One present as revealed in Christ. If we can believe that God is also in charge in this realm, then we can be joyful and free, believing that the One who has made heaven and earth neither slumbers nor sleeps (Ps. 121:4) — in all the ups and downs and back and forth of life. It is being allowed to believe, in a way that comforts, that what Zechariah 2:8 says is true for Israel, is also true for all others. This verse is what Calvin understood as the good news of the doctrine of providence:[33] "He who touches you touches the pupil of mine eye." We may believe this assurance in the face of the earthly happenings that confound us and in which we become entangled.

4. But does God stand by this assurance? The struggle of the soul caused by this question is called the problem of theodicy. Theodicy deals with the question of how the existence of God can be justified in view of the suffering in the world. Especially in modern times this question is persistently raised, in reversal of the Reformation question of how a human being can be justified before God. The reversal of the question is con-

33. J. Calvin, *Institutes* I.17.6.

nected with what C. Amery called "the end of providence,"[34] which was brought about because humans attributed the function of providence to themselves. In this state of affairs, these same humans, as soon as they no longer know what to do, or as soon as the "merciless consequences" of their arrogating this function to themselves become too much for them, go for help to the God they thought was powerless, or question God accusingly: "Why do you let this happen?" What right do people have, when the calculation they have made without God again and again does not add up, to turn to God for help? This is a God they as a rule thought they did not need, in the assumption that they want to pursue their own happiness, which they are capable of creating. What right do they have now to call on God for help or to accuse God of being untrustworthy? What right do we have to expect that God would do anything else but pass over in silence such calling for help, or such accusation, as long as the beginning point of our ways, the arrogance of wanting to play "providence" ourselves, remains uncorrected? With what right can a Christian German, for example, after Christians (including theologians) have allowed or supported the racial delusion that forgot God, then dare to ask, "Where was God in Auschwitz?" Yes, was the murder of Jewish people not bound to come, when in central Europe, so intellectually and technically developed, the "end of providence" had been announced?

Granted, this latter question raises a problem that again goes beyond that of deep human guilt. It is also beyond the blind alley of humans taking over the function of "providence." And here the heart of the problem is not first of all the general question of why God allows suffering in the world. There is a question thornier still, and only when we look at it and perhaps get at least a little clarity here, will it throw light on that general question. What is this thornier question about?

God's assurance is given first of all to those who belong to God, to God's people, the ones chosen out of all peoples. This assurance is not simply a general, blanket promise to all and everyone. "Can a woman forget her nursing child? . . . Even these may forget, yet I will not forget *you*" (Isa. 49:15-16). God has sworn faithfulness first of all to God's own people. It is promised first to them, not in order that the others go away empty-handed, but that the others may see in the support of those first singled out how God then and therefore wills to support these others also. Yes, but

34. C. Amery, *Das Ende der Vorsehung: Die gnadenlosen Folgen des Christentums* (Hamburg: Rowohlt, 1972). Cf. pp. 251ff.

is not the whole assurance of God, even God's own self, shown to be a lie when things do not go well for God's people? It is this very people — as the Old Testament shows — who again and again get into shadows and abysses. Why? Why? The explanation that they are so battered because of special sins does not suffice, any more than the moralistic one that rests on the lack of tolerance of their fellow humans, not to mention pointing to general human frailty. How should these theories explain why God's faithful servant Jeremiah and before him righteous Job were thrown into such darkness, while the godless are successful and happy in the world (Ps. 73)? Why is the obedient servant of God himself "despised and rejected by others, a man of suffering and acquainted with infirmity" (Isa. 53:3-4)? And Tevye, the milkman, sighs: "Is it true that we are the chosen people? But could you not choose another people for a while?"[35] And here in the midst is the one to whom the voice from heaven says: "This is my Son, the Beloved, with whom I am well pleased" (Matt. 3:17). But he of all people was so greatly burdened that he "began to be grieved and agitated. Then he said to them, 'I am deeply grieved, even to death'" (Matt. 26:38-39). He of all people "cried with a loud voice, 'My God, my God, why have you forsaken me?'" (Matt. 27:46). Why? Why does God let *this* happen? Why did God "not withhold his own Son" (Rom. 8:32)? To this question, scripture gives an answer — one that Christians see as the divine pointer in the dark mystery of that other Why-question: It was "necessary that Christ had to suffer these things" (Luke 24:26, 46; Matt. 17:12; 18:7; Mark 8:31 par; John 3:14; 12:34; Heb. 2:17). That is to say, in fulfillment of God's good intention for us, and in carrying out God's love for us sinners, and for our reconciliation with God, he "had to" interpose himself all the way to this extreme.

The fact that Christ had to do this does not mean that the evil deeds of the humans involved are counted as good, for those involved also needed and received his intercession. It will also have to be said of Jesus' own people, who suffer so enigmatically, "Woe to those by whom they are betrayed" (cf. Matt. 26:24). But you will not be able to say about them that they *"had"* to suffer in the same sense that he did, or that they suffered "for our sins," or that this came upon them because of their own sins. Yet you will have to say that they suffer in such an incomprehensible way *as his people.* They are his people because he is so close to them and they are so near to him. Their nearness to him is shown in their sufferings and in the fact that in fellowship with them he bears his cross, such a scandal to the

---

35. *Fiddler on the Roof,* a musical by J. Stein after Scholem-Aleichem. Act 1, Scene 5.

world, and to the "Christian world" as well. Sufferings dare not be heaped on this people because they are Jesus' people. But if in the enigma of their suffering there is a light from God, then it is this: that in it they are definitely *Jesus' people.*

5. From here, a light falls on all our experience of suffering, which so often sorely tries our trust in God's promise. Yes, this is the one really comforting light. Article 26 speaks about "evil God sends to me in this troubled life." Literally, it speaks of a "vale of tears" in which we find ourselves. And according to Article 27 there are in this vale of tears not only fruitful, but also unfruitful years, not only leaf and blade, but also rain and drought, not only health, but also sickness, not only prosperity, but also poverty — and so not only laughter, but also crying, not only birth and living, but also dying. We have not even mentioned yet the injuries, poverty, and death that human malice inflicts on others. Even if there were not such malice, there are in life both aspects, as well as dark shadows and hard mysteries that God sends our way. These are features of that nothingness out of which God has called us in our creation and which hovers about our creatureliness just because it is creaturely. But those who experience these shadows and know how quickly they can unexpectedly attack us and cause us deep spiritual struggle will find the way the Nazis mocked the Christians' talk of "this vale of tears"[36] to be inhumane.

Yet they will then above all cry for God, as Psalm 42 says, like a deer for fresh water: Where are you now? Then they may sigh:

Oh why does God sometimes keep still . . . when all the while our will and heart in fears are wrapped; seek here and there, find not a mite; they yearn to see, but lack the light; want freedom from harsh binding; the way, they are not finding.[37]

Is it supposed to be a comfort, then, to know that it is God who lays these burdens on me and "sends [them] to me in this troubled life" (Art. 26), and that these things "come to us not by chance but by God's fatherly hand" (Art. 27)? Is this not a ghastly Almighty who sends both kinds of events, yes, also evil and misery? Does not everything in us rebel against

36. "Idee und Tat" ("Idea and Deed"). From the teaching material for the total worldview education of the NDASP, in O. Söhngen, *Säkularisierter Kultus. Eritis sicut deus* (Gütersloh: Bertelsmann, 1950), p. 61.

37. Stanza 6 of the hymn "Du bist ein Mensch" ("You Are a Human Being"), by P. Gerhardt.

accepting this as willed by God? Would we not want to give in to the prompting of Job's wife, and "curse God" (Job 2:9)?

We will indeed have to reject that ghastly Almighty one. But not God! For only from the One who puts us before the enigma can the solution come. This is why Job does not simply lament, but laments in prayer to God. The One who kills and makes alive, makes poor and makes rich, abases and exalts, is one and the same (1 Sam. 2:6-7). If what is hard comes out of God's hand and not out of another hand, then it is still the hand of the One who intends good for us, and does good. In what way God intends and does good even in this hard experience we will perhaps not understand for a long time, and perhaps never understand on earth. We will at any rate often have long ways to go until we are able to understand a little. But God's help in distress is not only that it will go better for us after a while, but that already in the midst of the darkness we are not abandoned by God — and that because of this it now is going somewhat better for us. Even in the throes of feeling abandoned, we are not abandoned by God. This is so because God in the cross of Jesus Christ has abandoned Godself to our suffering, to the drought, the poverty, the Godforsakenness, and because the Easter truth was therefore revealed to us, that neither death nor life, nor height nor depth can separate us from the love of God which is in Christ Jesus our Lord (Rom. 8:38; cf. Art. 28). And though I can never understand death, abasement, and suffering, not to mention "manage" them, I may still be sure that all this is not great enough to separate me from the love of God. I must then say, as Ulrich Bach has impressed on us, that also the handicapped person is a good creation of God![38] I can even say as Dietrich Bonhoeffer did at the end of 1944:

> Should it be ours to drain the cup of grieving
> even to the dregs of pain at thy command,
> we will not falter, thankfully receiving
> all that is given by thy loving hand.[39]

6. Yet we humans are in the habit of making life endlessly more difficult than it is. We make the earth more than ever into a "vale of tears," a place of

---

38. Cf. U. Bach, *Getrenntes wird versöhnt: Wider den Sozialrassismus in Theologie und Kirche* (Neukirchen-Vluyn: Neukirchener Verlag, 1991).

39. D. Bonhoeffer, *Widerstand und Ergebung* (Munich: Kaiser, 1959⁹), p. 275. ET: *Letters and Papers from Prison* (New York: Macmillan, 1971), p. 400.

misery which God does not send us, but which we humans ourselves send by our evil tendency "to hate God and my neighbor" (Art. 5). We make the world into a place of misery, caused by us humans, but immediately also suffered by us — a world in which each one is somehow the culprit and also somehow the victim. Human evil does not always have to be equally evident. Often it takes its course indirectly. Out of concern that God may not care well enough for them, people take it into their own hands to intend good and do good, and so they set up a war of good against evil. The venture gives the impression of being justified, even when it turns out that it has become dangerous for everyone and has caused a real vale of tears because its fighters are only too similar to the ones fought against. Where has something beautiful, lovely to contemplate, and promising ever emerged that has not one day turned out as something sinister, soiled as though by a curse in the grasp of covetous people seeking prestige, hungering for power, furiously looking for more wealth, lusting for battle, and brutalizing others? Finally, at certain historical moments everything floods out into a sea of dilemmas — in reaction to which the game begins anew![40]

But where in all this is divine providence? The question is all the more urgent since God's providence is not carried out directly, straight out of thin air, so to speak, but indirectly. The use of God's creatures is involved, and human capacity is not shut off, but put to use. Where, however, is such a human capacity that would be a fit means for God's intention and action? If humans are by nature inclined to hate God and their neighbor, how can God make use of the intentions and actions of these humans? These are the very ones who have produced that ocean of dilemmas, including when they thought they were concerned for "peace and order" and even for a "new world order"! Those who get in their sights the disparity between what humans want and what God wants will surely pray with utter seriousness, "Thy will be done on earth as it is in heaven." In heaven it already takes place, in the concurrence of God's will with the service of God's pure witnesses and messengers, the angels (Art. 124).

But how can God's will be done on earth in any other way than by God prevailing against what opposes God's will? In what other way than this: *Hominum confusione dei providentia regitur* — "in the midst of our mistakes and tangles God's care for us rules"!?[41] How else can God make use

---

40. Cf. K. Barth, *KD* IV/3, pp. 501ff. *CD* IV/3, pp. 436ff.

41. A Swiss saying from the time of the Thirty Years' War; cf. K. Barth, *Eine Schweizer Stimme 1938-1945* (Zollikon/Zurich: Evangelischer Verlag, 1945), p. 233.

of such desires and actions than by *crossing* them out? We cannot believe God's leading in world events without recognizing it also as God's judgment, as God's governance, in which God is not mocked. We need to recognize that God's governance is also God's contradiction of the ways we take without God, and is the divine No to the misery we thereby prepare for ourselves. As we, in faith that God leads us while we are suffering, find comfort in the fact that nothing can separate us from the love of God, so in the same faith we must accept with regard to our sins that the love of God adamantly separates us from our opposition to God's love. But this way it becomes clear that the judgment with which God crosses our mistakes and tangles is still a form of God's love. For this crossing is manifestly an image of the "word of the cross" in which God, in the midst of judgment, above all saves. In saying No to the old, perverse human being, God loves the human being. Would not a church that really knows something of God's providence have had to bow under the gravity of God's judgment, say in 1945 as the Third Reich went down in horrors? Would it not have had to bow so low that it would have given thanks that God had not let the war against God's grace, and therefore against the chosen people, and therefore against humanity, succeed? For God's judgments also secretly contain, in all seriousness, something comforting, which is the quintessence of the Joseph story, so brimful of tangles. "As for you, you meant evil against me; but God meant it for good" (Gen. 50:20).

> But God, who loves us without end, makes good what our hands maul,
> Gives joy when we depress ourselves, and lifts us when we fall;
> All this is from his caring heart and pure creative Father's art
> in which we needy sinful ones are borne as daughters and as sons.[42]

7. The doctrine of providence is not only about God's actions in the realm of the creature. It is also about God's making use of creaturely capabilities, and especially human capabilities. For this reason, trust in God's providence does not make us irresponsible. It puts us in a place of definite responsibility. As we recognize at this point, the self-disclosing God who is our beginning sets us in a place where we are not puppets mechanically pulled by strings. God wants to win us as free coworkers. Because God does not shepherd us poor sinners as God's children in vain, our activity,

---

42. Stanza 5 of the hymn "Du bist ein Mensch" ("You Are a Human Being"), by P. Gerhardt.

which God uses to serve the divine governance, does not always have to be the behavior of rebels. It can also be the action of those who willingly let themselves be taken into God's service, not as marionettes, but in active affirmed harmony with God's governance of the world. Not all Christians will do this, and none of them will do it always. And again and again people can also be found outside the church who actually do this, and perhaps better than many Christians. Article 28 describes active behavior in which we can and should take part in God's governance of the world with three adjectives: "We can be patient when things go against us, thankful when things go well, and for the future we can have good confidence in our faithful God and Father."[43] We will try to understand this in a more extensive way than the Heidelberg probably had in mind!

(a) *Thankful* — not only in hours in which we feel "blissful." We may take such hours as signs that we always have every reason to be thankful to God. They are signs that remind us: "Do not forget all his benefits" (Ps. 103:2). They are signs that teach us: "Give thanks in *all* circumstances!" so that even in our helpless sighs we still come before God "with thanksgiving" (Phil. 4:6)! Thankfulness does not correlate directly with the high moments of our life. So it cannot be completely lacking in its low moments. It correlates with the love of God in Christ, from which nothing, neither height nor depth, can separate us. In view of this we may "rejoice in the Lord always" (Phil. 4:4). Thankfulness means joy — in God's redemption, but also in the fact that God gives me existence, "that I am and that I have a human countenance."[44] Thankfulness means active affirmation of my bodily-spiritual life and the abundance of life around me. In this way I take part in God's preserving of creation. This participation is the *cooperation* God affirms and desires from us. God expects that we, in correspondence to God's affirmation of creaturely existence even before it exists, take seriously that all affirmed and wanted life is worthy of life, and that we not turn this sentence around and say that unwanted life is not worthy of life, lacking the right to life. And God expects of us that we "till and keep" the "garden" which we have not made, and into which God has "put" us. By expecting this of us, God trusts that we will have a free, responsible relation with what is given us and surrounds us. The tilling and keeping are to be kept in balance, so that we till in order to live, and keep

---

43. Translation by the Christian Reformed Church (Grand Rapids, 1998).

44. M. Claudius, *Sämtliche Werke* (Darmstadt: Wissenschaftliche Buchgesellschaft, 1987[6]), p. 149.

the garden without destroying the environment and the social fabric. But tilling and keeping get out of kilter as soon as we forget that we are not co-creators of God's creation, but only coworkers in its preservation by God, and when we forget that even this cooperation is only our thankful answer to God's governing and sustaining of creation. Everything gets out of balance when we, like Prometheus, wrest the ownership of the earth out of the hands of the jealous gods. Or, like Atlas in the saga, we think we must carry the burden of the world — whether it be in the attempt to replace God's creation by a better one, or in the attempt to save it from its fall into nothingness. Human cooperation in building and preserving within God's creation, when done rightly, will always be the action of "poor sinful ones" who live from and according to the fact that we are God's and are "borne as daughters and as sons."

(b) *Patient.* Here we are not being guided to simply accept "adversity," and surely not to accept without opposition injustice which militates against God. Articles 107 and 110 will say that God commands us to avert harm as much as we can. And Article 26 says that I should not submissively bear what goes against me, but rather trust that God may "transform" it. Just as real thankfulness does not make us blind to all the objectionable things that prevail in the world (including what we ourselves cause, perhaps even while giving thanks for what is given to *us),* so real patience does not reconcile itself to what is objectionable. Patience hopes for its overcoming. It hopes however first of all in God's help and not in our own attempt to avert harm. We are commanded to do this, but only in a way rooted in God's help. The attempt dare not, then, resemble the self-help of Moses when he struck that Egyptian dead (Exod. 2:11ff.), which indeed did not liberate from adversity, but only made it worse. Liberation first broke out when God let it break out, whereupon the people started to move. With regard to God's defeat of adversity, we may take part in the liberation — but only in cooperation with God's action.

We take part, however, in *patience.* Patience means accepting the objectionable situation in which I find myself, without fleeing from it in wishful dreams. I can accept it, however, because I do not accept the adversity in itself, but accept that God loves me already, and not just when the adversity is past. Acceptance lets us hang on in adversity in the assurance that the adversity will one day stop. The opposite of such patience is thus not resistance against adversity, but weak conformity. Patience shows itself not in submission to adversity but in opposition to it. "One who is slow to anger is better than the mighty" (Prov. 16:32). Having patience is the strongest thing we can do. Patience means taking a long breath — in calm confidence trusting God. Patience means not satisfying oneself with premature solutions by means of rash attacks, but being able to wait — until "help breaks in with power"[45] and until it is thus shown that lies have short legs, and pride goes before a fall. Patience also means not resigning in view of the infinitely small steps we take, which are far from measuring up to the immensity of the opposition — in trust that God can grant that nothing of such "faithfulness in small things" (Luke 19:17) is done in vain.

(c) *Confident* — toward the future. Is there any reason for confidence? Is not the future of humanity this: the last human being returned to the trees from which we once came down?[46] And what waits for us personally — other than the grave and decay? For how many is this end already foreshadowed — in suffering, in pain, in tears! And is everything that we say and undertake against it anything more than a drop of water on a hot stone? Is it not all powerless and out of place like the speeches of the friends of Job to this man stricken in so many ways? Are slogans of confidence anything other than conjuring up a mirage in order to stay on our feet a little longer, although in the end we will be lost after all? Do we not with good reason begin mistrusting all those who constantly hush our suspicions and assure us that they have things in hand? Yes, genuine confidence will have at its side a thorough mistrust of all the false prophets who speak peace where there is no peace (Jer. 6:14). Real trust has no trust — except "in our faithful God," except that humans, whatever they do or suffer, can never cause God to stop being God. God is the God who is faithful to the creature, who has thoughts of peace for us and not of harm (Jer. 29:11), and who does not desire the death of sinners, but that they turn and live (Ezek. 18:23). Where there is hushing of suspicions, there is blindness to human misery. Where there is only agitation, you see only misery without end. But where there is trust in the faithful God, you see the piteous situation, but beyond that see in what is piteous the pity of God.

Whoever has such confidence, and lives and walks in it, is in accord with the promise of God to be close to those in misery and not to leave them. This person can no longer simply stride "confidently" over a sea of suffering and tears. She will be ready to *suffer with* those who are afflicted.

45. From stanza 6 of the hymn "Gott will's machen" (God Wills to Do It), by J. D. Herrnschmidt.
46. E. Troeltsch, *Glaubenslehre* (Munich/Leipzig: Dunker & Humblot, 1925), pp. 320-21, 324. ET: *The Christian Faith* (Minneapolis: Fortress Press, 1991), pp. 255-56, 258.

She can take her place only there, alongside all that grieves and sighs, without being above it all and distanced from those involved. She can only stand with them and be where no other hope is left for her than that God is her hope. With the people next to her, and for them, she will call "out of the depths I cry to you, O Lord" (Ps. 130:1). But even there, and especially there, she will not sigh without limit. She will say, "I wait for the Lord" (v. 5). So she will live in a confidence that enables her to hang on. She will also hope for the best for those around her, will stand by them and ease their distress as best she can. She will move forward in a way like that which Calvin describes in his doctrine of providence, when he says of Christians: "Often, indeed, are they distressed, but not so deprived of life as not to recover; they fall under violent blows, but afterward they are raised up; they are wounded, but not fatally; in short, they so toil throughout life that at the last they obtain the victory."[47]

3.2. The God Who Comes for Relationship with Us

3.2.1. Jesus Christ (Art. 29-36)

We are speaking about the free God. But God's freedom is different from the disconnected freedom in which the "enslaved" free will resides and is active in sin. God's freedom is not disconnected freedom. If it were, God would have nothing to do with us — except having to watch jealously so that we, as God's competition, did not come too close to treading on the divine independence. And perhaps God might want to prove divine superiority and get rid of our competition by making us oppressed creatures instead of independent ones. But God uses freedom differently. God uses it in order to form a bond with us humans, in order to set up a relationship between God and us. Instead of using it as freedom for and in competition, God uses it as freedom for and in *coexistence*. God turns to us humans and stands up for us, because God wants to live with us.

However, this is not about applying to God a general principle according to which everything must be in relationship. Under such a principle probably no real relationship could be set up at all. At any rate, we by no means already stand in such a relationship to God. And God has such a re-

47. J. Calvin, *Institutes* I.14.18.

lationship to us only by setting God's own self into relationship with us. We come into relationship with God only by God's action. The establishment of a relationship between God and us is an event that issues from God and comes entirely from God's free grace and love. God does not wait until we put ourselves in relationship to God. Bent into ourselves as we are, we could not do this at all in our own strength. But what we do not do, and cannot do, God does. In contrast to our independent freedom, and in overcoming it, God's freedom is freedom for coexistence. As the three in one, God is by nature the coexisting being who *can* do this and who is free to will to enter into relationship with a different entity and to bring this entity into relationship with God. And in love God *wills* to coexist with this entity different from God. For this purpose God comes to us before our life begins. To this end God creates the precondition, by bringing about the creation. Because God sets the divine self into relationship with us, we are brought forth as God's creatures. God's will for coexistence with us is the ground of our existence. So everything has as its goal, its origin, and its center, wonderful and holy beyond all telling, this one fact: that God sets God's own self into relationship with us, and in this way is revealed as the God who comes into relationship with us and bonds with us in a binding way. From the very beginning we could not avoid talking about this God continually. And to the end we will continually be renewed in talking about God.

What has been said so far is summed up in the message of the angel to Mary. She will bear a son, "and they shall name him *Immanuel*," which means, "God is with us" (Matt. 1:23). Note well that he is *called* this because he *is* the Immanuel. His name is not merely a symbol for a truth that stands even without this particular instance. His person is not merely like the letter carrier for a message that is independent of the one who delivers it. The message "God is with us" has its reality in his person. God is with us because God is with us in *him*. God has set Godself in relationship to us in Jesus Christ. God has done this by becoming a human being in him. Not that God has metamorphosed into a human being! But in the form of a human being, God has placed Godself with us, and us with God, in the most intimate, indissoluble companionship. In doing this, God did not do something that was strange to Israel. God did this in fulfillment of what had already been promised and assured to Israel: "I will be their God and they will be my people" (Ezek. 37:27; cf. Rev. 21:3).

In Jesus Christ, God has set Godself in relationship with us, and in him is God with us — although we are far from God, and sinners. God's being with us is more than simply a reaction to our sin. Someone who reacts puts himself or herself under the law another person dictates. God does not merely react; God acts, taking the initiative. God's setting Godself in relationship to us is not a constraint laid on God by us, through our sin, for example. Rather, it comes from the freedom of God's love. God's bond with us does not depend on the fact that we are sinners — that would have the consequence of making sin eternal. No matter what, God wills to bind Godself to us in free love. This is why God's love cannot be stopped when in this bond with us God comes upon the fact of our sin. This fact can only mean that in spite of it, and all the more, God is with us. God's setting Godself in relationship with us surely means something important for us — namely, an immeasurable blessing. But above all it means something for God, and costs God something — namely God's self-binding and self-limiting. In this sense it is God's self-definition, to be definitively always and eternally this one and no other — the Immanuel, the God with us and not without us, who even when it is necessary to be against us, is above all with us. Our thinking about God is mistaken if we do not think in this way. We think of an idol if we do not think of God as the God with a human face, the God bound with us humans.

The gospel of Jesus Christ has this as its content: God with us. And this content of the gospel is the reality of Jesus Christ. Rightly reflecting on and proclaiming this gospel has special relevance in view of a crucial point of modern thought: atheism, or godlessness. Atheism is only in small part, and not even necessarily, the theoretical argument that assuming the existence of a highest being is an illusion. Godlessness does not have to combat the assumption of a highest being. It can be content just to interpret this assumption, or it can simply ignore it. Atheism does not have to be anti-religious, but can certainly also have a religious shape. Even the atheist believes something. Godlessness, however, is not just a theory, but also a particular praxis. In this praxis, humans understand themselves, define themselves, and conduct themselves, as apart from God, separated from God, without God. Godlessness is the theory, and still more the praxis, of understanding and dealing with the human realm as the realm *only* of humans, a realm in which God is not to be found.

Since the nineteenth century, church and theology have to a large extent reacted apologetically to modern atheism. That is, they have taken a defensive posture. They have done this by trying to secure for God a niche in the world of these humans detached from God. They have done it by trying to prove to humans who define themselves without God that there is within them a corner or a void where they still need a God; yes, that in their psychic makeup there is a feeling of being born to something higher. People then called this "religion." This move could probably give atheism an emotional depth it did not have in its theoretical form, but it could not actually overcome atheism. It could not root out the sense that these humans, even in their deepest sinking into themselves, and even in their boldest elevation to what is higher, are always only dealing with themselves.

It was a mistake for church and theology to react so apologetically to atheism instead of asking: Have not we ourselves called forth this atheism? Is not this the natural consequence of a false god we have presented? It certainly is a false god who is a being by himself, absolute, detached from humans, essentially concerned with himself. This conception of God is that of a being without humans, who to be sure is secondarily, but only secondarily and incidentally, concerned with humans. This god is a being only in the realm beyond, where humans are not to be found.[48] And if God is such a being, why should not humans be correspondingly beings who are only concerned with themselves, who really come to themselves when they get loose from God? Why should they not be beings in whom God is absent? Modern atheism in its most perceptive forms has surmised that the God who is without humans, because concerned only with himself, is the mirror image of humans who are godless because they are concerned only with themselves.[49] A thoughtfully self-critical theology should admit that this God, who is a mirror image of humans absorbed in themselves, is in fact an idol. It is an idol because the true God is not a God without humans. God has come forth as the Immanuel, as the God with us, as the God who because of setting Godself into relationship with us, is not to be thought of in any other way than as the God who sets Godself into relationship with us.

On this account it is always a blind alley when theology gets involved in the question of *whether* "there is a God." As though many who are considered God were not idols! As though a god who depends on our proof, one who "is there," as other "things" are, could be God! The decisive question for Christian theology is always *who* God is. Only in connection with the answer that God is this one who is self-revealing to us and self-binding with us does light come on the question of God's existence.

48. E. Jüngel, *Barth Studien* (Zurich/Köln: Benziger/Mohn, 1982), pp. 332-47.

49. L. Feuerbach, *Das Wesen des Christentums* (1841; Leipzig, 1957), chap. 1, n. 3, e.g., pp. 45ff., 92ff., 270ff. ET: *The Essence of Christianity* (New York: Peter Lang, 1989), e.g., pp. 50ff., 87ff., 263ff.

Ask'st thou who is this? Jesus Christ it is,
Lord of hosts alone, and God but him is none.[50]

Now we probably understand better why confessing Christ is the center of the confession of faith. It is the center because he is the Immanuel, because in him God sets Godself in relationship, and because in this way the revelation comes to us that God is the One who sets Godself in relationship with us. We understand now too the good sense of the ancient church formula about Jesus as the "true God" and the "true human." This does not make the nonsensical claim that he is a chimera — half God, half human. It asserts: here in him you can recognize who the "true God" is, in contrast to every idol, namely this one and no other, who binds Godself with humans and is bound with them, who will not let humans go. This God is definitely not apart from humans: this is the God who is not found in any other way than with humans. And from this it follows who the "true human" is: not the godless one, not the one deserted by God. This is the true human: the human bound to God, the one who is with God. The fact that we humans live in contradiction to this truth, that we on our part do not live with God, creates special problems. But these are problems that can be solved only in the course of the history that in Christ the true God is the God with us, and that therefore in Christ the true human is the human who is with God. For the proclamation of the gospel of Jesus Christ in view of atheism, this means that it should not oppose atheism directly, and not apologetically. The proclamation of the gospel opposes atheism in a helpful way only when it self-critically opposes its *own* false images of God as a God without humans. And it does this by calmly and clearly delivering the gospel of the Immanuel, in whom God is bound with humans and does not let them go.

We will now look more closely at the Christology of the Heidelberg, which forms the main part of the second section of the catechism. Looking at this part's structure, we can see that Articles 29-36 speak about the *person* of Jesus Christ as the word of God become flesh. The following articles speak about his work, namely in his abasement on the cross, Articles 37-44, and in his exaltation at Easter, Articles 45-52. This makes three sets of eight articles each. Perhaps this threeness intends to mirror the threeness of the trinitarian God: the *Father,* from whom the Son, "anointed" by the Spirit,

---

50. From stanza 2 of the hymn "Ein' feste Burg," by Martin Luther. ET: "A Mighty Fortress Is Our God," in *LW* 53:285.

is what he is; *the Son,* who according to the will of the Father and "poor in spirit" gives himself up for us; and the Holy Spirit, in whom the Christ, resurrected and exalted by the Father, comes to us. This threeness surely also expresses what Article 31 presents: the threefold office of Christ as Prophet, Priest, and King. On the cross he carries out the priestly office toward us and for us and in his resurrection his kingly office toward us and for us. That leaves us to surmise that the text in the first Christological part, which speaks of the person of Christ, has Christ as Prophet in view. This would be a clue for the interpretation of this part: he is Prophet in that he discloses who he is in person and for us.

To review, the text speaks in a first step about the person of Christ, and in the second two steps about the work of Christ. Certainly the person and work of Christ cannot be separated from each other. For only in light of his work, and not prior to it, do we ascertain that he is an extraordinary person who is therefore able, for instance, to do various extraordinary things. Who he *is* in person, that he is true God and true human, is shown fully in his *work,* his humiliation on the cross, and his being raised to God, his heavenly Father. Therefore the person and work of Christ cannot be separated. For this reason, Articles 29-36 speak of the person of Christ in a way that always includes his saving work and what this means for us. Still, the text also distinguishes between the person and work of Christ. If it would not also make this distinction, the person of Christ would dissolve into its function, into its meaning, into the value and purpose which the fruit of his work has for us. It would then be hard to guard against the danger that the fruit is viewed removed from the tree on which it grew, that his work is viewed detached from his person. We would suddenly no longer have to do with him. Without being aware of it, we would again be dealing only with ourselves. We would no longer see that he is the Immanuel and that it is God who in him is with us in a gracious way. We would all at once be simply with ourselves. For this reason, the person and work of Christ, although they are not to be separated, still need to be distinguished. And for this reason, the discussion is first about the person of his work and then about the work of this person. Articles 29-36 speak first of his person. This again takes place in three steps.

First step, Articles 29/30: he is not only one, but *the* One. He is the One in the unity of the "Son of God" with the man Jesus. If God so loved the world that God gave the Son, this means that yes, the giver of the love and the gift of this love are to be distinguished, but not separated. For in the gift, the giver's own self is given. The gift is to this extent one with the giver, or in the old theological language, the Son with the Father. We must now go further: the gift, the Son, in whom God loved the world so much, is one with a particular, concrete human by the name of Jesus, datable in a particular time and place. He is bound so indissolubly with this name that we can also say conversely: we misunderstand this human being when we see him simply as one human among others, detached from, and not one with him who is the gift of the giver, the Son of the Father. "Even though we once knew Christ from a human point of view, we know him no longer in that way," says Paul in 2 Corinthians 5:16. This cannot contest his incarnation, or imply that it is no longer important for us today. But it contradicts the separation of this human from the One who is the gift of the giver: the only begotten Son of *the* Father whose self-giving in him is the demonstration of God's definitive love for the world. So he is *the* One and not just one among others.

So Jesus is qualitatively different from the sort of person who is one among other exceptional human beings. There are such persons. Article 30 calls them "saints." There are more such saints than one might think. There are also Protestant saints: Martin Luther King and Dietrich Bonhoeffer are often mentioned as examples. Why are we not accustomed to mention those who do not appear at all in books and newspapers? Paul calls the whole congregation a gathering of saints, without any irony (1 Cor. 1:2). Saints are people who are in some way impressive, whom we can well take as models — so long as they do not bind us to themselves. Such models are helpful so long as they are strictly only witnesses of the One who on his part is also a witness, also a model, but qualitatively more and different than that. If we do not see this difference, if on the one hand these models captivate us all too much and if on the other hand we see Jesus only in this roster of model human beings, then what the Heidelberg says applies to us: "Even though they may boast of belonging to him, they deny the only savior Jesus by such actions" (Art. 30). He is distinguished in just one way from such models and from our interpretation of him as just a model. But this difference is basic. Jesus is not distinguished by a spiritless "claim of absoluteness," which is always maintained only in murky delusion. He is different because he does, and is able to do, what the others neither do nor are able to do: "He saves us from our sins," as Article 29 quotes Matthew 1:21. Those "saints" also depend on him. And if they are genuine saints they will know this and not deny it. He is what they are not: the Immanuel, the God with us, as Matthew 1 later states. He is with us so completely that in his great love he is with us sinners in such a way that sin can no longer separate us from him. Rather, because of his being with us, sin, which is what really separates us from God, must really depart from us. In this way he is the One.

Second step: The special *names* of Jesus — he is called Christ (Art. 31), Son of God (Art. 33), and Lord, *Kyrios* (Art. 34). It is a productive idea to develop Christology, the doctrine of his person, not by means of the old doctrine of the "two natures" of Christ (true God and true human), but by means of his *names*. This says: He, the One, is no anonymous principle. He, as the subject of his work, is really a person, so that he is namable and addressable, can be called by his name. If we confess that we are his, we confess his name. The early church did not "attribute" these names to him, as is claimed again and again. This may be historically correct, but theologically it is extremely incorrect. For then you would have to understand the whole process as parallel with the name-giving right of parents, who in the exercise of this right declare a child as theirs, as their progeny. But Jesus as the Christ, the Son of God, the Lord, is not the progeny of early Christianity. Just the reverse: it is his progeny. If you want, you can say that the early church attributed these names to him, but only because these names apply and belong to him. The Heidelberg gives a helpful clue in this matter by connecting Jesus' person with his office of Prophet. Far from being who he is because we ascribe all kinds of titles to him, he lets us know who he is in a prophetic way, as God reveals it through him. His name, which according to Philippians 2:9 is above every name, "God . . . gave him . . . ." Therefore he has a name above all names and there is "no other name under heaven given among mortals by which we must be saved" (Acts 4:12). So we have to understand what his names connote not by what these names connote or connoted independently of him, but as they are interpreted through the reality of his person and his work.

The key statement of the second step is Article 31, which presents Jesus Christ to us as the one who holds and carries out a threefold office: Prophet, Priest, and King. The conjecture that calling Jesus by the three names — Christ, Son of God, and Lord — stands in an inner connection with these three offices may not be far off the mark. In the name "Lord," or *Kyrios*, the connection with his kingly office is obvious (Art. 34). He is Lord and deals with us in a royal way by acquiring us as his possession. Yet he does not do this in an authoritarian, proprietary way, as earthly power-holders are wont to do. Rather, he does it in a way that follows his own rule: "You know that the rulers of the Gentiles lord it over them . . . . It will not be so among you, but whoever wishes to be great among you must be your servant" (Matt. 20:25-26). Accordingly, he makes us his possession by giving himself to be ours and offers himself for us. So, to become his possession does not mean our enslavement, but rather redemption, having our freedom bought, our liberation from slavery, out of "sin and the power of the devil."

Correspondingly, the explanation of the name *Son* in Article 33 could be linked with the exercise of the priestly office by Christ. How does it come about that we are so close to God, that we may be called God's children, beings with whom God is so closely bound that we are God's? No, it is not just naturally so. We are so near to God only because God has come so close to us — so close that in the eternal Son God has become our brother in time, and that God has come in him to aid us in a priestly way. God has come to us who are endlessly distant and alienated from God. Therefore it is because of "grace" that this is so.

Following through on this analysis, it seems to make good sense to see Article 31 as related to the prophetic office of Jesus. The initial statement about who Jesus is shows by its contents that it is indeed the key statement, because it says that Jesus in his prophetic office as "the Anointed One" discloses who he is, and who he is for us. The answer goes: he is the holder and enactor of the threefold office as Prophet, Priest, and King. In this statement, four things are important to note:

1. It is crucial that the person of *the* work in which God is demonstrated as the God who is with us is not in the plan simply by his own initiative. Here God in person is at work, the threefold God. Otherwise it would not really be God who is with us. To be sure, it is the "Son," but he who was "ordained by God the Father" and "anointed by the Holy Spirit." Clearly his three offices are also specially correlated with the trinitarian three: as Prophet he reveals the "will of *God*," as Priest the *Son* advocates for us, and as King he rules us with "Word and *Spirit*." Insofar as Christ unites these three offices in himself and exercises them for us, his threefold office is a parable, an analogy of the threeness of God. And it is presented in such a way that Christ does a threefold work, but does not do three different things. In this threefold work he does just one thing: he functions thrice as our one savior, who as prophet reveals God's counsel for our salvation, who as priest gives himself for our salvation, who as king protects and preserves us in the same salvation.

2. Article 31 presents itself as an interpretation of Christ as the title of Jesus. "Christ" in English means "anointed one." In Hebrew the word is "Messiah." This name brings out directly the connection of his person with

the Old Testament and with the history of Israel, a connection that is not immediately obvious in the names God's Son and Lord. Already in Article 19, which understands the Old Testament as a witness to the gospel, there was in its unique threefold structuring of the Old Testament witness an allusion to the threefold office of Christ. At any rate, the three offices are Prophet, Priest, and King, the three typical functions that already in the history of Israel are carried out alongside one another, complementing one another. And now the assertion is significant that Jesus the Christ is the Messiah in that he actually is nothing other and does nothing other than what in its way already took place in Israel. It is new that he unites these three functions in himself. It is new that these three functions receive a new, radical sharpening. For what takes place here in one and the same event, in one and the same person, is the revelation, the sacrificial fulfillment and victorious affirmation of the self-giving of God for our salvation. But even this newness is actually nothing strange to Israel. It is not the founding of "another religion," or the eliminating of the history of Israel. On the contrary, it is the definitive confirmation of the assurance by which Israel has already been living, and the fulfillment — the completion and fullness of what has been promised to it. This fullness is witnessed to by the fact that through it the "full number of the Gentiles" (Rom. 11:25) now also has admittance to the people of God.

3. On the content of the statement: Christ carries out the priestly office in his humiliation, the kingly office in his exaltation; both together are the one work of Christ. In this double work God is with us in that Christ steps in for us. In his priestly task he is more than just a priest; he is the "sole high priest." For he does not simply offer something, but rather, as the Son of God, gives himself — for our good. In this way he saves us; in this way he sets us free from our separation from God. For this reason his exaltation does not mean that his humiliation, and thus his priestly function, are over and done with. He carries on these functions continually in that he "ever" intercedes before God for us. Therefore in his kingly function as well he is no abstract holder of power. He is not one of those who try to get results with the carrot first, and when that does not succeed, bring out the stick. This is why he is the king with the crown of thorns (John 18:37), the Lamb that was slain for us, on the throne (Rev. 5:12). This is why the instruments of his power are not decrees and machine guns, but "Word and Spirit."

In his exaltation and kingly function Christ does not surpass the work of our salvation with yet another and allegedly more powerful act. No, he "defends and sustains us in the redemption he has gained for us"; he guards us from the constant temptation of looking for our salvation in something else; and he keeps us *in this salvation,* holds us fast and does not let go those whom he has set free from their separation from God. In this way he towers above all earthly power-holders. In this way he is not one, but *the* "eternal king." And in this way he is not one, but *the* prophet, the "ultimate prophet." He is this not just because he "reveals to us God's secret counsel and will" — all decent prophets do that. He is the chief prophet because the "secret counsel and will" of God that he reveals is identical with the saving work of Jesus Christ. He "reveals" that what *he* does there is the deed and will of *God.* In doing this he is the one prophet who reveals himself, who discloses his own work as God's salvation for us. The perception that his work, his priestly humiliation and kingly exaltation, is our liberation by God, is an understanding that does not rest on our own arbitrary interpretation. We owe this knowledge to the prophetic work of Christ alone, that is, to the fact that he tells us this and reveals it.

It is therefore not the case that the "secret counsel and will" of God is at first hidden from us, and then after it has been revealed is no longer hidden at all. Just as Christ in his kingly office does not cease carrying out his priestly office, so the hiddenness of God's will does not entirely cease for us after Christ reveals it. We do not know anything about the hiddenness of God's will if we do not know who the God is who is hidden from us, that is, if God's will is not already in some measure revealed to us. As it is revealed to us, we know that there is more that remains hidden. God is continually inaccessible to us, and is knowable only as we always depend on having disclosed to us again and again that the work of Jesus Christ is God's salvation for us. In this way Christ is now also the "ultimate prophet," as he is the only high priest and the eternal king.

4. Article 32 brings to light that Jesus' intervention "for us" in his work aims totally at being "with us." A great deal of intervention by humans for others means the disenfranchisement of these others. The intervention of the "Führer" for the German people meant that the German people were rendered mindless and speechless. And some people today would understand democracy in a way that has the people give their voice away to politicians, or let the media say what their opinion is. But Christ's action for us is of another kind. In him God intervenes *for* us in order to be *with* us. God's purpose is not to turn us off, but to grant us participation and voice. God intervenes for us not so that we are disenfranchised, but so that we are included as responsible partners. God steps into our place so that it may truly be our place, in which we are with God and God with us. The sense of

the uniqueness in which Christ carries out the threefold office is not that he is alone, over against us. Rather, the uniqueness consists in the fact that only in his stepping in *for* us does he come to be *with* us. If you were to dispute the "for us," then you would dispute that we really need salvation. If you were to dispute the "with us," then you would say that Christ's intervention for us does not lead to freedom. But the fact that Christ's intervention for us not only aims at our participation, but produces it, shows that the issue is our freedom. Christ's work brings about our active sharing in his threefold office.

By faith in Christ we are so bound with him that we ourselves are anointed, called, ordained, and installed as prophets, priests, and kings. This holds for us *all*. The clergy are no more anointed and ordained than the so-called laity, the laity no less than the so-called clergy. This is part of the newness of the New Testament form of the covenant. All are installed by Christ, in whom they believe, and because they believe in him. They are not competitors with Christ, but are under his primacy and leadership, and so with him are prophets, priests, and kings. They are prophets by virtue of the fact that they confess the savior — that they *themselves* belong to *him*. They are priests in their giving thanks for his priestly intervention for us in order that we might be saved. But this giving thanks includes nothing less than their stepping in *themselves* and becoming engaged. And they are kings in that they live as people redeemed, as those who are free within *themselves* — "with a free and good conscience." Here the Heidelberg is quoting Calvin's Geneva Catechism: *avec liberté de conscience,*[51] that is, "with freedom of conscience." This emancipating concept appeared in the midst of the Reformation. In this freedom of conscience they are engaged in battle — not with this and that person, but with sin and the devil, with injustice and hardheartedness. They will no longer have to battle this way "in eternity." For then they will be completely at peace. In this sense they will "reign," as the Lamb on the throne and with him as "the meek" who will "inherit the earth" (Matt. 5:5). So God's being for us is fulfilled in God's being with us. Thus talk about who Christ is belongs with talk about what we become through him.

Third Step (Art. 35-36): the wonder of Christmas. Will we ever be in a position to look at the wonder of Christmas without its being distorted by Christmas shopping and Christmas customs? The wonder consists simply

---

51. According to *Bekenntnisschriften und Kirchenordnungen der nach Gottes Wort reformierte Kirche*, ed. W. Niesel (Zurich/Köln: Theologischer Verlag, 1985), pp. 7, 21.

and yet incomprehensibly in the positive answer to the question: "Are you the one who is to come, or are we to wait for another?" (Matt. 11:3). Christmas says: This is the one who is to come. The prophet, the priest, the king — is this child born in a manger, Jesus of Nazareth. " To you is born this day . . . a Savior" (Luke 2:11).

Whom all the world could not enwrap
Lieth he in Mary's lap;[52]

God's own child, infant mild, is bonded with our blood.[53]

This blood that binds Jesus to us is first of all *Jewish* blood. He is the "descendant of David." He belongs to this people whom God has graciously chosen and whose election God does not revoke in Christ, but more than ever bases on divine grace, which is as free as it is faithful. In Christ the "Lord God of Israel . . . has looked favorably on his people and redeemed them"; in him God has "shown the mercy promised to our ancestors and has remembered his holy covenant, the oath that he swore to our ancestor Abraham" (Luke 1:68, 72). In Christ, God has fulfilled this covenant, and not made it obsolete. God has so fulfilled it that by virtue of the grace that reconciles sinners, Israel cannot be excluded from the covenant. By virtue of this same grace, the "light for revelation to the Gentiles" has now appeared (Luke 2:32) and they too are no longer excluded from this covenant. The savior is born for *them* also.

In this one person, the "true and eternal God took upon himself" *our* blood too, *ours* as well — yes, "human nature" *itself.* God has done this by taking on a human being who "in all things, except for sin" is like us *all.* God has done this by becoming, as the one "true and eternal God," *our* brother in this one man, and so accepting us as his "sisters and brothers." God has done so by taking this one person as our representative, and thus not simply *one* human, but in him nothing less than "human *nature.*" Therefore what this one person encounters, and what he does, benefits all humans. It is not the case that humans have exalted a human to godhood. That would be idolization of Jesus. Nor in this taking on of human nature

52. From stanza 3 of the hymn "Gelobet seist du, Jesus Christ" by M. Luther. ET: "Praised Be Thou, Jesus Christ," in *LW* 53:241.
53. From stanza 2 of the hymn "Fröhlich soll mein Herze springen" ("My Heart Leaps with Joy"), by P. Gerhardt.

has human nature been transformed into divine nature. That would be idolization of humanity. But the true God, without ceasing to be God, without self-transformation into something else, but in carrying out the divine nature, has united Godself with humanity in this one Jewish human so inseparably that *the* human being is not without God and God is not without *the* human being. This took place not through human skill and not on the basis of an aptitude of human nature. It was rather solely God's work, the wonder of God's pure, gracious mercy. This took place solely "through the action of the Holy Spirit," which is the spirit of being a child of God. This is underscored in a symbolic way by language about the virginity of Mary. It would be nonsense to understand this language to mean that the child in the manger is the product of a marriage of the Spirit and Mary, still more to say that this establishes the God-humanness of Jesus. In that way what would have come about would be a chimera, and not what actually happens, which is that the true God, in and with the one human being, takes on true human nature. That this happens is the wonder of Christmas. Genuine wonders we cannot explain without missing their meaning. We can explain them neither by biological laws nor by other laws of nature, nor by the suspension of these. Genuine wonders we can only point to. The story of the virginity of Mary we can, without qualms, call a legend, which furthermore has little backing in the New Testament. But there are deeply meaningful legends. And this could be one — as a pointer to the fact that it is purely and solely God's work and wonder that in the One born for us *God* is with *us*. As a sign of *this*, Mary is lifted up here. This is done in such a way that the male, who often thinks he can make history because of his potency, here for once can make no history. The virginity of Mary is a pointer to the fact that the incarnation of God in Christ is a divine gift and not a human product. And the preferential treatment of Mary is a pointer to teach us that all humans are what they are only through God's grace, and not through what they make of themselves. It is a serious question whether the cult of Mary, which oddly is so zealously carried on by the male-dominated Roman Church, does not miss the point of the legend. The same question could be put to the thesis of mysticism, that each pious soul carries in itself the power to be a bearer of God. For the legend wants rather to be a pointer to the fact that God alone brings it about that the true God, in the one who has become like us, is our brother and so has taken on our human nature, our being human.[54]

54. Olevianus later distanced himself from Article 36. Cf. W. Hollweg: *Neue Unter-*

3.2.2. God's Severe Visitation (Art. 37-44)

The coexistence of the free God and the free human does not come about by two partners standing on the same level uniting in a common life. The human being is not available from the outset to be a partner. Rather, God first of all creates the human being. Yes, God loves humans before they are even here. What precedes the existence of humans theologically, however, takes place in history, in the middle of time: in the incarnation of the Word, or of the Son of God. No greater affirmation of humans can be imagined than what takes place in the incarnation. In it God does not declare from afar: "It is beautiful that you are there!" Rather, God takes on humanity *itself* in this one human person: God takes humanity into fellowship. In the incarnation, God is not transformed into a human, nor are we humans transformed into gods. In it God is intimately bonded with us and we with God. But what does God enter into when taking on humanity so radically? God comes for relationship with us. But we are *sinners*. We humans are not where we belong. We are far from God, lost in a strange land. For God to join with humans would in these circumstances mean that God searches for and finds them so that they come home out of their distance and alienation. But for God to join with humans means something for God too. It means for God — a visitation without parallel, suffering in which an abyss of pain is inflicted. Nevertheless, God joins us. From this we can see that God is actually our God, and to what lengths God goes for us.

We are speaking of the humiliation, of the cross of Jesus Christ. Not for nothing does this stand in the center of the Christian confession of faith. Paul writes: "I decided to know nothing among you except Jesus Christ, and him crucified" (1 Cor. 2:2). In the same context: his message is "about the cross" which "to us who are being saved . . . is the power of God" (1 Cor.

---

suchungen zur Geschichte und Lehre des H. Katechismus (Neukirchen-Vluyn: Neukirchener Verlag, 1961), chap 1, n. 14-124ff. One does not have to deduce from this that he is not co-author of the Heidelberg, as Hollweg thinks. That would be to maintain that a good writer dare not later revise his or her work! Nevertheless, Olevianus's critique is perceptive: We have to distinguish between the person and the work of Christ. To be sure, the two are not to be separated. But Article 36 goes a step too far by saying: this person as such is the saving work of God; by means of its constitution out of two natures "he removes from God's sight my sin." That is a step toward an orthodoxy in which Christ does not free us by stepping in for us, but in which faith in the equipment of this person with a divine and a human nature is in itself salvific.

1:18). Martin Luther holds that there is "in Christ crucified the true theology and knowledge of God."[55] John Calvin called the cross the "transmutation of nature."[56] The same view is expressed in the old Roman Good Friday liturgy: "Greetings, cross, you who are our only hope."[57] Clearly we enter the holy of holies when we confess in the Christian faith: "Christ died for us." What important confession do we make in this statement?

In answering this question, we also have in mind opposition to a theology of the cross circulating in the church today. We hear something like this: it is inconsistent with God's love to have sacrificed God's own son in order to be able to love humans. That is a distressingly cruel God who forages on the blood of a murder victim and then claims that this is to achieve a good purpose. And people who believe in such a God thereby become used to cruelty, to sadism, and so smilingly count suffering as necessary for allegedly higher purposes. This opposition to a theology of the cross claims that Jesus' death on the cross was nothing but a wicked murder that stood in contradiction to the love of God that Jesus himself modeled for us. It was a murder in the long line of other cruelties of humans to their fellow humans. Therefore, we have to work hard at practicing the love of Jesus today so that this kind of thing does not happen again. It is almost as though these objectors want to say: if *we* had been there, we would have prevented this murder, and world history would have taken a happier course. And God? Well, God rates as demonstrably powerless, and therefore should be partly accused, and partly excused, insofar as God regrets what happened there.

As a matter of fact, this view has been around for a long time,[58] and it must be said that it sketches a crude caricature of the biblical theology of the cross. But as so often happens when people make a distorted portrait, the purportedly corrective view throws out with the distorted portrait the good substance as well. In this case it is the gospel in "the message of the cross." For this critique of the theology of the cross, already in its first appearances long ago, had its backbone in a twofold protest. On the one hand the protest was against the idea that in the suffering on the cross something took place "for us," something we ourselves could not do, and yet was needed for our salvation. That was considered "immoral." What

55. M. Luther, WA 1:362. LW 31:52-53.
56. J. Calvin, Institutes II.16.6.
57. U. Bomm, ed., Das Volksmessbuch (Einsiedeln/Köln: Benziger, 1947⁴), p. 361.
58. K. Aner, Die Theologie der Lessingzeit (Halle: Niemeyer, 1929), pp. 285ff.

that meant was: we become good persons not through what someone else does "for us," no matter who it is, but only by means of the good that we *ourselves* accomplish. Modern society, in its obsession with production, achievement, and success, spreads this idea with proud slogans like: "What costs me nothing has no value." If no one can intervene for us, and what is more, dare not intervene for us, then the death of Jesus cannot, dare not, have the meaning that I depend on something I do not myself achieve. Then this cross is really not needed. So I must attribute a new meaning to it — a meaning that will definitively bar the cross from being understood in that old sense. Perhaps it will then be understood as a regrettable death, or perhaps as an example of the law of nature always and everywhere valid, to which we all have to resign ourselves, as expressed in the phrase "die in order to become." This critique, in its core, excludes what the gospel of Jesus Christ tells us in its core, that we definitely live not from what we do, but from what God does "for us," that we exist solely by God's compassion for us.

That older objection's insistence that only the good we ourselves accomplish counts was nevertheless able to refer also to the love of God, or to the example of the good man of Nazareth. But the objection had a second point. This was directed against the idea that God's love could have anything at all to do with anger or judgment on God's part. That was rejected as a sub-Christian, cruel "image of God" — a Jewish image of God, as one said until 1945. Today one says: an image of God that is cruel toward Jews, anti-judaistic. In one way or another, what God could be angry about slips out of view: human sin. What could God be angry about if sin is not very great after all?! In this way, God's love threatens to become an ideal, and so an ethical challenge to emulate this ideal of love. And since we are not really such sinners, we are capable of rising to the challenge. This excludes an understanding of the cross as God in divine love dealing effectively with human sin. We no longer need God to step in for us. No, God does not have to; *we* shall step in — for suffering people. The cross is now interpreted as a general symbol for their pain and their appeal to our sympathy. Or we are supposed to step in for God who is there shown to be powerless. Notice that this is after we have declared God powerless because we no longer need God to intervene for us, because we have denied God the role of redeemer in order to attribute it to ourselves. So in place of redemption *through* the cross appears redemption *from* the cross. The love given by God and Christ is indeed spoken about, but spoken about in such a way that it is no longer about God's free act of grace for us. Rather, it is about a demand on us, and about our salvation depending on the fulfillment of this demand. The price required by this view is too high. It abandons the gospel.

To be fair, we have to recognize that this critique of the "cross" is nevertheless very much aware of an older view of the cross widespread in Christendom. This older view offered a picture of the cross of Jesus Christ no less distorted. Here also the cross became a symbol — of battle against other people. The belief was that you should understand the cross as a commission to exact revenge on Jews or other "unbelievers" for "the murder of God." Thus the word "cross" came into impossible word combinations: "crusade," "army of the cross," "knight of the cross," "hooked cross" [swastika]. The symbol of the cross became blurred with that of the drawn sword and was then painted on steel helmets and tanks. On the basis of the "blood" of the crucified one, people glorified infernal bloodthirstiness, and put a hero's death for one's native land and one's own people on a par with the sacrifice of the crucified one. So the cross became the "symbol of the Christian West," and its manifold decorative uses today should not blind us to how much shock and horror this symbol has already spread. In light of this grotesque misuse you can understand Luther's anger, in which he declared: "for this reason I would that all crosses be knocked down."[59] But we also have to ask: Have not even some of the best theologians contributed to this misuse? Have they not done so when they took the cross to mean all kinds of troubles that confront us? By doing this they made the cross into a general, transferable matter that is for *us* to carry! After it had been made into our cross, could it not then be arbitrarily taken into our hand, or rejected?

We will not be able to deal with that critique of the theology of the cross without also dealing with this misuse. If in the former the gospel is not understood, in the latter it is covered with a dark cloud. In order to understand the *gospel* rightly we will try to spell out "the word of the cross" anew. The New Testament testifies to us "that Christ died for sins" (1 Cor. 15:3) — or as Article 42 says: "Christ died for us," namely for us sinners. What does this mean?

1. The phrase "for us" is to be understood here in the strictest sense. What we can do "for others" is always necessarily, and often also luckily, very limited. They are perhaps at the moment not able to do it for themselves, but in principle they can do it. Our help should aim to enable them

59. M. Luther, *WA* 10:3, 335.

to get in a position to once more help themselves as much as possible. But on the cross of Jesus Christ something was accomplished "for us" which we fundamentally could never do for ourselves. We are always and eternally dependent on it being done "for us." The cross of Christ is for this very reason a "stumbling block" (Gal. 5:11; 1 Cor. 1:23). The "for us" certainly also means: without our help. It is therefore a judgment on our efforts for self-justification and self-redemption. This is not because we are supposed to be kept weak, but because in these efforts we blind ourselves to our actual unrighteousness and unredeemed lifestyle, because in the self-idolatry we thereby commit, we can only come to ruin. The "for us" rules out that here simply a person like ourselves dies, and rules out classifying this death simply as an execution. It also rules out the idea that the uniqueness of this death is to be seen in the fact that here more was suffered humanly than in other cases where humans have been tortured to death by humans. The uniqueness of this death lies fundamentally, and in a way that shakes the foundations, in the fact that it is "the death of the *Son of God*" (Art. 40). This means that we can understand the uniqueness of this death only after the fact, only in the light of Easter, in which Jesus is shown to be the Son of God, and only by the faith in him thereby awakened. If we do not see this, we do not see anything of what it is all about. We see only a murder, which we lament, or whose perpetrators we accuse, and one way or another see the task of preventing this kind of thing in the future.

In the judgment of H. J. Iwand, modern theology "has stricken the divinity of Jesus in order to understand his death, and has thereby canceled the very point on which everything depends"; as a consequence, it has "made the death of Jesus simply an ethical matter."[60] The point on which everything depends is that here (in unity with the human taken on by God) the Son of God exposes himself to suffering, death, and abandonment by God — no apparent death, but real death (Art. 41), not simply our mortality, but an accursed death (Art. 39). The point on which everything depends is that here something takes place "for us," for our human nature, taken on by God in Christ — for us sinners. This we can never do ourselves, not because we are not "the Son of God," but because we are sinners. But just think what this means: God "did not withhold his own Son, but gave him up for all of us" (Rom. 8:32)! "Here is the Lamb of God who

---

60. According to *Diskussion um Kreuz und Auferstehung*, ed. B. Klappert (Wuppertal: Aussaat Verlag, 1971), p. 292.

takes away the sin of the world!" (John 1:29). Just think what it means — if in this gift the Giver's own self is given, if here suffering, death, and abandonment by God are inflicted on God's own self! "Unimagined dread, *God himself* lies dead."[61] Then in this suffering, death, and abandonment by God, God is present in person, and not absent! Then the conception that held sway among the ancient Greeks, and also for a long time in the church, that God is too lofty to be affected by such things, is shattered. If in view of the cross you can talk about a sacrifice, then it is first of all in the sense that God — without ceasing to be God — sacrifices being untouched by suffering and death.

2. But here a human being suffers as well. According to Article 17, the Son of God, who is "true God," must "bear in his humanity the burden of God's wrath." What is the significance of the Son of God's bearing this weight in his *humanity,* even though a burden is involved which "no mere creature can bear" (Art. 14)? Without understanding that here a human being suffers as well, we will not understand that the suffering of the Son of God "*for* us" really takes place "for *us.*" This includes the assertion that he suffered as a human *for* us, and not only *like* us. Surely, he also suffered as others do — otherwise he would not be "like his fellow human beings in all things, except for sin" (Art. 35). But this "except for sin" indicates to us that in his humanity he suffered something more than even the most tortured person, which he did not have to suffer, except that he suffered it for us. Think about the mystery of the humanity of Jesus! It consists in the fact "that the eternal Son of God . . . took upon himself" *a* human being, to be sure, but in this one human being took "our true human nature" into unity with himself (Art. 35). This is a bold statement. But if we did not say this, how could we say that in him God has chosen, loved, and reconciled us? Still, we do not need to believe this statement before we attempt to understand the cross. The statement just interprets the "for us" of the death of Jesus on the cross. The "for us" has to do with what the old concept of substitution asserts. This concept shuts the door on all Christian claims of wanting to represent Jesus. It counters them with the reverse assertion that he has represented us in order to do and suffer something we neither can nor need to do and suffer. What is said about him, that he has died to take away the sin of "the whole human race" (Art. 37), cannot be said of the death of any human being, however sacrificial. Can this be said meaningfully in any other way than that this has befallen humanity, whom the Son

61. J. Rist, *Himmlische Lieder* (1641/42) (Hildesheim/New York: Olms, 1976), p. 13.

of God in the one man Jesus has taken into unity with himself? So that now precisely in the place where "the human being," "human nature," "the whole human race" stands, it is not only one person who stands, but in truth we are there as well! He stands in our place, not so that we disappear, or so that we once again need to suffer what he has suffered. Rather, he stands in our place so that what he does and suffers there really encounters *us,* really takes place for us.

3. "Christ died for us" and "for our sins." This means that in this death God's Son steps in for us in such a way that God's own self is wounded. This means in turn that in this death the man Jesus steps into our place in such a way that this has validity and consequence for us — for the whole human race. If this is so, then this death is by no means simply a regrettable accident that would have been avoidable with some good will on the part of his contemporaries, or for which we dare accuse them in particular. Then what takes place here is God's will. This is underscored in Article 37 by a formulation that explains the strange fact, observed since the early days of the Apostles' Creed, that this old confession goes directly from Christmas to Good Friday, leaving out the earthly life of Jesus. The formulation explains that the whole earthly way of Jesus was a run-up to Good Friday, because what was laid upon him at that time "he bore in body and soul . . . during his entire life on earth." His whole earthly way is from the beginning (Art. 36) to the end one single humiliation of the Son of God — descent, offering, suffering, hiddenness of God.

That it is the Son of God who is confronted with this and who bears it, is first shown by the light of Easter, when the disciples, looking back at Jesus' earthly life, were finally able to recognize what had been breaking through. Yet on the whole, the gospels are passion narratives with introductions.[62] And it is as the Christmas song of Paul Gerhardt says: "You have come to be with us to suffer in our place."[63] Or Jochen Klepper: "Before your manger yawns the grave."[64] As Jesus says in Matthew 20:28: "The Son of Man came . . . to give his life a ransom for many." The cross, the goal of his earthly life, determines the way to it so much that the "passion nar-

---

62. M. Kähler, *Der sogenannte historische Jesus und der geschichtliche, biblische Christus* (Leipzig: Deichert Verlag, 1892), pp. 59-60. ET: *The So-called Historical Jesus and the Historic Biblical Christ* (Philadelphia: Fortress Press, 1964), pp. 80-81.

63. From stanza 4 of the hymn "Ich steh an deiner Krippen hier" ("I Stand Here by Your Manger"), by P. Gerhardt.

64. From stanza 3 of the hymn "Du Kind, zu dieser heilgen Zeit" ("You, Child, at This Holy Time"), by J. Klepper.

rative" under Pontius Pilate only fulfills and seals what has long since been announced. To the assertion of Pilate that it stands in his power to crucify Jesus or let him go, Jesus answers: No, "you would have no power over me unless it had been given you from above" (John 19:10-11). This shows that his death on the cross is no coincidence and no accident, no breakdown, which God or we would have to regret, to avenge, or to make good for. His death on the cross takes place with divine consideration because God wills to be subjected to this treatment; yes, not only wills, but more: "Was it not necessary that the Messiah should suffer these things?" (Luke 24:26, 46; Matt. 17:12).

4. But why this "will" and "must"? More pressing than the question that so often presses upon us: "Why does God allow this and that?" is the other question, which is really the only genuine key to the first question: Why does God require what is required in not sparing God's Son? Let us not muddle everything with the thought of divine masochism! Suffering is not fun, not for God either. A person for whom it is fun is sick and needs to go for treatment. But God lays Godself open to suffering for this reason, and this reason only: God does not want something for Godself, but for us. This is why God is exposed to suffering — because God joins with us. Yet it is not only the fact that God joins with us that causes God suffering. God gladly grants existence to us creatures, so different from God. Why should it cause God pain to join with us creatures and not instead — joy? God affirms our existence in the incarnation. Creaturely existence is not alienation from God, but rather God's loving intention. God's joining with us in the Son surely includes God's joining with the mortal, time-bound human, for whom it is appointed at some time to die. In the incarnation of the Son, God affirms not only our existence, but also affirms us in the limitation of our existence, and so discloses that our end does not have to be an end with terror. Yes, in this way God discloses that our wish to make ourselves immortal is a delusion that gives rise to horrors without end. By entering into the life of us mortals in the incarnation of the Son, God shares our mortality from the heart and assures us of God's nearness and bond with us in our passing. Furthermore, in the fact that Jesus died a violent death, God now stands in *one* line with all those who become the victims of human violence. The particular form of his death assures them that while humans cast them out, God is in solidarity with them. God's suffering in solidarity with them is the clear sign that it is not only an act against humanity, but is godlessness when humans cut short the life of other humans. All of this can be said because the suffering of this one person

means being "with us" as well. His suffering for us includes also a suffering with us.

But with all this, Christ's suffering for us is not yet seen and not yet explained. The meaning of "for us" first dawns on us when the fact of human sin dawns on us. It is not a perverse matter to be human, but we live in a perverse humanity. It is not that our creaturely existence is bad, but the way we live and the condition we are in are bad. Because our life is therefore a life with horrors, our death is also an end with horrors. And into this, our common lot, the Son of God, and in him God's own self, enters. God's own self is exposed to this in the human being taken on for us and in our place — "during his entire life on earth, but especially at the end of it" (Art. 37). What causes him pain is our perversity. This is what makes life suffering for him, and his death a cross. God would not seriously join with humans if God did not enter the human condition the way it is, and precisely because it is the way it is. And God would not really be able to bond with us without exposing Godself to this fact, and dealing with it: the fact of our sin and its misery.

5. This is what God exposes Godself to: our sin. Our sin does not just lie around like trash on the street, which you only have to pick up in order to get rid of it. God is exposed to our sin in such a way that it exposes God. God joins with us sinners as we sinners actively reject being joined with God. God dies *for* sinners as God is killed *by* sinners, as humans become concretely guilty in relation to God. God dies in such a way that around the crucified one a series of sinful humans press forward into the light. It is a representative selection out of humanity that does this — and indeed out of the better part of humanity: individuals from God's chosen people, representatives of church and state, members of the inner circle of Jesus' disciples, all of whom believe they can wash their hands in innocence. It is not some rascals who are involved here, in contrast to whom we could immediately think that we are better than they. It is nothing but well-intentioned people, who in their good intentions do not see their own sin, who think they can help themselves, and who on this account think they do not need his stepping in for them, who therefore do away with him. In these representatives, moreover, are the human beings of every age of history, perverse humans, who in their cave do not want their circles to be disturbed, and who try to send the disturber into the great beyond. This is why, in response to the question of guilt in the death of Jesus, it is evil foolishness to point at particular scapegoats, for example, at "the Jews." This is the damnable wickedness of sin, always looking for guilt in others, and so absolving oneself. This wickedness does not get any

better if, after we have absolved ourselves, we also good-naturedly absolve all others. This perverse foolishness is judged at the cross along with all the rest, so that here I can only say with Luther:

> *Our* huge sin and deep transgression
> On the cross nailed God's true Son.
> So on you, poor Judas, and on all called Jew
> We dare not heap abuse in hate;
> The guilt is ours, 'tis true.[65]

What will keep our finger from pointing at others, and turn it instead toward our ourselves, and what will make us stop accusing or excusing others in order to excuse ourselves, is to turn from concentrating on the sin of those who took part in the death of Jesus and instead look at the one who suffers and carries sin away. What sin is, and that it is so great that we cannot free ourselves from it, becomes clearer at the cross of Christ than anywhere else. It becomes clear by the fact that it takes nothing less than intervention on our behalf by the Son of God and the man Jesus bound with him in order to deal with sin — and us with it. "If we believe that Christ has redeemed men by his blood, we are bound to confess that the whole man was lost."[66] If he gives himself on the cross for *all*, then it is obvious that we *all* are under the more or less thick sheet of ice that is our self-righteousness and our struggle to redeem ourselves. We are all people in misery who fundamentally cannot help ourselves. And if on the cross he bears the sin which is directed at him, the very one who brings the grace of God to us, this shows clearly that the hard core, yes the hardest core of our sin is this: our hostility against grace, our No to the mercy of God. Sin is not primarily various kinds of misdeeds, but the denial of the goodness of God toward us misdoers. This sin is always much stronger where we do not transgress any law at all. And it asserts itself much more stubbornly among those who are close to him than among those who are far off.

6. By joining with us, God is exposed to our sin — and it is no accident that sin breaks out especially visibly and actively where God joins with us sinners. In a way, the Son of God is "patiently," that is, powerlessly exposed to this sin. If he were not, then at the very moment he joined us, he would have to withdraw from us. "No one keeps this misery from coming upon

65. M. Luther, *WA* 35:576.
66. M. Luther, *WA* 18:786. ET: *LW* 33:293.

you"[67] — least of all one of us. It is sheer religious arrogance on the part of sinners intent on self-redemption if they dare to want to save Christ from this, his powerlessness. But just as we dare not understand the almightiness of God in an abstract way, but only as the power of God's love, so now we dare not understand the powerlessness of God abstractly, as just passive suffering. God gives Godself for the cause of salvation, but God does not abdicate. We have to see God's powerlessness completely in the context of the power of God's love. If we omit this, we are able to say only that the Son of God became the innocent victim of some people who were responsible. We would need to say that he died *because of* the sin of these few, but not that he died *for* them. We would then not understand what everything depends on: that sin, which is more powerful than we, is at this very point not more powerful than God. We would not understand in what way this suffering, of all sufferings, affects God, and in what way it is here "the lamb of God who takes away the sins of the *world*" (John 1:29), really "*our* sins" (1 Peter 2:24), also the sins of those who were then no longer or not yet living. The New Testament witnesses to nothing less than this.

However, this becomes understandable only when we get clear in our heads that in the action of humans on the crucified one, God also is acting on him. In the verdict of the "worldly judge" it is also "the severe judgment of God" which takes place (Art. 38). In the powerlessness of God's Son, God is indeed powerful — powerful in "wrath." The Son of God not only suffers under the burden of these sins, he "bears" them, and does this because and in that he bears the just verdict of God on them, "the wrath of God against the whole human race" (Art. 37). He bears the No of God to the sin of all humans, and by virtue of this verdict, bears away all their sins. God's anger is no crazy outburst of rage that once it has blown its steam, and God has gotten a clear head again, God could become regretful about. God's anger is the unconditional, completely just verdict, which in its very justice is the annihilating condemnation of sin, of unrighteousness, of human misery. It is the No of God to humans themselves as doers of evil. If God were not in this sense angry and just, then God's *love* would be powerless and would always only put up with sin, but not do away with it. This is why it would be absurd to call the anger of God cruel. Sin is cruel in its hate against "God and my neighbor," and so against myself (Art. 5). To hate this sin without any ifs, ands, or buts, and to condemn it, is in truth the greatest boon that can ever come to the human race. The just anger of God

67. J. Rist, *Himmlische Lieder,* p. 13.

against the sinner is not only just. It is also a form of the love of God. This No to sin is full of a secret Yes to the sinner. This anger is the hidden form of the love of God for "the whole human race." On the cross it is only a *secret* Yes and a *hidden* love. For as the *manifest* No and the *manifest* anger it means what is without doubt horrible, that "the death of the cross was cursed by God" (Art. 39).

7. We come to the decisive point: by joining with us sinners, God is exposed not only to our sins, but above all to God's own No, which for the sake of God's justice and love must be spoken to our sin. By pronouncing the No, God is not automatically exposed to it. But because God loves us to whom the No must be spoken, God in love takes the harshness, the deadliness, the "sting" (1 Cor. 15:55) of the No to our sin onto God's own self, and into God's self, and locks it into Godself. Nowhere are we shown more exactly who God is than here, where God does this: takes away from us what separates us from God, what condemns us, by putting it onto Godself. What Article 37 calls the "atoning sacrifice" is exactly that — not that God sacrifices "something" for God's appeasement, but rather that in the Son, God sacrifices God's *own self.* God gives Godself away so that the divine No, exactly at the place where it would have to strike us and destroy us, instead falls only on God, wounds only God, so that it can no longer strike us. This is the "joyful exchange" of which Luther spoke,[68] and the "reversal of all things" of which Calvin spoke.[69] As the Heidelberg Catechism puts it, "he took upon himself the curse that lay on me" (Art. 39); the just judge "has already offered himself to the judgment of God for me, and has removed all the curse from me" (Art. 52). For by taking this upon himself for the sake of us people of sin, the Son of God has taken it away from us humans, and this burden is no longer on us. We are set free from it. This is why Christ "bore in body and soul the wrath of God against the whole human race": "so that through his suffering, as the only atoning sacrifice, he could redeem our body and soul from eternal damnation and could gain for us God's grace, righteousness, and eternal life" (Art. 37). It is not only true that "no mere creature can bear the burden of God's eternal wrath against sin" (Art. 14); none has to bear it anymore. We are unburdened from it, redeemed, liberated, because the Son of God did "bear" it (Art. 17).

The fact that God in the Son loads the whole No to our sins completely onto Godself means that the No is *for us* secretly a pure Yes, nothing

68. M. Luther, *WA* 7:25.
69. J. Calvin, *Institutes* II.16.6.

but love for us. And what is given us is not only love, but also God's righteousness! For God on the cross does not practice grace instead of justice, or love without judgment. Rather, God uses grace *in* judgment and love in a form that does justice. According to righteousness, God says No to our sins, and at the same time, according to the divine mercy, God does not let this No strike us. In this way we count as completely righteous before God, but on the basis of a righteousness given to us. For this reason, God does not first exercise judgment on us and then show us grace. Then God would be at first a harsh God, who would have to be "reconciled" and have the divine anger reacted to before being able to practice love. Then God's love would stand under the condition that it is only possible after penance has been accomplished through a sacrifice. Then it would be an open question whether God is satisfied with a sacrifice, or whether with new anger new sacrifices may be required and swallowed up. But the truth is that everything is just the reverse! It is not God who needs to be reconciled. "God was reconciling the world to himself" (2 Cor. 5:19). Not *in order to love* it, but *because* of loving it, God says No to sin and does this by making the burden of this No God's own concern, and by saying Yes to the sinner. For this reason, God's Yes, the love for us which God validates in judgment on sin, is irrevocable. Therefore the suffering, the "atoning sacrifice" of the Son of God, is the "only" one (Art. 37) — otherwise it would not be valid.

8. We dare not imagine this "joyful exchange" simply by the picture of shifting a burden from one shoulder to another, although as we have observed there is truth in this way of thinking, and nothing is to be taken away from it. But the truth of the cross goes beyond this picture, insofar as it has to do not with shifting guilt, but with abolishing it. Yes, it has to do with abolishing the very existence of the human being as the one who has brought about this guilt. In order to see this, we must look at the man whom the Son of God has taken into unity with himself and who in unity with him dies on the cross. This man is here in our place. He bears a burden that is actually foreign to him, since in his own person, he is without sin (Art. 38). And still he bears this burden entirely as his own, so fully does he step into our place. In that joyful exchange our sin is taken from us, yet not just for our relief. In this action, the human as the one who commits sin is taken away, is made into an old, outmoded, obsolete human. The action platform is pulled out from underneath this old sinful human. For in the dying of this one man, it is not only this one who dies. In this one man *the* human being dies (2 Cor. 5:14-15), the one whom the Son of God in his bonding with "true human nature . . . took upon himself" (Art. 35). In the

death of this one man on the cross, the existence of *the* sinful human being is crossed out. If he is there in our place, then we are also there in him, as the sinners we are, who have become an "old," obsolete, abolished human. "We know that our old self was crucified with him so that the body of sin might be destroyed, and we might no longer be enslaved to sin" (Rom. 6:6; cf. Art. 43). He removes our sin by removing us, its perpetrators, in himself. He ousts our human perversity by ousting *himself* as the perverse one, so that sin no longer has a claim on us. So we are freed from the delusion of having a capacity for it.

But in all this we belong to him in a completely different way than our sin does. Our sin is his in order for him to reject it, and so, as rejected, as destined to pass away, he takes it upon himself. We, however, are his in such a way that he does not reject us, but affirms us, and as affirmed by him destines us to life, to life with him. He affirms us and binds himself with us in the way he separates us radically from the separating power of sin. He makes us his possession in the way he dispossesses us of our sins. They no longer belong to us; therefore, we belong to him.

9. God's stepping in for us in the Son this way has practical consequences for us that make clear that faith in the crucified one by no means allows us to stand back as uninvolved spectators. These consequences mean that what took place on the cross impinges mightily on our life. The fact that Christ interposed himself "in body and soul" for the redemption of our "body and soul" leaves its traces. It is intended to shape our living and dying, and it does shape the living of those who believe in the crucified one. But let us be clear that all the various, deeply formative consequences are expressions of the one consequence: that we no longer have to bear what Christ bore on the cross, and that what he suffered there we can never suffer.

This has consequences — (a) for our relation to our own dying (Art. 42). To be sure, we still die. But this death is no longer for us a curse, no longer laden with the terrors of a separating power. Yes, Jesus says in John 5:24 that those who believe in him actually have death no longer before them, but behind them: "Very truly I tell you, anyone who hears my word and believes him who sent me has eternal life, and does not come under judgment, but has passed from death to life." Whatever the dying that lies before me will mean, it can no longer have the meaning of separating me from the love of God, since in Christ God has taken away the anger and curse, that is, what separates us from God. Since our old human nature, which was detached from God, has died in the death of Christ, our ceasing to live in time will not mean that we cease belonging to him.

194

(b) (Art. 43) Christ's bearing the No of God to the sinful human being in our place means that the ground is pulled out from under the feet of this human being. This one's right to exist is withdrawn. To be sure, this human being projects itself into our life again and again, but in a completely unauthorized way. Therefore we cannot believe in the crucified one without fighting against this devilment in our earthly life. In doing this we do not fight against others, as the old human being loves to do, but against the old Adam in ourselves. So we fight against the domination of sin (the lusts of the flesh, that is, the egoistic wishes of the old human being) within us. We do this so that "we may offer ourselves to him [Christ] as a sacrifice of thanksgiving." This means that we confess thankfully our dedication to the *ending* of all sacrifice of God's creatures by human hands. In this battle we do not once again carry the cross of Christ. But we follow the crucified one, so that we "take up our cross" (cf. Mark 8:34). In this battle we cannot abhor enough all human cruelty that wounds and kills, or have enough sympathy with all who sigh and wail. In this battle we cannot stand up enough for life, for a life in love and in a form worth living.

(c) (Art. 44) The fact that the Son of God on the cross, by interposing himself for us, exposed himself to our sin, our misery, and our lostness, has yet a final consequence: he thereby exposed himself to our being abandoned by God, and in this suffered "unspeakable anguish, pain, and terror" in his soul. This is the descent into Hell: "My God, my God, why have you forsaken me?" (Matt. 27:46). But he suffered that for us too — for comfort in our struggles of the soul. To be sure, we plunge again and again into these dark struggles, hellish "anguish and torment." Sometimes they last through long days and nights, sometimes so that we are brought up against mysteries and wind up in shadows where we have no idea what to do. But if there is something that can help us in all this, and help us out, it is this knowledge: he is in the midst of this desperate struggle with us — he who has suffered through abandonment by God. So we cling to the promise, and guide ourselves by it, that even in the deepest darkness God does not let go of us.

3.2.3. Our Return Home (Art. 45-52)

Easter is no doubt the highest holiday for Christians. Really, every Sunday is a celebration of Easter. For in the exaltation of Jesus, the crowning of God's liberating work is set before our eyes, the fulfillment of God's moving into relationship with us. The meaning of Christ's humiliation can be summed up in this sentence: In the crucified one God steps into our situation so decisively that God is exposed to our sin and deals with it. The meaning of Christ's exaltation can be summed up in a corresponding sentence: In the extreme situation into which God steps and is exposed, God retrieves us in such a way that we are brought to God, taken in, and enfolded in companionship with God, and thereby drawn out of sin, death, and abandonment by God. The bringing home of us human beings by God at Easter corresponds to God's stepping in for us on Good Friday. While God's entering into the human situation brings home to God unspeakable anguish, the retrieval of humans by God means their finding home, their homecoming to God.

The truth of Easter, like the truth of the cross, is not a general truth that holds just as well independently of Christ, and for which his story is at most a parable. As soon as his exaltation is only an example of an idea or a law that can also be discovered everywhere, it is a matter that functions completely without him. Then in truth he is no longer to be found, and so the meaning of his exaltation is also no longer to be found by us. We humans then remain by ourselves and in a world that according to the Easter message "has passed away" (2 Cor. 5:17). God's stepping in for us on the cross then points into emptiness, as though it had happened "in vain." Then it would be as though "Christ has not been raised" (cf. 1 Cor. 15:14). We then have a "truth" that basically needs no resurrected one. In short, we run into all possible kinds of wrong paths if this is not completely clear to us from the very beginning: the one who says "I was dead, and see, I am alive," *he* has "the keys of Death and of Hades" (Rev. 1:18). He has wrested from their guards the keys to the prison gates behind which we would always be abandoned by God. So to us all *he* vouches for the promise of life.

> If he had remained entombed, the world and all therein were doomed. But he is ris'n from death's dark ward; so praise we Jesus Christ our Lord.[70]

The truth of Easter is concrete in the sense that it takes place in him, and in him has its reality and validity. It is true exclusively in him, and it holds for us only because he as the Son of God has taken on humanity in his unity with the man Jesus, and because he is here in our place and acts for our

---

70. Stanza 2 of the hymn "Christ ist erstanden" ("Christ Is Risen").

benefit. What is involved in this truth? Two matters are involved that need to be distinguished, but not separated; they must be seen together.

On the first aspect (1): The truth of Easter says that God reaches us who are sinners and in misery, takes hold of us, and brings us in. God does this so thoroughly that we cannot ever fall away and escape, so that our return home to God becomes our only future. This truth does not abrogate the truth of Good Friday. It confirms this truth, underscores it, bears it out, highlights it — the truth that God steps in for us and takes our sin upon Godself. The Easter exaltation of Jesus Christ is no superseding or correcting of his humiliation on the cross. We do not think rightly about either his humiliation or his exaltation if we understand them as two stages that simply follow one another. Easter does not reverse Good Friday; God does not try, as it were, to make right a breakdown that occurred, whether it be by having Jesus return for a little while into his old life, or by enabling his soul to fly directly into heaven, which many people hope for themselves regardless of Easter. If you wanted to understand Easter as a divine reversal of Good Friday you would need to have completely hollowed out the "word of the cross" and changed the meaning of the death of Christ for us into a dying like our own, or into a senseless murder of somebody. Or you would need to have the natural-biological annual cycle from winter to spring in view.

Instead of a succession, in which the exaltation of Christ replaces his humiliation, the Gospel of John actually sees both within each another. His exaltation is his being lifted up on the cross. Later, the risen one is known by his nail prints. Similarly, according to Revelation 5:12 the final judge of the world is "the Lamb that was slaughtered," the king with the crown of thorns. If God in the Son and in the Son's uniting with the man Jesus steps into the human condition so radically as to be exposed to human sin and the divine No against it, through what other truth should this truth be superseded? Remember that in doing this God has not just let justice rule instead of grace, but rather the justice of his grace, grace in judgment. God says no, and it is good that God does not let sin have its way, but crosses it out. God accepts sinners and takes their sins on God's own self. If all this is true, what other truth could take its place? Certainly not the Easter truth. It bears it out. The Easter truth does not put the Good Friday truth in the shadows. It brings it into the light. Easter does not suppress Good Friday. It lifts it up as truth for eternity.

Easter announces the same truth as Good Friday, but in different language. It declares: the fact that God has stepped in for us and is exposed to our condition, *means* that God brings us into God's own presence. For this is what happens at Easter. By the fact that God does not "let your Holy One experience corruption" (Ps. 16:10; Acts 2:27), that God does not abandon him to death, God pronounces a verdict. And with this verdict God stands with the one who has died this way, and takes his part. God affirms him as God's own. So God makes clear that this one who is forsaken by all, yes even by God, and is cast out to death and Hell, is not forsaken and abandoned by God, but is one with God. This is how God "identifies" with him.[71] By this Easter verdict of God, what happened on Good Friday is brought to light. It is disclosed as truth and put on the lamp stand. By this God reveals that the one who dies in misery is actually the Son of God and that he, and in him God, so enters into our condition as to be exposed to our sin and the just No of God to it, the "curse" (Gal. 3:13) which embitters our death. The fact that this is made clear in the light of Easter by the divine verdict on the one who died on the cross establishes the eternal validity of what took place on Good Friday. This shows that God, by such a strong demonstration of being our God, has declared that we belong to God. In this way the Yes of God hidden in the cross becomes God's unveiled Yes on Easter morning. The grace and love hidden in judgment become manifest grace and love. So God crowns the redemptive work in which God comes into relationship with us.

On the second aspect (2): Although Easter does not reverse Good Friday, yet we dare not go back behind Easter morning as though it had not happened, in order to look at Good Friday in itself, abstractly. That will not do, if for no other reason than that we would then be looking at it apart from the verdict of God. Then Good Friday would be offered up to our arbitrary judgments and impressions, and what it is according to God's Easter verdict would no longer come into our view. But it also will not do because when at Easter the meaning of the cross came to light, something new happened on the other side of Good Friday. While we cannot separate the humiliation and exaltation of Christ into two stages, in which the second makes the first no longer necessary, there is nevertheless in the substantial unity of the two a difference. The difference involves an irreversible movement between the two: from Good Friday to Easter.

What is new? Just this, that the God who in the Son has been exposed on the cross to sin and has borne the divine No to it, in this way actually

---

71. E. Jüngel, *Tod* (Stuttgart/Berlin: Kreuz, 1971), p. 137. ET: *Death, the Riddle and the Mystery* (Philadelphia: Westminster Press, 1975), p. 109.

gathers in the human being and brings it to God. What human being? The human being whose sin, and whose self as the perpetrator of sin, God, by taking the sin away, does not simply condone. Rather, God condemns this human. To this human as such God can only say No, and lead to the deserved end. It is about the human into whose place Jesus has stepped, so that he is now located in our place, and we in his. It is about the human to whom God, in the form of the one who has stepped into our place, actually has said No. On the basis of this No, this human has come to the end of all possibilities, and is an "old self," a "lost son," one who has disappeared. It is about the human who on Good Friday was exposed not only to death, but also to the Abyss, because abandoned and rejected by God. To this human being God says at Easter: Come out! Come to me! This can only happen by virtue of the divine verdict that it is God who on the cross has been exposed for us sinners and in person has taken the brunt of the divine No. That this human, despite everything, does not fall out of God's hands is not on account of the creative fantasy of certain people. No, it is because of the creative power of God's verdict. Just where this human is at the end of all possibilities, and not only physically ceases, but where God says No, and where this human can therefore only disappear, God delivers the verdict that saves the human from falling away. At this very place God carries this human into the divine presence. At this very place it happens that this one, separate from God, is not separated, but bound with God, so much so that nothing at all can separate this human from the love of God. At this very place, what Luke 15 tells in parable happens in reality and truth. This one who was totally lost does not stay lost, but is enfolded in the arms of his father. "For this son of mine was dead and is alive again" (Luke 15:24). This holds for the human Jesus who is in our place, and so holds for us who are in the place Jesus takes.

The fact that this one who was dead lives does not mean returning into the old life and getting a little extension for it. Rather, it means that God has made this human, who as the old, perverse character this person was could no longer exist before God, into a new human being (cf. Rom. 4:17). The lifting up of this new human is what is new in the Easter exaltation. In it God calls the human into a new life, which has death behind it — death as the sign of the power of sin that separates from God and divine love. The human now has this death behind, and ahead is life in the hand of God, out of which nothing more can tear us (John 10:29). Being a new human and no longer the old one from before — the human of sin — does not mean, however, being a morally faultless person. That would mean that for this person the truth of Good Friday — the forgiveness of sin through the personal intervention of God — would no longer be relevant, because it would be only in the past. What is past for the new human being is only the attempt to live without living from this forgiveness. The new human being is none other than the same old one, yet no longer the same old lost one. For marvelously, this one is not lost, but is fetched home by God, brought into the presence of and into relationship with God. This does not cause something new to be added to the normal existence of this human, so that over and above human existence there would be a dimension of the beyond not connected with this world. The human is not absorbed into God and so made divine. That would presuppose that the old human of sin is the normal, true human. *Then* the new human would be so by virtue of something that lifted this person above being human. The opposite is the case. To be sure, the new human is beyond the old one. But this old one is not at all the true, normal human, but rather the one alienated from God and other humans and self — the perverse human. On the other hand, the human who has been found, who experiences belonging to God, who has turned around in order to live at home with God, and thereby has been wrested from perversity and alienation from God, is the normal, true, truly human person. In returning home to God, this human also returns home to self. Martin Luther's words about this are exactly on target: "God became human so that we supposed gods would become humans."[72]

So much for an attempt to describe the fundamental meaning of the Easter exaltation. It basically describes only one of the truths that encounter us there: that God, who in the crucified one enters radically into our situation, is shown on Easter Day as the one who carries us from being closed in on ourselves into new life in fellowship with God. If we sense something of the truth of this event, in which God crowns our liberation and our reconciliation, then we understand why the celebration of this Easter exaltation is the highest Christian holy day.

For a long time, however, Easter has been more of an embarrassment for Christianity than a joy, more an occasion for puzzling than for celebrating. It is more likely to arouse discomfort (and therefore in evasions like the Easter Bunny) than Easter laughter, which is the custom in the Eastern church. Perhaps this discomfort is connected to the fact that we do not make clear to ourselves that in hearing the message of the Easter exaltation we are dependent on witnesses. "Witnesses of the resurrection" is

72. M. Luther, *WA* 5:128, 36ff.

what they are called in the New Testament. We do not know the resurrection without witnesses, who belong insolubly with it. So we need to be very clear about this term: (a) Witnesses must not themselves invent, in free imagination, what they witness to. In the case of Easter this holds true: the witnesses did not create the resurrection; rather, the resurrection "created" them as witnesses, and brought them forth. (b) Witnesses are signposts, which may differ according to age, color, or lettering, but which lose their meaning if you examine them with regard to these differences instead of being guided in the direction in which they point. (c) Where do they point? Not to some historical facts. Historical facts are always facts among other facts, all of which relativize one another. Our interest can easily turn away from some facts and turn to others. But how can what we are trying to get in view as the truth and reality of the Easter exaltation be one historical fact among others? No, what these witnesses testify to is the verdict that God has pronounced at Easter on the one who died on the cross. In this verdict, God affirms this crucified one and stands by him. According to this verdict it is God in person who takes away the divine No to our sins. On account of this verdict the old human of sin is disposed of in the one who stepped into our place, and may, thanks to the *awakening* by God *arise* as the new human who belongs to God, whom nothing can any longer separate from God's love. Whoever hears nothing of this verdict of God which the witnesses testify to us, cannot be helped by the mere news that there once was allegedly an exception to the rule that the dead stay dead. Even if this exception is correctly reported, what else could it reasonably mean than that in this case the exception proves the rule (that we all must die)? But in doing this, how we would mishear and misunderstand those witnesses! They are not historical reporters. They are witnesses of this verdict of God the judge, commissioned by God to hear this verdict and to make it known to us.

If we disregard these witnesses, if we do not take them seriously (in the threefold sense just sketched) as "witnesses of the resurrection," then the Easter exaltation necessarily dissolves for us into nothing at all. Or worse, we dissolve it into all kinds of general views about death and life. These views swarm through our heads without any Jesus Christ, and we may favor one or the other of them according to taste and temperament. We may then apply such views to him, but they are valid independently of him. They all finally wind up explaining the exaltation testified to us by those witnesses as superfluous. One of these views is the *idealistic* one. It says that the human being in death casts off what is bodily, concretely human, and becomes pure spirit. Death is here no serious death; it only uncovers the indestructible spirit in the core of the human being. Applied to Jesus, this means: the man Jesus is passé, but his world of ideas, his religious or ethical body of thought, his spiritual legacy, "the cause of Jesus" goes on.[73] Another view is the *pragmatic* one, which is convinced that there is no exception to the rule that one who is dead is dead. But *we* live ("They celebrate the resurrection of the Lord, for they themselves are resurrected out of the dull rooms of lowly houses . . ."[74]); and those who are dead live on in us, in our memory, in our pious imagination. But in truth they do not live on at all. It is only we who live (according to the motto: "there is life before death"). Applied to Jesus, this means that his exaltation is a flowery metaphor signifying that we keep a remembrance of him, along with others. So we hope that when we are no longer here, someone still kindly remembers us.

Whatever stance you take toward these two views, one thing is sure: they have not been given you by the witnesses of the resurrection. These views are a totally foreign body over against what the witnesses testify to. So as soon as you put it into the frame of these views, what these witnesses call "the resurrection from the dead" is lost without a trace. These views cannot be combined with what is testified to by the witnesses of the resurrection. In the idealistic view, one expects too much of humans, and in the pragmatic view, one expects too little of God. In the former no serious No is said to humans, a No so great and definite that only God can bear it away. And in the latter no serious Yes is said to humans, a Yes so great and strong that beyond the possibilities of the old human there appears the new human, whose newness comes from being bonded with God. The former does not see the exaltation of Christ in its unity with his humiliation, in which God speaks and carries out the No. This is not a No to the body of the human, while the spirit comes away undestroyed. Rather it is the No to the perversity of the human, body and soul, the No to the old human, who under this No can only pass away. And the latter does not see the newness of Easter, in which God in Christ opens new life in fellowship with God beyond the end of the old human. It is not a conserving of the old life, in which I am alone for myself with my remembrances of people long since gone. The former depends on a potential of humans that does not expire

---

73. So W. Marxsen, *Die Auferstehung Jesu als historisches und theologisches Problem* (Gütersloh: Mohn, 1964), p. 34. ET: "The Resurrection of Jesus as a Historical and Theological Problem," in *The Significance of the Message of the Resurrection for Faith in Jesus Christ* (Naperville, IL: Allenson, 1968), p. 50.

74. J. W. von Goethe, *Faust*, Part 1, Before the Gate, 921ff.

with death. And the latter depends on a potential of death that humans, with their notoriously short memory, try in vain to spite. The former knows nothing about the end of all human possibilities, and the latter does not know that beyond all human possibilities the human person is not dropped by God.

In either of these ways, humans are hopelessly alone, caught in their own possibilities. Both views are comfortless because in one way or another they do not see "that I belong, both body and soul, in life and in death not to myself, but to my faithful savior Jesus Christ" (Art. 1). And both are basically godless, because they take account of death and life without God. They reason without the righteousness of God in which the judge pronounces the just verdict on us and without the mercy of God, in which the judgment falls on God, without God's thoroughgoing No to the old human of sin, and without God's creative Yes beyond all human possibilities to a new life with God. All of this the witnesses of the resurrection contradict categorically. If we listen to their witness, they tell us that where we are completely at the end, where God can only say No to us, we do not fall away from God, because God takes into the divine self the force of the No. At this end we are brought to God, and lifted up into fellowship with God.

Up until now we have spoken about "the Easter exaltation" in an undifferentiated way. Actually, the New Testament speaks about it in three temporal dimensions: He has (perfect) risen, he is (present) exalted to the right hand of God, and he will (future) come visibly as the exalted one for our exaltation. The New Testament sees these three aspects together, without making an effort to divide out their relationship to one another chronologically, as our modern historical ears would so desperately like to hear done. While John (12:32) understands the exaltation of Jesus as his being lifted up on the cross, and Acts has a period of time between the resurrection and ascension, according to a series of other passages his resurrection and his exaltation to the right hand of God happen practically together (Rom. 8:34; Eph. 1:20; 1 Peter 1:21). Philippians 2:9, in speaking of his exaltation, apparently means both of these, and also his exaltation to eschatological judge. In still other places, what follows Good Friday is only his exaltation to the right hand of God (e.g., Heb. 1:3; 10:12; 12:2). In Acts 4:11, talk about his suffering immediately moves into talk about the coming ruler of the world.

In short, the New Testament language about the exaltation is so varied that you could see yourself forced to hold only one or the other as valid, and then cut out the others, "sachkritisch" *[with scholarly objectivity]*, to use a word that is as handy on the tongues of us *[academic German]* contemporaries as the Colt on the hip of the cowboy. But the New Testament findings do not hinder us from recognizing that there is a warranted conclusion we can draw. In fact, the variety of perspectives help us see it. In talking about the Easter exaltation we dare not think only about a happening at the tomb of Joseph of Arimathea. It is about an event that has a past, a present, and a future dimension. It is an event that, holding together all three dimensions, is as a whole the exaltation of Jesus Christ.

A strength of Article 45 of the Heidelberg is that its language about the resurrection envisages all three dimensions. The following articles, which speak of the "ascension" of Christ (46-51) and then of the "return" of Christ (52), all work together to throw light on the meaning of resurrection and exaltation. Further, this elucidation is strong in its grasp of the fact that these three dimensions are not simply temporally distinct. They describe three different aspects of the one exaltation. These three dimensions bring up their own problem, and answer it. Let us look at this more closely.

1. Article 45: "By his resurrection he has overcome death, so that he could make us share in the righteousness which he has gained for us through his death." What is involved here? Christ by his *death* has won for us righteousness. He has done this in love for us by taking upon himself the righteous divine No to the old human of sin and thereby has set this old human free from the burden and condemnation, and has pronounced this human righteous. This has taken place in him *for us,* but also for us *in him:* in him we are free, in him righteous, in him people to whom God can rightly say not No, but Yes.

But how does what is true for us *in him* come *to us?* How does the righteousness which applies in him *for us* become *our* righteousness? In faith? Yes, good! But is this faith a condition to be fulfilled by us in order that what Christ has won will count for us as righteousness? And is this faith such that we retrieve it, as it were, from the grave of someone who has died, like a dead stone lying there? Can we simply grasp for it, which otherwise would lie there and which we at any rate would have to acquire for ourselves? Then we would be right before God not in him, but through ourselves. Then, in the final analysis, we would have obtained the acquittal by ourselves and given it to ourselves. Then our faith would have no genuine, living person facing us, but would be literally without an object. This is in fact how it would have to be without the wonder, "Jesus came and stood among them. . . . Then the disciples rejoiced when they saw the Lord"

(John 20:19-20). 1 Corinthians 15:14: "If Christ has not been raised, then our proclamation has been in vain and your faith has been in vain." But Christ has been raised. Therefore neither our proclamation nor our faith is in vain. Therefore we have a living counterpart who gives us a share in the righteousness he has won. We cannot and need not from our side make ourselves share in it. He obtains it for us and gives it to us. We do not obtain it on our own for ourselves. His resurrection is not about a corpse who happens to be moving around again. It is about Christ himself living and sharing with us what he has won, which takes away the "curse" from our living and dying under that curse. It is about our being pronounced righteous and free only in him, but in such a way that what is valid for us in him becomes *our* righteousness through his action.

2. The text deals in most detail with the present form of the resurrection (Art. 46-51): with Christ's being "taken up" (Latin, *ascensio*). We might better talk about the ascension of Christ to the right hand of God. What is this about? The point is already indicated in the second step of Article 45: "by his power we too are raised up to a new life." *He* gives us "life before death." The answer to the question of what this is about is this: what in Christ is already reality for us now reaches into our present life. The result is that in us the old human of sin becomes past, and before us is only new life with God, life in harmony with our Creator. But how might this be taking place? Where in our present is this new human? In most people — must we not say, in everybody around us? — we do not see this new human. Not even in ourselves! The old life reigns so strongly, reaching into our life everywhere, that we can doubt whether our sin is really already done away with in Christ.

We do not need to be ashamed of this doubt. It is part of the very difficult provisional nature of Christian existence in the present. If we try to elbow our way out of this doubt, or if we simply maintain: I am the new human already, we deceive ourselves. Besides, we miss the comforting answer to this doubt which is given us right here in the knowledge of the ascension of Christ to the right hand of God "on our behalf" (Art. 46). In what way does it benefit us? Here we need to spell out what is said in Colossians 3:1-3, which Article 46 specifically refers to. "So if you have been raised with Christ, seek the things that are above, where Christ is, seated at the right hand of God. Set your minds on things that are above, not on things that are on earth, for you have died, and your life is hidden with Christ in God." What does this mean? For one, "at the right hand of God" means that on behalf of God, Christ is carrying out God's reign, not only in heaven, but also on earth (Art. 47), not only in the church and for its protection (Art. 51), but also in the world (Art. 50). This reign intends to usher out the old human and bring in the new. His church may and must trust, in the face of all powers, that to *him* . . . "*all* authority has been given" (Matt. 28:18). For another, it means that his way of reigning is not that of armed force. Rather it is the abiding continuance of his priestly intervention and intercession before God for us, who still fall prey to the old human (Art. 49). And it is his distribution of his spiritual gifts to us (Art. 51). The new human does not have to be invented. In Christ the new human is already here, and we are the new human already in him. He is already at the right hand of God (Art. 49) as a sure pledge that this human is not an empty promise, but is already really here. This is why the gift of the Spirit consists of lifting up our eyes and hearts to where the promise of the new human is already fulfilled (Art. 49). This is the reason for the answer we get to the question, "Where then is this new human in me?" The answer is: I am this new human being in that I "set my mind" on him, stretch out toward him, orient myself to him and am on the way to him. I am the new human in God's assurance that I really am who I am in Christ.

An incidental theological remark may be added here. From what has just been said, we understand the interest of the Heidelberg in emphasizing that in the uniting of the Son of God with the man Jesus, God is not transformed into a human, nor is this human transformed into God. This is why Article 48 declares that the divinity of the Son of God is the same both outside the human nature that has been taken on as well as within it. Since the sixteenth century, this conception has been designated the "Extracalvinisticum" and rejected in Lutheran polemic[75] by arguing that on the basis of the uniting of the divine with the human nature of Christ, his human nature has itself received divine qualities; therefore his divinity no longer exists outside the human nature that has been taken on, but only in the bonding of both. The anti-Reformed polemic against the "Extracalvinisticum" has some deficiencies: 1. The Reformed view in this matter is no Calvinist specialty. It has long been the ecumenical consensus in theology. 2. The Reformed view does not claim, as Lutheran zeal often says, that the divinity in the Son of God did not take on human nature but is always only outside of it (therefore the Latin word *extra*, used to mean that divinity is outside the man Jesus). The Reformed position claims that his

---

75. Cf. F. Loofs, "Kenosis," *Realenzyklopädie für protestantische Theologie und Kirche*[3], 10, pp. 246-63.

divinity is both within and outside the human being. 3. It is not the case, as Lutheran polemic supposes, that behind this position stands only a philosophical captivity on the part of Reformed theologians. The Lutherans charge that Reformed theologians are bound by the philosophical dictum: "The temporal can never contain the infinite."[76] This statement is theologically just as untenable as the Lutheran one held in opposition to it: "The temporal is capable of containing the infinite." Behind the Reformed view stands a decisively theological concern. Only if the distinction is maintained in the one Christ between the God who takes on the human and the human who has been taken on, is it clear that it is God who redeems us. And only if the human taken by the Son of God into unity with himself is like us, "our brother," including when he is exalted to the right hand of God (Art. 49), and is not made exclusively divine, can he be a sure pledge for our being destined to be new humans.

3. Article 52 looks at the future form of the exaltation of Christ. Article 45 has already spoken about this when its third step calls his resurrection "a sure pledge to us of our blessed resurrection." The question that presents itself here is this: Who has the last word — God or death? Must not death, which brings everything else to silence, also take away the word from God? Must not death, in which we fall away from everything, and also from ourselves, mean that we also fall away from God? "The last enemy . . . is death" (1 Cor. 15:26). Is it not therefore also stronger than God? The Heidelberg is helpful here in its recognition that the answer to the question of whether everything does not end with death depends on the answer to the question of whether our limit is also God's limit. More exactly: our death would in fact be only end, silence, dropping away, if God would let us fall, if God would have to say No to us definitively: "Away from me!" But this means that the question of the divine victory over the "last enemy," over death, depends completely on the question of the divine victory over the *first* enemy, over the separating power of sin. But this victory is already won on the cross, in which God has carried out the No to the old human of sin, and has carried it out in love, by bearing the hard force of this No in person. So on Easter Day the love of God, from which nothing can any longer separate us, became manifest. On the cross the final judge himself "has already offered himself to the judgment of God for me and has removed all the curse from me" (Art. 52).

---

76. Cf. T. Mahlmann, "Endlich," in *Historisches Wörterbuch der Philosophie*, ed. J. Ritter, vol. 2 (Basel/Stuttgart: Verlag Scheidegger und Spiess, 1962), pp. 487-88.

Because the victory over this first enemy is already won, therefore I "with head held high can go toward the last, the ultimate day. I can do this, not because I have a nice, positive balance sheet to show for my life. Rather, though that will not be the case, I can still hold my head high because there the same one "who has already offered himself to the judgment of God" will always be there, will be there again, will "return." On the basis of the divine verdict, God will not say No to me, but Yes. God will not say "Away from me!" but "Come here to me!" The same action that disarmed the first enemy will therefore also disarm the last enemy, death. So I will live, and what will die off will be only "all his enemies" which are therefore also "mine." By this is meant, according to Article 127: "the devil, the world, and our own sinfulness" — evil, and the perverse old human and that human's world. They will then be definitively divorced from us, and will disappear forever because they cannot tear us out of God's hand. God's love *gives* life *after* death. For "Who will separate us from the love of Christ?" (Rom. 8:35). If that first enemy, the power of sin cannot, how *then* should the last enemy, death, have the power to do it! What will there be then? We cannot say it better than to quote 1 Corinthians 13:8: "Love never ends." This is the whole of glory.

3.3. The God Who Brings Us into Relationship

3.3.1. The Holy Spirit (Art. 53)

The doctrine of Christ stood under the heading: The God Who Comes for Relationship with Us. Correspondingly, the doctrine of the Holy Spirit will be summarized here with the title: The God Who Brings Us into Relationship. This indicates the close connection of the doctrines of Christ and of the Holy Spirit. It also indicates how the works of the two are distinct, and complement one another. God aims at coexistence with the creation distinct from God, namely with the human who has fallen into sin. To fulfill this aim, God comes to be in relationship with us, as we have said. But now we must not suppose that after God has done this, we on our side have to put ourselves into relationship with God. This is excluded because God's making Godself to be our God already *includes* our belonging to God. But what this action of God includes, the Holy Spirit *opens up* to us. This unfolds within us, not in our grasping for it, but in our being grasped. This too is God's work on us, the work of God's Spirit. The Holy Spirit is once again God, God in another form than the Father and the Son, but not less than they, rather together with them the one God. "What do you believe about the Holy Spirit? First, that the Spirit is eternal God equally with the Father and the Son" (Art. 53).

But the Spirit is God in special and unique form! The Spirit is God who sets us in relationship with God, as the Son of God is God who comes to be in relationship with us. When Article 24 calls the work of the Holy Spirit "our sanctification," it means essentially the same thing. For "sanctification" means that God takes hold of certain people, draws them close, and gives them a task. Essentially the same thing is meant when we say that the work of the Spirit is to bestow on us the status of children of God (a status already won in Christ). For this is the relationship with God into which the Holy Spirit brings us, and this is the closeness to God into which the Spirit draws us. It is not that the Spirit makes us divine, but that the Spirit brings about a change so that we become what we in ourselves are not: God's children. "For all who are led by the Spirit of God are children of God. . . . It is that very Spirit bearing witness with our spirit that we are children of God" (Rom. 8:14-16). In the first place, this is not our work. God does not come, as it were, only halfway toward us and then require that we come up with what is still needed for the other half of the way. This opinion would represent God's position this way: after I have come to be in relationship with you, it is up to you to do the rest, so that you bring yourself into relationship with me. This way we land again at that problematical idea of faith as condition, with its miserable thesis that all the glories of Christ are of no use or validity for us if we do not contribute our part to them. No, the truth is that God comes the *entire* way toward us. Not only toward us! God comes to us. God does not only come to be in relationship with us. Beyond this, it is God's concern that we come into relationship with God, that we are sanctified, that we become God's children. Only those who see this latter step, which once again God does in us in the Holy Spirit, really know what God's grace is.

This is the presupposition: God is self-determined to coexist with us. But now in regard to this blessing, surely a great one, God is not satisfied with only wanting its fulfillment. God does not stand idly by to see if we will one day perchance be inclined on our part to coexist with God (and then also with all with whom God coexists). God could wait a long time for this, even to St. Never Ever's Day! For we are by nature inclined to hate God and our neighbor, and in addition inclined willfully to overlook the fact that this perversity has become objectively impossible in Christ. Of ourselves we are inclined, in spite of all divine light, to creep into our caves, in the supposed free will of our independent freedom. But now God does something more, and also takes personal responsibility for seeing that we become "willing and ready" (Art. 1) on our side also to become such coexisting beings. So God searches for us in our caves in order — person to person, so to speak — to bring us into the light. God does this in order to let us see in this light that the perversity that has become impossible in Christ is *really* impossible for us, that there is *really* nothing left for us but to coexist with God. This is the work of the Holy Spirit. For a closer understanding of it, we will underscore five points.

1. To the work of the Holy Spirit belongs a certain negation. This negation is involved in something we have already touched on, that first of all and decisively we do not bring ourselves into relationship with God, because this is God's concern and work on us. This negation also lies behind the formulation of Article 53: the Spirit has been "given" to me. This rules out taking and having the Spirit by my own effort. Perhaps this negation is intended in the strange statement in John 16:8 that when coming to us, the Spirit sent by Jesus "will prove the world wrong." In his interpretation of the third article of the Creed, Martin Luther lifts up this negation very sharply. "To believe in the Holy Spirit . . . what is this? I believe that *I cannot* in my own reason or power believe in Jesus Christ my Lord or come to him."[77] Luther is probably thinking of 1 Corinthians 12:3: "*No one* can say 'Jesus is Lord' except by the Holy Spirit." This statement of negation is a truth we will always contest so long as God's Holy Spirit has not touched us. Why should I, so we think, not have the ability to put myself in relationship to a divinity? This claim no doubt belongs to the natural endowment of every religious self-understanding. Those to whom the Holy Spirit comes have this claim taken away. They no longer contest what on their own they would always contest, because through the Spirit they are convinced that "in my own reason or power" I cannot put myself in that right relationship with God. And so long as I think that I can put myself into it, it will never be the right relationship with God. "We must already have the Spirit of God in order to recognize that we lack the Spirit."[78]

77. *Die Bekenntnisschriften der evangelisch-lutherischen Kirche* (Göttingen: Vandenhoeck & Ruprecht, 1956³), vol. 3, pp. 511-12.
78. H. J. Iwand, *Nachgelassene Werke*, vol. 4, *Gesetz und Evangelium* (Munich: Kaiser Verlag, 1956), pp. 151-52.

This recognition rules out the pattern of thought on which so much moral or religious zeal is nourished: before I did not have it — now I *have* it! The claim (mentioned earlier in this work) is that before the revelation, God was hidden from me, and after the revelation God is hidden no longer; now I have God in my grasp and at work, so to speak. Or, before I was weak in spirit, but now I am Spirit-filled, or gifted by the Spirit. Before I could not come to God, but now *I* come! This pattern lies at the base of all needless, and precisely therefore dangerous, confrontations. For persons must apparently confirm the certainty of their present form of light by the distance from those whom they see as still lying in the night in which they themselves had previously been. It is always those who are well-meaning, right-thinking, filled with ideals, capable, or Spirit-gifted who distance themselves, who build fences, and who now either exclude the other poor folk or try to bring them to their side. It is those same well-meaning ones who either in a metaphorical or literal sense wage war: always "just" wars, always wars for "a good cause." In this chapter belongs also the proverbial "*rabies theologorum*," the theological lust for quarreling.

The gift of the real *Holy* Spirit is able to resist this mentality of confrontation. The gift is able to do this because it makes us who supposedly have, and who have the right on our side, and who are well-meaning and filled, into *poor people*. It makes out of us people who are "poor in spirit" (Matt. 5:3), literally, those who "in the Spirit are poor," beggars with empty hands. We become those who depend on and wait for the Spirit to help in our weakness and to intercede for us "with sighs too deep for words" (Rom. 8:26). The Spirit makes out of us persons who do not think we are in a position to set ourselves in relationship to God and who do not think we are already set in this relationship. Rather, we live from this, and recognize that we live from this: that the Spirit creates this relationship for us and in us. Spiritual people are "humble in spirit" (Isa. 57:15). The presence of the Spirit in them is shown in the fact that they become asking, praying people. Yes, the distinguishing mark that the Spirit has been given to me is that instead of saying "I have the Spirit," I sigh "Come, Creator Spirit."[79] I *have* the Spirit only in laying hold of the promise of Jesus that "the heavenly Father [will] give the Holy Spirit to those who *ask* him" (Luke 11:13).

Yet we dare not confuse "poverty of spirit" with mere limpness or passivity! For these who are asking for the Spirit are in a new way also fighters — in a new confrontation that is really needed. This is the battle of the

---

79. The beginning of the Pentecost hymn by Rhabanus Maurus.

"Spirit against the flesh" (Gal. 5:16-17). Those who try to end that old confrontation mentality by recommending tolerance on all sides may well miss the battle in this needed confrontation. They propose the well-meaning concession that just as I naturally claim the Spirit for myself, so all others somehow, in their own fashion, already possess the Spirit. Where there is such possession, the one battle necessary is in one way or another not engaged. This battle does not pit those on high moral ground against those on a lower level, so that we are God's fighters waging war against the children of darkness. For one thing, the nature of this battle is completely different. This battle puts us in the battle of *God*, which proceeds in the reverse direction. God casts down the lofty and lifts up the lowly, makes the first last and the last first, fills the hungry with good things and sends the rich empty away (Matt. 19:30; Luke 1:52-53). For another, the battle of the Spirit against the flesh is different in method from that unnecessary battle. Its method does not consist in counting "flesh their strength" (Jer. 17:5), that is, not by means of one's own capacity, by using the tools of power of an unredeemed world to prevail against others. This battle is fought strictly with spiritual means, that is, with strict trust, which was the core of the "Holy War" in Israel, with reliance on the promise "The Lord will fight for you, and you have only to keep still" (Exod. 14:14; cf. Isa. 30:15).[80]

2. Though the Holy Spirit makes us into persons who are "poor in spirit," the Spirit does not leave us empty. Emptiness is in itself not a guarantee of divine nearness. What matters is that the Spirit gives us what we cannot procure for ourselves. All the wealth which the Spirit gives is included in the Spirit's "making me participate in Christ . . . through a true faith." Because I participate in Christ, I participate in "all his benefits" (Art. 53). As Martin Luther says: the Spirit "brings Christ into the heart."[81] Or as Calvin says: "The Holy Spirit is the bond by which Christ effectually unites us to himself."[82] This is so much the work of the Spirit that the Spirit is called in the New Testament "the Spirit of Jesus Christ" (e.g., Rom. 8:9). And 1 John 4:2-3 even declares flat out, "By this you know the Spirit of God: every spirit that confesses that Jesus Christ has come in the flesh is from God, and every spirit that does not confess Jesus is not from God." There are all kinds of spirits: the human spirit, the spirit of life, the spirit of

80. Cf. G. von Rad, *Der Heilige Krieg im alten Israel* (Zurich: Zwingli-Verlag, 1951). ET: *Holy War in Ancient Israel* (Grand Rapids: Eerdmans, 1991).
81. M. Luther, *WA* 17; part 1:436.
82. J. Calvin, *Institutes* III.1.1.

the times, the spirit of a people, the spirit of comradeship, the spirit of sport. They do not have to be evil. But they become evil when they make themselves out to be holy spirits. The Holy Spirit is always to be recognized in bringing Christ close to us (1 John 4:2). Because the Spirit is the Spirit of Christ, the Spirit is a benefactor. For the Spirit's benefits are "his [Christ's] benefits." Because Christ in his death has "redeemed" us, therefore "where the Spirit of the Lord is, there is freedom" (2 Cor. 3:17). Because Christ is resurrected from the dead, therefore it is "the Spirit that gives *life*" (John 6:63, 68) who gives us a share in the resurrection life of Christ, which makes life worth living and is life affirming. Because by virtue of his living and dying "Christ wills to be our comfort," therefore the Spirit is our "Comforter" (John 15:26), who assures us that in living and in dying we belong to Christ.

The Holy Spirit is the Spirit of Jesus Christ. Let us make this clear with reference to our formulations: In Christ, God comes to be in relationship with us, and in the Holy Spirit God brings us into relationship. God's coming to be in relationship with us *aims* to bring us into relationship, and God's bringing us into relationship is *based* on God's coming to be in relationship with us. The work of the Holy Spirit corresponds to the work of Christ in that it brings us into relationship with the God who comes to be in relationship with us. The Spirit *brings* us! We do not bring ourselves; God brings us through the Holy Spirit into relationship with the God who comes to be in relationship with us. This is why whenever the question is raised of how we come into relationship with God, the answer must always be: only through God's turning to us. The Spirit lets the One who has come into our world come directly, personally, to each of us. This is why it is the Spirit of *Jesus Christ*. This is why the Reformers insisted unyieldingly that Word and Spirit, that Christ and the Holy Spirit dare never be separated from one another. Not that the Holy Spirit is withdrawn from the Israel of the Old Testament! Christ is no stranger to Old Testament Israel. As Immanuel, as God with us, he is the fullness of the covenant promise given and assured to Israel: "I am your God, and you will be my people." How can this be promised and assured to Israel without the Holy Spirit already working in it?

Moreover, the conviction that the Holy Spirit is the Spirit of Jesus Christ stands critically against the proposition formulated some years ago that wherever people are enthusiastic about something, the Holy Spirit is working. Clear examples appear in German history of human enthusiasms that even diametrically contradict the Spirit of Christ. Karl Barth's dictum no doubt aims at these: "The Holy Spirit does not blow on mass gatherings."[83] We also need to be careful about a more recent idea: everything that lives and moves is enlivened by the Holy Spirit of God. Why should we not be allowed to believe this? But insofar as this is the case, it is the most hidden aspect of the Holy Spirit. To begin with this in seeking to understand the Holy Spirit would be like trying to tame a horse starting at its rear end. If indeed this idea is supposed to mean that we are to reckon with a Holy Spirit of *God* which just drifts around through everything alive, independently of the covenant with Israel and independently of Christ, and only now and then also wafts in Israel and Christ, then for this at any rate we will not have the backing of the biblical witness. This idea would mean that we have a relationship from ourselves to God that is not mediated through, and is not owed to, God's setting us in relationship to God beforehand out of pure grace and love. The result would be that this supposed Spirit no longer *corresponds* to this gracious, loving act of God, so that this Spirit is something other than the God who brings us into relationship with God. This Spirit would then be the creaturely capacity to set oneself in relationship to God, and even on one's own to be always in such a relationship. Blunders like this arise when it is not clear that we cannot draw knowledge of what the Holy Spirit is out of any of our own experiences. We "experience" it on the basis of holy scripture.

3. From what has been said in these first two points there arises a unique two-sided stance of Christian faith to the world of *religions* in which it finds itself. Although the church in its manifestation as "Christianity" is only one among other religions, the Christian faith, if it is awakened through the Holy Spirit, is unavoidably a *stranger* in this world, yes, a *troublemaker*. It is a troublemaker in response to the question so characteristic of the world of religions: Are there many ways to God, which need to tolerate one another and which can perhaps enrich one another, or is there only a single way, which may therefore lift up a "claim to absoluteness" over against the others? Christian faith is a troublemaker in this matter because it has to deny, simply but imperturbably, the presupposition of this controversial question. For what Christian faith lives from is neither the only way to God nor one among other ways to God. The Christian faith itself is no such way either; it is the contesting of all such ways. Christian faith is dissuaded from seeing itself as a way by the Holy Spirit, and told that humans cannot "come to God." That is excluded by the fact that God has taken the

83. K. Barth, *Gespräche 1964-1968* (Zurich: Theologischer Verlag, 1996), p. 424.

opposite direction. Jesus says "I am the way. . . . No one comes to the Father except through me" (John 14:6). This says there is in fact no way — neither an absolute nor a relative way to God. There is only the opposite direction of the gracious God who comes to us sinners. By imparting to us God's action in this opposite direction, the Spirit denounces every vision of another way, and always denounces first of all the error of those who should know better in this matter, and still do not know. The Spirit condemns the attempt of sinners, in denial of being sinners, to think up such human ways to God and then to practice them reverently.

But in hearing the gracious Yes and the condemning No of God to us sinners, faith is also a sign of the *promise* in the midst of the world of religions. If there is only the way of God to us, and if God in the Holy Spirit opens this way to us in controversion of all our ways to God, what obstacle could be laid in God's way by humans now or in the long run? If even our way of being the church is not an insuperable hindrance for God, then how would resistance outside the church be able to stop God? How can Christians not reckon earnestly with the affirmation that God "knows many thousand ways to save out of death"?[84] They will not be able to explain how this takes place. They will therefore not be able to come up with theories about it. They can only let it be said to them: "The Spirit blows where it chooses" (John 3:8). So they will listen carefully and openly in the world of religions — not trusting in the amazing skill of humans with regard to such ways to God, but trusting in the One who is more amazing, whose way and "work no one can hinder."[85] Free from the cramping effect of open or hidden competition about the true way to God, they will listen attentively in this world with the question of whether they may not hear in this or that extraordinary word an echo of the voice of the Good Shepherd. They will listen in readiness for being surprised that here and there the voice of the Good Shepherd may even be heard more clearly than in the church. This way they may repentantly learn to be the church of Christ in greater faithfulness than heretofore, in the power of the Holy Spirit.

4. What does the Holy Spirit accomplish? Article 53 answers with a quotation from John 14:16: The Spirit's role is "comforting me, and abiding with me forever." Now we saw already in Article 1 that for the Heidelberg all

---

84. From stanza 3 of the hymn "Du meine Seele singe" ("Sing, My Soul"), by P. Gerhardt.

85. From stanza 4 of the hymn "Befiehl du meine Wege" ("Direct My Ways"), by P. Gerhardt.

comfort lies in the fact that we belong to Jesus Christ. So we need to read Article 53 this way: the Holy Spirit enables us to share in Christ, gives him to us as our own, so that we may *be* his own. The Spirit brings close the God who comes to be in relationship with us so that we can be in relationship with God. From this we understand why the Spirit brings Christ close to us *with his blessings* — namely his righteousness and mercy demonstrated on the cross for us, his love revealed at Easter, from which nothing can separate us. In disclosing and opening up *these* blessings to us, the Spirit also opens the door on our side — so that by God's being close to us, we are now close, so close that we know ourselves as "God's own." To be God's own does not mean that we are simply a mass of stuff at God's disposal, or that we become absorbed into God. "Belonging to God" means — and herein lies all comfort — that we, in Christ and through his Spirit, are *God's children.*

This is probably the sense in which we are to understand the image of God in humans, to which, according to Article 86, "Christ renews us in his own image through his Holy Spirit." Just as rulers in the ancient Orient used to have their images posted in regions to which they laid claim, so this is what the "image of God" means — not that we look like God or that God looks like us, but that we belong to God as God's children. And if the Spirit comforts us by making us Christ's possession, and God's image, children of God, then this is clear: in the working of the Spirit we can always be only receivers. But the Spirit does not treat us as mere receiving objects. We become our own autonomous subjects, not set loose from God, but autonomous subjects within the relationship opened to us by God, autonomous subjects as God's children.

The Spirit's making us into this kind of people is to be understood in a twofold sense. For one, we are humans who are treated as having come of age. Our coming of age, our maturity, is shown most clearly in free access to God and in use of the permission to address God personally and directly as "dear Father" (cf. Gal. 4:1-7!). This maturity, so highly activated and expressed in our communication with God, is the very thing that includes the freedom to use our own reason. It is a perverse conception of the Holy Spirit which holds that the Spirit nestles only in the irrational and extraordinary. The Spirit directs us also to do ordinary things in an orderly way. In the genuine Holy Spirit we are not raving outside ourselves, but come rightly to ourselves. The genuine Holy Spirit does not bring us away from our understanding, but to our understanding.

The second sense in which we are renewed in God's image is that as children of God we are brought into solidarity with one another. For there are children of God always only in the plural. Whoever knows them only in the singular does not know the Spirit of God. A perverse idea of the Spirit is holding sway also when the feeling of being more Spirit-filled makes people run out of the church into some special club or other. The Holy Spirit, who according to Acts 2 blew at Pentecost, in a movement counter to that of the story of Babel, led people together to *one* community, against their drive to scatter. Children of God will always be very different from one another, but they are children of God only as they are all in solidarity (cf. Gal. 3:26-28). — In correlation with these two aspects of being in God's image, the doctrine of the Holy Spirit will also include the doctrine of the church and of the life of the individual Christian.

But there remains to be underscored the last statement in Article 53, according to which the Spirit is "abiding with me forever." It is better not to understand this as though I receive the Spirit on a certain day and then simply possess the Spirit, as though at a particular hour I become a child of God and then always remain such! The biblical perspective comes from the opposite direction. In the work of the Spirit eternity dawns, and the eschaton, the final act of God, the future, the life of the future, breaks into our temporal existence. For the work of the Spirit is the fulfilling work of God, beyond which nothing further is to be awaited. "The Kingdom of God is the Holy Spirit."[86] What could there be to await beyond God's dwelling with mortals, and their being God's people? According to Revelation 21:3-4, everything is included in this: the new heaven and the new earth wherein righteousness dwells and all tears are wiped away. Moreover, according to Paul in Romans 8:19-20, everything is included in the "revealing of the children of God" and the liberation of the creation to the "freedom of the glory of the children of God." This is the future, eternal life — the fulfillment of the work of God in the existence of the new human, of humans as children of God, who as God lives with them, now in response live with God.

But this future is not simply future. It comes to us already now. In the Holy Spirit the future begins already, breaks into our temporal life and takes hold of it. The Spirit makes people into children of God already now. Yet we also have to add the converse: where this happens, it is all only the first anticipation of the future, as Paul says: installment, guarantee, pledge of what is to come (2 Cor. 1:22; 5:5; Eph. 1:14). What does this mean? The fulfillment

86. Gregory of Nyssa, *Fünf Reden auf das Gebet,* Bibl. d. Kirchenväter, ed. F. Oehler (Leipzig: Engelmann, 1859), p. 261.

of Joel 2:28-32 quoted in the Pentecost story in Acts 2:17ff. is not yet here: "In the last days . . . I [God] will pour out my Spirit *upon all flesh*." Until then it is time for proclaiming the gospel to all peoples. But the Spirit is far from having been poured out on all flesh. And it is far from being fully poured on those who believe in Christ, except as only a beginning. Those on whom it does begin know that they are far from being in the harbor. They get into an open sea, where there are storms and headwinds, much sighing and groaning, but in all of this there is joyful anticipation of the future liberation of the creation to the glorious freedom of the children of God. In these storms they will not be alone. They will be bound with others who have already heard their calling to be children of God. They will ask with them for the coming of the Spirit, that the Spirit come "on all flesh." And together with them they will turn to all the others who seem not to have heard their calling to be children of God, in faith, hope, and love.

5. Yes surely the Holy Spirit makes us into children of God, into persons who have come of age, and into the kind of persons who live in the community of the children of God — on the way to the final, eschatological freedom of the children of God. But this means that this community, the church, depends utterly on the moving and coming of the Holy Spirit. This puts the church *as a whole* in that "poverty of spirit." This is a poverty the church apparently has again and again not tolerated. Its binding to the Holy Spirit, necessary for the church to keep its essential nature, has been abruptly reimagined and twisted into a binding of the Spirit to the church. This view does not see the Spirit being imparted to the church, but the church, or a ruling caste within it, imparting the Spirit to others. It is not the Spirit who binds them all to God as God's children, but instead the church sees salvation in binding people to itself. In this way the Holy Spirit, in the hands of the church administering it, was changed "from a flame-thrower to a fire extinguisher."[87] So a whole system of being the church arose that stands before our eyes as so much a matter of course that we no longer can imagine it any other way.

This church poses now as the earthly embodiment of the grace of Christ and his Spirit. In doing so, a small group of consecrated and initiated persons have the part of the givers, distributors, "real" speakers and actors, while the rest are silent. The rest are the greater number of the so-called church people, who are deliberately called church people. To them is

---

87. M. von Galli, from a television sermon at Pentecost. The phrase has become proverbial.

assigned the role of receivers, of "addressees," of listeners and passive on-lookers. It is only a variation of this "medieval" division of the church when today it is between (male or now also female) counselors and clients, between managers and those managed, between full-time leaders and the right and left hands of the pastor, between officials and those who when needed offer them some service. For this church system the peculiar way it gains members is indicative. It consists, at least among [regional churches in Germany] without exception, in this church's making people members without asking them, over their heads, so to speak. Today this is not done as it was at one time, when the church "Christianized" whole peoples and tribes by force. Rather, the church integrates people into itself as tiny children. In one way or another, the church does this with the assurance that this is an act of wonderful grace. People accept this probably because of the concession that if they are just church members, they can hold whatever ideas and opinions they like, including being able to carry on all kinds of heathen customs under the mantle of "Christian symbols." This is no doubt what some church people today call "pluralism."

If any sort of criticism is to be made against this church system, it cannot be in the name of the free human personality that does not want to see itself administered in this way. This principle actually wrecks the *church* and is partly responsible for this false *system,* under certain circumstances cooperating very well with this system. The one who actually raises a protest against this system is the Holy Spirit. For the work of the Spirit, in binding the church to the Spirit, struggles against the church's binding the Spirit to itself. The Holy Spirit is the troublemaker for this church system. No wonder the church is so concerned to keep the Spirit in chains by binding the Spirit to itself. The Spirit's movement is *really* grace, over which neither the church nor any other power has control. The church and *everyone* in it can only *ask for it.* But it is *grace,* for which neither the church nor anyone in it asks in vain, which indeed comes before we ask, and makes the asking possible. It is grace that also sets right the false picture of it in that church system, according to which what corresponds to grace on the receiving side is mere passivity. "Grace . . . means neither that men can or ought to do something, nor that they can or ought to do nothing. Grace means that *God* does something. Nor does grace mean that God does *everything.* Grace means that God does some quite definite thing."[88] This is

---

88. K. Barth, *Der Römerbrief* (Munich: Kaiser, 1923), p. 196. ET: *The Epistle to the Romans* (London: Oxford University Press, 1968), p. 215.

the very reason why grace also means that humans — in answer to it — on their side also do "something." In the Holy Spirit God makes us, without distinction, God's children by grace. And God's grace is truly gracious in that it makes us all come of age, puts us on our own feet and sets us in motion. And as the Spirit binds the church to itself, the church's drive to bind people to itself fades away. Instead, the Spirit binds the church to people outside of it, pushes it out over its walls to them in order to stand by their side and await among them future brothers and sisters. Where the Spirit moves, there the church *lives*.

3.3.2. The Community (Art. 54-55)

God's bringing us into relationship in the Holy Spirit and making us children of God means first of all that we are placed in solidarity, in the fellowship of the children of God. Christian faith is directed to the God who sets the divine self into relationship with us, and us into relationship with God. So this faith is, from the beginning, faith in relationship. Therefore it manifests itself in the way Christian believers consciously live in such relationship, and engage in it. This is what will be discussed here: the Christian church.

To link up again with what was said previously, assuredly the church is the work of the Spirit. But the church is not the final work of God. The church is not yet that "great multitude" that will be gathered around God's throne and that "no one could count" (Rev. 7:9). It is only an initial preview of this promised people, only a gathering of the "first fruits of God's creatures" (James 1:18). The church is not the promised kingdom of God. It can only pray for the kingdom's coming. Where it forgets this, and so forgets its provisional and relative nature, an ecclesiastical imperialism threatens. However, this does not begin at the point where people customarily start to accuse the church: in brutal enforcement against people who believe differently, and in keeping company with powers bent on conquest. It always begins where we put forth our own cause as the cause of God because it seems so "lovely and lively" to us, like something we ourselves may and should take to be at our disposal, under our management. Now, such an ecclesiastical imperialism is never a *real* anticipation of the kingdom of God, but only a premature encroachment on the kingdom. It is in truth a form of the accommodation of the church to the way and the method of this aeon, to the spirit of the world — an ecclesiastical secularism. Then again, the secularization of the church can have many forms, by no means only the form of lust for power. But secularization always consists basically in the church's no longer waiting for what is more than the church, for the fulfilled kingdom of God. Where the church no longer waits, it will always be inclined to conform to the structures of this world, even if it limits itself to a sacred realm of its own (and especially then!). It will tend to make pacts with the ruling powers and movements of this world. There it changes from being a waiting and petitioning pilgrim band to a church of possessing, and indeed of abundant possessing. There it loses its meaning. It makes no difference whether the church keeps its possessions for only itself to enjoy, or gallantly distributes them to the "people." It does not matter whether in administering them the church conforms to the spirit of the times, or uses its giving to subject people to itself. Against this church we cannot be on guard critically enough.

But even more important, the church does not stand first of all under our judgment. We stand — with this church — under the judgment of the Spirit of *God*. Against this church is directed the hard word of God that Amos (5:21-23) had to deliver against the temple cult in Bethel in writing: "I hate, I despise your festivals! . . . Take away from me the noise of your songs!" This church needs to be reminded that "It was the Church, not the world, which crucified Christ"[89] and that "there is no sinner so great as the Christian church."[90] It has not been the worst people who have chafed at and been vexed by the church, who have wanted desperately to run away, and have indeed run away because the church is always so little a foretaste of the promised kingdom of God. But however desirable it is that some individuals be discontent with the shortcomings of the church, this needs to be said to these impatient persons: because we can now receive the Spirit only as a beginning of what is to come, therefore we wait for the kingdom of God by not running from the church in its completely and thoroughly awkward provisional nature, but by staying in it. Luther, though he accused it so much, could even call the Roman church "holy" — with the curious explanation: "You [Lord] will rule in the midst of your foes" (Ps. 110:2).[91] So "the idea of leaving it [the Church] or renouncing his orders would be even less intelligent than to take his own life."[92] This does not

89. K. Barth, *Der Römerbrief*, p. 373. ET: *Epistle to the Romans*, p. 389.
90. M. Luther, *WA* 34: I, 276, 7.
91. M. Luther, *WA* 40: I, 69-70. *LW* 26:24-25.
92. K. Barth, *Der Römerbrief*, p. 320. ET: *Epistle to the Romans*, p. 336.

mean any kind of ban on the idea of criticizing and reforming the church. The church needs constant criticism and ongoing renewal. But even this we can undertake appropriately only if we do not look at the church from outside, and certainly not peevishly like Jonah, who under his bush wanted to see the downfall of Nineveh. Rather, we contribute to constructive change by taking part in the church with all our strength. We would deny the Holy Spirit, who makes us children of God, if we would be ashamed of the fellowship, however questionable, with the others who are called to be God's children in the church. — What then is the Christian church? Articles 54 and 55 give a threefold answer.

(1) *The Head of the church.* Article 54 speaks of the church by decidedly *not* speaking of the church, in order to speak rightly about the *church.* To the question of what you believe about the church, no definition follows, such as: the church is . . . Instead comes an answer that almost sounds misplaced, but in truth is the one fitting answer: "That out of the whole human race . . . the Son of God . . . "; and the Son of God remains the subject of the whole statement about the church. The article on the church does not confess belief in the church, but in Jesus Christ, and only in a subordinate clause then also in the church. He is the Head, the leader, the office bearer, the pastor and bishop of the church (cf. 1 Peter 2:25; John 10:14), besides whom there is no need for a proxy. What the church is, and that it is the church of Christ, is determined and understood completely from this its Head. It is comprehended not by what humans do in it, but by what Christ does for it and to it and in it. If there is a church, then it is not because it is here as a given, but because Christ is here. It is not because he once was here, but because in the Holy Spirit he comes today, too. There is a church because he lives and calls it into life and holds it in life. The church does not make him present; he makes himself present to the church, and so the church is present also, as the band of his people. The church is the "creation of the Word,"[93] as the Reformers used to say in citing James 1:18. They meant: it is the creation of Jesus Christ who is proclaimed in it, the creation of the voice of its "Good Shepherd." To hear his voice is the "sacrament," the "spirituality" that it owes to him. He brings the church into being — not sometime or other, to then leave it on its own, but in such a way that it continually lives from his creative Word, from his

---

93. Cf. M. Luther, *WA* 2:430, 25, 361; further: Thesis 1 of the Bern Reformation of 1528, according to Müller, *Bekenntnisschriften,* p. 30; further: *J. Calvins Auslegung der Heiligen Schrift* (Neukirchen-Vluyn: Neukirchener Verlag, n.d.), vol. 14, p. 420 (on James 1:18).

creative presence. Where the church does not live as the creation brought forth by him, it will inevitably become a religious cult that functions in the opposite way, creating its own deity.

When the church becomes an entity rotating about itself, this is worse than all persecution and contempt from the outside. Then its mere presence becomes the only determinative measure of its self-understanding. It will then simply assert: because this entity is here, and because it calls itself the church of Christ, therefore it must somehow be the church of Jesus Christ. As the church and theology have tried, more than once, to view Creation without the Creator, the historical Jesus without the Son of God, and so-called spiritual experiences without the Holy Spirit, and afterward futilely thought that in these matters, conceived without God, nevertheless God is somehow included, so the church and theology have tried to look at the church first as a given, sociological structure. The result has been that the church has gone from one embarrassment to another on the question of what inner right it has to be called the church of Jesus Christ. And even if it is able to arrange an answer, the answer will still not change the fact that not in theory, but in practice it does not need "Jesus Christ" at all for its operation and sustenance. It is then sufficient in itself because in practice it gathers itself, protects itself, preserves and provides for itself, and manages itself, because it has in its own hands what it effectively lives from. It then strives, contrary to the word of Jesus (Matt. 6:31-32), first of all to keep itself alive, as the Gentiles do, and is convinced that in this way the kingdom of God will come to it. Such a church is like a chicken that occasionally flaps its wings, but does not get airborne. Yet it pretends to others, or at least to itself, that this flapping is already flying, or that flying is not necessary at all, because it can flap so nicely. . . .

But where the church of Jesus Christ is, all this thinking of the church about itself is recognized as its great problem. Here such thinking is turned on its head, or rather, turned from its head onto its feet. Here is unerringly spoken: "The Son of God . . . gathers, protects, and preserves for *himself* . . . a chosen community [i.e., called out of the rest of humanity, but also out of its churchly circling in itself]." Here it is clear that the church does not have its ground of existence within itself, but that it lies outside. Then it does not live out of itself. Then it lives because the Son of God says: "Because I live [therefore, and on the strength of this], you also will live" (John 14:19). This is the structural law of its existence: "You did not choose me, but I chose you" (John 15:16). Here the existence of the church is not the first thing. Here the first, determining, actual reality of the church is the hidden, believed presence of its Head, Jesus Christ. For where he is, there is the church also. But Christ and the church are not interchangeable in this formulation. For if Christ is not present, the church is not present either. Even if it calls itself that, it is only an illusory and false church. But where he is, there the church is too, and it is the true church, even if in itself it is so unlikely, so hard-pressed, and so questionable. This has consequences:

(a) That I, to my comfort, "belong . . . not to myself, but to my faithful savior Jesus Christ" holds also for the church as a whole. It does not belong to itself. It is Christ's possession. Belonging to Christ means that the church does not have its own authority over what it is and has, what it says and does, and what it can do and should do. The decisive criterion in all these matters is not what human needs the church is supposed to meet, nor what those who give the money might think, nor what loss of so-called chances and privileges might result. This way the church could easily become the playground of all kinds of foreign interests, which are foreign even if they look good to us. Rather, the decisive standard was formulated admirably by Augustine: "In the church what counts is not: this I say, this you say, this that person says, but: Thus says the Lord."[94]

(b) It is not the case that the Lord exercises imperial power over the church! Nothing contradicts more the church's attempt to arrogate power to itself than what Matthew 20:28 says: Christ has come, not to rule but to serve for our good, as a demonstration of God's mercy and justice. So it is no sinister claim to power, but a genuine comfort, that the church belongs to him and not to itself. This is why the directive to orient itself by "Thus says the Lord" is the command of the gospel. This is why the calling of the church out of circling around itself is the call of the Savior: "Come to me, . . . I will give you rest" (Matt. 11:28). This is why the call of Jesus to seek first the kingdom of God includes the assurance that the question of our needs is not neglected. And this is why the church that has the ground of its being outside itself in Christ is built on rock and not on sand.

(c) This is also why Christ's three actions for the church are true blessings for it. He does them in the exercise of his threefold office. As the prophet who announces the will of God for our redemption, he *gathers* to himself a community he has called and chosen. As the priest who has given himself for us and stepped in for us, he *protects* the church — first of all not from ominous outward enemies, but from itself, from the devastation it causes to itself. He protects it by covering its sins. As the king who rules it

94. Augustine, *De unitate ecclesiae*, chap. 3.

"by his Spirit and Word," he *preserves* it — not necessarily as an outwardly stable entity, and not necessarily in old familiar tracks. But he preserves it by holding it fast through his good news. What people in the church do is often terribly boring and even sad. The church would be lost if it were not true that thanks to Christ's intervention, "It wavers, but it does not sink."[95] In, with, and under, and despite what people do, I dare believe that here the Son of God gathers, protects, and preserves for himself a community.

(d) Christ does this "by his Spirit and Word." This means above all that it actually takes place. The church can rely on it. It is not abandoned by him. This does not take place in a mysterious way. It takes place where his Word is heard by means of holy scripture. But the church cannot assure that his Word is really listened to. It can only ask for this, and it takes place in the fulfillment of this request — in the enlightening of our hearts and minds through God's Spirit.

(2) *The church as the body of Christ.* Of course, the church also means the fellowship of particular humans. One can foster religious convictions on one's own, but we have Christian faith only in the fellowship of the church. Private Christianity is wooden iron. A church that is like a restaurant, where all kinds of customers sit at individual tables and are served by waiters who rush here and there attempting to meet their wishes, is wooden iron too. If my comfort consists in the fact that I do not "belong to myself," then there is no comfort for me without having my circling around myself taken away from me. Where the church is, there a redemption comes into view that redeems me not simply as an individual, but redeems me also from my individualism. So to be a Christian means to be in the church.

Article 55 expounds this. It says rightly first off that all Christians together and each individually — as members of Christ — "share in one fellowship with Christ" and in his gifts. For the Head of the community is not only the key to what the community is. He is also the reason that Christian life is life in fellowship. Jesus Christ is Immanuel, God's guarantee to be God in fellowship with us humans. As such, Jesus Christ is also the fulfillment of the double command of love, in which the vertical and the horizontal, the God-human relationship and the human-human relationship are insolubly linked. If the Holy Spirit brings us into relationship with this God who in Christ keeps fellowship with us, then faith means: "fellowship with Christ." If we come into fellowship with him, we come into fellowship

---

95. "Fluctuat, non mergitur" — M. Luther, *WA* 31, part II.

with all with whom he keeps fellowship. None of us can be a child of God in the Holy Spirit without being together with other children of God who now may and should discover one another as sisters and brothers. That "the Son of God . . . gathers, protects, and preserves" the church does not take away the responsibility of those who experience this, or make them passive. This action calls them forth and calls them out to answer in word and deed and to confess themselves part of the church gathered and supported by him. They do this because they no longer belong to themselves, but to their faithful savior, in preparedness for using their gifts "willingly and with joy for the benefit and welfare of other members."

Here we understand in what sense the church is visible. The fact that it lives from its invisible Head who is present and believed in does not mean that its spiritual essence is invisible, while its visible appearance is simply a secular form. The proclamation of the gospel is most notably "visible." The invisible Head uses this to make known his presence in the church. The Spirit uses it to produce "fellowship with Christ." Without this proclamation the church would in fact be invisible, and the outwardly visible church would become a merely secular matter. The church of Christ is recognizable first of all in its delivering the message of Jesus Christ. But the Heidelberg also places importance on the conviction that fellowship with the Lord Christ, its invisible Head, is visibly manifested in the binding of people into *one* community, called forth and supported by him. For this reason, the manner in which the church is visible is not a matter of indifference. Of course, the order and form of the church at any given time are made by humans, and those who are gathered can do this only according to their insight and from the point of view of what is useful at the time. But if it does not arrange its form according to the gospel proclaimed in it, then in the visible realm it hides its light under a bushel, and becomes wide open to all kinds of foreign influences. Its visible form can and should give witness to its faith that its fellowship is "with Christ." And it gives witness to this faith insofar as thoroughly visible mutual sharing of human life takes place in its arrangements. "By this everyone will know that you are my disciples, if you have love for one another" (John 13:35).

The church gives this witness when its basic order is that each member feels "obliged to use these gifts willingly and with joy for the benefit and welfare of other members." According to its basic order the church is a *diaconal* fellowship. It is diaconal in the fundamental sense that everything done in the church can only be service, action in the service of its Head Jesus Christ. It serves him, and therefore does so especially for "the least of these who are members of my family" (Matt. 25:40). Everyone is responsible for this, and all may and should take part in their own ways. So the church, according to its basic order, needs also to be a fellowship *of sisters and brothers*. There is no one who dare be here only to be served. And there is no one who does not have gifts that can be used in the service of the others. Not everyone has the same function to provide; yet the variety of gifts dare not be an excuse for rescinding the fellowship of sisters and brothers. For there is no one here who does not also need to accept being served by others. To dispense with being served would mean dispensing with mutuality in togetherness, and then some would soon make themselves heads over the others. They all conform to their one, unique, invisible Head in that no one poses as another head. "Serve one another with whatever gift each of you has received!" (1 Peter 4:10; cf. Gal. 5:13). "The greatest among you will be your servant!" (Matt. 23:11).

Are there limits to the fellowship in the church?

(a) Yes, there is one limit that goes right through the heart of the church. It is mostly hidden, and usually even goes through the hearts of all members. It breaks out and becomes a problem especially where being "in the unity of the true faith" is obviously called into question (Art. 54) by "those who call themselves 'Christians,' but espouse un-Christian doctrines or live in an un-Christian manner" (Art. 85). But let us add immediately that unity is not called into question by lively variety in understanding and practicing faith. The unity of the church is not the uniformity of a barracks. Neither dare the calling to unity be a straitjacket for the taming of critical spirits. Yet there is a limit to the "unity of the true faith," because in this unity there dare not be love at the cost of truth. For when truth is harmed, love is also harmed. So the church must take very seriously a calling into question of its "unity in the true faith." But it must take it seriously in a spiritual way, and not with the tools of worldly power. This means first, trust in the Son of God, who through his Spirit and his Word is himself at the forefront of looking after the unity of true faith. The church does not have to give additional help; it can only try to follow him. And second, this means the church has to follow him in an attitude of repentance about itself because the roots of the invasive error can be found in the church *itself*. Therefore the church has first of all to separate *itself* from this error.

(b) Another limit of the church is addressed with the words about the community chosen "out of the whole human race." It is the boundary between church and "world." Of course the church itself is also a part of the world. But this dare not be a basis for clouding over the fact that to be called into the church is to be called out of the compulsions and false bonds of the human race — a break from devotion to the golden calf, power, Mammon, and Moloch. To be the church dare not mean an avoidance of the seriousness of the decision: "They left everything and followed him" (Luke 5:11). To be sure, the Heidelberg lacks instruction that the boundary between church and world is there precisely for the purpose of being crossed again, not in order to go back to those compulsions and bindings, but to go out to the people who live in them. The election of the community dare not be understood as an end in itself. Just as it dare not live in conformity to the rest of the world, so it dare not exist in isolation from it. If God in Christ is not for God alone, then neither can God's church be for the church alone. Then its members also have to turn together to the people around it, in missional and diaconal responsibility. One dare ask: Is the relation of the Christian community to the rest of the world distorted by the traditional relation of clergy and laity? And is it not distorted in such a way that the break in becoming a Christian is clouded, and awareness of the mission of all Christians in the world outside the church walls is suppressed?

(c) However, the church is not limited by living in various places and at various times. Rather, it experiences an unparalleled breaking of limits because through its Head it has a span "from the beginning to the end of the world" (Art. 54). It is always the whole church in every place and at every time. But it is at the same time the ecumenical church. In it even the geographically most distant are in fact our neighbors, mediated by the love of Christ. In it also the temporally most removed, long since dead, are factually our contemporaries by virtue of the resurrection from the dead, and have the right to be listened to by us. And if the chosen community existed already "from the beginning . . . of the world," then Israel belongs to it as well. Yes, it is the first fruits of this chosen community. Israel is for the church not "another religion." According to Article 19 it is bound with the church through the gospel, and not separated from it. That Christ according to Article 54 gathers to himself the chosen community does not have as its only meaning that Christ now stands separating the church and the synagogue. This is correct too, and it is the most burning wound in the ecumenical community of God. But it means also that the church basically owes the synagogue only this one witness, that the same Christ as the one who has come into the world in Israel binds the church inseparably with Israel.

3. *Participation in the church.* Article 54 says finally: I believe of this

community "that I am and forever shall remain a living member of it." So I cannot believe that the church is the church of Jesus Christ without thereby at the same time believing and confessing that I am its member. Just as I cannot hear the voice of the good Shepherd without also recognizing myself as a sheep in the herd, I cannot make the faith statement "church of Christ" without therewith expressing my belonging to it. "There is no uninvolved faith with regard to the church. You cannot know it and acknowledge it and at the same time distance yourself from it."[96] This includes awareness that in the fellowship of the church each and every one counts. "It takes many to be intelligent."[97] If I can be a Christian only in fellowship, then it is only genuine fellowship when each member is involved as one who has come of age. Otherwise the individual would be spoken for by some sort of authority, and would become an object administered and "cared for," instead of being a free subject. God redeems us in Christ not only from the false way of a private Christianity, but also from that of a mass Christianity.

It is conspicuous that Articles 54 and 55 do not specifically mention the office of pastor. Of course, they do not dispute "the office," the ministry of the divine Word, the service of the Word of God.[98] But this special office, which is needed and is to be welcomed by the community, functions within the framework of the calling promised to each and every member. These church articles stand against the picture of the church that recent empirical research on the church [in Germany] has shown.[99] According to this research, what hold sway among "church folk" today are extremely clergy-centered conceptions of the church, in which *the* church is automatically equated with the "office bearers"; these *(the* church) are called on by the people when they feel the need for certain religious performances. Yet to recognize that many people think this way is one thing; to ask whether this is right is another. It surely is not right this way. For if the work of the Holy Spirit has to do with our becoming children of God, and if the eschatological goal of this work has a foretaste in the church, then it

96. W. Kreck, *Grundfragen der Ekklesiologie* (Munich: Kaiser, 1981), p. 34.

97. Cardinal Suenens, *Die Mitverantwortung in der Kirche* (Salzburg: Müller, 1968), p. 81. ET: *Coresponsibility in the Church* (New York: Herder & Herder, 1968), p. 100.

98. Cf. the First Helvetic Confession, acc. to Müller, *Bekenntnisschriften*, p. 105, 1. ET: in *Reformed Confessions of the Sixteenth Century*, ed. A. C. Cochrane (Philadelphia: Westminster Press, 1966), pp. 105-6.

99. Cf. K.-W. Dahm, *Beruf: Pfarrer. Empirische Aspekte zur Funktion von Kirche und Religion in unserer Gesellschaft* (Munich: Claudius Verlag, 1972), p. 2.

can be that there are very different children with different gifts and tasks. But it dare not be that a few regard themselves as though they were parents, while most of the others rate as lay children not yet come of age. For all — not all in the same way, but each in his or her own way — are called to responsible living as children of God.

Here we need to remember Article 32, according to which the faith of each Christian means being "a member of Christ." This is identical with the calling of everyone to active participation in the threefold office of Christ, that is, for oneself to be with him a prophet, priest, and king. The basic, inclusive concept is that of prophetic action, which consists in confessing the name of Christ before people (cf. Matt. 10:32). This confession results in, and is shown in, the twofold form of "resistance and surrender," of revolt and sacrifice. It is not a matter of revolting against this and that person or group, but against the root of evil we see first of all sprouting up in ourselves. And it is about sacrifice, not of something, but through the engagement of oneself. Revolt is the kingly action, and sacrifice is the priestly one. Both belong together. Revolt without sacrifice would become a forceful pushing through of one's own way. And sacrifice without revolt would become weak accommodation. Both belong to the twofold form of the action in which we confess the name of Jesus and the humiliation and exaltation fulfilled in him, his sacrifice and his revolt. All our action can consist only in our thankfully confessing Jesus Christ before other humans. We can all do no more; we all dare do no less. All members of the community may and should *themselves* take part in this confessing the name of Jesus Christ. If they are called through the Holy Spirit to be children of God, then they are declared free and mature. In this maturity they carry out their participation in the church.

And *in this way* they live together in "reconciled diversity."[100] Galatians 3:28: "There is no longer Jew or Greek, there is no longer slave or free, there is no longer male and female; for all of you are one in Christ Jesus!" In 1933 leading German New Testament scholars interpreted this to mean that human differences, which count in the world and which we are to acknowledge, are abrogated (only) in the purely spiritual realm of the church.[101] This does not get at what this is about. The problem for Paul lies

---

100. Johann à Lasco, acc. to J. R. Weerda, *Nach Gottes Wort reformierte Kirche,* Theologische Bücherei 23 (Munich: Chr. Kaiser Verlag, 1964), p. 98.

101. H. Liebling, ed., *Die Marburger Theologen und der Arierparagraph in der Kirche* (Marburg: Elwert, 1977), p. 17.

not in the human differences mentioned, which in his view are not to be denied, including within the church. The problem lies in the supposed superiority and inferiority, in the disparity between the advantages of the one group and the disadvantages of the other that are derived from these differences. This disparity is so unyielding because it is presented as the natural consequence of those differences. However, this apparently unavoidable consequence is abolished in Christ. In him and in the community determined by him the advantages of one group, like the disadvantages of the other, based on these differences, cannot continue. Every ground and justification for this is withdrawn, and withdrawn so strongly that this disparity from now on is completely groundless both within and outside the community. But there is no better way for the community to witness that this disparity is groundless outside the community than to practice its abolishment within the community itself.

Paul names first (a) the theologically weightiest difference between humans, the difference established in salvation history between Jews and "heathen." The former have a favorable position that cannot be made up for by the latter (Rom. 9:4-5). They hold this position not by any human advantages, but by their being chosen to be God's people, to which the "heathen" do not belong. But the greatness of the grace of Christ is shown in the fact that now in the church of Christ, Jews *and* Gentiles are together (cf. Rom. 11:5-7; Eph. 2:11-18). What does this mean? It does not mean the abolishment of the difference between Jews and Gentiles set in salvation history, but the abolishment of a "wall" between the two deduced from it. It means that in spite of the fact that the Gentiles were chosen only later to be in the people of God, no second-place status develops in relation to those who were first chosen. "You — who have come in later from outside — are no longer strangers and aliens, but you are citizens with the saints and also members of the household of God" (Eph. 2:19). This is what Paul in his time fought for. Soon the situation was reversed, so that now it was much more the case that in the church "Jewish Christianity" was demoted, yes, even "overcome," so that the question of whether it was "a factor in the development of Christianity . . . is to be answered in the negative."[102] According to Paul, however, it is obviously harmful for the church itself when it is merely a band from the Gentiles. For Paul, the relation to the Jews who are not Christians is to be understood this way: "As regards the gospel they

---

102. A. von Harnack, *Dogmengeschichte* (Tübingen: Mohr, 1922), p. 60. ET: *History of Dogma* (Boston: Little, Brown & Co., 1899), p. 290.

are enemies for your sake; but as regards election they are beloved, for the sake of their ancestors" (Rom. 11:28). From this statement we can understand why Jews who find themselves in the Christian church dare not be subordinated, or have their voice taken away. They, who with their Yes to the gospel have not stepped over to another religion or been unfaithful to the election of Israel, are needed in the church. They are needed as a continual reminder that a Jewish No to the gospel of Christ can really not be grounds for a Christian No to the Jews, beloved by God on account of their election.

In the second place Paul names (b) a difference that is the sum of all unnecessary differences, not set by God, but in fact present between humans. This difference, however, maintains itself all the more stubbornly on the basis of the "normative nature of the factual." It was not even set aside by the fine sentence of the USA Declaration of Independence that "all men are created equal."[103] It is the difference between those who are on top and those who are underneath, between the rulers and the ruled, between "slave and free." All of us can hardly escape having our vision hampered by this difference: for "one sees only those who are in the light, those in the dark one does not see."[104] The Bible teaches neither a divine sanction of this difference, nor nourishes in us the illusion that it can be set aside by overlooking it. But it does say that through Christ in his community this difference is contested as completely impossible for its favoring one group and holding down another, thereby dividing Christians into respected people and "little people." Community would be impossible if such a division were allowed (cf. James 2:1-13!). Division is resisted, however, not merely with the theoretical statement that all are equal. It is resisted with the practical recognition that God chooses not those who in the world are wise, noble, powerful, advantaged, but rather the weak, the despised, the overlooked (1 Cor. 1:26-31). Therefore the "little people" in the community are encouraged to stand up and must have voice, and the otherwise respected people must come down from their high horses and have no other future than beside these "little ones." By resisting such division in this way, the community rattles the bars of this whole differentiation and exposes it as unnecessary.

103. Cf. O. Müller, *Denkwürdige Vergangenheit*, vol. 1 (Aarau: Kantonaler Lehrmittel-verlag, 1968²), p. 241.

104. Concluding stanza of the play "Die Dreigroschen Oper" ("The Threepenny Opera"), by B. Brecht (1928).

In third place Paul names (c) a structural human difference: that of man and woman. All the goodness of God is reflected in the fact that the human has not been created alone (Gen. 2:18). It is not simply *the* human, but the human in this duality, "as man and woman" (Gen. 1:27). How could this difference be denied in the community, and not much rather be given honor? But what dare not take place in the community founded on Christ is the conclusion drawn from this difference of the kind of order in which the man speaks and the woman is silent, the man commands and the woman follows. If in the community founded in Christ, interdependence and the maturity of all members are not recognized, then this conclusion contradicts its head Jesus Christ. Then we have to say, as Calvin wrote in his letter to women who had been imprisoned because of their witness: "Since it has pleased God to call you as well as men (for in God's sight there is neither man nor woman) so you must also do your duty and you dare not be cowardly. Since we all have our salvation in him, we must be united in carrying on his work."[105] Just as Jewish Christianity was hardly a serious factor in church history, and just as the offensive against deference to the high and rich had little success, so this recognition of the equal calling of woman with men has not been observed. The church was and is to this day a church dominated by men. This is a shameful fact. This business has no ground in Christ. It is good that in our day, because of the pressure that women (being "not cowardly") are exerting, it is gradually beginning to lessen.

In view of all that has been said, the question arises: Where is there actually such a community as has just been described? It was not the description of a verifiable community existing in 1563, when the catechism was published. But how then is what has been described to be understood? You have to say here what has been said previously. If you look at the visibly present church first, and take it as the given, and then only afterward look at its relation to its head Jesus Christ, there is no way except to see the teaching of the catechism as a Utopia, a wishful dream about which we today, under the given circumstances, can do little. But when the order is reversed, and the latter view is first, there is a crucial difference. When, while standing in our present place in the church, we believe in the Son of God, who is the leading subject the church needs to focus on, then what has been said about the church is neither an empirical description of the pres-

---

105. *Calvins Lebenswerk in seinen Briefen,* trans. R. Schwarz (Neukirchen-Vluyn: Neukirchener Verlag, 1962), chap. 1, n. 12, p. 915.

ent condition of the church, nor a fantastic wishful dream, but the *promise* given to the church. If you believe that the Son of God is gathering, protecting, and preserving a community for himself in our church today, then you have the promise that this church may be and become a community in diaconal solidarity, with responsible participation by all its members. And if you have this promise, you will work modestly but assiduously for this kind of a community: a community whose visible form witnesses to the Head in whom it believes.

3.3.3. Our Membership

Baptism (Art. 65-74)

It may sound surprising, because quite a few doctrines of baptism do not include it in their thinking, but baptism is about our church membership. In particular, it is about how people become what they formerly were not: members of the church. Or, from the viewpoint of the church, it is about how the church expands by receiving a new member. How does this take place? Now comes what is really surprising: it takes place neither by people's joining the church, nor by the church's incorporating them, possibly even against their knowledge and will. It takes place as people become *Christians* — that is, persons intimately related to Christ, persons who belong to their faithful savior Jesus Christ (Art. 1), each of whom is "a member of Christ" (Art. 32). Humans do not become this by themselves, by their own decision. They do not become it by the intrusion of the church upon them either. They become it only through Christ in the Holy Spirit. He makes them into those who belong to himself, into "Christians." By becoming a "member of Christ," each becomes a member of his "body." As the voice of Christ comes through to people by his use of the church's ministry, they become Christians. Where this fundamental conviction is disregarded, the result is one of two possibilities. On the one side is that imperial church, which incorporates people without asking. This church probably lightens its aggressiveness by assuring those so manipulated: you can believe whatever you want, and can be passive members; the main thing is that you are attached to the system. On the other side, people can react against such a dominating church by understanding faith as a matter of one's own religious self-determination. Here too I can believe what I want. Only here I can join the church at my pleasure as well as leave it, because I can just as well believe in Christ as in anything. I can make myself into a "member of his body" just as I can join with anyone.

In contrast to both these alternatives it is essential to hold fast to this: Christ himself, and only Christ, makes us Christians, those belonging to Christ, members of Christ. Neither the church nor I myself make me this. And only by Christ's making me his member do I become a member of his church. What takes place for us then, when we become a member of Christ and so a member of the church? What was our situation previously? Not all people are members of Christ and members of the church — and we all were not members at first. For no one is born into the church. Let us not try to make the problem of people's status before and outside of being members of Christ easier by resorting to the argument: as I grant to myself the right to believe what I want, so I have to grant others the same right, even if their use of it does not lead them to a Christian conclusion. It may well be that outside of Christ we believe what we want. But being a person who belongs to Christ is not something I am because I grant myself the right to be, and choose to be at my pleasure. With regard to this, the word of Jesus holds strictly: "You have not chosen me, but I have chosen you" (John 15:16).

Yet the Heidelberg has brought darkness into the question of the situation before and outside being a member of Christ. It has done this by the bare No with which it answers the question of Article 20 about whether all who are lost in Adam are saved, reconciled with God, and loved by God. Faith in Christ itself forbids us to pronounce this No. "The Word became flesh" (John 1:14), that is, a *human being* — not a Christian! "In Christ God was reconciling *the world* to himself" (2 Cor. 5:19) — the world, and not just the believers or those whose names are on the church membership rolls. "But God proves his love for us in that while we still were sinners Christ died for us"; "while we were enemies, we were reconciled to God" (Rom. 5:8, 10). Not that people believe what they want, and that this is their right, but that Christ has stepped in for all — *this* is the reason why we may see all humans in the light of a great hope.

Now we can understand better what is at issue here. The fact that Christ has died for all and that God has in this way reconciled them does not mean that all on their part belong to Christ, are Christians, members of Christ, and so members of the church. This is something special that takes place in the work of the Holy Spirit. In the Spirit, the God who has come for relationship with us works on our side to bring us into relationship and makes us into Christians, those who belong to Christ, children of

God, and so members of the church. In the work of the Holy Spirit what is true in Christ intervenes in our lives so that it becomes effective for us and in us. The work of Christ opens itself up to us and we are open to it. From this point a twofold truth becomes understandable.

First: While the work of Christ for us holds even when we are still enemies and do not yet believe in Christ, the work of the Spirit takes place in us in such a way that we participate in it in faith. Namely, we are empowered and awakened to faith in Christ, in his mercy and righteousness. To become a Christian, a member of Christ, a child of God, and to come to faith in Christ are all one and the same. All our emphasis on the fact that we cannot make ourselves Christians any more than we can give ourselves faith dare not cross out this point — that in this faith the saving work of Christ opens itself to us. If we would cross this out, the work of the Spirit would turn up empty — the work of bringing us into relationship with the God who has come for relationship with us. By coming to faith through the Spirit and becoming a member of Christ and a child of God, we on our side are brought into relationship with God.

Second: We also understand in this context the extent to which belonging to Christ and to the church go together. We do need to distinguish between the two, since becoming a member of the church does not necessarily mean that one is also a member of Christ. But it does work the other way around. If by the Spirit we become a member of Christ and so a child of God, then we are included in the fellowship of the children of God and can no longer withdraw from the church of Christ. We are therewith added to *it* as a member.

Now look at Article 65. "Where does such faith come from? The Holy Spirit awakens it in our hearts by the preaching of the holy gospel." This is common Reformation understanding: the Holy Spirit does not come from somewhere out of the air. It comes together with the Word, bound with the gospel of Jesus Christ proclaimed to us. And faith does not come in any old way. Faith comes from hearing the gospel (Rom. 10:17). It is not our hearing that makes faith. But in the hearing God does this, "the Holy Spirit awakens it" through the instrument of proclamation. It may be noted that within this common understanding there are different Lutheran and Reformed accents (which will come to light more fully in the understanding of the sacrament). While the Lutheran view puts more emphasis on the Spirit's being bound to and dependent on the instrument of proclamation, the Reformed view emphasizes proclamation's being bound to and dependent on the Spirit: only where the Spirit (as the subject of the whole process) makes use of this instrument, does the Spirit bring about faith. In this way, what was pointed out above becomes a little more understandable, namely that a person's belonging to the church comes about only by belonging to Christ through the Holy Spirit, and not the other way around. But in principle the two views are united.

Yet in the continuation of Article 65 a difference between Lutheran and Reformed tradition is often seen. The view is that according to Luther faith is first given in the sacrament, while the Reformed position is that faith is presupposed in the sacrament, as Article 65 apparently indicates: the Holy Spirit (does not effect, but rather) "confirms it by the use of the holy sacraments." Yet there really is no serious difference here either, so long as you are clear about one understanding held in common by the Reformation. Over against Roman sacramentalism, the Reformation held that the sacrament gives us nothing other than what the Holy Spirit gives us through the sermon: the assurance of the grace of God which is received in faith, yes, which itself awakens faith.

But here the question arises: Why then is the sacrament needed, when the same thing is given through the sermon? To this Luther answered plainly and succinctly,[106] because Christ has commanded it. The Reformed leaders offered a somewhat different explanation: they said that the sacrament is needed as a clarifying help for understanding alongside the sermon. Article 66 says sacraments are "holy signs [i.e., signs that point out to us something true] and seals [i.e., authenticating confirmations of what is said to us] instituted by God so that God may use them to more fully reveal and seal to us the promise of the gospel." This explains why the sacrament is needed alongside the sermon: the answer is that the gospel that is proclaimed in the sermon and that awakens faith is made clearer, confirmed, and provided with a seal. Correspondingly, Article 65 declares that through the use of the sacrament the faith brought about by the Holy Spirit through the preaching of the gospel is confirmed and strengthened. As a matter of fact, Luther could also say it this way.[107] Hence in his baptismal liturgy of 1526 the candidate for baptism is asked about his confession of faith before the act of baptism (in which, according to more recent teaching, faith is supposed to first be brought about), and an affirmative answer is foreseen.[108] Likewise, according to the Augsburg Confession, the

106. *Bekenntnisschriften der evang.-luth. Kirche*, pp. 698-99.
107. M. Luther, *WA* 24:256.
108. *Bekenntnisschriften der evang-luth. Kirche*, p. 540.

sacrament, like the sermon, is "witness of the divine will toward us" and is given in addition to it "to awaken and to strengthen our faith."

So, a first point about the sacrament, according to Reformation understanding, is that it belongs together with the proclamation of the gospel, and in principle does not give anything more than the proclamation does. But now we must ask what is special about the sacrament. It makes sense to do this by speaking first in the singular — about *the* sacrament. This is close to the way the Heidelberg proceeds, although we depart from its language. In form, the sacrament is an act tied to an earthly, visible sign — with water and with bread and wine. Or we could say, it is tied to the suggestion of washing by means of water, and to the suggestion of a meal of bread and wine. These signs are taken from daily life, but receive a function in the sacrament they do not have in everyday life. Therefore a warning needs to be raised against seeing too much significance in the fact that the elements of this sign are water, or bread and wine. According to the sober explanation of the Reformers, these elements have been chosen because Christ instituted and commanded the sacrament this way, and not because the elements by their nature carry a special symbolic power within themselves. This indicates that the elements are separated from their usual meaning and receive a new meaning. They *become* signs. Not only is a person not actually bathed in baptism, or filled in the Lord's Supper, but also there is no meaning already latent in the elements that is simply expounded.

This understanding is not uniquely Reformed. According to the Augsburg Confession, as has been noted, the sacrament is "sign and witness of the divine will toward us."[109] Yet, more strongly than the Lutheran position, the Heidelberg puts great emphasis on the conviction that this sign in the sacrament is *only* a sign, an earthly sign, and is not transformed into something divine (cf. Art. 78) — any more than the man Jesus in his bond with the Son of God is transformed into someone divine! Therefore, the sign does not bring something divinely salvific to us. It is not the water, bread and wine in themselves that do anything. To be sure, Luther also says: "Water of course does not do it [the divine act of blessing], but the Word of God."[110] The Heidelberg however, conceives this so radically that it cannot say, as Luther then does, that the water, bread and wine give . . . (on the basis of a bonding of the Word of God with these elements) but only: *God* gives, the *Holy Spirit* brings about . . . . As in the case of the ser-

---

109. *Bekenntnisschriften der evang-luth. Kirche*, p. 68.
110. *Bekenntnisschriften der evang-luth. Kirche*, p. 516.

mon, it is not the sermon but the Holy Spirit through it that brings about faith. There is in baptism as in the Lord's Supper no delegation of the divine action to the earthly sign, so that then the sign does what God does. But there is in the action and working of the Holy Spirit a divine putting into service and using of the elements, so that these thereby do become signs. These signs witness and seal for us visibly not what they, but what God in the Holy Spirit does to us. More exactly, these elements are not in themselves signs. Because they are about witnessing to a divine *act* toward us, the use of the elements, the *act* (that suggestion of washing and that suggestion of a meal), is this sign. On the basis of divine use (so Art. 73), these signs are not merely symbols and parables of the divine action, but *holy* signs, pledges of assurance for God's action. On the basis of the divine use of the signs for witnessing to God's action I can then also say (Art. 69) that "as certainly . . . as I am washed outwardly with water that commonly washes away the filth from my body," so certainly am I washed by Christ "with his blood and spirit from the corruption of my soul." Yet what is actually effective for salvation, what is in this sense sacramental, is not this sign, but the action of Christ in the Holy Spirit upon us, which is signified in the sign. Luther's suggestion (not followed up on by him) points in a similar direction: according to scripture there is strictly speaking only one sacrament, namely Jesus Christ in his Word and Spirit, and baptism and the Lord's Supper are signs of him.[111]

For determining the content of the sacramental act, Article 67 is important. The way the question is put already gives a hint of the answer, which just confirms the question. "The word and the sacraments," that is, the preaching of the gospel as well as baptism and the Lord's Supper have basically the same content. They point "our faith" to the same thing: "our whole salvation is based upon the one sacrifice of Christ on the cross for us." For this is the very thing that "the Holy Spirit teaches in the gospel and confirms by the holy sacraments." The Heidelberg remains true to this basic principle, so that the explication of baptism as well as the Lord's Supper consists primarily of elucidation of their relation to the cross of Christ. Article 67 calls what was done on the cross "the one sacrifice of Christ." This definitely means that it needs no repeating. So baptism and the Lord's Supper are not repetitions of what happened on the cross.

But then what is the relation of baptism and the Lord's Supper to the unrepeatable, once-for-all event on the cross on which "our whole salva-

111. M. Luther, *WA* 6:86, 501.

tion is based"? Article 67 speaks somewhat brusquely and cryptically about this, saying that both sacraments "direct our faith" to the sacrifice, and that the Holy Spirit "teaches" us this in the preaching of the gospel, and "confirms" it in the sacraments. Article 70 unlocks the meaning of this for us, here with reference to baptism. It summarizes the meaning of Good Friday in the formula "forgiveness of sins from God, through grace." Naturally, to understand this we have to keep in mind all that took place in the humiliation of Christ. Forgiveness is not a weak and conciliatory overlooking of guilt, but the event in which God in righteousness says No to the sinful human, and at the same time in love takes this negation onto God's own self in order to say Yes to us. It is the event in which our old person of sin is ended as Christ steps in for us in order that in him, instead of an old person, the new person in covenant with God is lifted up, as Easter reveals. This is what Article 70 is pointing to when it says that I have "forgiveness of sins from God, through grace, for the sake of Christ's blood which he shed for us in his sacrifice on the cross."

And now Article 70 goes on to say more about the Holy Spirit: that we are "renewed by the Holy Spirit" and "sanctified as members of Christ." In the Holy Spirit we are brought into relationship with God. This relationship is with *God* because it is *God* who has come for relationship with us. In short, the Spirit brings us into relationship with God who in Jesus Christ steps in for us, giving the divine self for us. And God's self-giving is so effective that in Christ the old, lost human, separated from God, is done away with and the new, redeemed human, bound with God, is brought forth. To this end God in the Holy Spirit brings us into relationship. In the Holy Spirit all that God has done for us is brought to us, so that what is already true for us in Christ now also begins to be true in us. What is true in Christ is the death of that old human and the bringing forth of the new human. In us this is not yet true. In contradiction to the Christ-reality, the old Adam and the old Eve live on all too jauntily in us. But the Holy Spirit reaches into our life, awakens us to faith, makes us children of God and sets us apart so that we are "sanctified as members of Christ" (Art. 70). In doing this, the Holy Spirit begins to take us into the turn from the old to the new human "so that we may more and more die to sin and lead holy and blameless lives." So the process of bringing us into relationship with God that is carried on in the Holy Spirit does not only bring us knowledge of what has taken place in Christ. It not only points us to this but also brings what has taken place into our life. This is the working of God in the Spirit. And this is what is sacramental in the sacrament. This is what the sign — the washing with water, the eating and drinking of bread and wine — testifies as true, confirms, seals.

We have described the heart of the Heidelberg's teaching on baptism. It may have become clear in the process that the Heidelberg, together with other Reformation doctrines of baptism, has a weakness in that it says about baptism only what — apart from the use of water — can just as well be said about the sermon and the Lord's Supper. This weakness is the reverse side of a strength. The strength is that the Reformers wanted to rescue the sacraments out of the realm of mystery play and to understand them as acts of proclamation. But this still leaves us in the dark about several matters. First, what specifically does baptism do that is not done in the sermon? Second, why is baptism given? And third, why is baptism especially connected with the beginning of the Christian life and entrance into the church? If a baptismal doctrine does not explain these points, it runs the risk of opening an inner split in which baptism is consciously made out to be proclamation, but unconsciously a host of mysteries are smuggled in without theological reflection. Yet to explain these open questions does not require a whole new theory, but only taking more seriously the understandings already presented. The following can then be said:

1. The sign of the sacrament according to the Heidelberg does not lie in the element but in the act. In baptism, for example, the sign is not in the water, but in the washing. The sacramental, divine matter to which the sign points is an event, namely the cleansing and renewing which comes to us sinners from God. From here we can say that there is an essential difference between the sermon on the one hand, and baptism and the Lord's Supper on the other. This difference means that they complement one another, but are not simply the same thing. The difference can be formulated this way: the sermon tells us *what* God does for us and with us; baptism and the Lord's Supper tell us *that* God *does* this to us and with us. Both sermon and the two acts relate to the same gospel. But the sermon works with a view to its contents, whereas the two acts relate to it as event.

2. According to our description, the work of the Holy Spirit consists in causing what is true for us in Christ to reach into our lives, and to reach in such a way that it makes each of us "a member of Christ" and a child of God. Baptism differs from the Lord's Supper because it has especially to do with the beginning, in which a person becomes a member of Christ and child of God, and thus in which this person's membership in the church begins. This beginning puts us on a path in which we have again and again to turn down the old Adam and to go toward the new person. On this path,

what counts is (Art. 70) "that we may more and more die to sin and live holy and blameless lives." Our continuation on the way opened by this beginning is what the Lord's Supper is especially concerned with. Its particular role is to sustain us on our way. Encouraging us to keep on is, however, also a purpose of the participation of the congregation in the celebration of baptism during the worship service.

3. At this point the following should be clear: baptism and the Lord's Supper both have to do with the same thing — what took place on the cross, in which God turns our sins away from us and turns God's love toward us. But in the two acts we have to do with the cross in different ways. What took place on the cross is "one" (Art. 67), unrepeatable. Baptism witnesses to this in its character as the beginning event in our Christian life. It is therefore a one-time act, unrepeatable. But what took place on the cross is also intended to reach into our life and thereby sustain us on the way of renewal. This is witnessed to us by the Lord's Supper, which strengthens us on this way. So the Supper is intended to be celebrated again and again.

4. The order in which proclamation and sacraments are named should be taken more seriously than the Heidelberg does, although the Heidelberg itself does recognize it in Article 65. "The preaching of the holy gospel" goes before "the use of the holy sacraments," thus before baptism. This order is also that of the New Testament, even in the oft-quoted passages about baptism of a whole household. The gospel is spoken to the head of the household and to all in the house and thereupon he has his house and himself baptized (Acts 16:31ff.; cf. 10:44; 16:14). Matthew 28:19-20 only apparently contradicts this order: baptize them and teach them to observe all that I have commanded you. For both these actions are included within the "Great Commission" according to which the apostles are to make all peoples *disciples*. The apostles are here made responsible not only for the proclamation of the gospel, but also for what then becomes of the hearers of the proclamation: they are to be baptized and thereby begin a walk according to what Jesus has commanded. The order "sermon — baptism" makes clear that becoming a member of Christ includes becoming a (full) member of the *Christian community* in baptism. The Holy Spirit, who makes us members of Christ, comes to us by using the preaching of the gospel done in the church. If the Spirit brings about in us faith, then this faith is by this very fact involved in *the* church whose proclamation of the gospel the Spirit has used to awaken our faith. So baptism *following* this proclamation is certainly also the confirmation of our coming into the Christian community.

Finally let us ask about the recipients of baptism. The Heidelberg comes to this last, and only in connection with the question of whether one should also baptize little children. The fact that this became a problem at all is something unique to the baptismal teaching of the Reformation. It is no problem within Roman baptismal doctrine, according to which a child should be baptized as soon as possible in order to wash it from original sin and so protect it from dangers that threaten in the beyond in case of childhood death. The Reformers rejected this view out of concern that baptism might become a magical rite.

Infant baptism is no problem either for the recent freely invented teaching that baptism is a "rite of passage."[112] According to this view, the human being requires a sacral act of consecration corresponding to each of the four stations of the natural rhythm of life: birth, sexual maturation, mating, and death. Baptism is supposed to be such an act for the natural birth of a person. It should be said briefly and bluntly that this view does not stem from holy scripture. It is copied from some history-of-religion text and is fundamentally opposed to Reformation teaching. Reasons for this judgment are: 1. Baptism is not related to natural birth, but to the incorporation of a person into Christ, and so to the dying of the old human and the rising of the new. 2. Baptism does not belong in the context of sexual maturation, mating, or burial, but in the context of sermon and Lord's Supper. 3. Baptism is tied to the acceptance of a person into the Christian church, which is not accomplished by the fact that parents rejoice because a person has come to see the light of day. The rite-of-passage thesis can prove only that in order to receive such a rite a person must be a baby, but not that this rite has anything to do with Christian baptism. We can discuss whether such a rite has nevertheless a useful meaning, as for example a church wedding can. Both of these can have the specific effect that persons are accepted into the intercession of the congregation. But there is no theological basis for naming this rite Christian baptism.

However, in the Reformation environment infant baptism did become a problem, and it is not accidental that the Anabaptist movement, with its rejection of infant baptism, arose here. This Anabaptist concern was by no means disposed of by the Reformers' condoning of the bloody persecution of Anabaptists. Why did infant baptism become a problem for the Reformers and their descendants? Because here it was recognized that baptism stands in the context of the work of the Holy Spirit. So it is not

112. Cf. K.-W. Dahm, *Beruf: Pfarrer*, pp. 124-25.

enough to say: Christ died for us, God loved us "while we were still enemies" — while we were not yet Christians, did not belong to Christ, and so
were not yet members of the church of Christ. The work of the Holy Spirit
is to bring what is true in Christ into our life, so that the gospel is not only
spoken to us, but comes into us, so that we become Christians. This is why
the work of the Spirit is inseparable from what it brings about in us: faith.
Therefore baptism is inseparable from the faith of the one baptized. This
understanding distinguishes the Reformation teaching on baptism from
the Roman position, as well as from the rite-of-passage thesis, and this understanding is the result of seeing faith as the work of the Holy Spirit. So
Martin Luther says in 1520 that the sacraments are fulfilled, not by their
taking place, but by their being believed, so that it is not baptism which
justifies us, but only faith awakened by the Word of promise,[113] and that
baptism is of no use to us without the faith that accepts this promise.[114]
Yes, "before we take the sacrament of baptism we must have faith."[115] So
according to the Augsburg Confession the sacraments "require faith," and
their right use consists in "one's receiving them in faith and having faith
strengthened through them."[116] In its own way, the Heidelberg says this
with its thesis about the confirmation of the faith brought about by the
Holy Spirit through the use of the sacraments (Art. 65). Therefore, according to Article 74, in baptism children are "promised" redemption in Christ,
and the Holy Spirit who brings about faith. They are thereby "distinguished from the children of unbelievers." Yes, they are baptized, as the order for baptism that accompanies the catechism makes clear, only because
they already have received "the Holy Spirit who awakens faith."[117]

If the gift of the Spirit is inseparable from the faith it brings about, and
if, according to Article 21, faith is sure knowledge of what is revealed in
God's Word and heartfelt trust in the forgiveness and blessedness given me
by God out of grace for the sake of Christ, then it may be asked how this
can be meaningfully asserted with respect to a baby. On this question the
Reformers fell from one embarrassment into another, without completely
giving up the fundamental principle that only faith makes baptism effective. They answered to this question: 1. We can never ascertain the faith of
another, so we cannot deny that the baby already has such sure knowledge

113. M. Luther, *WA* 6:532-33. *LW* 36:66-67.
114. M. Luther, *WA* 6:517. *LW* 36:39.
115. M. Luther, *WA* 24:330.
116. Cf. note 106.
117. According to W. Niesel, *Bekenntnisschriften*, p. 143.

and heartfelt trust in God's grace in Christ. For certain, we cannot look into the hearts of others. But faith expresses itself in confession of faith. For this reason in Luther's baptismal liturgy the child is rightly asked (already before baptism) whether it believes in the triune God and renounces the devil. So after all, without confession of faith by the baptismal candidate, no baptism! Baptism is instituted "so that one confesses faith."[118] Answer 2: But in the place of the one baptized, the parents and Godparents vicariously affirm the confession of faith for the child. Good, but then it would have to be shown why particularly in baptism (in distinction to the Lord's Supper) it normally has to be the case that those baptized believe in such a way that it is not they who believe, but others who do this for them. Answer 3: Faith is no achievement to be produced by us in order to make ourselves worthy to receive God's grace. Right, faith does not look at itself, but looks at Christ and his stepping in for us. But this has to be made clear by the right preaching of the gospel. The need to get rid of a false understanding of faith is no argument for making faith so invisible that you can no longer make clear that it is relying on Christ and his forgiveness. If this were an argument, why then not undertake similar attempts with relation to the Lord's Supper in order to thwart scrupulous reflection about the worthiness of the recipients? Answer 4 — and this is explicitly stated in Article 74: As in Israel children, more accurately little boys, came into God's people through circumcision, so children of Christian parents come into the community through baptism. But in Israel little boys did not become members of God's people by circumcision, but just as little girls, through birth. In the church, on the other hand, children do not become members of Christ and so members of the church through the faith of their parents, let alone through their birth: see John 1:12-13. Answer 5: Oh, ultimately faith is perhaps not so important after all! For God's promise does not fail, even when faith is lacking. Yes, indeed very comforting: God's promise does not fail, while our faith is often shaky. But this does not prove that in baptism, of all places, faith can just as well be there as not, because God's promise is so sure.

These arguments thought up in defense of infant baptism cannot be called convincing. Still, the Reformation got mixed up in these difficulties only through their new insight that in receiving baptism, faith cannot be lacking. For if baptism is not about expressing the truth that God in Christ loves everyone, whether Christian or non-Christian, churched or un-

118. M. Luther, *WA* 12:481.

churched, but is about our becoming Christians, those belonging to Christ; and if baptism relates to the work of the Spirit who makes us members of Christ and so members of the church; and if baptism is about our discerning the faith brought about by the Spirit through the hearing of the gospel; and if according to Article 65 this faith is confirmed in the use of the sacraments, then the faith of the one baptized, and confession of faith as well, belongs to baptism. Then the practice of infant baptism cannot be justified, and the adherence of the Reformers to this practice was inconsistent.

The Lord's Supper (Art. 75-85)

To be a Christian means to be a member of a fellowship. In what sense? What holds the people gathered in this fellowship together? What gives the fellowship its basis for existing? Should we understand the church fellowship as a social group, which is founded on and has its basis in certain interests or ideals about which its members are united? A social group ordinarily occupies people only part of the time. As a rule it is something alongside one's vocation, which it doesn't much affect. It is typically part of leisure-time activity. And usually after people leave its meeting place the group evaporates into thin air, so to speak, even though its members greet one another politely when they meet on the street. And generally, even though there are those who have been members for many years, people are prepared to revoke their membership. If a person can no longer identify with what unifies the group, or if certain other members are not agreeable, one leaves. Is the church such a social group? We should not say No too quickly here. For the church understood as a social group is after all able, in considerable measure, to motivate and engage its members. This is a justifiable concern, which it would be foolish to ignore. There can be liveliness here that an established church gets going only with great difficulty. And yet we must say No to this view at its core. What binds the church into a fellowship is not what its members agree on — what is identical in their interests, ideals, basic principles, or sensibilities. What binds them together does not lie in themselves. It lies outside themselves, and binds them together in a way that holds even when they move out of their meeting place and apart from one another. It binds them in such a way that something within them resists if they want to leave. It brings together people who otherwise could hardly be brought under a common denominator. A social group is based on the principle: "Birds of a feather flock together." But the mark of the church's fellowship is that in it very different people are gathered together.

Is the church then a *pluralistic* structure — perhaps in the style of modern society, in which people of the most varied convictions and practices live together? Must we not describe what binds people together in modern society by using the very least common denominator, so that no one is excluded? Except those who want to exclude others from this society! What binds people together here is that on the basis of historical conditions they live together in a certain area. And what binds them together is a common agreement to grant one another their varied views and practices without excluding one another. Is the church such a pluralistic society? It would then be a realm of society — not precisely definable over against other realms — in which people on the basis of their presence in the Christian West, for example, factually live together. They have to live together in such a way that in their varied opinions and actions they do not exclude one another. In such a church the uppermost principle would be that no one, not even clergy, dare make rules about what its members have to think and do. On the contrary, its office-bearers would have to orient themselves to the "needs" of their varied members — in the way that K.-W. Dahm has wished: "The church [meaning the official church] must, in the concert of the competition, bring a consumer-oriented offering to the market."[119]

We will call this church, in distinction from the church-as-social-group, the warehouse church. Its concern, over against that of the church-as-social-group, is to take into account the variety of Christian life, and it is not to be looked down on. Just the same, a No also has to be said against the core of the understanding of the church as warehouse. The warehouse church can no doubt rightly claim that in it *diverse people* are gathered together. But it cannot state in theological seriousness what the spiritual basis is that *gathers* them together. What unifies it is the coincidence that we in the West find ourselves in a common "Christian tradition." But to what extent this church is "Christian" by accident of where we live, or perhaps by what our color happens to be, must remain open. And it is supposed to stay open, for the sake of its orientation to satisfying the needs of its members. This view of the church rests on the false reasoning that if the church *calls* itself Christian, it *is* Christian. So this view suffers basically from the same malady as the church-as-social-group, in that it ascertains what

119. K.-W. Dahm, *Beruf: Pfarrer*, p. 112.

makes the church a Christian fellowship by observing its own present state and self-understanding.

To both these conceptions No has to be said — not only because they cannot explain particular matters theologically: the first view cannot explain that *diverse* people are to be gathered into the church; the latter cannot explain what *holds* these diverse people *together.* No has to be said to both views because they totally neglect the principle of faith that the church as Christian fellowship does not exist by its own doing. In these two conceptions Jesus Christ comes at most (and therefore not necessarily) as object of the activity and thought of the church people, but not as the determining subject of the church. That Jesus is the real subject of the church is the cardinal principle of the Reformation teaching on the church (cf. Art. 54).

This principle I am now going to highlight in a particular way — with the insightful formulation of J. Calvin, according to which it is no coincidence that the Apostles' Creed speaks of the forgiveness of sins right after speaking of the church. This means that "Forgiveness of sins, then, is for us the first entry into the church."[120] So we do not understand what the church as a Christian fellowship is if we do not understand what the forgiveness of sins is. If we understand *this,* then we also understand the fellowship of Christians. It clearly owes its existence and endurance completely to the truth and reality of God's forgiving sins. If we disregard this truth and reality, there is nothing left except something like a church-as-social-group-for-piety-or-virtue or a church as warehouse. If on the other hand we do not disregard it, then we stand before a church that is more inclusive than a church-as-social-group and more solid than a warehouse church. We see it then, in the words of the Barmen Declaration, "as the Church of pardoned sinners . . . in the midst of a sinful world."[121]

What brings the church together into a fellowship, as a group of sinners in the midst of other sinners, is fundamentally this one thing: they are a group of sinners saved by grace. This unites them more strongly and deeply than agreement among human views can hold "birds of a feather" together. The barrier to belonging together does not lie in diversity, which could be overcome by making everyone the same. The barrier lies in the fact that its

120. J. Calvin, *Institutes* IV.1.20.

121. *Die Barmer Theologische Erklärung: Einführung und Dokumentation,* ed. A. Burgsmüller and R. Weth (Neukirchen-Vluyn: Neukirchener Verlag, 1983), p. 36. ET: *The Theological Declaration of Barmen,* in *The Book of Confessions,* Part 1 of the Constitution of the Presbyterian Church (U.S.A.) (Louisville, 1994), p. 257.

members have been uncovered by God, and before God, as sinners, that is, as enemies of God and therefore also of their neighbors (Art. 5). But God in Christ, the crucified one, has not only exposed their sins, but has at the same time covered them. In this way God has removed not only what separates them from God, but also what separates them from one another. On this basis they are allowed to discover themselves as people who belong to God, and who thereby also belong together with one another. They have ultimately nothing to hold against one another, but have to give one another their hands, and hold fast. For this reason, none of the differences between the people gathered in this church can any longer be cause for separation — the differences of race, class, gender, and nation. But also the differences of schools of various theological convictions, not to mention other convictions, yes, not even the differences in confessional traditions can be cause for separation. Therefore these differences in the church do not need to be removed (apart from the case of an error that devastates the church). They can have validity in life together, and can, because of the freedom that flows from forgiveness, make one another more fruitful. Whatever may otherwise separate people must not separate them here.

The grounding of the church in forgiveness shows itself in the thankfulness in which people gathered through this forgiveness now do what corresponds to the grace of God shown to them. Because of grace, people who are very different from one another accept one another as Christ has accepted them (Rom. 15:7). What unifies these vastly different people into a fellowship is not something they are able to give themselves. Nor is it a given on the order of my being a person of the technological era and standing in the tradition of the Christian West. It is not that kind of given at all — it is an encounter that is imparted to this fellowship and makes it into a fellowship in the first place. What unifies it is the encounter on the basis of which they may thankfully confess themselves as a group of sinners saved by grace. What makes them a Christian fellowship is this: the crucified and exalted Jesus Christ persists in having fellowship with them again and again, and through the Holy Spirit places them in fellowship with himself. And this is despite the fact that in the midst of a world of sin they are a band of sinners! Yet because Christ overcomes their sins by forgiving them and showing mercy to the sinners, they are in fellowship with him. What brings them together is Jesus Christ's gathering them to himself in the Holy Spirit, and showing himself to them as the friend of sinners. This makes them a Christian fellowship. This lends their fellowship existence and endurance. This also moves them to that thankfulness in which they show their bonding with him by forgiving one another. In this way they themselves make it impossible to let one another go. For this reason they also "bear with" one another.

After Calvin calls the forgiveness of sins the first approach to the church, he continues: "Accordingly, we are initiated into the society of the church by the sign of baptism. . . . Not only does the Lord through forgiveness of sins receive and adopt us once for all into the church, but through the same means he preserves and protects us there."[122] The first part relates to baptism, the latter to the Lord's Supper, about which we are to speak here. If we keep in mind the context that has been described, then it is clear that the Lord's Supper has its indispensable place in the existence of the Christian fellowship. Then it can become clear to us that the celebration of the Lord's Supper is the central celebration of the Christian fellowship and the high point of its worship. It is understandable also that along with baptism, which is a one-time event, the Lord's Supper is to be celebrated "again and again." However, it is also clear that removing the Lord's Supper from the normal Protestant service is an arbitrary act. There is no excuse for doing this, not even the Reformation argument for such omission, that the service of the Word is in itself a complete worship service. This argument for the absence of the Lord's Supper in the regular worship service can easily give rise to an unclear feeling, not theologically supported, that perceives the meal with a kind of numinous fervor, as though it offers much more than proclamation. It now becomes a mysterious procedure that becomes more sacred the less one knows what is really going on, and more "holy" the less frequently one is exposed to it. And we have not yet mentioned that with the absence of the Lord's Supper in the normal worship service, a diffuse feeling can set in that "something" is missing. And then come attempts to satisfy this feeling in false ways with all sorts of arbitrarily introduced frills! But if we understand the Lord's Supper in the context described, then it has a clear, sober, namable, valuable meaning that distinguishes it beneficially from such mystery cults.

What is its valuable meaning? Let us describe it with the thoughts that have been presented — and so make ourselves aware of the central role of the Lord's Supper in the church's life. Its meaning is the celebration of the ground-laying event for the church which gives the Christian fellowship its existence and duration. It is the event by which the church "in the midst of a sinful world" is called out, called together, and maintained as "the church

122. J. Calvin, *Institutes* IV.1.20-21.

of pardoned sinners." As in Article 54 to the question of what the church is, the surprising answer is given that Christ gathers, protects, and preserves it, so in Articles 75ff. for the understanding of the Lord's Supper the question of the existence and the upholding of the Christian fellowship is raised — albeit implicitly. But it is only implicitly raised because right away everything is overshadowed by the answer that in the Lord's Supper *Christ* keeps fellowship with us sinners and brings us sinners into fellowship with him. He does this by letting what he has done on the cross for the forgiveness of our sins come to benefit us through the Holy Spirit. He does it in that, as the one who gave himself for us on the cross, he binds himself with us and us with him by the Holy Spirit. He does it, not by giving us something just to satisfy our appetite, but by giving us himself as food and drink, as truly as he promised us: "*I* am the bread of life" and "*I* am the true vine" (John 6:48; 15:5). In this way he gives us food and drink "for eternal life." For if our sins are forgiven, nothing, not even death, can separate us from him and his love.

This event above all is what the Heidelberg describes in its articles on the Lord's Supper. In them an extraordinary doubling stands out. For one, the promise is made to us in the Lord's Supper that he whose body is given for us and whose blood is poured out for us is present. For another, the promise is also made that he is not only held out before us, but also brought close and shared, so that through him and with him we are given food and drink for eternal life. Article 76 says that for one thing, we receive forgiveness and eternal life thanks to the one who has been given up for us; and that for the other, the Holy Spirit comes to us and unites us with Christ, yes, with his body exalted to the right hand of God, with the new human given in him. So what takes place is like the first creation! As, according to the creation saga, Eve was flesh of Adam's flesh (Gen. 2:23) so we are completely from him, and not only from him, but with him, because he and we together "live and are governed forever by one Spirit." Article 79 says that for one thing, his crucified body and poured-out blood are food and drink for us, that is, we live by his offering of himself for us, for our forgiveness; and for the other "that we share in his true body and blood through the working of the Holy Spirit," and are bound with him so that what has been done for our good comes to benefit us. The two aspects are gathered together in Article 80, which says "the Lord's Supper testifies to us that we have complete forgiveness of all our sins through the one sacrifice of Jesus Christ . . . on the cross . . . and that through the Holy Spirit we are ingrafted into Christ."

How does this take place in the Lord's Supper? As in baptism, so also in the Lord's Supper, the Heidelberg sees a distinction between the sign and the substance, and also a relationship. The substance is the event, Christ's forgiving our sins in binding us to himself in the Holy Spirit. The signs are not actually the elements of bread and wine in themselves, but their use, the eating and drinking of bread and wine. This action takes place in correspondence to Christ's giving of himself to us in the Spirit to eat and drink. In this, the sign is only a sign and not the matter itself. Christ in the Holy Spirit is the subject of the celebration of the Lord's Supper, which does not cede its action and delegate it to the sign, let alone to the elements. It is not the sign that works redemptively on us. God, Christ, the Holy Spirit does this — with the accompanying sign, nevertheless in such a way that not the accompanying sign but only the one who accompanies the sign works here for our good. Therefore we assert that just as the water in baptism is not transformed into something divine, so also the bread in the Lord's Supper is not transformed (Art. 78). For this reason we must dispute the consequence Roman teaching drew in the Council of Trent[123] that as a result of a transformation of the elements, Christ is to be worshiped in these elements (Art. 80). We must also join the Heidelberg in disputing the Roman view that this meal, beyond witnessing to the one-time sacrifice of Christ on the cross, means its (unbloody) repetition, and the view that the presence of the one-time sacrifice of Christ through the Holy Spirit is not effective in itself, but becomes so only through the ecclesiastical official who is therefore literally to be called "priest."

(Article 80, which vehemently disputes Roman positions, was inserted into the Heidelberg in the fall of 1563. It reacts against the teaching on the mass that the Counter-Reformation in the Council of Trent in 1562 made dogma.[124] What the Heidelberg Catechism says against it is in order, as far as its positive affirmation goes. But you can be right and let your position escalate into being absolutely right, which actually makes your right wrong. The condemnation of that teaching on the mass — a condemnation adopted by Calvin, by the way[125] — as "condemnable idolatry" is simply a break in style in this catechism. It is so obviously written in a momentary rage about this latest news from Rome that we must hold James

---

123. H. Denzinger, *Enchiridion Symbolorum* (Barcelona: Herder, 1961^{31}), p. 888.

124. Denzinger, *Enchiridion Symbolorum*, pp. 938ff.

125. J. Calvin, *Kleiner Abendmahlstraktat* (1541), in *Calvin-Studienausgabe*, vol. 1/2 (Neukirchen-Vluyn: Neukirchener Verlag, 1994), p. 488, 7. ET in *John Calvin: Selections from His Writings* (Garden City, NY: Anchor Books, 1971), pp. 531ff.

1:20 against it: "Your anger" — even understandable, grounded anger — "does not produce God's righteousness." But this is only a secondary matter. At any rate, it is important to hold fast to this conviction: it is not the sign or the action connected with the sign that forgives. It is only the crucified Jesus Christ signified by the sign who forgives us our sin by sharing himself with us and binding us to himself in the Holy Spirit.)

When the distinction between sign and substance is clear, the relation between them needs to be emphasized. Because of this relation, the eating and drinking of bread and wine has to do not with an empty sign, a mere simile which could be lacking, or be replaced by something else. The use of bread and wine is of course first of all an act of obedience to the command and institution of the meal by Jesus Christ (Art. 75 and 77). But within the obedient use of bread and wine, these elements have their usual meaning and function taken away and receive a new one. They are linked with what Christ through the Holy Spirit does for us. In this linkage, it is no longer we who use the elements in order to interpret a spiritual event in a tangible way, through the significance of these signs. Rather, Christ uses their significance (so Art. 79) in order through it "to assure us by this visible sign and pledge that we share in his true body and blood through the working of the Holy Spirit just as certainly as we receive with our mouth these holy tokens in remembrance of him, and that all his sufferings and obedience are as certainly our own as if we ourselves had suffered and satisfied God." So the signs in the celebration of the Lord's Supper are not empty signs. They also give us something: through them Christ gives us, in a visible way, the assurance that the Spirit really gives us what they signify. So they are, to speak with 1 Corinthians 10:16 (Art. 77, 79), "fellowship," *koinonia,* our participation in the body and blood of Christ.

Seeing Article 80 as a later insertion, it is evident that the passage about the Lord's Supper in the Heidelberg comprises two groups of five articles each. The five articles 75-79 speak about the fellowship into which Christ enters with us in the Holy Spirit, as the Lord's Supper tells and assures us. The five articles 81-85 speak about the fellowship of Christians in the church. The first five articles talk about the *grace* of Jesus Christ (about his *charis*) witnessed to us in the Lord's Supper, in which he binds himself with us and us with him. The second five articles talk about the response called forth by this grace — our *giving thanks* for it (about our *eucharistia,* from which word comes the most fitting designation of the Lord's Supper as "eucharist," i.e., thanksgiving celebration). Both belong inseparably in the celebration of the meal. The purpose of the meal is not only to assure the community of the grace that has called and held it together, but also to have the community thankfully hear and receive grace. Grace is here in no other way than that the Christian community that lives from it and is carried by it comes together in responding to grace. The community emerges in thankful answering to the grace that keeps it alive and forges it together. It demonstrates its true nature in giving thanks that Christ keeps fellowship with us sinners and that the church is thereby the "church of pardoned sinners." It becomes visible in confessing its head and so also his body, that is, itself, as the flock bound together by him.

Therefore the Christian community appears in its most concentrated form in the Lord's Supper. Here the claim is made on it to show itself worthy in all its members of Christ's keeping fellowship with it. Worthy means living in accord with the worth it receives by being in the bond of Christ. Through its bond with Christ the church is made worthy of Christ's fellowship. It is distinguished in such a way that as a whole, in the relation of its members to one another, and in their personal walk, it needs to correspond to this distinction. If it neglects this, it denies what is assured to it in the Lord's Supper — its bond with Christ. In this case, to prevent such denial and to call itself to order, the "office of the keys" (according to Matt. 16:19) must be brought to bear (cf. Art. 83). In a sense, this office is regularly brought to bear — in the "preaching of the holy gospel." But it is brought to bear particularly in "the Christian discipline of repentance," also called "church discipline." (The underlying Latin term *disciplina ecclesiae* also means "church order.") This latter concept makes sense because the question in this context is how the Christian congregation lives in accord with Christ's fellowship with it, and how then its members live in accord with what the congregation truly is. So it is understandable that church order has its origin in the gathered community of the Lord's Supper.

The crucial problem of church order that affects the whole life of the Christian community comes when disorder arises in the community because Christians do not live in accord with fellowship in Christ, when they "show by what they say and do that they are unbelieving and ungodly" (Art. 82). This is a very real problem. For the church cannot in the final analysis be threatened from the outside, by those living outside of it who are "unbelieving and godless." But it is all the more seriously threatened on its own grounds, by the errant teaching and ways of living that break out, and by the wolves in sheep's clothing who show up (cf. Matt. 7:15). In actuality they will as a rule hide their unbelief and godlessness behind the nice front of the claim that they also belong among the sheep of the Good

Shepherd. They will bring fine-sounding arguments for their perverse undertakings, so that their perversity is not obviously "demonstrable." And
they will be up in arms, claiming that their perfect right is being denied, if
you uncover their false appearance. They will not accept being merely sinners, as all in the community are again and again. All members of the community are unworthy, not better people. Totally dependent on God's grace
and yet not deserving it, all come again and again to the Lord's Supper to
be comforted by the forgiveness of their sins. Unworthy people are invited
to the Lord's Supper, and not excluded from it. They thereby acknowledge
that forgiveness holds for them, that they are those "who are dissatisfied
with themselves for their sins, and yet trust that these sins have been forgiven them and that their remaining weakness is covered by the passion
and death of Christ, and who also desire more and more to strengthen
their faith and amend their life. But the impenitent and the hypocrites eat
and drink judgment to themselves" (Art. 81). *They,* only these unrepentant
ones, are the "unbelieving and godless." And they can be recognized by the
fact that they do not, as the others do, acknowledge that they are likewise
totally in need of God's grace, and in it have all their comfort and renewing
strength. Their ungodliness consists precisely in their comfortless enmity
toward grace, and their disbelief consists in their unrepentant lack of insight into their dependence on God's grace. *For this reason,* though they
call themselves Christians, they actually teach or live in an un-Christian
way (Art. 85). Their error can express itself in both teaching and living, and
both are equally offensive: breaches of right teaching and worship, and
breaches of right living.

By thinking and acting in these ways, they "eat and drink" judgment,
and that not only to themselves. They harm the entire community: they
"profane the covenant of God" and bring it about that "God's wrath would
be provoked against the entire congregation" (Art. 82). By living contrary to
that by which the Christian community at its root lives, they make the entire life of the congregation before God a vexation and before the world a
thing unworthy of belief. Therefore, "according to the ordinance of Christ
and his apostles" (Art. 82), "the Christian discipline of repentance" in the
narrower sense must be used with these people. This practice is no Reformed specialty. Luther also spoke in favor of it, and citing Matthew 18:15-
17 as warrant, even calling it a mark of the church.[126] In this matter, Article
85 envisions three measures, the harshest of which is exclusion from the

126. M. Luther, *WA* 50:631f. *LW* 41:153.

Lord's Supper and from the baptism of their children. By this method the community makes known that it can no longer acknowledge those concerned as members in the body of Christ. Did this measure bring forth a hesitation to celebrate the Lord's Supper in congregations, as one often hears? This could only be the case where the connection of this measure with the gospel has been perverted into connection with moralism, so that only the morally better people are allowed to the Lord's Supper. This could only be the case where it is forgotten that *sinners* are not excluded from the Lord's Supper, but only *those* sinners who deny God's grace and their dependence on it and live contrary to this, thereby excluding themselves from the church of pardoned sinners. That harshest measure can therefore consist only of the church's ascertaining the self-exclusion of these persons from this church. Its goal is for this very reason not their exclusion, but the winning back of these persons who do not want to live as "pardoned sinners" so that they return into the congregation, and so that Christian fellowship is there in earnest. The more important measure, which historically has become more effective, is the one named first: loving counsel. This admonishing counsel is the origin of pastoral care and home visitation. Moreover, its practice is entrusted to the whole congregation, which means that the pastors also need it themselves: pastoral care for all members of the congregation with visitation of the places where they live. In short, the characteristic example of "church discipline" reveals a church order that is based on the statement of Ephesians 4:15-16, on which the thesis about the church in the Barmen Declaration of 1934 is also based: "Speaking the truth in love, we must grow up in every way into him who is the head, into Christ, from whom the whole body is joined and knit together."[127]

127. M. Luther, WA 12:481.

4. The Free Human Being

4.1. The New Human Being

4.1.1. Justification (Art. 56, 59-64)

The entire work of God has as its goal drawing the free human being. Especially the work of the Holy Spirit as the final, eschatological work of God, has its meaning in creating the new human being. The new human being is the one who is brought to the "freedom of the glory of the children of God" (Rom. 8:21). But who is the "free human being"? The free human being is the one who in correspondence to the free God becomes, and is, a free person. This includes a twofold reality.

First, this free human being is not simply here in every person you meet. These persons are not free until they *become* human beings who correspond to God. To do this, a person must become a different and new human being. The need is to become new, not better or higher, but rather a person who is freed from alienation and so at last is really human. We cannot make ourselves into such persons. We are made into new persons through Christ, who in committing himself and stepping in for us is our liberator. And we arc made new persons through the Holy Spirit, who brings us into relationship and into correspondence with our liberator, and so makes us children of God. So, through the work of Christ and through the work of the Holy Spirit, humans become *new* persons, who correspond to the free God by being themselves free human beings.

Second, the freedom of the free human being has a definite content. God's freedom, as we have tried to understand, is freedom for and in coexistence with what is different from God. It is genuine freedom, self-determination, in which God does not give up being God, but is really Godself. In this self-determination, God distinguishes the divine self from what is other than God, but not in order to be independent, living for self. Rather, God self-determines for togetherness, for living together with us who are other than God. If we become free human beings in correspondence to this free God, then the freedom opened to us can be only the kind in which our perverse habit of living to please ourselves, our unfree freedom, is overcome. In true freedom our free choice can be nothing other than the choice for coexistence, freedom in and for living together with God and with all loved by God.

Both of these realities are to be unfolded in this fourth chapter — that the freedom of the free human being is that of the *new* human being, freed through Christ and the Holy Spirit; and that the freedom of the free human being is freedom from the false freedom of independence and freedom for and in solidly united community. Because the freedom of the free human being has both these aspects, it is the foretaste of the promised "freedom of the glory of the children of God." Under the heading of "The New Human Being," I will begin by speaking about the first aspect: that the freedom meant here is not one we win for ourselves or arbitrarily assume for ourselves, but one given us by God in Christ through the Holy Spirit. Foundational for all that follows is John 8:36: "So if the Son *makes* you free, you *will* be free *indeed*." This is what the doctrine of justification emphasizes.

The statement of the Heidelberg about this in Article 60 is good Reformation teaching: I am right with God

> only by true faith in Jesus Christ. Although my conscience accuses me that I have terribly sinned against all the commandments of God, and have not kept any of them, and that I am still always prone to all evil, nevertheless God, without any merit of my own, out of sheer grace, grants and imputes to me the perfect satisfaction, righteousness, and holiness of Christ. It is as if I had never committed any sin or had ever had sinfulness in me, and had myself performed all the obedience which Christ has carried out for me, if only I accept such a blessing with a trusting heart.

This coincides materially with what is said in Article 56 about the forgiveness of sins. So we can say: what has just been quoted is exactly what is meant by "forgiveness of sins." And we must also say: forgiveness of sins is something much deeper than that weak excusing which is said to be God's business, because otherwise the dear God would have missed his calling.[1] Such excusing is weak because it either does not really look at what is to be forgiven or does not take it seriously. It is weak because in essence it simply overlooks what is bad, passes over it, forgets it, as you wipe a speck of dust from your clothing. So in reality it suppresses the bad into the subconscious, where it causes further damage. Such excusing would, for example, in regard to the murder of the Jews, mean simply acting as though it had not happened. Forgiveness of sins is no such excusing. Rather, it is justification.

What does justification mean? It certainly does not mean making a wrong that has taken place, such as the murder of the Jews, into something that did not happen, or somehow passing over it. Justification comes to a person who cannot be justified — and who is nevertheless justified. How can this be? It is not that when facing wrongdoing the question about making things right is dropped in order to let grace rule instead of justice. This grace would wind up treating the wrongdoing as harmless. It would definitely not be *just*ification. It could not mean that through it I am righteous before God (Art. 59) — and this is what really matters — a person becoming just in God's eyes. Since justification must mean becoming just in God's eyes, and dare not mean less than this — not merely that God "excuses" me — what justification is about is that I, who am in the wrong, and have done wrong, and who therefore cannot be justified, nevertheless become "right" with God. How does this come about?

The gospel witnesses to us that "I am righteous *in Christ* before God" (Art. 59). Our justification corresponds exactly to the fact that Jesus Christ, who as such is guiltless, has stepped in for us guilty ones. In our place he has taken on himself God's righteous No to our guilt, and thus in our place has done what is needed for righteousness. Our justification corresponds to this, since in it we who in ourselves are guilty and stay guilty, are, because of Christ's stepping in for us, and because of the righteousness which he has satisfied, not guilty, and stay not guilty. Our justification is what Luther called the "blessed exchange";[2] that we who have "grievously sinned" and are "still inclined toward all evil," in and through Christ are totally different, new persons, as though we "had never sinned nor been a sinner." Our justification consists in this: that in view of ourselves, and for our sake, we are poor guilty sinners, and that in view of Christ and his righ-

---

1. Voltaire, according to K. Barth, *KD* I/1, p. 442. *CD* 1/1, p. 421.
2. M. Luther, *WA* 7:25.

teousness and for his sake we are free children of God who are pronounced righteous.

From this consideration, Article 60 articulates the oft-quoted Reformation formula, that justified persons are *at the same time* righteous and sinners *(simul justus ac peccator)*.[3] This does not describe an abstract paradox. This signifies the truth of that blessed exchange on the strength of which we, who in ourselves are and remain sinners needing forgiveness, are "at the same time" for the sake of Christ and his stepping in for us, pronounced free and righteous. This truth excludes the deep-rooted misconception that we are only partly sinners, and are after all, on the basis of our well-meaning action or of a divine influence rising up within us, righteous. God's grace would then consist in graciously making up what we lack of complete righteousness. Instead, we need to understand the Reformation formula strictly, that we are at the same time *totally* just and *totally* sinners. This needs to be said so strictly because our being totally righteous is true only on the basis of that blessed exchange. This is true, and this holds "without any merit of my own, out of sheer grace" (Art. 60).

The righteousness in which I am completely right is thus one that is given and credited to me, not one that I have won, or that is due me on the grounds of my merits or my worthiness. Again, what is graciously given to me is not simply grace instead of justice, but is *justice*. So I, who in myself am completely a sinner, *am* at the same time through and through, and not just partly, "righteous before God." So in faith I may be altogether sure of this, and not merely partly sure. Not because of my faith (Art. 61)! Not because my faith itself instead of works of merit creates for me a right to grace. Not because faith itself, because of its not being a work, for example, has an advantage over human activity. Faith is literally the *self-abandonment* of the human being to what a person has not earned or won, but what Christ has won and gives. *He* is our justification.

This is the Reformation doctrine of justification, as the Heidelberg represents it. Indeed, it rates as the central doctrine of the Reformation, characterized by Valentin Ernst Löscher at the turn of the eighteenth century as the *"articulus stantis et cadentis ecclesiae,"* the article with which the evangelical church stands and falls.[4] So, for example, a few years ago a theologian could make the proposal that a theological faculty must have as

---

3. Cf. M. Luther, *WA* 56:272. *LW* 25:258-59.

4. According to W. Koehler, *Dogmengeschichte als Geschichte des christlichen Selbstbewusstseins*, vol. 2 (Zurich: M. Niehans, 1951), p. 329.

first in its list of duties that the study of theology be work on the article about justification. Meanwhile, the disconnect between claim and reality on this point is remarkable — that is, the gap between holding this doctrine as the highest treasure, and being embarrassed about explaining its practical relevance. The conference of the Lutheran World Federation of 1963 in Helsinki[5] is famous because this disconnect came to light in it. There this doctrine was touted as the foundation of the church, but it was quietly added that for now we do not know exactly why it is so fundamental today. Yet we do not need to go to Helsinki. An ordinary funeral sermon for an important Christian can demonstrate this for us very adequately. While praise is heaped on all the merits of the deceased, the absence of understanding of our justification by grace and not by works shows us how little in Christendom this allegedly wonderful knowledge is applied in practical terms. Therefore, an attempt will be made now to point to the practical range of help afforded by this understanding.

1. Justification means: *I do not have to justify myself any longer.*[6] I can, I may, be joyful and breathe freely. Before my justification encounters me, I stand continually under pressure and stress, having to "justify" myself. Beforehand, we live under some tribunal or other we must please, whose assent to us we have to safeguard. We must do so because only in this way do we gain the consciousness that our life is worth something and has the right to exist. It is a matter of indifference whether we call this tribunal "God" or whether it is a societal value or the psychological superego, or what Immanuel Kant called "the inner court" of conscience. Yes, it is part of this system that the tribunals we have to please can change, and are interchangeable. Now they are outer, now inner, now religious, now moral, now societal, now psychic. But however they change, the system remains the same. And this was not just a problem for medieval anxiety; it functions in the modern world even more mercilessly. You are the author of your own fortune: it lies in your hand; the duty to which you are condemned is to bring before the respective tribunal the evidence that you are worthy of living and have the right to exist. You may need to bring it before the eyes of the so-called god, before the eyes of the societal convention, or the authority of your social group, or before the eyes of your superego, or

---

5. Cf. W. Andersen, "Das theologische Gespräch über die Rechtfertigung in Helsinki," in *Helsinki 1963*, ed. E. Wilkens (Berlin/Hamburg: Lutherisches Verlagshaus, 1964), pp. 25ff.

6. Cf. to the following H. Gollwitzer, *Forderungen der Umkehr. Beiträge zur Theologie der Gesellschaft* (Munich: Kaiser, 1976), pp. 75-94.

your "conscience." You are really *nothing* if you do not get attention and esteem through achievement and still more achievement — such as in the
academy, with its law of "publish or perish." The respective tribunal holds
sanctions ready in order to drive us on: woe to you if you are a coward or a
slacker or a failure or someone who dances out of line!

In all this, I can never be sure whether I please the respective tribunal
enough or whether it might withdraw its favor from me, for example,
when I fail. And this drives me on unceasingly to produce *more,* to make it
better than before, until my death makes it impossible for me to make anything better than it once was. At bottom, everything I do always falls short
of what I ought to do, and this gives me a constant feeling of guilt. For this
I can try to get relief — in earlier times by accepting that divine grace
strengthens me in my pressure to produce, today by pretending to be more
than I am through an outward image. But these kinds of relief are only
provisional. For if I am supported in my achievements by grace, or if I appear to be so much more than I am, then suddenly all the more achievement will be expected of me.

To this whole system in which I have only as much worth as I acquire
for myself, the gospel stands diametrically opposed. For the gospel tells us:
you do not have to justify yourself. You are of worth, your life has the right
to existence and respect, not because you *make* it worthy by production
and still more production. The endless battle is blown away, the battle that
can never reach the goal because death, in which you cannot make anything better, breaks it off. Canceled is the battle in which those who lose are
actually of no worth. You do not have to make yourself worthy, because
you are already a person of worth. You are already affirmed and loved by
God in Jesus Christ, and this without any conditions you have to fulfill first
in order for this to hold. You are unconditionally and absolutely loved. You
are of worth because you are already affirmed — and affirmed just as you
are. So you do not have to appear to be more than you are. You are affirmed, not because you are so acceptable, but because, although you are
not acceptable, you are completely accepted, from head to toe. You are of
worth, not through what you try in vain to give yourself. You are accepted
through what God effectively gives you, not through your performance,
but out of grace. For this reason no one is worthless. So it is not the case
that a person's life is not worth living if that person has no achievement.
Who in the end has achievement when in death he or she can have no
more achievement? But you may breathe a deep sigh of relief, freely and
joyously. You do not have to justify yourself.

2. *Neither can you justify yourself* — you cannot do it, although we all continually try. But we can only try; there is no success that corresponds to the attempt. We should not understand our inability to justify ourselves in the universal sense that everything and anything we do takes place in a night where all cats are gray and everything is just sin and nonsense. Nor should we take it in the ridiculous sense that in spite of the grace of God we always stand under an unending demand, in view of which every honest effort is pointless because we can never do enough. The statement that you cannot justify yourself at all means concretely that it is a dead end to strive for worth through your own achievement.

This dead end, which shows up in sometimes rather crude, but often uncannily subtle ways, involves people's ceaseless drive to fence themselves off from others, to devalue as much as possible others' "achievements," to denigrate their worth, to make them look tarnished. Then against the dark background of the unworthiness of others, they aim to have their own worth shine forth all the more brightly. These people who are worthy through the worth they acquire for themselves, therefore need people *under* them: scapegoats, "little people," abject folk, underdeveloped people. They count on standing in the limelight as all the better and finer and more highly developed and educated people in comparison to the others. They are happy about this, and possibly thank God that there are "thieves, rogues, adulterers, or even [people] like this tax collector" so that they can really be happy and even thank God that they are "not like other people" (Luke 18:11). They *need* this to make sure of their own worth, to divert themselves and others from their own faults, of which they are probably more aware than they would like to admit. For this they need a worldview, in whatever variation, in which good and evil stand opposed to one another, and where they themselves of course stand always, always, on the side of the good, sometimes even with the impression that they alone stand on this side. Related to this is the unbridled desire to point the finger at others as well as the sometimes downright sick obsession to cut down others behind their backs.

To this whole system in which I make myself worthy by putting others down, the gospel once again stands diametrically opposed. For the gospel tells us this negative truth: you cannot justify yourself at all. This has the precise meaning that you do not have any breath to accuse others, to denigrate them, to put them down, because that breath is taken away. You cannot demand that others beat their breasts and sweep in front of their doors because now you have your hands full beating your own breast and sweeping in front of your own door. The same finger that is so terribly eager to point at others now turns around and points only at your own breast. As Gustav Heinemann said so clearly:[7] you discover now that while *one* finger points at others, at the same time three fingers point at yourself. This is also a healing discovery. For in this way with one blow the whole damaging wall comes tumbling down — the wall that had separated me from the others, the downgraded ones, those so-called evil people. The wall tumbles down so completely that I now come to stand on their side in solidarity with the sinners. Without God's grace, I no less than they am lost. But they no less than I have the promise of the mercy of God, by virtue of which they are not lost. This is what it means that I cannot justify myself.

3. *You are justified!* A doctrine of justification that one considers important and yet has to puzzle about, wondering if it is still relevant, is too sad for words. It can only be the other way around: there is a doctrine of justification because justification is relevant — otherwise it is like a rotten tree. Justification is relevant because it actually does take place that God in Christ through the Holy Spirit justifies human beings. The church lives, and does not become like a rotten tree, just so long as this is spoken to people in a helpful way, and they receive it to their salvation: that God relieves and frees them from the pressure and stress of making themselves worthy through their own achievements, because they are already of infinite worth without having to fulfill any conditions. And together with this, the church lives just so long as the artificially erected wall between good and bad, better and worse people is done away with by God, because only in solidarity with those on the other, evil side can we be redeemed and liberated. Because this *happens,* because you are assured again and again that you are justified, that you do not somehow have to take care of this yourself, but instead this holds for you, therefore something also happens *within* you. You become another person. You do not become better, more worthy than others, as the achievement way of thinking would have it. Certainly not. But you become a person who is different than before in that you move ahead on the ground that no matter what happens, you are affirmed and loved out of sheer grace and on the basis of God's love, and that you can therefore let go of your drive to wall yourself off from others.

If we have understood this, then we understand that the old charge

---

7. G. W. Heinemann, *Es gibt schwierige Vaterländer . . . Reden und Aufsätze 1919-1969* (*Reden und Schriften,* vol. 3), ed. H. Lindemann (Frankfurt am Main: Suhrkamp, 1977), p. 334.

against the doctrine of justification[8] is untenable — the charge that grace makes lazy people. What differentiates justified persons from high achievers and from those who are not in solidarity with sinners is not that the latter work, while the former work less or not at all. The difference is in the fact that justified persons work *in another way.* This is why Article 64 rightly says: "But does not this doctrine make people careless and depraved? No, because it is impossible for those who are grafted into Christ by true faith to fail to produce the fruit of thankfulness."

It is not enough to simply say that they work just like the others with the exception that their work, instead of coming from themselves, comes from divine inspiration. It is essential to understand that they actually work differently from the others. In what way? Well, what those achievers and those who are not in solidarity with sinners do, they always do basically for themselves, for their advancement, to put themselves in a favorable light, so that they get attention and respect, worth and self-worth. Yes, even when they do it for others, as in giving to charity, they do it "so that they may be seen by others" (Matt. 6:1, 5), so that they have something from it, so that they reap praise from others or produce inner satisfaction for themselves. Yes, even though no one else sees what good they do for others, still they stand alongside themselves all the time to value themselves and clap themselves on the back: "You really did a great job"; "Worthy persons think of themselves last."[9] Yes, but last and ultimately always of themselves. Altruism, in which they may well think of others, is only a form of their egoism. They are not free for the other.

Justified persons, however, are free for the other. They cannot justify themselves by their own actions. But this does not mean they do nothing. It means their action is now free from the compulsion to earn for themselves something praiseworthy. In just this way they are free for others. They do not need to produce their own self-worth by their achievements because they are already worthy and affirmed. So they are free to do what helps and benefits, and does good, not for themselves, but for others. In their action, therefore, they are not there for themselves, but for others. And they do not need the others as a negative foil against which they show up brilliantly. They stand alongside them, basically in a common predicament, the overcoming of which can only be experienced together. So they can be free too

8. Cf. H. Zwingli, *Schriften,* ed. Th. Brunnschweiler (Zurich: Theologischer Verlag, 1995), vol. 1, p. 365.

9. F. Schiller, *Wilhelm Tell* (1804), I, 1.

from the altruistic danger in which one thinks that the other person needs me, which can so easily lead to manipulating the other as an object of love. So they become free to understand that they too need the other. This is how persons act to whom it is said: You are justified! For this reason they bring "fruits of thankfulness." And in this way their action differs from that of those self-regarding achievers who do not live in solidarity.

Do we sense something of the relevance and worth of the doctrine of justification? It is in fact indispensable for describing the process by which God wins in us free human beings.

4.1.2. Conversion (Art. 87-90)

"Repentance or conversion," as Article 88 puts it, translates the Greek word *metanoia*. Conversion is more than the decision to adopt a different life-style, such as living without meat or alcohol, although this may be included. Conversion has a meaning different from what it had in the Greek world outside the Bible. Conversion for the Greek world generally meant a change of mind on the basis of insight I have won, or others have helped me to. In this conversion I admit having made mistakes; for example, I see that a course I have taken does not lead to the desired goal, so I change course.

But the conversion we are talking about here is something more foundational and incisive. It is about the complete turnaround of my life by 180 degrees. It is about turning away from the life I have been used to up until now so that this old life stays behind me and is done away with. And it is about turning to another, unfamiliar life, unknown to me until now, so that with every step I take, this new life is ahead of me. Or, as Article 88 says: conversion consists in "the dying of the old self, and the birth of the new." Our justification would be incompletely conceived and could wind up in the self's being held fast in its sins despite all the talk of God's grace if our justification were cut loose from our sanctification, which consists in this conversion. And conversely, our sanctification and conversion would conjure up anew the danger of self-redemption if it were cut loose from our justification through God's grace in Christ. So both belong together, and yet need to be distinguished from each other. Pietism has kept guard more carefully on the second concern than the rest of the church has. A church and a theology are ill advised if because of anti-pietism they let the legitimate question about our conversion fall under the table. Consider the fact that according to Hebrews 6:1 the theme "conversion" belongs to the fundamental articles of the Christian confession of faith and that according to Luke 24:47 the missionary task of the church consists in its preaching conversion and forgiveness among all peoples. Indeed, according to Luke 5:32 the purpose of the sending of Jesus is to call us to conversion.

How are conversion and justification related to one another? As we have seen, justification is that blessed exchange by virtue of which, though I am a lost sinner as the "old self," yet for the sake of Christ I am pronounced free and righteous, the "new human being," a child of God. This righteousness I do not win for myself. It is given to me. But as righteousness imparted to me by grace, it is nevertheless righteousness in which I as God's child, as one who belongs to God, am addressed and laid claim to. I *am set free to be* the new human being instead of the old. But I *should* also want to be the one I am allowed to be, and no longer the one I dare not be. In our conversion we do not add to our justification, but confirm it. We abjure from our side the old self, obsolete in Christ, and greet the new human being intended for us in Christ. Both stand opposed to each other in a dramatic imbalance: the old human being whose right to existence is withdrawn, and the new human being as the one who alone rightfully comes into consideration for us. To be sure, there is a lifelong conflict between the two, the conflict between "spirit and flesh" (Gal. 5:17). The old Adam in me simply will not resign, even though in Christ the ground is pulled out from under him. He fights with all kinds of tricks against the new human being who I already am in Christ. But his right to exist is now constantly challenged by the new life that Christ has provided for me. And in faith we confess that in this conflict the old self stands at a lost post, and its coveting a comeback actually consists only in rearguard actions of retreat. This is because Christ, with the new life he brings forth, has greater staying power and more leverage. So by faith in him I can be sure that the old self which still sows disorder in me must disappear, as according to Mark 5:13 the "unclean spirit" had to go out of that "possessed" man.

It really is the case that I do not lead the decisive battle against the old self. There is a danger of losing sight of this when you try to refute the well-known charge that grace makes people lazy. For in doing this you can easily concede the charge while trying to refute it, by supplementing grace with an appeal to good intentions. In this way, instead of getting rid of the objection, you get rid of grace itself. What is decisive is not done by us. The conflict of the new against the old self can only be carried on in prayer:

'Tis all in vain, do what we can, our strength is soon dejected.
But he fights for us, the right man, by God himself elected.
Ask'st thou who is this? Jesus Christ it is.[10]

This is so because the crucial battle is already done. In and with Christ our old self is already crucified and dead, and we are risen to a new life (Rom. 6:5-8). In Christ the old is already past and everything has become new (2 Cor. 5:17). But what is already true in Christ for us is not yet true in us. Here it is still contested by the retreating skirmishes of the old nature. Therefore what is already true for us in Christ, that our old nature has already been successfully combated, must still be fought out on the ground into which it has withdrawn: into ourselves. If we are already new persons in Christ, then the old self has no right to stay in us any more. The battle against its falsely arrogated right to stay is primarily not fought by me. I take part in it as K. Barth said, looking back at his life: "The conflict went on, the battle was fought, and I sat on the baggage wagon."[11] Still, I take part in this way, and not merely as an idle spectator. Article 88 refers to Ephesians 4:22-24, where on the basis of the indicative statement that by grace you have been saved the imperative follows:

> Put away your former way of life, your old self, corrupt and deluded by its lusts, and . . . be renewed in the spirit of your minds, and . . . clothe yourself with the new self, created according to the likeness of God in true righteousness and holiness.

Here we could also think of Galatians 5:24-25: "And those who belong to Christ Jesus have crucified the flesh with its passions and desires. If we live by his Spirit, let us also be guided by the Spirit." This is what our conversion means. Conversion is commanded, but commanded because it is grounded in the indicative that in Christ we already are converted and by the work of his Spirit in us will be converted from our perverse being to the new life as children of God.

We must look at the relation of indicative and imperative a little more closely. It would not do justice to the subject simply to speak of a paradox

---

10. From stanza 2 of the hymn "Ein' feste Burg ist unser Gott," by M. Luther. ET: "Our God He Is a Castle Strong," in *LW* 53, 285.

11. K. Barth, Word of thanks at the celebration of his 80th birthday, in *Evangelische Theologie* 26 (1966): 619.

and to say: on the one hand our old self is crucified in Christ and a new be-ing is already brought to light; on the other hand we still need to crucify this old self and renew ourselves in our innermost being. Conversion dare not mean that we have to undertake the latter as though the former had not happened. It also dare not mean that because the former has hap-pened, we do not have to undertake the latter. Rather, this is the way it is meant: *because* you have had your old self taken away, and have been changed into a new being — not partly, so that you have to produce the rest yourself, but completely — and are assured that this is true, *therefore* do not resist this any more, but recognize the line drawn marking the end of your old life so that a new life is opened! Show that this is so by assent-ing to this line, and so tracing the line yourself and underscoring it.

The question in Article 87 offers an inspired formulation for this. The conversion to be fulfilled is turning "to God *from* their unthankful and unrepentant lives" and thereby *to* a thankful and penitent walk. So the old self which has already been ended in Christ still lives on in us in the form of our impenitence, with all the terrible things of which the answer in Ar-ticle 87 speaks. And the new human being already risen in Christ is not yet here in us, as is shown by our ingratitude for what Christ has already prepared and intended for us. Still, in order to crucify our old self and walk in a new life we do not have to do again what Christ has already done. The way we put off the old self and put on the new is by turning away from our ungrateful, impenitent way and turning to a thankful and penitent way. This is our conversion, our repentance, our sanctification. It is not we who get rid of the old and create the new; God does this for us in Christ through the Holy Spirit. We struggle against this by not being thankful for it and penitent about it. But this is the new walk to which we turn, conquered by the love of God in its working on us, so that we begin to cease struggling against what God has done, and begin to become thankful and penitent persons. Some clarifications are in order about what conversion means.

1. How does this kind of conversion come about in the life of a person? It is notable that in the Old Testament prophets the theme becomes ever more intense that Israel not only does not want to convert to God, but also has no capacity to do it. "Can Ethiopians change their skin or leopards their spots?" No more can you change yourselves (Jer. 13:23). Matthew 19:24 points in the same direction when it says that it is easier for a camel to go through the eye of a needle than for a rich person to go into the king-dom of God. The disciples react rightfully when they ask, then who can be

saved? Jesus answers, "For mortals it is impossible." We can illustrate this inability by the almost complete lack of confession of sin in German post-war history — A. and M. Mitscherlich characterized this lack as "the inability to mourn."[12] We can also illustrate it by the present-day inability, so uncanny in its extent, to convert to a new lifestyle despite the frightening chorus of voices that tell us that with our present lifestyle we are preparing catastrophe for those who come after us.

Why this inability? Apparently the summons to turn around and thereby to admit the perversity of the life we have been leading constitutes such an insult to our self-esteem that we almost reflexively either water down such a summons, bring a countercharge, or shift it onto others. In one way or another we suppress it. Luther rightly remarked that sinners are not really capable of repentance and conversion. At most they are capable of fear of penalty, and so of ever-new forms of self-assertion.[13] The same Luther says: "The law says, you shall turn to me; the gospel says, I will turn to you."[14] This gospel also includes the statement: you cannot turn to me — "For mortals it is impossible." The gospel however says above all, because I turn myself to you, therefore it now holds that "for God all things are possible" (Matt. 19:26). Repentance, the conversion of the sinner over which joy reigns in heaven, consists in the encounter in which the Good Shepherd goes after the lost sheep and searches for it until he finds it (Luke 15:3-7). This is the way the gospel makes conversion possible. And in this way you can do what is otherwise impossible: "become converted."

A fable[15] tells about the wind and the sun arguing over who is the stronger. They agree on a contest to see who can get a wanderer to take off his coat. The wind cannot do it. The more it roars at the man and shakes him, the more tightly he wraps himself in his garment. But then the sun beams calmly, clear and warm, so that the man gladly and of his own accord takes off his coat. Just so, a person under the sun of the gospel thankfully puts off the old self and turns around. Under this sun, humans find themselves loved so much that the summons to admit the perversity of their previous way of life is no longer unduly burdensome for their self-

12. A. M. Mitscherlich, *Die Unfähigkeit zu trauern. Grundlagen kollektiven Verhaltens* (Munich: Piper Verlag, 1967). ET: *The Inability to Mourn* (New York: Grove Press, 1975).

13. M. Luther, *WA* 1:39. *LW* 51:17-23.

14. M. Luther, *WA* 18:682. *LW* 33:135.

15. *Mein grosses Fabel und Geschichtenbuch*, ed. L. Kincaid and G. Fischer (Erlangen, 1982, 1983²), pp. 36-38.

esteem, but becomes a real relief. In this relief they may make a new beginning and receive what D. Sölle has aptly called "the right to become another person."[16]

2. The first of Luther's 95 theses reads: "When our Lord and Master Jesus Christ says: 'repent' . . . he intends the entire life of his believers on earth to be a *continual* repentance."[17] Just as we do not, at some point in our lives, have our justification completed and behind us, so we never have our conversion completed and behind us. The only one-time event is the cross and resurrection, in which our old human being was crucified in Christ and the human being of a new life stepped into the light. But what took place there "once for all," took place "for all time," so that now "at all times," in every hour of our life is the turning point in which we exist, when what counts is for us to turn away from what has been done away with in Christ and to turn to what has been opened up in him. In this respect, all progress in the Christian life is always a new beginning, an ever-new fulfilling of this repentance, again and again sorrowful at having fallen so far short, and again and again glad to be allowed to try once more. And when we make progress in the new beginnings that come again and again, it is above all continuing education in how much we are actually dependent on God's kindness for each step, and how little we have deserved it, until perhaps finally, in a high moment of insight, we ascend to the recognition: "We are beggars, it is true. . . . I thank God that he has had sympathy with me, his poor creature."[18] This is Christian perfection, which is the complete opposite of the illusion of perfection with which we plague ourselves and others so much.

So the new life we turn to as we turn away from the old self also includes our readiness to repent. To the new life belongs that "godly grief (about oneself) [which] produces a repentance that leads to salvation and brings no regret," because in this repentance you are borne by God's grace, and in the light of this *grace* are ashamed of yourself, which brings you to hold fast to grace more than ever (2 Cor. 7:10). To the new life belongs the extraordinary experience: "The beginning of good works is the confession of evil

16. D. Sölle, "Das Recht ein anderer zu werden," in *Die Wiedergewinnung des Humanen: Beiträge zur gesellschaftlichen Relevanz der Menschenrechte,* ed. H. J. Vogt (Stuttgart: Steinkopf, 1975), pp. 189-99.

17. M. Luther, *WA* 1:233. *LW* 31:83.

18. M. Luthers letzte Aufzeichnung: *WA* 48:241; and J. Calvins Testament, in *Calvins Lebenswerk in seinen Briefen,* trans. R. Schwarz (Neukirchen-Vluyn: Neukirchener Verlag, 1962), chap. 1, n. 12, 1280.

works."[19] And the older we get, the more we become aware of this. It is not that we become anxious about avoiding the least little possible misstep (for we know about the forgiveness of our sins), and so not self-deprecating either. But we do become more aware of the brokenness and awkwardness in our nature. It is not as surprising as it might sound at first that the perversities of the old human being reach their highest point in the obstinate stance — the old human being calls it faithfulness to oneself — in which the self always wants to stay the same old person. In this person, the self constantly peers out defensively and always shakes off criticism from outside as simply misunderstanding, or trumps it by trying to nail the others at the vulnerable places it spies in them. Even if this old self is sometimes discontent and sorrowful about itself, it is so only within the limits of its own distorted nature, and therefore in such a way that it is soon content with itself again. Paul calls this "worldly grief [which] produces death" (and no saving conversion) (2 Cor. 7:10). Only where you find yourself loved under the sun of God's love do you become strong enough to see your faults, to grieve over them, to be ashamed of them. According to Romans 2:4, it is "God's kindness" which is "meant to lead you to repentance" that gives us a sense for our mistakes and makes us self-critical about the injuries we cause.

In the light of all this, a critical point clearly emerges against the idea that conversion takes place just once and is then behind us. Those who hold this view can feel they are so very much on God's side that they need no further conversion. Then the very same obstinacy characteristic of the old human threatens on a higher level. But part of the sanctification of the person caught up in conversion is "sincere sorrow over our sins, increasing hatred of them, and flight from them" (Art. 89). Furthermore, my own readiness to repent, a critical stance toward myself, is an essential requirement for being able to love others around me with openness and understanding. Without it, only a strained, condescending love develops. In this kind of love, someone who is almost, or completely a saint bends down to poor folks and imposes something on them that they perhaps do not want at all. The objects of this love always sense the distance between them and the one who is putting on airs. Genuine love comes from solidarity, in which the persons who love, no less than those who are loved, know their need for love.

3. In conversion, however, when we are given critical distance from the

19. Augustine, *Vorträge über das Evangelium des Hl. Joh.* 12:13. ET: *Tractate on the Gospel of John*, in *The Fathers of the Church*, vol. 79 (Washington, DC: Catholic University of America Press, 1988), p. 41.

old human being, it is distance not simply from our previous existence as individual private persons, but from a whole system of life, an old *world*. Once again, it is not we who overcome this old world. And although it is overcome in Christ, it is always protruding into our present, on the basis of our "unthankful and unrepentant lives." The only way we are drawn into the overcoming of this old world through Christ is by being thankful for the kindness in which Christ has said: "take courage; I have conquered the world!" (John 16:33). But within this context, it still needs to be said that our conversion, while it does not lead to a wholesale despising of the world (which would conflict with God's love for this world), nevertheless does lead us to a critical distancing from a graceless and loveless worldly reality which as such fights against Christ, and which he rejected. If our conversion did not include such distancing from this "world," then the conversion would become that problematic, individual "penance" which has so often been taught and practiced in the church. In this kind of conversion, sins against private morality, such as lying, promiscuity, drunkenness, stealing, or being rebellious, were denounced and "done penance for." But such "penance" allowed idols such as Mammon, Mars, and the Fatherland to remain prevalent, unassailed, and unscrutinized. Therefore this private penance led to people's being shrewder dealers than ever, all the more obedient soldiers, and still more devoted nationalists. The new way of life that was only private carried with it a thoroughly unconverted conformity to the old world. In contrast to this, we cannot make it clear enough that the "dying of the old self" and "sincere sorrow over our sins" relate not only to the old *human beings* individually, but to their rootedness in an old *world*. This calls for unlearning a "lifestyle" now seen to be perverse, and learning a lifestyle to be newly discovered. For our conversion does not make us better functioning wheels in the machinery of the old world. In conversion we are called out of conformity with this world into conformity with God.

4. Our conformity with God — this is the new human whom we are turning into as we turn away from the old human. The new human is the human who turns toward *God* — not to something or other, not to this or that convincing idea or ideal, not to a new program intended to remove a situation perceived as distress, but to God. Again, turning toward God is no partial, merely "religious" conversion, cleanly separated from a secular realm that is not involved. God gives attention to our whole life, body and soul. As the old human is rooted in an old world, so turning to God "embraces the whole walk of the man who is claimed by the divine lordship. It carries with it the founding of a new personal relationship of man to

God."[20] Article 90 describes the meaning of turning toward God this way: "What is the birth of the new self? Sincere joy in God through Christ and delight in living according to the will of God in all good works." The newness of the new humans is that they turn toward God and have joy in this turning. Joy, as release from tensions, from burdens, from oppressive bonds, is the fulfilled form of freedom, as genuine freedom is pure joy. Real freedom is after all not the ability of independent persons to do whatever they please. It is freedom in togetherness, since you cannot have true joy only for and by yourself. Joy is first of all joy in . . . joy most of all in God, in the One who prepares joy for us. "See — I am bringing you good news of great joy" (Luke 2:10). How can those "seriously" know God for whom the thought of God does not make them joyful? Moreover, you cannot keep genuine joy to yourself. It makes us glad when others are made glad. As the enslaved will dwells in capricious freedom, so the freedom to which Christ has made us free is situated in our being children of God and dwells in the "sincere joy" and "delight" of living for the joy of the one who has set us free, and so doing "the will of God in all good works." Jesus does not say, you shall not, but "you cannot serve God and wealth" (Matt. 6:24). In both cases we are serving: the old human serves the idol Mammon and the new human serves the will of God. But we see clearly that the two are mutually exclusive when we realize that we not only exchange the "masters" of our serving, but also that the character of our "serving" is qualitatively changed. With Mammon I am "possessed by a desire for possession";[21] in the will of God I am set free to give joy to God, who has made me glad by giving me Godself. And I give God joy by giving God nothing less than myself. When we turn away from our old self and its service to Mammon, it is to God we turn. "Serve the Lord with *gladness*" (Ps. 100:2, New International Version).

4.1.3. Hope (Art. 57-58, 52)

For what it has to say, Article 57 relies, among other texts, on 1 John 3:2: "Beloved, we are God's children now; what we will be has not yet been re-

---

20. J. Behm, "metanoeo," *Theologisches Wörterbuch zum Neuen Testament,* ed. Gerhard Kittel, vol. 4 (Stuttgart: W. Kohlhammer Verlag, 1942), p. 981. ET: "metanoeo," *Theological Dictionary of the New Testament,* ed. Gerhard Kittel, trans. Geoffrey W. Bromiley (Grand Rapids: Eerdmans, 1967), vol. 4, p. 1003.

21. M. Buber, *Das dialogische Prinzip* (Heidelberg: Schneider, 1962), p. 107. ET: *I and Thou,* in *The Writings of Martin Buber* (New York: Meridian Books, 1958), p. 59.

274

vealed. What we do know is this: when he is revealed, we will be like him, for we will see him as he is." The verse expresses that "already and not yet" which is characteristic for Christian hope. Before this verse comes the one that says: "See what love the Father has given us, that we should be called children of God." We are granted the right to call ourselves this already, because we are this already in Christ. But what is already true for us in Christ is *not yet* rightly true in us. Yes, we still live in that conflict, and so in that conversion which is still needed from the old to the new human, from the slave in the power of sin to the child in the hand of God. Above that conflict and that conversion stands the proviso: "What we will be has not yet been revealed." We are already children of God, but only in the promise. To speak with Romans 8:24: "For in hope we are saved." What we already are in Christ, children of God, in our lifetime always lies ahead of us, so that we are always going toward it and looking forward to it. In faith we dare hold fast to the conviction that we are already children of God, and so new persons, but we walk by faith, not by sight (2 Cor. 5:7). We do not have this in our possession. It is given us in hope. But this is true not only in the sense that what is given us in and through Christ is not yet a visible actuality in us. It is true also in the sense that those who believe in Christ and in what is given to us in him through the Spirit are also set free to reach out toward the promised glorious freedom of the children of God. The new self's belonging to God, to which we turn in conversion, begins to break forth in us, so that we become people of *hope*. We become people who venture forth in hope of the fulfillment of the promise that "we will be like him," and so similar to him and with him. We will be children of God not only in Christ, but also in ourselves. This is the Christian hope.

This hope stands in conflict with other hopes that people have. We can divide human hopes into two basic types. The first type of human hope can be described in the Latin proverb: *"Dum spiro, spero"* — "Where there's life, there's hope." Human beings hope as long as they live. And as long as they live, they create hope. The drive to *create* hope is so strong in us that we do not want to give up on it even when many hopes are disappointed ("If hope fails, never fail to hope").[22] Is this not convincing in light of the fact that a person who no longer has any hope gives up, and so is lost? What stimulates us to such hope is no doubt that in contrast to the past, which lies unchangeable behind us, the future appears again and

---

22. F. Rückert, *Die Weisheit des Brahmanen,* Book 16, section 5, no. 41 (Leipzig: S. Hirzel Verlag, 1870[7]), p. 599).

again as the land of a thousand possibilities. In this land we believe we can steer things for the better, or can hope for a gift of providence for the better. Yes, what stimulates us to such hope is the experience that the past which lies behind was so pitiful that one must simply say, "That can't have been all!"[23] The dream awakened through that bad experience, the dream that everything shall turn to the good, has to be fulfilled sometime. And in creating such dreams, humans try to make them come true. They can even fall into the illusion of being able to create what they want, always believing in constantly greater progress, always in the assurance that things which in the process go awry they nevertheless have firmly in hand.

But what happens when this creating stops because a person stops breathing and is at the earthly end?

Does hope stop when breathing stops? An observation of the history of religions is interesting: we come upon religion archaeologically where we come upon graves. They testify that for humans who create hopes for themselves, death does not have to mean any limit to creating hopes — hopes for a continuation of life after death, hopes for satisfaction there for this life that has taken an unsatisfactory course. The most widespread form of this hope in the West is the Greek idea of death as the redeemer. Death redeems the immortal soul from the mortal body.

The second type of hope stands critically opposed to the first type. It can be described with another proverb: "Hoping and waiting makes fools out of many." This type feeds on the skeptical thought that humans, in creating these kinds of hopes, are inclined to create what are actually illusions. So this type of hope turns against the idea of life after death. It sees in this idea only an empty consolation invented with the intention of getting people to fit unprotestingly into this earthly vale of tears by the promise of an allegedly better life beyond death. Against this the slogan is raised: "There is life *before* death" — or, as one can read in Heinrich Heine, not without being moved:

On earth we fain would happy be
Nor starve for the sake of the stronger . . .
To angels and sparrows we're quite content
That heaven should be confided.[24]

23. W. Biermann, "'Lied vom donnernden Leben': Das kann doch nicht alles gewesen sein . . . ," in W. Biermann, *Alle Lieder* (Köln: Kiepenhever und Witsch, 1991²), pp. 263-64.

24. H. Heine, *Werke in fünf Bänden* (Berlin/Weimar, 1967), vol. 2, p. 95. ET: *The Poems of Heine*, trans. E. A. Bowring (London: Bell and Daldy, 1866), p. 329.

Here the concern is not to wait for a better future, which, after all, not everyone will experience, but to fight for a better present, or to fully taste and enjoy the present. Here too, humans create hopes, but only for such a life before death. But when we do die, what then? Then that is the end, and "that has been all." This is just what makes the present moment so extremely precious, because nothing more comes afterward. But what is left for comfort at the grave? Either this: "Death was a release for him" — now not in the sense of release of the soul from the body, but in the sense of release from sickness and pain. It is somewhat pale comfort, because it means only that the suffering of a person is resolved by the destruction of the subject who is able to suffer. Death does not resolve, it dissolves. Or the other comfort left is: "In our hearts you live on." This is a well-meaning comfort, but just as powerless, because the one affected does not live on at all. What lives is only an image of her, which then fades more and more, until it completely disappears when we ourselves are gone.

We do not have to despise these two types of human hope, because in them is something genuinely human and even warranted, which is preserved in Christian hope. Christian hope, like the first type, will know about the "Not yet," about what has not yet come, what is insufficient and calls for fulfillment. And Christian hope, like the second type, will protest against all consolation that says "tomorrow, just not today," against a devaluation of the present moment, against contempt of what is bodily in favor of an allegedly immortal soul. Christian hope, without being limited to the one or the other, can certainly join in conversation with them. But we dare not confuse the two types of hope with Christian hope itself, because Christian hope at the decisive point stands opposed to them and contradicts them. The decisive point is that Christian hope can never, except at the cost of its own dissolution, understand itself as a hope that one *creates for oneself.* Hope is *created* for us, is "given" to us (2 Thess. 2:16). This is demonstrated by the fact that it carries us just at the places where hopes otherwise deceive, where there is nothing more to hope for (Rom. 4:18). This "hope does not disappoint us" (Rom. 5:5). Measured by this hope, those who do not have it, whatever they do hope, are in truth without hope (Eph. 2:12; 1 Thess. 4:13).

Christian hope does not hope for "something," neither something before nor after death. It hopes in *Jesus Christ.* He is, he gives, he creates hope for us (Eph. 2:12; 2 Thess. 2:16; 1 Tim. 1:1; Col. 1:27). It hopes in him because he has already come, and in the Holy Spirit comes to us, and without him we would fall into hopelessness. Epistemologically, this means that when

Christians hope, they do not first look into the future and seek to put themselves into some kind of relationship with it. They first look back, to the one who has already come, to the one who has not since disappeared, but who is present with us. They look to him who comforts us by letting us know that whatever happens we belong to him. In this way he puts himself and us into a relationship with the future and opens this to us as our future: that in it also he *will* come and that in the future also we *will* belong to him. For this reason and in this way we also look into the future and *hope* in him.

We need to make clear to ourselves that we readily carry around in our heads a "heathen" concept of time. This concept has some sort of picture of past, present, and future, and some way of connecting these three aspects of time. Sometimes the connection is more linear, sometimes more cyclical. Sometimes this concept includes the impression that the past has nailed down so much that the future is a matter of extending the lines that have already been set. Sometimes the viewpoint is of the present moment, which is seen as having decisive meaning for all time. And sometimes the future is seen as the field of unexhausted possibilities. These concepts of time are heathen because they are formed apart from faith in Jesus Christ. For in them he comes only subsequently — whether it be as someone who among many others also had his time, whether it be as the deliverer of ideas we consider valid or know how to actualize as ideas that go beyond his time and are timeless, or whether it be as an appearance that we believe capable of yet having a future. So Christ appears somehow in our time as one of its moments, but in a time not defined in a Christian way.

If we want to believe in a Christian way, we will need to get used to the biblical concept of time. Psalm 31:15: "My times are in your hand" — in the hand of the God of Israel, who in Christ has fulfilled the covenant, and so has opened it for all peoples. This is exactly the opposite of what we are used to thinking. What God's hand accomplishes does not stand somewhere as a particle in earthly time defined in one way or another by us. Rather, what this hand does is the true event in which my, our, all time past, present, and future stands and is borne by this hand. What does Hebrews 13:8 mean: "Jesus Christ is the same yesterday, today and forever"? And Revelation 1:8: "I am the Alpha and Omega, . . . who is and who was and who is to come"? Surely this, that he is not a moment of our time, but in being that as well, he encompasses all times and aspects of time. These are all moments of our belonging to our faithful Savior Jesus Christ. What is our past? It is what it also was, not first of all ours; it is carried by him, covered by him, kept in him. What is our present? It is not first of all ours, it is his present, in which he is contemporary with us, in which the perfect tense of his action is so relevant that it literally holds for us: "To you is born *this day* . . . a Savior" (Luke 2:11) and "*Today* salvation has come to this house" (Luke 19:9). And what is our future? It is not ours; it is his future. It is not a future time we have, or think up. It is his coming to us, not an empty or probable time, to be filled by us, but a time filled by him, fulfilled in him. — We look now particularly at the future aspect of time.

1. The fact that our *future* is not *our* future has a radical meaning in view of our death. With this meaning, the biblical understanding contradicts our secret or shared dreams. Our death is the real end and not just the apparent end of our earthly life. Our life is a limited existence, and when the limit is reached, we have no further time. Therefore death is not simply "the brother of sleep," but the end of our sleeping as of our waking. Therefore death is no mere interruption of the continuation of our life — whether it be in improved, otherworldly form, or whether it be in the repeat of an earthly life through a "rebirth." We "have" then no more future. And we have within ourselves no powers — no inborn, no achieved, no borrowed powers — and our soul is definitely no such power able to get over the limit set by our death and so "come into heaven." (Art. 57, in its older version, appears to be infected with the Greek notion of an immortal soul and not to deal seriously with the biblical understanding of death as the end of our existence.) This understanding is so strange to us, it hurts our drive for endless self-assertion even beyond death so much, that to make room for this understanding and not sidestep it, we need to pray rightly in accord with the guidance of the Bible: "Lord, let me know my end, and what is the measure of my days; let me know how fleeting my life is" (Ps. 39:4). Of course, once we grasp this, we easily fall into the other extreme and say: with death everything is over. If, in the wish for an endless existence, we previously desired an existence similar to God's, we now fall into a Godless way of thinking. For our end is only *our* end, but with our end God is not at an end. "They will perish, but you endure . . . and your years have no end" (Ps. 102:26-27).

It is important to take seriously this distinction between the Creator and the creature — not in order to hold on to an abstract superiority of the Creator, but in order to keep us from a fatal death fantasy. This fantasy can come over us after the breakdown of our fantasies of endlessness and almightiness: if I have to go down, then *everything* should go down. Then "after us, let a catastrophic end come!" We sense today something of the effective power of such fantasies of death. To our salvation, however, we will never succeed, even in the worse scenario, in dragging everything with us in our demise. God remains. And our going and God's remaining do not stand opposed to one another in an unconnected way as simply different facts. Rather, when our years come to an end we go to the One whose years have no end. When we have no future any more, then God, only God is our future. When nothing more is left for us, then only God is left for us. And if our earthly life was a fleeting existence, deeply fleeting also in the sense of fleeing from God, at our end this fleeing will have been in vain. For God will come forth as our last, our only refuge. Then we will fall, to be sure, but God will not fall from us and so we will not fall from God.

2. What is really the theological problem posed by our death? It does not consist of the question both types of human hopes plague themselves with: Then what will become of me? Can I assert myself even beyond my death? Or, because that won't work anymore then, can I concentrate on asserting myself now? In faith I am graciously relieved of the question "What will become of me?" because my only comfort is that with body and soul I belong not to myself, but to my faithful Savior Jesus Christ (Art. 1). The theological problem of our life's end presents itself on the ground of this comfort: In our end won't our belonging to him stop? What is really threatening in our end is not the dissolving of our earthly life in itself. It is the separation from God and our faithful Savior threatened in this end. And what makes it really more threatening than ever is that at our end we have no time any more to change anything in our life. Nothing can any longer be made good; nothing can be made better than it was. There is no time any more for conversion, for believing, for hoping and loving! However bravely we may have been caught up in the battle between flesh and spirit, the bottom line is more devastating at our end than the usual funeral sermon would lead one to suspect. Then the only thing that matters is, to speak with Calvin: "With your verdict, O Almighty God, we stand and fall."[25] This is the last, the final judgment. We are not the final judges. Against our eagerness and tendency to arrogate this role to ourselves we cannot impress on our minds enough: "Judge not!" — neither others nor, what can be just as devastating, oneself! But God is the final judge, who does not miss what was there, not even what was most hidden, what even the eagle eye of our neighbor may have over-

---

25. J. Calvin, according to K. Barth, *Gebete* (Munich: Kaiser, 1963), p. 85. ET: *Selected Prayers* (Richmond, VA: John Knox Press, 1965), p. 68.

looked about us. So must not God's verdict at our end be: No, for eternity you do not belong to me?

The problem at our end is not our end, but our sin. From this point we now understand the helpful meaning of the statement that Christians, when they look into the future, first look back to the One who has already come. For in him this real problem of our end, sin, is already solved. As Article 52 insightfully says: He is the coming judge, "who has already offered himself to the judgment of God and has removed all the curse from me." Because the coming judge is none other than this one who has been executed so that we may go free, therefore as our judge he will be at the same time our definitive advocate. He speaks justice, to be sure, but the justice of his grace. In his suffering of injustice on the cross he set up this justice of grace. And in the final judgment this will prove not to have been set up in vain. Then it will be remembered much more than everything that happened in our life. This is what the return of Christ will be: that with his gracious justice he will become openly present and eternal in the verdict of the final judge. Then his verdict will be fully just because it is fully merciful. In the judgment, nothing from our life will come out without being in the light of his eternal mercy on us. Nothing can be turned against us that is not under the sign of our eternal acquittal. So we can now recognize that it is good our sin is not swept under the carpet for eternity, but rather dare finally be brought to light. We can see it as good that God, by taking our sins seriously, shows us how seriously God takes us! But now that the real problem of our end is resolved this way, its reality is not taken away, but its power, its sting is. So we cannot treat death as harmless, but we no longer need to fear it as though it has the last word about us. This is why the New Testament can boldly say that those who believe in Christ and so have already heard the acquittal of the final judge have death behind them — even though they still must die — but have come from death to life (John 4:24; 11:25-26; 1 John 3:4; Rom. 6:6-8).

3. Death has its power taken from it. What does this mean? Its reality remains. It ends our earthly time so that we have no more time — no time for any sort of continuation of our life. The information in Article 57 is questionable above all because it apparently reckons with an ongoing time, so that immediately after our death our soul is united with Christ and only after a longer time is it then united with our resurrected body. But all the insufficiency of statements about "What then?" hangs together with the fact that everything we can think about is bound to space and time. Yet even here we do not have to be entirely speechless, because we may also say

that Christ "has ended the power of death" (2 Tim. 1:10, Today's English Version) — he has ended *the* power to separate us from God and God's love, from Christ as our "head," as Article 57 says. Although we are powerless against sin's rule, he who has taken away sin's power to separate us from God's love has by this action shown his superiority over the inescapable power of death to tear us out of his hand. The proof of this superiority of his over the power of death in our death consists in the fact that (so Art. 52), "He will cast all his enemies and mine into eternal condemnation," that is, they will be thrown far away from God. This does not mean that our shattered private relationships will be made eternal. What it does refer to, according to Article 127, are our enemies that attack us again and again in this life: "the devil, the world, and our own sinfulness."

These powers opposed to God attack us so much because we stupidly consider them again and again to be our friends. Because in the company of these false friends, we ourselves are enemies of God, therefore eternal condemnation indeed threatens us. Christ on the cross has redeemed us from this condemnation (Art. 37, 34), but in the conflict between spirit and flesh they keep on attacking us our whole life long. Their right to attack us is already canceled. But in the demonstration of the superiority of God's grace in Jesus Christ over the power of death that wants to separate us from God, they will be definitively separated from us. Then they, these enemies of God, will also become *our* enemies. Then they can no longer attack us. They can only disappear. Then we are "free from the storms of all enemies"[26] and are only friends, children of God. And then what in ourselves is split, the disintegration of body and soul, will be healed so that both are given to each other; and so our person will be whole and at peace. (In this sense Art. 57 can be accepted.)

In this way it will finally be clear that God's Yes spoken in Jesus Christ, humiliated and exalted for us, was not in vain. It does not need to be, and cannot be, superseded by any other word. Rather, it now comes more than ever to be recognized as of utmost importance. As this Yes factually precedes our creaturely existence, so it also follows our earthly existence — in such a way that at the end of our existence in time it brings us home and lifts us up. This is not done in a way that extinguishes our creaturely existence, but in the way of the good shepherd who, to everyone's joy, finds his lost sheep and lifts it onto his shoulders (Luke 15:4ff.). "There will be more

---

26. From stanza 2 of the hymn "Jesu, meine Freude" ("Jesus, All My Gladness"), by J. Franck.

joy in heaven" the text reads. This is the "joy . . . of heaven," "eternal joy" (Art. 52, 58). Similarly, this lifting up of our finished earthly life onto his shoulders is our eternal life. Or we can say it with the word of the Crucified One to the thief, to which Article 57 refers: "Today you will be with me in Paradise" (Luke 23:43). You the sinner together with your Savior are inseparable even in dying and beyond dying, because even death cannot disprove that he is our head, and that we therefore are and remain his members. This is eternal life: our ultimate coming (Art. 57) to him to whom we already belong (Art. 1).

4. Eternal life! God's love for us will not be without an object after our passing away. It will not become a love without us. Even after our death we will not be lost to God's love. It will always *hold* us dear. "Our death is our boundary; but God is the boundary even of our death."[27] It is not death that is eternal. God's love is eternal. It makes us eternal — us as those who were earthly-temporal, body and soul. It is not just about salvation of the soul, as though an allegedly immortal soul were the only worthwhile part of us, and as though our having bodies and being temporal were something to despise, that could be tossed away. Rather we who are temporal, earthly, beings of body and soul are not eternally lost; we are eternally accepted in God's eternal love. "*This* perishable body" says Paul in 1 Corinthians 15:54 — without its ceasing to be this perishable body (otherwise we would no longer be the persons we were) — will "put on imperishability." We will then be nothing more than that God is everything for us. But God not without everything! This is the last step, the "eschaton," that God will "be all in all" (1 Cor. 15:28; Art. 123). God's eternity is not the extinguishing of the temporal. "In eternity there is time enough."[28]

The fact that the Eternal has taken time for us in Jesus Christ will in the end not have been in vain. It is fulfilled when God conversely accepts us temporal beings who one day will have had their time. God will resurrect us, exalt us, bring us home: what God has already done in the resurrection of Christ to our "head," God will also do to us, his members, and in similarity with "the glorious body of Christ" (Art. 57). Then the conflict between flesh and spirit will be lifted. Then God will be "all in all" in such a way that what is already fully true in Christ will be fully true in us. Then

27. K. Barth, *KD* III/2, p. 743. *CD* III/2, p. 611.
28. S. Kierkegaard, *Der Liebe Tun,* in *Collected Works,* sec. 19, ed. E. Hirsch (Düsseldorf: Diederichs, 1989), p. 344. ET: *Works of Love,* ed. H. and I. Hong (Princeton: Princeton University Press, 1995), p. 312.

will come to light what we will be, what we then fully are: God's children, and so "we will see him as he is" (1 John 3:2). We will see what on earth we perhaps believed, but believed against appearance: that God has made everything good in love. "I shall possess after this life perfect blessedness, which no eye has seen, no ear heard, nor the human heart conceived, and so praise God forever" (Art. 58). And this is the fulfillment of the promises to and in us, that the hungry and thirsty will be eternally satisfied and the tears of the wounded will be eternally dried and for us sinners our sins will be eternally forgiven.

However, here we must look beyond an embarrassing narrowness of the Heidelberg. In the eschaton, not only the disparity between what is true in Christ and what is true in me will be overcome, but also the disparity between the fact that God has taken on "human nature" in Christ (Art. 35) and the fact that always only some (and even these always more imperfectly than rightly) accept this in faith. What is involved here is the very unsettling disparity reflected in the opposition and existence alongside each other of church and state, of church and society, of Christians and the rest of humanity. This disparity we can no more repeal on earth than we can repeal the conflict between spirit and flesh. It is a disparity, and will not be repealed by our thinking up all kinds of theories, now for a Christian world reign, now for just and peaceful living together. But when God in eternal life is "all in all," this disparity is overcome. Then the petition for the coming of the kingdom of God is fulfilled. Then, according to Revelation 21:22, there will be no temple any more, no special church, but rather only that "great multitude that no one could count" (Rev. 7:9), united by the love of God and united to "praise God forever." Then the acceptance of "human nature" in *Christ* comes fully into view in human *nature* itself. Then Christ has come to the goal that Colossians 1:20 boldly states: "Through him God was pleased to reconcile to himself all things" — all things, which beyond human nature include also all the fallen and violated plant and animal worlds.

5. We are not yet there, but we are on the way there. We hope for it. So Now and Then do not simply stand opposed to each other like darkness and light, despite the burdens under which we must still sigh, despite the sins that still take place, despite the conflict between spirit and flesh that still needs to be fought. But those who hope for it see in the midst of all that is contrary the "morning light of eternity" and can say, "I now feel in my heart the beginning of eternal joy" (Art. 58). And they already now begin to say that "in all troubles and persecution I, with head held high, may

look for the self-same one who has already offered himself," and walking uprightly keep on their way and go toward what is to come. They begin to live, think, act, and bear themselves differently than "others do who have no hope" (1 Thess. 4:13). In the hope that God will eternally keep them, they begin to take seriously this world, the temporal, the soul and also the body and material affairs, to value these things, to stand up for their respect and advancement, And they stop thinking and acting as though in the end both good and bad are all the same, whether it be because tomorrow we are dead or because finally everything winds up in a slipshod acquittal. They dare to be comforted that none of our efforts for the good here on earth are done in vain. This is what the biblical talk of a "reward" which we will receive at the Last Judgment means (e.g., Matt. 6:4; Luke 6:23; 2 Cor. 5:10; Rev. 11:18).

But does this not contradict the claim that in the Last Judgment only the gracious justice of Christ counts? To this point Article 63 speaks beautifully and rightly: "This reward is not given because of worthiness, but out of grace." Grace surely does do away with the calculating aspect of works righteousness. But grace for this reason is no shabby grace. It really is rewarding to risk ourselves for grace. Grace rewards in its own gracious way, without our needing to be envious of others because its giver is so kind (Matt. 20:15). Certainly the verdict of God in the Last Judgment will not depend on "what works have earned." But just because God's grace alone will rule there, it will also praise all human works in which grace has been praised, in which we have actively shown our thankfulness for grace.

4.2. The Engaged Human Being

4.2.1. Thankfulness (Art. 86, 91-93, 114-15)

The free human being is the one who reflects the freedom of God. A human being reflects God's freedom because God brings this person into correspondence with God. Such persons are now what in themselves they are not: new persons, whom God has pronounced right and free, who have turned around from their old being to a new one and who in hope lay hold of God's promise of belonging to God in time and eternity. This is what has just been discussed, and now the content of this freedom will be developed.

The freedom of God is freedom for and in relationship with human beings. Corresponding to this is the freedom of the free human being, because it also is freedom for and in relationship. It is *freedom* in community (the human is mature, so can make decisions — section 4.3 will deal with this). But it is freedom in *community*, freedom in sharing, in taking part in other life. This will be discussed first, in order to bring out the truth that this freedom is no variant of that "freedom for independence," which people basically have only for themselves, in which they are independent from others, and remain uninvolved with them. That kind of freedom is actually their captivity. They show that they have been brought out of this captivity first of all by stepping out of the mold of being for themselves alone, uninvolved with others, and becoming interested in the existence and living of others, that is, becoming engaged. The Heidelberg sets this forth in its exposition of the Decalogue, the Ten Commandments.

Freedom in engagement is active freedom. When people move out of themselves, and go beyond themselves in taking part in other lives, this activity is truly human. Such activity is not without passivity, because no humans would act rightly if they were not indebted to what has been done for them — not only by God, but also by other humans. But it is still true that our engaged freedom with other lives is active freedom. It is not the case that we first have freedom and then maybe also put it into practice, and maybe not. This may hold for that "freedom for independence," which you can enjoy by yourself, and which first becomes active either when somebody gets too close to your independence or when in order to show your independence, you reach out for others as objects of your desire. The freedom for which Christ frees us is of another kind. This freedom, unlike that other one, we cannot get for ourselves, in order to possess it. This freedom is given us to use. Unused, inactive freedom is not true freedom. This is summed up in Galatians 5:13: "For you were called to freedom, brothers and sisters; only do not use your freedom as an opportunity for self-indulgence, but through love become slaves to one another." The freedom rejected there is no longer freedom at all. It is a fall into the flesh, backsliding into the old human and its apparent freedoms. It is extinguished freedom if it is not freedom burning in love, which means freedom active in engagement with others. Freedom is active participation and participatory activity in relationship with others. This is what the divine command makes us aware of — the command announced in summary fashion in the biblical Decalogue and expounded in Jesus' Sermon on the Mount.

But are not freedom and a command that requires our obedience mutually exclusive? From the viewpoint of a person who desires freedom in order to be independent, this is an insoluble problem. For this person will react to every command coming from outside as an unwarranted expectation. And this person will feel confirmed in that conviction by the opposing stance of the legalistic person. For the legalist, conversely, scents behind every freedom the danger of licentiousness, which must be chained up. But we are talking here about another kind of freedom, about freedom in *community,* in relationship. Here the reality of the command does not contradict freedom, any more than being together with others contradicts freedom. It is just that here the command has another meaning than what that independent person and that legalistic person assume! The genuine command does not take away our freedom. It gives order to the common life of free persons. Real commands are for regulating our life together, opening a liberation "practised and developed as a freedom under obligation."[29] Yet people themselves do not give the commands. It is *God,* after all, who *gives* us this kind of freedom and who also *gives* us the divine command. The togetherness of God and humans depends on God's liberation of humans; therefore, it is granted and warranted by God alone. Hence *God* also decides how God's partners are to carry out this community on their side. Because God acts in this way, the command is an order of freedom and not of force. To set freedom and obedience over against one another is a false alternative. In truth, the alternative is this: Is human freedom fulfilled by humans obeying *themselves,* or by obeying *God?* The biblical answer is that true obedience is due *only to the One* who has given us the experience of "joyful deliverance from the godless fetters of this world."[30] True freedom is obedient freedom, freedom in the covenant founded and maintained by God. So then, freedom divorced from this is disobedient freedom, loss of freedom, falling back into "the slave house" of Egypt, even if it deceives us with its "fleshpots" (Exod. 16:3).

God's liberation does in fact not come without a binding claim on us. It lays claim on us for just that which God has graciously prepared for us. As such, it is also our introduction into the *order* of freedom. God's liberation is in no case our release into an irresponsible caprice (which would be only a new slavery and which would immediately call those anxious legalistic persons onto the scene who want to guard against willfulness by sub-

29. J. M. Lochman, *Wegweisung der Freiheit: Die Zehn Gebote* (Stuttgart: Betulius, 1995), p. 29. ET: *Signposts to Freedom* (Minneapolis: Augsburg, 1982), p. 32.

30. Thesis 2 of *Die Barmer Theologische Erklärung,* chap. 3, n. 118, p. 35. ET: *The Theological Declaration of Barmen,* Thesis 2, in *The Book of Confessions,* part 1 of the Constitution of the Presbyterian Church (U.S.A.), p. 257.

jecting us to foreign lords!). Rather, "they have been freed from miserable bondage that they may, in obedience and readiness to serve, worship him as the author of their freedom."[31] The call to such obedience does not subsequently limit once again the freedom given us. It calls on us to put it to work responsibly in the relationships opened for us by God. With the smallest step into disobedience to God we would lose this freedom. Likewise, by reshaping the divine command into a constraint that makes us unfree, into the obedience of a robot, we would cease to be *obedient* to God! For God is "indeed merciful, but God is also righteous" (Art. 11). And this means that as God makes Godself to be ours, so God makes us to be God's, and thereby makes a claim on us, as on Godself, to live accordingly. God has used merciful justice above all else in the way God has redeemed us in Christ. We are "bought with a price" (1 Cor. 6:20; 7:23) from our sin and distance from God to be God's free children. But because of this we also belong to God. In redeeming us, God makes a legitimate claim on us to reflect our belonging to God by listening to, that is, obeying God. And indeed, the claim is made in such a way that no exception is foreseen where we would be left to our own discretion instead of to God. There is no realm of our life in which we do not belong to God, and in which we are withdrawn from God's command. And there is no situation in which it does not hold true that "we must obey God rather than any human authority" (Acts 5:29).

But can we keep the divine command? Is there such a thing as what Articles 86 and 91 call "good works"? The Heidelberg itself knows this problem, and in Article 114 answers at first negatively to the question: "But can those converted to God obey these commandments perfectly?" Then in Article 115 it says more brusquely that "no one can keep them in this life." This is not yet the whole answer to the problem. But first we need to get some clarity about what the problem really is. It is obviously not the case that all people are constantly busy murdering, committing adultery, lying, breaking into jewelry stores, and so on. It is also not the case that people who are involved in these things never would do something good and loving, selfless and sacrificial. Must I then make everything out to be bad, and impute low motives to these people, just to uphold "my" dogma of the sinfulness of all people? But how can I then say of the Ten Commandments that "no one . . . in this life" can keep them, not any of them?

But we must look more closely. Are "good works" to be considered im-

31. J. Calvin, *Institutes* II.8.15.

possible only because otherwise our dependence on God's grace could not be alleged? On the contrary, really good works will be good because they confess the grace of God. If our justification by God results from grace, and not from what we have earned by works, this does not mean that there are no good works at all. Rather, it denies that specifically those works by which we want to earn God's grace are good works. Again, there are people striving to do good who admit their action is not perfect; but they do not therefore think of needing grace. Many would assert just the opposite! It is remarkable that Jesus makes a distinction between righteous people and sinners when he says that he is sent only to the sinners and not to the righteous (Matt. 9:12-13)! This does not mean that he views these righteous ones as any less in need of God's grace than those sinners. But it also does not mean that he holds God's commandments as completely unrealizable. He does not snoop around in the life of the "rich young man" of Matthew 19:16ff., who believed he had kept all these commandments from his youth on. Jesus does not say: well, at some time or other you too have lied or stolen and so have not entirely fulfilled God's commandments. Much less does he teach the man abstractly about an inability to keep the commandments. But Jesus says to him that he has understood God's commandments *wrongly* and kept them *amiss,* and *therefore* says to him: sell all your goods! Jesus does not thereby give him an eleventh commandment, but rather uncovers the meaning of all Ten Commandments. Their meaning is the instruction to submit ourselves completely to God and to live from God's kindness. But it is just this meaning that the rich man has not grasped. As Jesus' word disclosed, his heart hung on himself and on his possessions. On this account, while keeping all the commandments, he had in truth kept none of them. If, according to Article 62, our righteousness must be entirely "in conformity with the divine law," and if "even our best works in this life are all imperfect and tainted with sin" we should not understand this simply in this way: if I fulfill the Ten Commandments at the rate of 99 percent and transgress only 1 percent, then all my action is "sinful." Nor should we understand it this way: the better I keep the Ten Commandments, the less I need to depend on God's grace.

The reverse is true: the more independent from God's grace I think I am, the more I am a sinner, even if, like that rich man, I keep all the commandments, and so I am all the more that person who according to Article 60 has sinned "terribly . . . against all the commandments of God" and never kept "any of them." Real sin is transgression against the *meaning* of all the commandments: it is disregarding the grace of God. And this sin takes place not less, but more intensively, where persons think they keep all the commandments, and on this basis consider themselves good people who as such believe they are no longer dependent on God's grace. With this attitude they are all the more transgressors of all the commandments, and all their deeds are evil. So sin takes place not only in breaking individual commandments. In fact it reaches its high point in disregard of the grace of God based *in* its keeping the commandments. But once we experience God's grace, we see that we are entirely and unconditionally dependent on grace, when we break a commandment and even more when we keep it. Those who keep a commandment have a much harder time understanding this. These are the very ones who ask: "Should we keep it then? We ask, not because good works are in themselves impossible, but because in this light they appear superfluous or dangerous. Should we not rather sin and do no good works so that God's grace will shine all the more purely?" This question is one Paul wrestled with (Rom. 6:15).

We should take note of the fact that the New Testament responds to this question with an unqualified No! For Protestant ears, it is astonishing that the whole New Testament speaks very positively of "good works" (cf. Matt. 5:16; 26:10; Acts 9:36; John 3:21; 14:12). Paul too speaks approvingly about the kind of people who "by patiently doing good seek for glory and honor and immortality" (Rom. 2:7) and "share abundantly in every good work" (2 Cor. 9:8; cf. 2 Thess. 2:17). According to Ephesians 2:10 and Colossians 1:10 we are created in Christ "for good works" (cf. further 1 Tim. 6:18; Titus 2:14; 1 Peter 4:19; Heb. 10:24 and 13:21). It is right that we are pardoned before God "without the work of the law." But we in Protestantism have had this hammered into us so much that we have often overlooked the positive sense in which the New Testament, including even Paul, speaks of "good works" which we may and can do, and also should do.

Good works are what we are discussing here. But how can we talk about them meaningfully — so that on the one hand grace is not conditioned by our good works, and on the other hand this same grace spurs us on to good works? The Heidelberg, following the lead of Luther and Calvin[32] answers in this way: we understand our works as our active *thankfulness* for this grace. We confirm that our righteousness is a righteousness graciously *given* us (Art. 60) by receiving God's commandment as an invitation to *thankful* action for this gift. Our works are not good insofar as they disregard this grace, or insofar as we understand them as work to earn

32. M. Luther, *WA* 38:364-65. *LW* 43:200-201. J. Calvin, *Institutes* II.8.15.

grace. Our works are good insofar as they are a thankful response to God's grace. They are good when we in our action respond to grace *(charis)* with thanks *(eucharistia)*. What does this starting point of Christian ethics mean?

1. Thankful conduct in correspondence to the grace of God is conduct in dependence on God's grace. It is action in which we are in accord with God's will by trusting God's mercy. How could we earn God's grace by our action, when grace establishes the action to begin with! Beyond this, action so established is not a kind that, the better we do it, the more God's grace is superfluous for us. It is the kind of action in which grace is always needed more than before. While perverse behavior under the sign of sin can take place where people keep the commandments, and while sin happens there most intensively, namely in the form of disregard of God's grace, here the positive role of the commandments is affirmed. According to Articles 114-15, although conversion does not bring the ability to obey the commandments perfectly, and there is only a "tiny beginning" of obedience, nevertheless there is a beginning of living "according to all the commandments of God, and not just some of them" in the very people who do not "keep these commandments perfectly" and therefore "in this life" do not keep them. This beginning is there in people who admit they do *not* keep the commandments, but who listen to them so that "the longer we live the more we may come to know our sinfulness." How can it be that in them there nevertheless is a beginning of living "according to all the commandments of God"? Because they do not disregard the grace of God, but only "seek more fervently the forgiveness of sins and righteousness in Christ" and ask for the renewing grace of the Holy Spirit. Although they always remain sinners in need of forgiveness, and although they again and again, sad to say, do so much that in the sight of God and humans is not right, and although they themselves see this "more and more . . . all our life long," and tell themselves so, nevertheless their works are not simply perverse. Their works are a beginning of right action, a beginning which has its goal not in this world, but "after this life," where we will thank God in eternity because God's goodness endures forever.

2. If the doing of good works is our thankful response to God's gracious action, a question arises that ethical reflection often skips over, and which yet has decisive significance. Prior to the question of *what* is the right and good we should do stands the more important question *who* is the person in a position to do right? The answer to this question lies totally in our thankful response to the gracious action of God toward us. The "old

human" who we are in ourselves is not the person who is in a position to do right. But as those pardoned by God, we become and are in a position to do right. In grace, God's love meets us. It "does not find, but creates that which is pleasing to it."[33] They who have never experienced love cannot love, and will hardly conduct themselves in a way worthy of love. God loves us, to be sure, not because we are worthy of love. The fact that God nevertheless counts us worthy of love makes us into those loved by God. Through this we become the kind of persons who on their part can love — not as perfect, sinless humans, but in that "small beginning of this obedience." Without being made into such persons, we would not be able to behave in thankful response to God's gracious action. But God's love transforms us into such persons, because we are made into God's loved ones. Article 86, which denotes this transformation as the prerequisite for our thankful doing of "good works," says this in its own way: "Christ having redeemed us with his blood, also renews us in his own image through his Holy Spirit." He who in his self-offering for us has won his claim on us, renews us through the Holy Spirit. He begins to make us, through the Spirit, into his image, into the kind of persons on whose faces a reflection of his friendly countenance shines. Through the Spirit we catch and are ignited by Christ's love as those who, like Christ and with him, are beloved children of God. As such, we on our part can love, and thus show that we are thankful for God's gracious deeds.

3. Persons made capable of loving, and thereby capable of acting, through being loved by God, show that this is so in active behavior. Corresponding to the grace of God effective for us are the persons who reply "thankfully" to grace, stepping forward responsibly. In this sense let us interpret the remarkable comment in Article 86, that we "may be assured of our faith by its fruits." This could point in the direction of the infamous *syllogismus practicus,* with its problematic inference: because I am such a wonderfully active person, I am no doubt a believer and a beloved child of God. It would be better to understand the statement this way: where there is really grace, and faith in this grace, there is certainly also thankfulness for it, and it is impossible that a free, responsible, active, demonstrative response not be given. This does not contradict the grace of God. But it does contradict a dangerous notion of it. According to this notion, the grace of God shines all the more brightly the more a human being is quiet in passive idleness. This notion is reflected in that church system mentioned ear-

33. M. Luther, *WA* 1:365. *LW* 31:57.

lier, in which a passive laity faces a clergy that mediates grace. And the church deftly kept on passing this system off as an expression of divine grace. Of course the system could only be carried on in compromise with the powers of the "world," because the laity could not be passive in every area of life, but needed to act, and this was only possible for them outside that alleged realm of grace.

But do not protest against this system of misunderstood grace in such a way that you also lose sight of rightly understood grace at the same time! Rather, grasp the fact that grace itself, rightly understood, contradicts this system. What really matters is that the free God, in freedom for coexistence, achieves the goal of interaction with free human beings who on their side commit themselves to coexistence. The grace of God, which sets up this interaction, triumphs where human beings in thankfulness for it freely reciprocate. "None but those who are free are very grateful to one another"[34] and vice versa. God's grace is friendly to humans in that it enables the persons in whom it is effective to be effective themselves. Grace gives to persons gratis, and it gives them endlessly much to give thanks for "with hearts and hands and voices."[35] It would not be grace if it made persons irresponsible. Grace proves itself gracious in that it makes persons responsible and provides them freedom to act responsibly. And grace is so great that it does not need to dismiss persons to a different, graceless agency under whom they can act, but lets their activity reflect the gracious work of God. The object is not that they complete God's work! To be sure, in the coexistence of God and humans there is also cooperation between God and humans, but with the difference that we do not do the same thing God does. Rather, by our action we give thanks for God's action. In addition, thankfulness brings "fruits," not so *we* can quietly enjoy them for *ourselves,* but so *others* can enjoy — and we hope enjoy them so much that "our neighbors may be won over to Christ" (Art. 86). To *Christ!* Not so that they be impressed by *us,* and even become *our* supporters! Jesus says: "Let your light shine before others, so that they may see your good works and give glory to your *Father in heaven*" (Matt. 5:16). If they praise us instead of God, one may even doubt if the works were really good.

4. How shall we act? In a way that seeks to correspond to the action of God. We are to affirm what God wills and seek to follow it. In this way, and

34. B. Spinoza, *Ethica* (1677), IV.71. ET: *Ethics* (London: J. M. Dent and Sons, 1923[4]), p. 189.
35. From stanza 1 of the hymn "Nun danket alle Gott," by M. Rinkart. ET: "Now Thank We All Our God," by C. Winkworth.

only in this way, do we do what is good and right, though it be in ever so small beginnings and attempts. Article 91: "What are good works? Only those that are motivated by true faith [that is, trust in and attention to God's grace], in accord with the law of God, and done for God's glory; and not those that are based on our own opinion or on human tradition." Grace, in which God binds Godself to us, stands continually in antithesis to what our works deserve. But the good works in which we show our thankfulness for this grace stand in another antithesis: between what God commands us to do and what other authorities command us to do. Works are certainly not good to the extent that by them we want to earn a right to God's grace, to the extent that by them we want to do something to *our* praise. They are good insofar as they take place to the praise and honor of *God*, the gracious God, insofar as God is "praised through us" (Art. 86). So they are good insofar as they acknowledge what this God wants as ultimately binding for us — this *alone*, and not what we ourselves want, and what somebody else may order us to do. Works are not good insofar as in doing them we obey, but only insofar as we obey God in doing them. They are good as we acknowledge that God distinguishes the divine command from all other commands. There is no compulsion on this account to disobey these other laws — they can indeed be in line with the command of God. But there is also no compulsion to follow them unconditionally in every case. We are to "discern what is the will of God" (Rom. 12:2). When we follow these laws that we believe reflect God's, however, we will not be fundamentally obeying them, but above all God. We will give our heart to God and not make the desires of our heart the center and motive of our action.

In this sense, Article 113 (like Rom. 7:7!) understands the tenth commandment, "Thou shalt not covet," as the key to the basic meaning of all Ten Commandments: "That not even the least inclination or thought contrary to any one of God's commandments should ever enter into our heart, but that we should constantly hate all sin with our whole heart and take pleasure in all righteousness." Here God's command differs from all other commandments (as well as from any commandment of God misused to justify ourselves!). To follow God's command is not a burden, but is actually a delight. It is not the command of a tyrant, obedience to whom may be the obedience of a robot. To rebel against such a tyrant, as Prometheus did, could be celebrated as a heroic deed. But God's command is the command of the gracious God, and therefore is a law full of grace and never merciless. It is the law of the God who has set God's enslaved people free, as Article 92 indicates in quoting from Exodus 20. God does not enslave the people anew, but instructs it in the right use of its freedom. We follow this commandment gladly or not at all.

5. Article 92 asks: "What is the law of God?" — and answers by quoting the entire Decalogue. As we, in thankfulness for God's grace, make room for the will of God in our will, and actively follow it, we are not following diverse decrees, but the one command of God. We are following not the Decalogue, and not some letter of the law, but God. The Decalogue does not thereby become useless. For it drives home a twofold lesson. On the one hand, it shows that the one command of God includes a multitude of aspects. On the other hand, it shows that the one command of God does not pose an abstract "Thou shalt," but always in each particular time calls for a fully concrete response. Let us be clear about this: when God commands "Thou shalt not kill," for example, it would be nonsense to say that while trying to follow this commandment, I am not keeping the other nine commandments. Rather, in what is commanded of me each time, the whole question is at stake: "Will I follow the will of God or not?" Furthermore, the commandment against killing, for example, tells us something particular at any given point. For example, in 1939: Thou shalt not affirm Hitler's war of aggression, but thou shalt affirm the resistance against this war.

It would also be nonsense to say that God's command tells us only a general direction, and its particular application is a matter of our willful imagination. Then we would in effect not be following God's will, but our own interpretation of it. Where we conceive of the command of God as a legal code set down in individual laws, we run into endless conflicts which always lead to senseless compromises: now I can keep only this one commandment while I transgress against the other commandments, though it be only through omission, and now I keep even this one in such a way that I partly, or almost completely transgress against it. In opposition to this, we cannot make it clear enough: God always requires of us only *one* thing, and in each situation only a definite and particular thing. Of course we have to examine, each time exactly, and each time anew, what the will of God is now. And certainly we can miss knowing what it is. But this does not change the fact that this is the question we have to use in examining, and in measuring our misses: What does God want of me now? And in this question I am not confronted by many, or only one of many laws, but in this situation I am confronted with the entire command of God.

6. Though what God requires of us in each situation is open, and must

remain open, there is one thing that is not open. What is decided in advance is that the rightness of our action has to show itself in its being an act of thankfulness for God's grace. In God's grace, moreover, God's love meets us. Therefore whatever may be asked of us in a particular situation, it will always and everywhere be required that we, in correspondence to the love of God, also love. "Love is the fulfilling of the law" (Gal. 5:14; Rom. 13:10). To put it more exactly: whatever is asked of us will always guide us in two relationships in which love is commanded: in relation to God and in relation to our neighbor (Art. 93). There is, to be sure, also a rightful self-love. This does not get shortchanged, since it is only through being loved that we become persons who can love others. Behind the division of the Ten Commandments into the two aspects of the relation to God and to our neighbor we have little difficulty recognizing the twofold commandment of love taught by Christ (cf. Art. 4). We remember that sin is that perverted freedom which wants only to be independent, which is not free for God and neighbor. It is hate against God and against fellow humans, the sin of Adam and Eve and the sin of Cain. We are set free from it by the love of God for us and for our neighbor. We are freed from it through the just and merciful intervention of the true God in the true human Jesus Christ, our brother, not because we have earned it, but out of God's grace toward us. When this grace in the Holy Spirit becomes effective in us, the new human cannot fail to begin becoming visible: it is the human who thanks God for this grace. And we thank God by beginning to affirm actively the twofold relation against which we in our sin transgressed, and which we in our sin abandoned: the relation to God and to our neighbor. We affirm this twofold relation in that we, who previously were independent, become involved with God and our neighbor, and so love them. About this the two tables of the Ten Commandments speak. Now to the first table!

4.2.2. Love of God (Art. 94-103)

This section could also have the heading: Involvement with God. This is what love is: heartfelt attention to and interest in the life of another. In love a person moves out beyond self in order to associate with another, to live with that person, to be something for her, but also to let her be something for herself. Yet love does this without one's losing oneself in the other, or absorbing him into oneself. The first table of the Decalogue is about our love of God, our involvement with God. Love of God plays an important role in older hymnbooks, but in Protestant writing on ethics appears rarely or not at all. It has been pushed out of them with the groundless argument that the first part of the love command, love for God, is taken care of in our fulfilling the second part: love of neighbor. There is fear, so one hears, of falling back into medieval Catholic mysticism and its love poetry about God, where you would take seriously and literally: "You shall love *God* with all your heart, and with all your soul, and with all your mind." But we are never well advised when in fear of presumed dangers we suppress what dare not be suppressed, according to the clear meaning of scripture.

Protestant association with the command to love God, and so to attend to the first table of the Decalogue, has features of a massive sin of omission. Here we need new reflection. Can we even speak only a little prayer — whose primal cry according to Romans 8:15 is: "Abba, dear Father!" — without thereby loving God with all our heart? Does not our ethics, insofar as it has no room for love poetry about God, necessarily become an ethics of an uninterrupted workday? Does it not become an ethics of a kind of love whose crushing tentacles we would very much like to get free from sometimes because we have the feeling that the one who loves always knows better what is good for us than we ourselves? Further, is not the easy acceptance of recent theological argument that there really is no special *Christian* ethic connected with the fact that the first table of the Decalogue was simply forgotten, whereby the second table could all the more easily be put forward as the expression of a general natural law? And further, does not the Christian bad habit, mentioned earlier, of taking so lightly the forbidding of idol worship, the cult of images, the misuse of God's name and desecrating the Sabbath, have roots in the hidden Christian contempt of Judaism, which in distinction to our Christianity, lives with such a sensitive feeling for these four commandments?

But how can we love God as we are supposed to do? Is God not too exalted and too unimaginable for us to be able to enjoy? To this we need to answer that we are not talking about some god or other. We are talking about the one who has come close to us, who has taken on concrete form, who has become a specific person encountering us, a You. We are talking about the one who wants to associate with us, as was already said about Moses and Abraham: "as with a friend" (Exod. 33:11; James 2:23; in *this* connection read also John 15:14!). It is the God who is graciously turned toward us, who has come forth as our God. As such a one, God has loved us and keeps on loving us. God does this so well as to become lovable for us. Yes, God *is* lovableness. We would have had to do with another god if we would need to ask whether we can love God. This God we cannot know without already *doing* what we should be doing: loving God. Our action would not be a deed of *thankfulness* for God's action if it were not first of all love of *God*. What this means, the first four commandments of the first table illuminate.

The first commandment (Art. 94-95) tells us that part of our love for God is standing for God with *passion*, for the one true God who is completely unmistakable over against all gods and idols. The commandment dare not be understood as a general directive to a monotheistic faith in the sense of a theological knowledge that the Pantheon, instead of having many gods, has only one. It is also not meant in the sense of the Greek conception of God that has infiltrated Western theology in a dangerous way. According to this conception, God is the absolute One, unchangeable, beyond all manifold experience, whom we can think about only by eliminating any thoughts of number, measure, variety, and motion. Such a god I may perhaps be able to *think* as an extreme concept. I could perhaps also lose myself in this god, as the mystics want to do. This god is also perhaps the foundation for Nietzsche's "belief in a normal god" and the "teachings of a normal human type."[36] But to "*trust* in God alone, . . . expect *all good* from God alone, . . . *love* . . . God with my whole heart" (Art. 94), this I cannot do with such a god. About such a god I can have only conceptions, and only relative, inadequate conceptions at that. This picture of god gives life to the conviction, which so many people today have absorbed into their flesh and blood, that we may believe what we want, as long as we don't make any absolute claim about it. Behind this stands the view that God is the inconceivable One; therefore all our ideas of God do not fit, they are only *our* conceptions. Not only the familiar powers and values that we set as our absolutes, but also the opposite picture of God as the inconceivable One, belong to the idols that according to the first commandment we should avoid and flee from so that we do not lose our soul's salvation (Art. 94).

The first commandment does not see God's people in danger of religiously absolutizing the tribal God it happens to have. It does not see God's people in danger of believing that God is the One beyond our conceptions of God, an idea that could be remedied by clarifying our reasoning. It does not see God's people in danger of carrying its relation with

---

36. F. Nietzsche, *Die fröhliche Wissenschaft*, in *Werke*, chap. 2, n. 31, vol. 2, p. 135. ET: *The Gay Science* (Cambridge: Cambridge University Press, 2001), p. 128.

God too far, but it sees God's people in huge constant danger of carrying on with other gods, in danger of dividing its heart between God and the idols. Article 95: "What is idolatry? It is to imagine, cling to, or trust in something other than or in addition to the only true God, who has revealed himself in his Word." God's being so revealed means, however, that God is really distinguished from the other gods. Even in their powerlessness, these other gods are extremely strong powers, the more attractive, the more terrible — and sad to say, the more terrible, the more attractive. They have us in their hand. We cannot get ourselves free from them. But *God* makes us free from them. God *differentiates* Godself from them in turning to the people of Israel and freeing them from slavery. God will then also do the same for others, but for others only in the way it was done for Israel: not because Israel has an advantage over others, but as a demonstration of God's pure love and grace.

"I am the Lord, *your* God" — with this claim God elects humans to be God's people. They do not elect a god, and then set this god of their own choosing as absolute, or then again, because it is conceived as only their private god, as relative. *They* are always busy choosing other gods for themselves. And what humans choose on their own is always another god, not the God of grace, since such a choice is always a work of humans. We cannot in our own power choose for ourselves the God of grace. God chooses us. This God is one, to be sure, but not *the* inconceivable One behind and apart from all historical phenomena. God is the one in the history in which God chooses a people and remains true to the divine choice. For this reason the New Testament does not cancel the first commandment, but just makes it more precise. 1 Corinthians 8:4ff.: "there are many gods and many lords — yet for us there is one God, the Father, from whom are all things and for whom we exist, and one Lord, Jesus Christ, through whom are all things and through whom we exist." The New Testament says that God, graciously acting in this one born in Israel has even taken on human form — the human form worthy of being accursed. But God has really taken on this form so that no sinner any longer has to be excluded from God's gracious choosing. Even Gentiles can be included.

Only with this background does the *command* in the first commandment become understandable. It allows us and bids us to choose the God who graciously chooses us. We cannot do this on our own, but only in response to God's electing grace. And I give the response in that I "trust in God alone, humbly and patiently expect all good from God alone, and love, fear, and honor God with my whole heart" (Art. 94). Love always also means choosing. Love means saying with all the passion of love in the action of my life: this one and no other! In this way we may and should on our side reflect the self-differentiation of God from the idols and take part in this differentiation. This means for one thing that we need to keep ourselves open to the fact that God — because God is not that motionless One behind and apart from all historical phenomena — deals with us and meets us in ever-new ways and changes, in bright and dark hours, as helper and as judge, as supporter and as challenger. God and no other means also that we can trust that however God meets us, God is never a different God, but is again and again, in all the changes, the same: the one who is gracious to us, who loves us, who frees us. This God and no other has also, but only secondarily, the polemical meaning that we for our part distinguish this God from everything that is not this God. The God who chooses us is alone the true God, while all the gods chosen by us are only apparent and pretended gods. They are the images and creations of our fanciful imagination.

> Expel false gods with mocking prod;
> the Lord is God, the Lord is God.
> Give our God all honor![37]

These gods, though ever so imposing, stand on clay feet. They fall down by themselves if we only *love* God according to the first commandment.

The second commandment (Art. 96-98), according to the Reformed numbering the forbidding of images, tells us that part of the love for God commanded us is that we commit ourselves to God without preconceived notions. This is what is at issue here — not a question of good taste, about which people can argue, as we know. This is also not about a stance toward painting, which Calvin called a gift of God.[38] Furthermore, the most significant painters have arisen in Reformed territory, in which the forbidding of images was so important. Moreover, the impulse for attacking images in the sixteenth century was not simply hatred of art, but the battle against the symbols of an ecclesiastical power system perceived as thoroughly bad. Again, this commandment is not a matter of good advice, which one could also not follow. Rather, it is about setting specifications

---

37. Stanza 8 of the hymn "Sei Lob und Ehr dem höchsten Gott" ("Praise and Glory unto God"), by J. J. Schütz.

38. J. Calvin, *Institutes* I.11.12.

for God that can burden generations and through which the decision is made whether we love or hate God. It has to do with the prohibition of a serious "iniquity" (Exod. 20:5-6), which God, for the sake of love for us, strives against as fiercely as possible. What is the evil that threatens here?

Here before our eyes stands a sharpening of the sin against which the first commandment is directed — and therefore it must be named as its own commandment in the Decalogue. If the first commandment is aimed against our having an idol in God's place, the second is against the true God's being made into an idol by us. How can this be? The answer given by Immanuel Kant, who named this commandment the loftiest in Hebrew scripture, is that it warns us not to draw down the invisible God into the visible realm,[39] and implies that the more we speak of God in concepts purified of all we can see, the more appropriately we will speak. But if this were the meaning of the commandment, the Bible would sin against it on every page. However, the Bible does not sin against this commandment because the God it testifies to is not merely in the world beyond this one. In being beyond this world, God is also in it. This is why the Old Testament speaks about God in a way, objectionable for all idealistic philosophy, that is highly visible and human. It talks about God as one who has hands, feet, eyes, ears, and even a heart. More than ever in the New Testament it speaks of God as the one whose Word became flesh and dwelt among us, so that we could see God's glory (John 1:14). This person is, according to Colossians 1:15, the completely visible "image of the invisible God."

The prohibition of images cannot be applied to God's becoming visibly perceptible to us, as in a picture. It is aimed rather against our constructing pictures of what lives on earth, although this is already visible to our eyes. It is aimed against our habit of making preconceived images, which we call prejudices — preformed ideas we make about others that take the place of the living reality. These pictures grow so rooted in our minds that they become resistant to all better teaching by reality. For example, a Jew can be a hundredfold different from what fits our prejudice; our prejudice admits only one case that confirms our prejudice, out of a hundred cases. But in prejudice we not only fasten someone to a picture that does not really resemble the person, but we even try to remold the living reality of the person and subject it to our picture until it corresponds to the role we envision for that person. This very thing is what happens,

---

39. I. Kant, according to W. Luthi, *Die Zehn Gebote Gottes* (Basel: Reinhardt, 1950), p. 23.

yes, happens most dangerously, when we construct God for ourselves and relate to God according to a picture or prejudice we have made. We understand now why it makes no essential difference whether this picture is of a more spiritual, or of a more sensory sort. We understand further that these pictures exercise real power for generations, as in our patriarchal, militaristic, and egoistic pictures of God. But we understand that we do not ward off this evil when in place of the old pictures of God we quickly make new ones that suit us better. For this is the evil: we substitute for the living reality of God the picture we make, and we fasten God into that; then we consider this picture to be the way God really is. We probably pray to God with this picture in mind. And the more zealously we do this, the more we close ourselves off from realizing that in all this we are dealing only with *our* picture of God, and that the living God is not in it. However beautiful or serious our picture may be, it resembles those idols who

> have mouths, but do not speak;
> > eyes, but do not see.
> They have ears, but do not hear;
> > noses, but do not smell.
> They have hands, but do not feel;
> > feet, but do not walk. . . .
> Those who make them are like them. (Ps. 115:5-8)

In our pictures we no longer have God as living counterpart. In them we face only ourselves, our own reflections. We think we honor God and yet are without God. This is how God "punishes" this "iniquity."

How do we get out of this blind alley? In this way, says Article 96: "That we should not make any image of God or worship God in any other way than God has commanded in God's Word." I interpret this to mean: we can let go of this image-making by honoring God in the way revealed in God's Word. We honor God by letting Godself speak for and about God. So God leads us out of this blind alley, and does so in a way that renders our making of images superfluous because God takes care that we, who in those images give false information about God, nevertheless do get to know God. We receive what we need to know about God in the divine Word, in which God makes Godself known to us. And "we must not try to be wiser than God who does not want God's people taught by lifeless idols, but rather by the living preaching of God's Word" (Art. 98). According to Gerhard von Rad, this is the meaning of the Old Testament forbidding of images: "the place occupied in the pagan religions by the cultic image was in Israel taken by the word and name of Jahweh."[40] We can say that in God's Word, God becomes perceptible to us, in speaking pictures, or in picture language; this is how Christ is "before your very eyes . . . portrayed" (Gal. 3:1, New International Version). In this way God does become *indirectly* perceptible, visible as the One who is hidden. We always depend on the self-revealing of God's living reality. We can never see God directly. We can only first believe and listen in order after that to be able to see God as "before your very eyes . . . portrayed," as in seeing by faith. Other than in such indirectness we will not get to see anything except our own self-made images. Only through believing and listening to God's Word do we keep the second commandment. We love God by keeping ourselves open for God to make perceptible to us who God is, instead of hanging on to our own images of God.

The third commandment (Art. 99-102), the prohibition of the misuse of the divine name, tells us that part of the love for God commanded us is *carefulness* in relating with God, sensitive unintrusiveness. This obviously has to do with a very serious matter. For in the case of the breaking of this commandment a divine penalty is added. Article 100 declares that "no sin is greater or more provocative to God than the profaning of God's name." What is so bad about it? The name of God is not just sound and smoke. In the Name, God is open for relation with others, addresses them and lets them address God, entrusts Godself to them and allows God to be bound by them. In the Name, God is your and my God, *our* God, and designates us as persons belonging to God. God's name is God's reliable presence with us, so that we can have interaction with God and call God by name. God's name is called a holy name. "All that is within me, bless his holy name" (Ps. 103:1). God's name is "holy" because in the very closeness into which God is brought, yes delivered to us by the Name, it is nevertheless the name of *God*. The familiarity God wants to cultivate with us dare not turn into a coarse familiarity. The use of God's name dare not turn into a misuse. God's approachability, in which God is here for us, dare not mislead us into using God's name as a thing at our disposal, which we can manipulate. By doing this we would not only disturb the relationship with God, but destroy it. In relationship with God, the closeness of the interaction calls for carefulness, sensibility, and restraint.

40. G. von Rad, *Theologie des Alten Testaments* (Munich: Kaiser, 1957), vol. 1, p. 218. ET: *Old Testament Theology* (New York: Harper & Row, 1962), p. 219.

Obviously, the name of God can only be misused where it is *used*. Yes, misuse is all the more threatening the more intensively God's name is used. It is not the people who stand far off, but those who stand near who are the evil transgressors of this commandment. Not only cursing and perjury, which the Heidelberg is especially concerned about, are the objects of this commandment. Unobtrusive, subtle misuse is the most dangerous misuse of God's name. Where could it be misused more badly than where, without cursing and swearing, it is used ardently: for example, in the pulpit or in a theological lecture hall. "When words are many, transgression is not lacking" (Prov. 10:19). The closer people stand to the holy fire, the more likely they are to burn themselves. What then is this misuse? It consists in the attempt to make one's own cause out as God's, or vice versa, to subordinate God's cause to one's own. The misuse consists in using the name of God as support for reaching our own goals, set by ourselves, and without God. These goals do not have to be egoistic; as a rule people will maintain that they are for the common good. Nor do these goals have to be militaristic and colonialist. They will in any case be interpreted as carrying out an idealistic program or as satisfying a legitimate need. In one way or another, the procedure is always the same: humans are using the name of God not "in order to serve God," but because "they want to use God in their service."[41]

The Lord, however, "will not acquit anyone who misuses his name." Let us not think of this punishment in a childish way! The misuse of God's name always carries the punishment within itself. The punishment lies in the fact that the name of God becomes an empty concept. We then have, by using God's name falsely, "God" *without God*. While we fancy that we hitch God to our wagons, God is already no longer with us, but has withdrawn from us. In this way, God hallows God's name. In this way God is able one day to open our eyes for the holiness of God's name. God does this by giving us part in the hallowing of God's name, which comes about in the following way: just as God withdraws from our use of the divine name for our own interests, so we on our side also withdraw from such use. We will then look with respect at the carefulness of the Jews, who would rather not speak God's name at all than sin against it. We will also respect the carefulness of the Anabaptists, who would rather not swear at all than take a false oath, which would hinder them from loving God above all else. But in such carefulness we must not renounce the use of God's name, for even such a

41. L. Ragaz, *Die Revolution der Bibel: Die Zehn Gebote* (Zurich: Religiös-sozialen Vereinigung, 1964²), p. 11.

resolution would not be sure protection against misuse. We escape the misuse of God's name only through the *use* of God's name, but through right, careful use. So, as Article 99 says: "We must use the holy name of God only with fear and reverence, so that God may be rightly confessed and worshiped by us and be glorified in all our words and works."

The fourth commandment (Art. 103), the Sabbath commandment, tells us that part of the love of God commanded us is also *joy* in God. This commandment also belongs to the first table of the Decalogue. It is important to note this, because people alienated from God become upset at what is commanded here. To honor the Sabbath is not to do nothing — that would be nonsense, since a divine commandment always calls for human action in response. But what is commanded is that we not do our own work, but instead refrain from and distance ourselves from it. Again, people ask in exasperation, "What's the use of this?" In response, recent theology takes perhaps too much trouble to answer in a satisfactory way: yes indeed, this is helpful to people for their recreation or their social life, and helpful to the animal and plant world which otherwise is so overused by all of us. All this does no doubt belong to the consequences of the Sabbath commandment. But the commandment itself, as part of the first table of the Ten Commandments, aims at our relation to *God*. There is such a thing as Godless rest, which rests on the illusion that humans are able "all the better to rest, the more time for rest they have."[42] In this respect the Reformers were right when in treating this commandment they thought first of the worship service. Article 103 therefore lists the elements of the worship service: sermon, sacrament, calling on God, and — this too is an integral part of the celebration — the offering "for the needy." What times those were, when people said: "Indeed, nothing is to be preferred to the Work of God [*opus dei:* regular term for worship in the *Rule of St. Benedict*]"![43] And what times where this holds: "we dare do nothing, least of all in matters of the worship service, in which we are not assured that we do it according to the word of God!"[44]

Still, with the invitation to the church worship service the meaning of the Sabbath commandment is not yet exhausted. Why does God here lay special claim to each seventh day, to a seventh of our lifetime? This is why:

42. G. Ebeling, *Die Zehn Gebote. In Predigten ausgelegt* (Tübingen: Mohr, 1973), p. 97.

43. Benedikt von Nursia, cf. *Die Benediktinerregel. Eine Anleitung zum christlichen Leben* (Zurich, 1980²), p. 224. ET: *The Rule of St. Benedict* (Collegeville, MN: The Liturgical Press, 1981), p. 243.

44. P. Bartels, *Johannes à Lasco* (Elberfeld: Friderichs, 1860), p. 35.

to let us take part in the rest in which God rested from God's works on the seventh day after the six-day work of creating heaven and earth. What does God's rest mean? It means that God is free from a necessity of working endlessly, free from letting work consume God, free to be Godself. "Only those beings are free who are able to limit their action."[45] The fact that God limits the divine action is not a deficiency. The fact that everything created by God is "very good" underscores God's staying away from further work. God does not need always to work restlessly to make it better. The better is actually the enemy of the good. If God would always have to make every-thing better than before, God would never be able to be satisfied with any of God's works, and would hurry past all possible partners of God's love. Love always has a particular, a limited vis-à-vis. By the fact that God did not continue working on the seventh day, but rested, God found the object of God's love. In God's rest, God is also free to rejoice in the created being vis-à-vis God, and to love it.

Since God commands us to rest on the Sabbath, as God does, this is apparently because God wants us to take part in what God's rest from di-vine work means. Humans too are released from having to work endlessly. They too are free to be themselves. They too may limit their own action and do not have to make everything better. They may be content, but not on the basis of their own achievements! For the Sabbath of Genesis 2:2-3 is indeed the first day of human life, on which the first humans cannot look back at any achievements at all. Rather, it is the day for letting ourselves be satisfied with what God has done in advance. Therefore we are to rejoice that God is here and encounters us, and to rejoice in God's beauty in the divine works. We are commanded here to live out of a loving Yes to God. What we are forbidden to do is to live out of the Yes we would like to say to ourselves on the basis of our achievements. This commandment must also determine our other days, the workdays: we should simply make the effort to provide what we need to live, without by our action wanting to "make" ourselves; otherwise our work becomes a curse. What is imparted to me on the Sabbath day I have to receive joyfully and thankfully in such a way that from there "I will stop doing evil works all the days of my life, allow the Lord to work in me through the Spirit, and so begin in this life the eternal Sabbath" (Art. 103).

This last statement presupposes the other explanation of the Sabbath commandment, in Deuteronomy 5:14-15: it is for the remembrance of the

45. K. Barth, *KD* III/1, p. 243. *CD* III/1, p. 215.

liberation of Israel out of Egyptian slave labor. This reminds us that in the meantime the world created good by God has been overshadowed through the Fall, and that human work, from which that first day of life released us, has thereby become alienated work: now there are servants and maids and cattle put to work by humans. In view of this, the Sabbath, with its remembrance of the liberation out of Egypt, now becomes a sign of the promise of a new liberation. Yes, it becomes a sign of the promise of a final liberation out of a twisted life in twisted circumstances to a new life in a new world. This is the "eternal Sabbath." We do not celebrate this yet. For the Sabbath celebrated under the shadow of sin has to mean that we stay away not only from our *work,* but also from our *perversion* of work. How could a rest from our perversion of work help us when after the Sabbath we just devote ourselves anew to our perverted work? The danger here is that the Sabbath instead becomes lost in further perverted work. But now Christian faith confesses that the promise of a new life is already fulfilled: in the One risen on Easter we are a new creation, freed from our perverted work (cf. 2 Cor. 5:17). This is why Christianity celebrates its Sabbath on the day of Resurrection, on Sunday. Because what is valid for us in Christ is not yet true in us, liberation from perverted work is a promise only to be fulfilled in the eternal Sabbath. But because the Holy Spirit begins to bring what is valid for us in Christ into our life already now, there may and should also be a joyful beginning of what is promised in our life on this side. So the Sabbath commandment tells us in fact: that — from Sunday, from the assurance of the gospel received there — "I will stop doing evil works all the days of my life, allow the Lord to work in me through the Spirit, and so begin in this life the eternal Sabbath."

4.2.3. Love of Humans (Art. 104-12)

The freedom to which Christ has freed us is freedom in community — first with God, but therefore also freedom in community on the horizontal plane with all with whom God wills to coexist. The priority of the vertical plane, the love of God, is important in order to understand that the fulfillment of our freedom in community necessarily has to take place also in the horizontal, in love of fellow human beings. Why then should we practice love of neighbor? This is not as obvious as we often think. Should we do it, for example, because we consider others worthy of love; or because we regard them as needing love? But would that not mean that they become objects of our surplus energy, so that they do not get what they need, but only what we get rid of onto them that we do not need anyway? Or is our supposed love of neighbor not secretly self-love, because in truth we only want the others in order to have something for ourselves: a higher enjoyment or even a handy usefulness, so that even where we attend to them we actually are thinking only of ourselves?

However, love of neighbor flows freely where in response to the demonstrated freedom of God for community with us we become free to live with God and so to love God. For then it becomes clear to us that the God who is self-revealed as ours thereby makes us God's, not only alone, but also with others. God coexists with them and me together. In doing this, God makes us humans into fellow humans, neighbors. We do not have these neighbors by our own will. We do not seek them out for ourselves. God places them with us — and thereby they become, and are, our neighbors. Yes, because they are given this way we can no longer withdraw from them. We would no longer be free for God if we were not also free for them. We would no longer coexist with God and love God if at the same time we did not coexist with them and love them, with whom God coexists. There would always be doubt whether we should and can really love — not some objects we desire, but the neighbor — if we did not love God with our whole heart. When we do love God this way, it becomes clear that "whatever the character of the man, we must yet love him because we love God." It would be a perverse kind of love for God if it were not unquestionably bound with love for neighbor. "Where God is known, there human kindness is practiced."[46]

The objection to the command of neighbor love is an old one: that it requires of us a harmful selflessness. For this reason people recently have been expounding Matthew 22:39 this way: you shall love your neighbor *as yourself* means that to the extent that you love yourself, you can also love others. But this goes against the meaning of the words of the command. To love your neighbor as yourself means that the neighbor steps into the place of the self so loved by you. And this is the situation: in the sin of wanting to be independent, we have falsely put ourselves in the place, not only of God, but also of our neighbor. And our motive in doing so is to seek and find *ourselves* in this very place, to direct our attention and love to ourselves. On this account, there can be no other way but that we who have been

46. J. Calvin, *Institutes* II.8.55, and *Auslegung des Propheten Jeremia* (Neukirchen-Vluyn: Neukirchener Verlag, 1937), p. 332.

made free from sin make free this place that we have falsely taken for ourselves. Right in this place we are to discover anew the other, who by rights
belongs there, and so direct our attention and love to the neighbor.

What is right about this objection is the insight that an unloved,
unaffirmed, and in this sense self-less person can have no loving relationship
with another. But the objection is questionable if it means that I need to provide love and affirmation for myself before I can think of others. Then we
would never get ourselves together so well that we could ever love others. But
I cannot and must not by my own efforts provide for my being loved. Think
of the often-overlooked point in the parable of the Good Samaritan with
which Jesus answers the question: "Who is my neighbor whom I am to love?"
Answer, Luke 10:36-37: the merciful Samaritan! This tells you that the neighbor is first of all a gift for you, and not first of all a task. Because love has en-
countered you, who are like the man who fell among the murderers; therefore love him who loves you, and *do the same thing* as he did.

This point is underscored by the most immediate meaning of our
command. The neighbor does not mean simply every person, but the
comrade in the people of God. Please do not take this as a directive to love
only like-minded people and exclude others. Rather, understand it as a
clue that genuine human love normally can be carried out only in sisterly
and brotherly togetherness, and so only in *mutuality,* only in a milieu of
being loved and loving. This is also the sound wisdom from Jesus' mouth
in the Golden Rule (Matt. 7:12), cited in Article 111: that you do to others
"as you would have them do to you." In this way care is given on the human plane as well that I do not have to love selflessly, that is, without myself being loved and affirmed. From here Jesus' instruction about the problematic borderline case of neighbor love becomes understandable: dealing
with the person who stands outside the normality of mutual love — the
enemy. "Love your enemies" (Matt. 5:44). How can we love the kind of
people who do not love us? Jesus answers: "Pray for them!" This means:
come before God together with them! And think and behave toward them
from there! That is, act in a way by which you do not return their enmity,
do not pick it up from them. Treat them now as what they are not yet, but
as you want them to be and act toward you: as your future brothers and
your future sisters. How could you not be waiting for this, since God loves
them long before you can even consider whether you want to love them?

A further consideration is that the word "love" as the governing concept
for our behavior in relation to the neighbor dare not have that weak, senti-
mental meaning which the word often has come to have. Love is active in-

volvement in the existence of others for the furtherance of their well-being. Therefore we have to rid our thinking of three misconceptions. First is the idea of love as almsgiving. This is love like a few leaves of salad to garnish a plate of cold cuts. It is love as a partial easing of an otherwise hard reality. But just as God's justice and mercy are actualized together, so our love of neighbor is only believable and helpful when justice also comes to people, when the human rights of their human dignity are given their due. The objection raised against this, that one can demand rights, but not love, is convincing only if you understand by love merely subjective, private feelings for someone, and not active involvement in the existence and situation of others.

Second is the related misconception that a Christian ethic based on the concept of "love" has to make a distinction between an individual and a social ethic. The commandments of the Decalogue are to be consulted not only with regard to their meaning for the single individual, but at the same time also for their social import in the community. From this we have to draw the conclusion that people's humanity comes to light where they are free in community and in community are free. We also need to draw the conclusion that conversion, in which the Christian life takes place, is the rejection of the old world and the acceptance of the new person in a new world. And we have to draw the conclusion that God's command reaches to all realms of our life and not simply to a private precinct.

Third, the death of all love is that patronizing love of which "Mr. K." in Brecht's work speaks. He says that to love people means: "I make a sketch of the person . . . and make sure that one comes to resemble the other." "Which? The sketch?" "No," says Mr. K., "the person."[47] This kind of love violates the other person. "In order truly to help someone else, I must understand more than he — but certainly first and foremost understand what he understands. If I do not do that, then my greater understanding does not help him at all. . . . then basically instead of benefiting him I really want to be admired by him. But all true helping begins with a humbling. The helper must first humble himself under the person he wants to help and thereby understand that to help is not to dominate but to serve, that to help is a willingness for the time being to put up with being wrong and not understanding what the other understands."[48]

47. B. Brecht, *Gesammelte Werke*, vol. 12 (Frankfurt: Suhrkamp, 1967), p. 386. ET: *Stories of Mr. Keuner* (San Francisco: City Lights Books, 2001), p. 27.

48. S. Kierkegaard, *Der Gesichtspunkt für meine Wirksamkeit als Schriftsteller*, in *Collected Works* (Jena: Diederichs, 1922), pp. 19-20. ET: *The Point of View for My Work as a Writer* (Princeton: Princeton University Press, 1998), p. 45.

The commandments in the second table of the Decalogue also describe aspects of the love we are commissioned to give. In this table, they are about love of neighbor. The commandment to honor parents tells us that our *respect* and *consideration* in view of those who have gone before us, who have been given to us before we were here, are part of our love of neighbor. The Reformation exposition of the commandment, like the one in Article 104, suffers from applying the commandment all too directly to the hierarchical relationships that obtained at the time: parents-children, master-apprentice, teacher-pupil, pastor–church people, and rulers-subjects. In this framework, those who in each case stand above are the instruments of divine governance, and the ones below have to subordinate themselves willingly. This simply does not work. Take notice of how the 12-year-old Jesus brought to bear against his parents the conviction, "You must obey God rather than humans" (Luke 2:49; cf. Acts 5:29)! Bear in mind the sharpness with which Jesus then attacked the grasp of familial authority in relationships: not "parents' will equals God's will," but the reverse: "Whoever does the will of God is my brother and sister and mother" (Mark 3:35; cf. in this context the harsh words in Luke 14:26 and Matt. 10:35). Only when this clear relativizing of all earthly authorities comes into view, and stays in view, can the concern of the Reformation exposition be taken up positively as well. But then it must be done in a deeper and more comprehensive sense.

It is part of the humanity of persons — in fact, to a considerable degree — that they always stand on the shoulders of others: on those of people who have gone before, who have been given beforehand — physical, intellectual, spiritual ancestors. No one can choose this: the parental home, the culture, the age, the milieu into which he or she is born, and so the natural tendencies, skin color, gender, which are thereby given. We can accept these far-reaching givens uncritically. But we can also chafe under them and want to get rid of them. Certainly we would deny the gospel's declaration of freedom if we were to maintain that we are mere marionettes of our ancestry. And we would misunderstand the claim of God's gracious command if we confused it with our being determined by our origin. God's gospel and God's command make us free in relation to where we have come from — but not free from it. So the gospel and command also make us free from the illusion that we could ever get rid of our ancestry. Rather, they make us free for responsibly dealing with it. And this includes the sober affirmation that I am a child of this and no other origin. Whoever is ashamed of it, and in shame suppresses it, or dreams up another origin, whoever in this sense, with regard to the earthly conditions from which he or she comes (to speak with Art. 104) does not want to "submit myself with due obedience," and does not also "bear patiently with their failings," whoever does not meet his or her origin with respect will never be able rightly to respect himself or herself. Such persons will also not find their way to what is surely needed — dealing critically with one's heritage in a constructive way. Without this they will obey God in a way that is not helpful and brings about only confusion. They will then also in turn not stand up responsibly for the conditions of the heritage of future generations. And in all this they will not learn that the neighbor given us to love is not the one sought out by us, but the one placed before us by God. Therefore, and to this extent, there is no neighbor love without the honoring of "father and mother."

The prohibition of killing (Art. 105-7) tells us that part of neighbor love is also our readiness for peace in relation to the life that meets us — also in relation to non-human life, we should add today. If, as H. Ruh says, a questioning of our massive consumption of meat would also mean a questioning of our high standard of living,[49] then our standard of living stands on clay feet. Furthermore, this standard of living is purchased at the price of a dramatic dying off of species. We gradually begin to grasp that we cannot live without "reverence for life,"[50] for *all* life, for one's *own* life too, so that "I am not to harm or recklessly endanger myself either" (Art. 105)! We begin to understand on the other hand that my own life is bound together with the success of a sustainable, protected common life. But this is deeply threatened. It is threatened by the inhumanity which, from the absolutely correct statement that every life must be affirmed, infers that every unwished-for life is in principle disposable. And this conclusion is even made out to be human freedom. Sustainable, protected common life is threatened by the fact that the hidden root of living without others and against others is tenaciously embedded in us all, "the root of murder" in "envy, hatred, anger, and the desire for revenge" (Art. 106). So then: *principiis obsta!*, "resist the beginnings!" Where there is not vigorous resistance against the root of readiness for violence against others (and against oneself!), this root will express itself in all kinds of discriminating thoughts, words, and works, and it often takes only an outward, sometimes

49. Nach G. Altner, *Naturvergessenheit. Grundlagen einer umfassenden Bioethik* (Darmstadt: Wissenschaftliche Buchgesellschaft, 1991), pp. 238, 92-93.

50. A. Schweitzer, *Kultur und Ethik* (Munich: C. H. Beck, 1960), pp. 328ff. ET: *Civilization and Ethics* (London: A. C. Black, 1923), pp. 251ff.

ridiculous incident for the direct, murderous use of force to ensue. And because this use of force has that root, simple rejection of violence, abstaining from killing, is not enough (Art. 107).

For this reason, everything humanly possible must be done to resist the beginnings of violence. This includes the positive creation of a relaxed, peaceful climate to prevent the eruption of readiness for violence. It includes positive action, "to show patience, peace, gentleness, mercy, and kindness toward our neighbor, to prevent harm to our neighbor as much as we can, and also to do good even to our enemies" (Art. 107). It includes also the scrupulous acknowledgment that omissions too can be murderous. "If you see anyone suffer hunger, and do not feed him, you have let him starve."[51] And what is humanly possible *can* be done where it is clear to us that the freedom to which Christ has freed us is freedom in coexistence, and this means also in peaceful coexistence. Of course, the Catechism is mainly concerned only with individual prevention of outbreaks of resort to violence, and not social prevention. To be sure, it does say at the end of Article 105: "The civil authorities are armed with the sword in order to prevent murder." After all, the state's monopoly of the use of force is well determined by its function: the state's monopoly on force serves to *limit* the use of force. This is a criterion for making sure that the state's monopoly on violence dare not change it into a violent state. In personal relations too, peaceful coexistence does not have to mean simply putting up with whatever unjust dealing is carried on by unpeaceful contemporaries. Above all, this must be added: in analogy to the individual's task, the state has the task — not only of lawfully checking violence, but also of hindering it by the creation of a just peace in just conditions. The old proverb says: "He who desires peace, let him prepare for war."[52] This means: where you show military weakness, the lust for aggression awakens; therefore in times of peace you must make a show of strength through armaments. But in fact, armaments have again and again led to their being used in war. That proverb needs to be composed in a new way: "If you do not want war, prepare for peace." That is, not weakness, but social discord and injustice awaken the desire for war. This is why there is no better way to prevent war

51. M. Luther, *Grosser Katechismus*, in *Bekenntnisschriften der ev.-luth. Kirche*, chap. 3, n. 75, pp. 608, 30-31. ET: *The Large Catechism of Martin Luther* (Philadelphia: Fortress Press, 1959), p. 35.

52. Vegetius Renatus (A.D. 383-450), *Anleitung zur Kriegswissenschaft* (Halle: Hendels Verlag, 1800), p. 116. ET: *Epitome of Military Science* (Liverpool: Liverpool University Press, 1993), p. 63.

than by building a just peace — as Isaiah 32:17 says: "The effect of righteousness will be peace."

The seventh commandment, against adultery (Art. 108, 109), says that part of love is also *partnership*, specifically in our sexual relationships. From time immemorial these relationships have brought much delight and much suffering, the most beautiful and the most cruel moments, the most exalting and the most humiliating events, the most exciting and the most repressed experiences. It may be that we are unaccustomed to thinking that in this area too the guide for Christians is not some old or new morality, but God's command. God's command is not identical with either an old or a new morality. So we do not keep the commandment by holding on to this or that morality. And God's command is not only for married people; it applies in every respect to the relationship of man and woman, "whether in holy marriage or in the single life" (Art. 108). But God's command is a compassionate command. For in this regard especially it has its basis in God's covenant of grace with God's people. Although this people breaks the covenant again and again, and carries on "whoredom," which in the Bible refers mainly to falling into idolatry, God forgives them and remains faithful to the people. It is a reflection of this gracious covenant of God when the Creator declares about the difference and togetherness of man and woman: "It is not good that the man should be alone" (Gen. 2:18). This means also: it is good that the man is not alone! You could call this statement "the Magna Charta of humanity."[53] It keeps on being the bright light, even if we humans, men and women, transgress against this Magna Charta in many ways, as we do against that covenant of grace. "Let anyone among you who is without sin be the first to throw a stone," says Jesus to those who accuse the woman caught in adultery (John 8:7). In the relation of man and woman, both within marriage and outside it, there is in fact no person without sin, but there is also no one who may not be comforted by forgiveness. On the basis of this forgiveness, however, everyone is also told: "Go your way, and from now on do not sin again" (John 8:11). In the power of forgiveness they may venture again and again to keep the commandment, and so to "live chaste and disciplined lives" (Miller and Osterhaven) (Art. 108). What do these two words mean?

"Chaste" means having respect for the inviolable worth of another person whom I come to know and with whom I am together. It means respect for her mystery, which is not at my disposal, and which sets a limit

53. K. Barth, *KD* III/2, p. 351. *CD* III/2, p. 291.

against my treating her as an object. It means respect for her otherness, in which I again and again need to allow her the *freedom* to be herself, without losing myself in her, without subjecting her to myself. Only in such mutual respect will we be able to be partners for one another who acknowledge and attend to one another in our uniqueness and equality. The other word, "disciplined," is the same word by which the early Christians understood our sanctification as a whole in the metaphor of lifelong school attendance. "Disciplined" refers to a way of learning in which we never finish becoming responsible persons — here in particular responsible in our sex life, responsible for our sake and for the sake of the other. For coexisting in partnership takes a discipline that learns and practices responsibility. In such discipline our togetherness may become a lasting coexistence in *faithfulness*. Faithfulness means taking a path together. On this path we can fail. Yet on this path we may venture the attempt to say Yes to a partner discovered in love in a way so comprehensive that we can seriously do it only one time in our life. Faithfulness is risking saying yes to his strengths, but also to his weaknesses, which soon come to light, and become ever more noticeable. Although you know him so closely, you still do not say No, but Yes: Yes to him in the days of blossoming and maturity, as in the days, if God gives them, of frailty. "To love a person means consenting to become old with him" (A. Camus). It is to be feared that persons who withhold this total Yes to their partners also want to flee from their own weaknesses — and from their own growing old. And it is to be feared that when they do not say this Yes to the other, they could be rejecting the prize of their own maturing to full humanity. Today the chance for mutual partnership seems to be greater than that of mutual faithfulness. God's commandment calls us, however, to give this lesser chance a chance too. There is a blessing in it. For it is in this area especially that the mystery of all love shows itself: in love, the reasons we initially had for thinking we could love someone steadily decrease, but through loving we continually receive new reasons to love.

The eighth commandment, against stealing (Art. 110, 111), tells us that part of our love for neighbor is also standing up for *social justice*. For this commandment "forbids not only the theft and robbery that are punished by the civil authorities" (Art. 110). God's command reaches deeper and is more thorough than the state's command usually is: "God also regards as theft all evil tricks and schemes by which we seek to get for ourselves our neighbor's belongings, whether by force or by pretence of fairness." For example, it includes a person's acquiring property through exploiting others, or using property in such a way as to squander God's gifts, or dining while disregarding poor Lazarus at the door (Luke 16:19ff.). What is upsetting about this parable is that this poor man is favored by God on no other ground than that he is poor, while the rich man sinks into Hell on no other ground than that he is rich.

Originally the commandment was aimed against stealing people, that is, against the inhumanity in which people have others at their disposal as property. As in the prohibition against killing, where God's command tackles first the "root of killing," so in the case of stealing, it tackles the root of theft. And this root is the twin pair: envy and greed. Envy is the wish to "get for ourselves our neighbor's belongings" (Art. 110). Envy means: I begrudge the other what belongs to him or her. From envy comes a life at the expense of and to the disadvantage of the other, by such means as "phony weights and measures, deceptive merchandising," and "excessive interest." Put in modern terms, these could be price-fixing, exploitation of countries with low wages, and redistributing from the bottom to the top. Greed is to refuse the proposal "that I promote my neighbor's welfare wherever I can and am able to" (Art. 111). Greed means that I do not wish for the other what has been given to me; and I provide myself with a good conscience for having more than others by charging them with being envious if they do not want me to have it all. In this way a "sharp elbow" society arises in which some people who live by the motto "the more he has, the more he wants"[54] have success. It is an uncanny experience that the richer people are, the more they stand in acute danger of being transgressors against this commandment.

Are envy and greed the claws of the "predator" human?[55] Or are they the plague that befalls the person who is in the hand of the evil god Mammon? In either case, the gospel can heal us from the root of the evil with its message of the God "who can wish me nothing bad,"[56] who instead has a heart that wants for us every good we need, of whom we may boldly sing: "thy desires e'er have been granted in what he ordaineth."[57] This gospel has

54. From the folk song "Was frag ich viel nach Gut und Geld" ("What Should I Care about Possessions and Money?")

55. Cf. O. Spengler, *Der Mensch und die Technik* (Munich, 1931), p. 1. ET: *Man and Technics* (Westport, CT: Greenwood Press, 1976), p. 19.

56. From stanza 4 of the hymn "Was Gott tut, das ist wohlgetan" ("God's Actions, Always Good and Just"), by S. Rodigast.

57. From stanza 2 of the hymn "Lobe den Herren, den mächtigen König" ("Praise Ye the Lord, the Almighty"), by J. Neander.

the power to so disarm the force of "Mammon" over us that our basic principle will become: "the person does not have to serve things, but things have to serve the person."[58] In thankfulness for God's desire for our good, which is free of envy and greed, this gospel makes us free to become *human beings* who in turn want everything good for their neighbor and who do all they can for their neighbor's welfare, and "work diligently" so that they "may be able to help the poor in their need" (Art. 111). Though they do gather together money and means, they do not do so in order to take it away from others or to sit on it, but to share it. In doing this they will no doubt have Jesus' parable of the Last Judgment before their eyes (Matt. 25:31-46), whose point is the criterion by which the judgment will be carried out: How is your relation to Jesus? But to Jesus as brother of the sick, the hungry, the imprisoned! So nothing helps you except your becoming a brother, a sister, to these people who are in need! Here again, the action of the individual is a sign for what only the society as a whole through its government can do: see to it that there is social justice. In his Reformation theses of 1523, Zwingli already identified a measuring rod by which Christian understanding can measure whether justice rules in a society: justice rules when the laws "protect the oppressed, even when they do not protest."[59]

The ninth commandment, against false witness (Art. 112), connotes finally that a quality of the love for neighbor commanded us is our *reliability.* "Your Word is truth," says Jesus (John 17:17), which means that it is reliable. But I can rely only on someone who comes near to me. That God talks with us is the most human thing that is told us about God. Yes, this is what God's becoming human in Christ entails (John 1:14). Correspondingly, the most human thing we can say about humans is that we can talk with one another. But this most human characteristic is harmed at its most fragile point if we talk with one another without being able to rely on one another. "Whoever tells a lie is not believed anymore."[60] The terrible thing about the lie is not the dirtying of one's own tongue, but that I no longer can rely on the other, or the other can no longer rely on me. Now something has become broken in our relationship. Where people can no longer

---

58. K. Barth, *Christengemeinde und Bürgergemeinde* (Munich, 1946), 23. ET: "The Christian Community and the Civil Community," in *Community, State and Church* (Garden City, NY: Doubleday, 1960), p. 172.

59. Cf. H. Zwingli, *Schriften,* ed. Th. Brunnschweiler (Zurich: Theologischer Verlag, 1995), chap. 2, n. 84, vol. 2, p. 371.

60. Phaedrus, *Fables* I.10.1.

rely on one another, human community goes to ruin, and with it, humanity. The original position of the commandment in the situation of a trial reminds me that by my statement I can do terrible damage to my neighbor. The lie causes almost irreparable damage. Wanting to take it back is like trying to put toothpaste back into the tube (Lore Lorentz). So the Bible is right when it sees the most devilish aspect of the devil in the fact that he is "the father of lies" (John 8:44).

The devilish nature of the lie is that only its most harmless form is an untruth you can see through. The lie really becomes dangerous and insidious because it loves to make itself invisible as a lie. Then it masquerades as reliability, so that we only too gladly give it credence. Certainly, it consists (Art. 112) in our twisting words, slandering others, joining in condemning anyone without a hearing or just cause. As a rule, we do these kinds of things to put ourselves in the best light by contrast. But this all goes on in such a way that the really serious lie stuffs itself so full of nothing but correct propositions that it has the aroma of nothing but truth. And what gives the lie so much success over against the truth is that it drapes its assertions in forms that flatter us, and tell us what we like to hear. In this way it is able to manipulate us so that we finally get to hear only what other masters want us to consider right. Yes, in just this way the lie is the crowning of all evil, in that it understands how to hide evil as evil. Is it not so? "All those who once have proclaimed violence as their method must inevitably choose the lie as their principle."[61]

We need to make all this clear to ourselves in order to understand that even a well-meaning attempt to keep the ninth commandment is not up to defeating the power of the lie. But God is up to it. God deals with the power of the lie by speaking with us and giving us the Word "full of grace and truth" (John 1:14). Grace and truth here are not two sorts of things. God's grace is pure truth, and God's truth is pure grace. In just this way, God's truth is completely reliable. It heals the damage of our lying work with its reliable gracious truth and its reliable true grace. In thankfulness for this we will attempt taking little steps, but steps in the direction of a life in truth. By doing this we will understand above all that we can do nothing better against the "great power and abundant deceit" of the lie than to keep from pursuing all its rats back into their holes and exposing all its juicy untruths and disproving them. Simply "the attempt to live in the truth" will

61. A. Solzhenitsyn, Nobel Prize winner, in *Frankfurter Allgemeine Zeitung*, September 15, 1972. *Nobel Lecture* (New York: Farrar, Straus & Giroux, 1972).

threaten the system of lies.[62] We can do nothing better against the system of lies than letting the truth to which we straightforwardly witness speak for itself. Only as we become people who love the truth and speak the truth in love, in correspondence to the divine Word, full of grace and truth, will lies be reduced. For the truth, the right witness that we have to speak to our neighbors and about them, will always show itself as right and true by being helpful for them. It will be truth that sets them free, helps them to stand upright, brings them to the right, and is merciful. I tell the truth when I "defend and promote my neighbor's good name as much as I can" (Art. 112). I tell the truth when my hard-pressed neighbors discover in me someone to whom they can entrust themselves. I really love my neighbors rightly when I do not deceive them, do not lead them astray, but rather relate to them on the basis of openness.

4.3. The Mature Human Being

4.3.1. Prayer (Art. 116-21)

The freedom to which Christ has freed us, and to which he calls us, is freedom in *community*. We have to be clear, however, that this community is genuine, right, and vital only when in it we are really *free,* and *stay* free. Freedom and community belong together, yet they are to be distinguished from one another. A freedom that is not freedom in community will wind up being individualism, in which individuals next to one another and in competition with one another try to realize and protect their freedom. And a community that is not community in freedom will wind up being a collectivism, in which the individual does not count, but only the mass, in which our freedom is sacrificed in favor of a large anonymous whole. What is more, a freedom that is not freedom in community is not real freedom, but only that questionable freedom of independence. And a community at the expense of freedom is also not real community, but merely a submissive mass, without lively interaction. Precisely for the sake of true Christian community, we have to say that this community would be dead without the freedom of individual Christians. This is what is to be dealt

---

62. Cf. V. Havel, *Versuch, in der Wahrheit zu leben. Von der Macht der Ohnmächtigen* (Hamburg: Rowohlt, 1980), esp. p. 81. ET: *Living in Truth* (London: Faber, 1990), esp. p. 62.

with here. The thesis to be explained is that this freedom comes forth most intensively, and with most consequences for Christian living, in prayer to God. In this conviction, we turn our attention now to Articles 116-29 of the Heidelberg and its exposition of the prayer of Jesus. First, six fundamental considerations are in order.

1. Freedom means *self-determination,* or *maturity.* According to Immanuel Kant's famous formulation: "Enlightenment is the human being's emergence from self-incurred immaturity. . . . Have courage to make use of your *own* understanding! is thus the motto of the enlightenment."[63] This motto is directed, as Kant remarks, "chiefly"[64] against a Christianity in which "guardians have taken it upon themselves to supervise them [human beings]. Having made their domesticated animals dumb, and carefully prevented these placid creatures from daring to take a single step without the walking cart in which they have confined them; they then show them the danger that threatens them if they try to walk alone. . . . The officer says: do not argue, but drill! . . . The clergyman says: do not argue, but believe. . . . Everywhere there are the restrictions on freedom."[65] Does not the free self-determination of the person rule out faith, which is determination by another? Is not prayer in particular the most subjugating act a person can be engaged in, and therefore the exact opposite of human maturity? Is this not obvious, if praying means (Art. 117) "that we grasp our need and misery so that we may humble ourselves in the face of the divine majesty"? Is not the praying person unfree, because dependent on another?

We need to look more closely into this matter, and must insist against the above objection that what goes on in prayer is indeed an act of genuine human maturity. As the old human being we were "under guardians" and were "minors" (Gal. 4:1ff.!). However, as the new human being who we are in Christ through the Spirit, we are no longer that, but we are children of God. And this is shown in the prayer: "Abba, dear Father!" According to the beautiful statement by Hendrikus Berkhof, "the main fruit of the Spirit is that he opens our mouths."[66] This is the original meaning of maturity [*Mündigkeit*]: opening your mouth without timidity, using one's own vo-

---

63. I. Kant, *Werke,* 10 vols., ed. W. Weischedel, vol. 9 (Darmstadt, 1968), p. 53. ET in *Immanuel Kant: Practical Philosophy* (Cambridge: Cambridge University Press, 1994), p. 17.

64. Kant, *Werke,* p. 60. ET: p. 21.

65. Kant, *Werke,* pp. 53ff. ET: pp. 17ff.

66. H. Berkhof, *Theologie des Heiligen Geistes* (Neukirchen-Vluyn: Neukirchener Verlag, 1988²), p. 40. ET: *The Doctrine of the Holy Spirit* (Richmond, VA: John Knox Press, 1964), p. 36.

cal equipment to express what one has grown to understand. The maturity of a praying Christian is not any less maturity than what Kant defines. Granted, it is a different maturity. It is indeed also emancipation from guardianship, but it is not the self-sufficiency of a person that leads to an individualistic existence. It is maturity *face-to-face with . . . ,* in relation to . . . , in correspondence with. . . . It is maturity that essentially takes place in a duality of I and Thou. It comes about through an experience of being called upon which opens our mouth so that we can and will answer in a mature way. As an act of freedom, it is also an act of freedom in togetherness. If God's whole work with humans has as its goal that as God lives with them, so also they live and have community with God; if it aims at the free human being who is free, not for detachment from God, but for correspondence with God, free to give one's own answer, and in this way to associate with God, then we can see that prayer is "the most important part of the thankfulness God requires of us" (Art. 116). It is "the original form of all human acts of freedom in the church."[67]

2. But in prayer do we not carry on a *monologue,* a conversation with ourselves? Do we not talk as though to a wall or into the empty air? People have often asked this kind of question. In our day, some have made a virtue out of this distress by declaring that the benefit of prayer is that it is not talking to someone, but is an act of human self-reflection, a meditation, a sinking into oneself. And it is to be recommended on the grounds of spiritual hygiene, in order to come clean with oneself. It is to be recommended also perhaps because of the opinion that in it people may discover in themselves something divine, a divine spark. But this facile thought, which leaves people only to themselves, makes a virtue out of what in truth is a quandary. In this view, even if one reckons with a god, this god would resemble those idols that have ears, but do not hear (Ps. 115:6). If God wants us to live in maturity, but cannot hear what we say, or ignores it, there cannot be association of the free God with humans. This whole question about whether our prayer is a monologue makes sense only in the framework of a human maturity that understands itself as emancipation, as making humans self-sufficient apart from God, and not as maturity in the duality of I and Thou, in the relation of God and human beings. How could prayer be anything but a human conversation with oneself, if such maturity does not need to have a divine partner?!

But if instead prayer is an act of our thankfulness toward God, then

67. K. Barth, *KD* I/2, p. 782. *CD* I/2, p. 698.

according to its whole character it is human response: reply to the word of God that we have previously heard and received. Then it is the result of God's calling on us and speaking to us. But then we have to say with Psalm 94:9: "He who planted the ear" — so that we hear the word of his mouth — "Does he not hear?" According to Matthew 6:8, God already knows what we need *before* we ask. Therefore Article 129 can say confidently that "it is much more certain that my prayer is heard by God than I am certain that I do desire these things from God." So the hearing of my prayer is surer than my praying itself. This suggests that the problem is not on God's side, but on ours. The question is not whether God hears us because the right ears are lacking *on God's side*. The question is whether God can hear us at all because the right mouth for praying is lacking *on our side*. To this, Article 117 makes three helpful points:

(a) It is essential that in prayer we do not direct our speaking somewhere or other, but right to the One who has spoken to us beforehand. Otherwise prayer has no genuine partner.

(b) In prayer we must not, and should not, appear better and different, more pious, more holy, than we are. In the right kind of prayer we should admit to the distress and misery, the calamity in which we find ourselves.

(c) What prayer is worthy? Which one will not resemble the empty phrases of the Gentiles (Matt. 6:7) or the wish list of the little ones for St. Nicholas? What is God to make of all this? Yet "in spite of our unworthiness, God will certainly hear our prayer for the sake of Christ our Lord." God will do this by forgiving us for the empty phrases and so purifying our prayer from its distortedness.

3. Who is the God to whom our prayer is addressed? There is occasion for the question, because the Enlightenment has infiltrated and confused our heads with an apparently pious, but in truth completely un-Christian view. It is the consideration that God, because of divine wisdom, has ordered everything and makes everything happen in accord with the divine plan and guidance so that it would be childish cockiness or egoistic overestimation of self to ask God to change anything in this plan according to my wishes. If there dare yet be a prayer, it would be only adoration that reverences God, be it in God's unsearchable purposes, or in God's wonderful arrangements in Creation. Pious as this sounds, it nevertheless speaks at cross-purposes with God. And humble as it sounds, it is a perverse humility. We can make clear to ourselves by referring to Article 120 that the god this view has in mind is at any rate not the One who "has become our Father through Christ." It is rather the god of that sheer almightiness who

does whatever he wishes. Such a god has people simply as disposable objects, and ultimately carries on quite apart from humans, because they are not necessary as partners who speak with God and so join in conversation about God's actions.

But just such a god is contested when we know God as revealed in Jesus Christ. "God has become our father through Christ and will much less deny us what we ask God in faith than our human parents will refuse us earthly things" (Art. 120; cf. Matt. 7:9-11). God in Jesus Christ is the Immanuel, the God with us. Therefore God wants not only to associate with us, but also to have us associate with God. God wants not only to talk with us, but also for us to talk with God. God wants to listen to us and to let us have a say in what God wills and does. Certainly, in all this God remains God, and we dare "have no earthly concept of the heavenly majesty of God" (Art. 121). We continue to be human beings, and do not edge into God's place. Certainly it is God alone who wants to, and is able to, "give us all that is good," to whom we pray about these things. And surely on this account we will praise God's holy name forever (Art. 128), and not praise ourselves because we have prayed to God about them. But presupposing all this, it is still true that while we may not think of God's majesty as something earthly, yet nothing earthly is foreign to God. So we may and should pester God with the earthiest things, bringing before God "all things necessary for body and soul" (Art. 121). It is also true that it is the superbly wonderful humanity of God which makes it possible that God can be talked with! God can be interacted with! God is ready to accept our answers, our petitions, to take them seriously, to consider them, and to incorporate them into the divine reign over the world. This is how earnestly God takes our freedom, the maturity to which God has freed us in Christ. And from here we can understand that the primal form of prayer is not humble adoration, but petition laid before God with great abandon, yes, petition that besieges God.

4. Why do we pray at all? Do we not confuse Christian prayer with a natural thrust of the heart that comes into play where we do not know how to go on, where we are not able to get something, and instead try to get it from a higher power? This would mean that prayer is shifting our unsolved problems onto someone else, who then almost like a magician, like a *deus ex machina,* has to serve what is desired as on a platter. And this would mean that we pray only once in a while, when we feel the need, and then likely less and less, because with the advance of technology we know how to do more and more things ourselves (as the saying goes: "In earlier days people prayed when there was a thunderstorm; now we have lightning rods"). Immanuel

Kant called such praying a "superstitious illusion," because "nothing is accomplished by it and it discharges none of the duties to which as commands of God we are obligated."[68] The moral is clear: we should not substitute prayer for action, but should act rightly instead of praying. Prayer for Kant was in fact the inner moral reflection that accompanies our right action.

Though we cannot go along with this, neither can we go along with what Kant is separating himself from. No, Christian prayer takes place not from an inner need, but because we are *commanded* by God to pray. As prayer is the primal form of all acts of freedom, it is also the primal form of all acts of obedience. Nowhere is it more clearly expressed that persons let themselves be graciously *claimed* by God than where God actually *makes a claim*. We often know only too well what we want to do, yet in actuality "we do not know what to do, but our eyes are on you" (2 Chron. 20:12). All estimable action always begins with prayer like this. Because we are commanded to pray, we have to pray independently of whether we feel a need to or not. This is why prayer has to take place regularly, and not just in time of need. As Paul says, we should pray "without ceasing" (1 Thess. 5:17) "in all circumstances," whether it seems at the time that we ourselves can do something about the circumstances or not (Phil. 4:6). Article 116: "Why is prayer necessary for Christians?" Because it is the most important aspect of the gratitude that God requires of us, and because God will give grace and the Holy Spirit only to those who earnestly and unceasingly beseech God and give thanks for these gifts. In brief, God wants to be prayed to. This is why we pray. This is why our praying is following the will of God, and this means, practically, following a pattern for prayer given us by God, connecting with the prayer of Jesus (Art. 119). When in our praying we connect again and again with the "Our Father" prayer, we do it because we thereby align ourselves with Jesus — as the one who goes before us in prayer, as the one who in his intervention for us has opened for us free access to God. If prayer is commanded of us, this means that we acknowledge it as the good will of God for us. Thanks to this free access opened up to us and in thankfulness for it we devote ourselves to God. When the Heidelberg goes so far as to call prayer "*the most important* aspect of . . . *gratitude*," we have to remember that for the catechism "gratitude" is the summary of all that God commands of us, all action corresponding to God's

---

68. I. Kant, *Religion innerhalb der Grenzen der blossen Vernunft* (Hamburg: Meiner, 1956), pp. 229-30. ET: *Religion within the Limits of Reason Alone* (New York: Harper, 1960), p. 183.

will. Prayer is the most important aspect of thankfulness, but not the only part! For living according to the Ten Commandments also is part of thankfulness. Praying and working belong together. What we have prayed for, we also have to work for. (Praying in a thunderstorm does not make the installation of a lightning rod superfluous, and vice versa. Praying against world hunger does not make development help superfluous, but establishes it.) But when prayer rates as the most important form of thankfulness, this means that it is characteristic for *all* action in the Christian life. It is not the case that we devote ourselves in prayer to God and then turn away from God and devote ourselves to our ethical tasks. No, we *remain* in each and every action to which we may devote ourselves, at the same time devoted to God. In these actions we are not far from God, but near: comforted, gladdened, strengthened, guided by God's goodness. It is not as though we had the divine in our hands. Rather, at each footstep and handgrip we depend on God and the divine goodness.

So we understand the significance of the Reformed recognition that our daily tasks in our earthly vocation are genuinely and seriously *service of God,* quite literally "thankfulness." They are not this automatically. They are this when they are formed by our devotion to God in prayer. So we can say with Kant that our prayer is not a lazy substitute for the action we are commanded to do. But prayer itself is the most important form of this action. And against Kant it must be said that our moral behavior dare not supplant prayer or swallow it up. For our works are not good in themselves, but only as thankful response to God's action. And this is only clear when prayer is and remains the first, "the most important aspect of the gratitude that God requires of us." No work is in itself service of God, but only work determined by our devotion to God.

5. When we say that praying is an act of genuine human maturity, the concept "maturity" is used in a different sense from its usual meaning. For praying always also means expressing one's *neediness;* it means *owning up* to one's neediness. But this does not narrow the meaning of "maturity" or make it flimsy. Rather, it becomes more complete than ever. It signals a lack of freedom when a person denies and glosses over his or her neediness. It is inhuman to think you are, or to want to be, without needs. So it is no weakness to admit your weakness. On the other hand, all human strengths are always ominous and dangerous when they gain their stiff backbone by suppressing their own weaknesses — and in this very way increase their lust for finding out the weaknesses of others. Similarly, people's giving becomes problematic when they cannot also receive, when

they cannot ask to be allowed to take! At the beginning of this book, I said that I would take a course decidedly different from a theology that deduces its truth from previously identified human need. Here, in the context of prayer, the concern of that kind of theology gets its due after all. But it gets its due in corrected form. Only when persons know God do they know in a right and clear way that they are needy, and in what ways, and to what extent. And only then can they rightly admit their neediness. It is not the other way around, as theology that has an interest in things going badly for people loves to have it, so that it can make people all the more dependent on God! Nor is true prayer a process by which people identify certain needs within themselves, and then search for how and with whom they can satisfy them most conveniently. What they identify this way they can for the most part take care of by themselves. At any rate, it is not the God of the Bible who delivers to them what they wish for. "Your Father knows what you need before you ask him" (Matt. 6:8). And when we ask God, we share in this divine knowledge. Since Christ summons us to prayer, and since our prayer is answering God's call to us, we know not only *that* we are needy persons, but also *what* we need. Yes, we not only need this and that, but this and that solely in the context that above all we need this one thing, this one person: God, God's care, God's presence. Only then do we understand that our neediness, in which we need this one thing above all, is part of our humanity, so that we can affirm our neediness without shame. The statement of Kierkegaard is profound: "To need God is a human being's highest perfection."[69] Consider in this connection what L. Helmbold had already sung in the middle of the sixteenth century.

> For God there's nothing pleasing but help for me in need;
> God's love for all, unceasing, gives Jesus, who has freed
> Our captive human race. Through him God keeps on giving
> For soul and body's living. Praise God's amazing grace![70]

6. If our neediness, which we own up to in prayer, is not a godless desire that we then connect with a "god" in order to have it filled, and if this neediness is discovered and awakened in the face of God, then we finally

69. S. Kierkegaard, *Vier erbauliche Reden* (1844), in *Ges. Werke*, vol. 13 (Düsseldorf/Köln, 1952), p. 5. ET: *Four Upbuilding Discourses*, in *The Essential Kierkegaard* (Princeton: Princeton University Press, 2000), p. 85.
70. From stanza 4 of the hymn "Von Gott will ich nicht lassen" ("From God Can Nothing Move Me"), by L. Helmbold.

understand as well that in prayer we necessarily call on God as "*our* Father," and not merely "my Father." Doesn't maturity conceived in a godless way, as having a voice in my own destiny, stand in danger of being a mentality that seeks to advance my career, so that I orient myself toward those who are "above," and I *too* must be "above," and if possible, *first?* And doesn't a neediness I detect in myself, apart from God, promote a kind of thinking in which "I" always think of myself, only myself first, and others always last, if at all? But by praying to the God witnessed to in the Bible, I am always praying to the One who "raises up the poor from the dust" (1 Sam. 2:8; Job 19:25; Ps. 113:7; 103:14). This is certainly speaking of God's comfort and help. But it is speaking also of the fact that God, with this comfort and help, always passes by those who are above — rich, proud, and lofty, those who think they can come through fine without God. Instead, God heads toward those who are in the dust, who are underneath, who are at the end, in order to make the last first (Matt. 19:30), to fill the hungry with good things, while letting the rich go away empty (Luke 1:53). "God chose what is foolish in the world to shame the wise; God chose what is weak in the world to shame the strong" (1 Cor. 1:27). If we pray to this God, we recognize ourselves as the kind of people who are underneath: poor, beggars. And we confirm this recognition by seeing in the same moment others next to us whom we did not see before, or did not see in this way: needy people, the kind who are underneath and at the end of their rope. We confirm this recognition by realizing as we see them that we are near to them and that we can no longer distance ourselves from them. We confirm this recognition by praying for them and so consciously putting ourselves alongside them — in solidarity with the obviously needy. Naturally, we do this not by praying for them only to forget them afterward. Rather, because we had to pray for them, we can no longer overlook them. If we refuse to pay attention to them, do we not also refuse to pray as those who are ourselves really needy? And do we not then make prayer a ritual of cultural religion in Sunday garb? If we no longer refuse, we will understand first of all what it means that we have no private relation with God; but that God is in all seriousness "our Father in heaven."

4.3.2. Having a Say with God (Art. 122-24)

The Lord's Prayer has two parts. Three times it says *your* — your name, your kingdom, your will; and three times it says *our* — our bread, our debts, our temptation by evil. The first part of Jesus' prayer, like the first part of the Decalogue, relates to God, and the second part, like the second part of the Decalogue, relates to us, to our fellow humans and our world. From this we understand anew how praying and working belong together. If prayer is the most important form of thankfulness, then we do not arrive at a right love of God and neighbor, according to both tables of the Decalogue, if we do not above all *pray* in both directions — about the things of God and about matters in our world. Again, we will not pray convincingly in both respects if we do not also — within the limits of what is possible, but with all our strength within these limits — become engaged in what we have prayed for. Yes, our action is only done worthily when it is imbued with the character of calling on God to make right what we are trying to do, rather more roughly than rightly. Right action stays step by step in a Thou-relationship with God. And conversely, right praying is not something like idleness, which, as is well known, is the root of all evil. Praying is the beginning of all *virtue:* in the form of petition it is itself already active engagement for what we pray for. The Heidelberg takes this recognition so seriously that in its exposition of the individual petitions of the Lord's Prayer it asks each time for God's helpful intervention, and then also for God's strength for corresponding intervening action on our part for God and our world.

It makes good sense that, according to the prayer of Jesus, we are to pray first about God's concerns and only then about our own human concerns. We humans with our concerns will not in this way get short shrift. "Strive first for the kingdom of God and his righteousness, and all these things will be given to you as well" (Matt. 6:33). The fact that the matters of God are so conspicuously placed prior to ours impresses dramatically on us that in prayer we can allow ourselves no narrowing of horizons. Praying in general means that we step out of the circle of what is our own, including when we are praying about our human concerns. Praying is not lifting ourselves up and getting our way — even though it may be in a religious sense. As a sign of this, the threefold "thy" comes before the "we" gets its turn. But what shows that it is not a self-seeking God who bids us pray this way is the fact that the "thy" and the "our" are immediately put together and interwoven in a wonderful way. Our being called to make petition for *God's* concerns means that God does not push divine causes through in opposition to us. Rather, God lets us take part in divine causes. God does not want to be alone in caring about these causes. God makes room for us to care about them with God. And our being allowed also to bring *our* concerns to God means that God is not only interested in divine concerns, but is also very much interested in ours. God wants to take part in them and care about them. In praying this way, we take God up on the divine claim to be our God, and we let God take us up on the claim that we are God's. So the circle of relationship is closed between God and us and between us and God.

Consider too, that as we can see the act of praying *as such* in relation to our participation by faith in the *prophetic* office of Christ, that is, to confessing his name, so we can see intervening in prayer for the matters of *God* in relation to our partaking in the *kingly* office. And we can also see intervening in prayer for human affairs in relation to our participation in the *priestly* office of Christ. Although it is not the only place, prayer is the first place in which each Christian person carries out and practices his or her participation in the threefold office of Christ, and this is full of implications for all further action and behavior.

In what way does our participation in the kingly office of Christ have special meaning for our freedom to speak *with God?* Because of our participation in the kingly office, speaking with God has the powerful meaning of being entitled to have a say in God's affairs. Having a say with God means to reign together with God. We unspeakably poor beggars are supposed to be allowed to take part in deliberation with God! This assertion is so powerful that we probably should ask whether we dare risk it at all. Naturally, we have to add immediately that a reigning by us over God is certainly not included. We would misjudge with whom we have to do if we would not fundamentally understand that in this speaking with and reigning, God always has the priority, and we can only afterwards link up with what God is doing. And we are talking here, to be sure, about an eschatological possibility that lies beyond all our human possibilities (Art. 32). But this final goal is already foreshadowed in *prayer:* in the prayer in which, according to Jesus' bidding, we are called and allowed to speak with God about God's concerns and so to have a say.

But is it not better for God to take care of these things alone, without us? Will we not cause confusion without end if we have a say in them? Does God in any way depend on our contribution to them? As far as that goes, it is surely not as though God's concerns would be refuted or suspended if we were to refuse God. Religious pride has indeed, in its uncanny extreme, contrived the idea of the "redeemed Redeemer." According to this idea, it depends on us to help a god, lost without the power of our will, out of distress by bestowing our positive support. The God of the Bible dampens this pride because with the biblical God it is always the other way around; humans do not redeem God, but God redeems humans. We will need to keep this in mind as we have to say, all the same, that the good will of God toward the creature (who is only creature and not secretly God, who is a sinner in need of redemption and not secretly also redeemer) would be deeply shadowed and would seem to come to naught if we did not have some say with God. But this is God's good intention, as manifested in Jesus Christ: God becomes ours so that we might become God's. But would we be God's people if we were not given a part, and were not allowed to share in God's concerns? At any rate, this is the way it is with Jesus Christ, who is God's own person: he actually takes part in prayer in God's concerns by praying and has a say in them. His heavenly Father lets Jesus' praying matter, so that God grants him opportunity to talk things over. In following Jesus and his prayer, we too may have a say with God and may have in God the One who grants us the opportunity to talk things over. If this opportunity did not come to us, God's good intention would not yet have been realized. Contrary to God's intention, we would still not be God's people. But we do belong to God, and so as God's children also take part in that which is of God.

Granted, God is not yet at the goal. The first three petitions by no means assume that we are asking for something already stored up, as it were, in some supply cupboard, just out of our view. These three petitions presuppose that God's work for and with humans still faces stiff opposition. God's work is still being held back. It is being contradicted and resisted. In many ways the work is sore beset and impaired and seems to us to be weak, yes, powerless. So the king, who God in the work of salvation surely is, stands before our eyes in the picture of the one who wears a crown of thorns. God's concerns, which are shown in God's gracious turning to us, are marked by all the opposition that God is exposed to by turning to us. When in the first three petitions of the Lord's Prayer we devote ourselves to these divine concerns, this does not mean that we help to spare God from affliction. But it does mean that we step out of this conflict against God, which also takes place within ourselves, in order to stand by God. Then we do indeed pray that God will be victorious in the battle and God's way will win out. But this means for us at the same time that we put ourselves in the shadows of the one who is afflicted, and in discipleship of the king with the crown of thorns. Our talking things over with God will then indeed be to a large extent sighing with God, and our reigning with God will be to a large extent entanglement in the conflict "against sin and the devil" (Art. 32).

Now let us look more closely at the content and meaning of the first three petitions. Again, you could see and interpret them in analogy to the threefold office of Christ as Prophet, Priest, and King.

1. *"Hallowed be your name."* In the context of the Third Commandment we have already talked about this — and the closeness of that commandment to this petition reminds us once again of the way prayer and work belong together. We cannot fulfill that commandment without calling on God to make right what we are working at, though our work be questionable. On the other hand, we cannot call on God without doing what we can to see that God's name "be hallowed." So it is no coincidence that this petition stands at the apex of all those to come. For how can God's name be hallowed more fittingly than by our calling on God in prayer? And from God's side, the fact is that we can call upon God only because God has a name. A nameless "It" can perhaps stimulate me to meditation and introspection, but I cannot call upon it. I can call upon no principle, no system, no idea, no concept, and no thought. All these I can discuss, suppress, contemplate, but only a counterpart I can call by name is someone I can call upon. The biblically witnessed God *has* a name. God has presented the divine self as well known and worth naming "in all your works" (Art. 122), and finally in a name "that is above every name" (Phil. 2:9). We have not attributed this name to God. So we cannot take it away from God or distort it by giving another name. In this name God has presented the divine self to us and made God accessible, namable, addressable — and thereby also distinguishable from others, who bear another name, or want to sneak in and get intimate with us under an assumed, false name.

God's making Godself addressable by us in the divine name means also, however, making the divine self open to attack, and vulnerable. For in doing this, God exposes the divine self to our association, and thereby to the danger and peril of the profanation, the *dishonoring* of God's name. This danger and distress become actual as God presents the divine self in the encounter with a world of sinners. They show themselves to be sinners in the way they dishonor God's name. Dishonoring can consist of humans' neglecting God and God's name, their renouncing it and not using it at all, and then even thinking they should prove why we must or can get along without God. This is theoretical atheism. The worst dishonoring of the name of God, however, is practical atheism. This appears where God's name is "blasphemed because of us" (Art. 122). There the use of God's name is not abandoned at all. There it is used, perhaps even very zealously, not to call upon God, but to use God, to put God to service, to misuse God for our purposes, decided on without asking God about them. This avenges itself in God's becoming anonymous for us, nameless: in place of God's name comes an idea of God. God's "You," which we can call upon, turns into an "It" that can be called off at our pleasure. We may illustrate how subtly this can happen by taking the perfectly true biblical statement: "God is love" (1 John 4:16)! Do not we sinners understand this statement almost inevitably in such a way that it does not designate God's free self-interpretation; instead, in place of the name of God, which seems so strange, we insert a concept referring to something of value to us even apart from God? Then the word "God" actually adds nothing to this desirable thing except at most its confirmation. This way the word "God" is replaced by "our desire," by something we ourselves can put to use. In comparison to the non-use of God's name, how much more grievous is the dishonoring of the name by such misuse, and by its replacement by a conceptual idol which such misuse results in!

This dishonoring is of course so subtle that we probably would not even notice that the name of God is being dishonored if Jesus did not put the petition on our lips: "Hallowed be your name!" Only then do we realize how much God truly is blasphemed "on our account." Only then do we grasp the helpful significance of God's reply to the question Moses anticipates his people will ask, "What is his name?" God gives the divine name in the form of a refusal to name: "I will be who I will be" (Exod. 3:13-14). This means that God always reserves the right to tell us "what his name is." And so the hallowing of God's name is taken care of by the divine *self*. Only in this context is the wonderful meaning of the first petition understandable. It means nothing less than this: that although God reserves the right to the divine name, God nevertheless lets us share in this right. And we share in it above all in asking God: "Hallowed be your name!" If we ask this of God, we actually are taking a first step. We, who have also misused God's name and will probably do it soon again, throw in our lot with the One whose name is profaned and dishonored in so many ways. Then it cannot fail to happen that we too step into the shadow that falls on God through the dishonoring of the divine name. Not in such a way that we have to carry the cross of Christ again, but that in his discipleship we receive *our* cross to carry (cf. Mark 8:34). Blessed are we if we do not let ourselves be led astray on this account into a denial of God's name instead of "confessing his name" (Heb. 13:15; Rev. 3:5). Blessed are we if we then say: though God's name may be profaned and dishonored, this will not be done by me. Blessed are we if we "so order our whole life in thought, word and deed that your name . . . may always be honored and praised" (Art. 122)!

2. *"Your kingdom come"* (cf. Section 2.1.3). This is "the full coming of your kingdom" which is promised, which is still being resisted, toward which we are nevertheless underway, where "you will be all in all" (Art. 123). This is the kingdom of God: God's good, gracious will come to its goal, not alone, not without us, but with us, and in such a way that we are not alone, without God, but with God. This is the kingdom of God: God fully with us and we fully with God — "He will dwell with them as their God, they will be his people" (Rev. 21:3). They will not engulf God, nor will they be absorbed into the divine. But beyond all that divides, everything will be gathered into a great irreversible togetherness: God and human, human and fellow human, human and the rest of creation. "Now there is great peace without end":[71] a peace with *justice,* unlike a merely apparent peace, with an unjust status quo and the roots of future hostilities written into its law. In the Bible, God's kingdom of peace and God's justice belong together (2 Peter 3:13; Matt. 6:33; Isa. 32:1). Here justice means much more than securing private right; it means that certain *conditions and relationships* are just. The justice of the kingdom of God consists entirely in conditions and relationships that are set *right.* Here *God,* whose ways so often seem puzzling and unjust, is first of all shown as just. God justifies God's *own self.* But fittingly, God does this by definitively "not forsaking the works of God's hands" (cf. Ps. 138:8). Yes, God does it by "dwelling" with the fallen and miserable creature. In doing this, God makes a dwelling place available to us. God at the same time justifies *us.* God brings us, whose "righteous deeds are like a filthy cloth" (Isa. 64:6), to justice, and in doing this gives justice to those who have suffered so much injustice and twisting of justice. In this way, in this kind of justice, God *has mercy* on the creature — for "true justice consists in pity toward the poor."[72] So there is now "great *peace without end.*" In this peace the tears of all are wiped away to everyone's full satisfaction; all problems are solved, all the hungry are filled, all wounds are bound up, but also all those who have dealt out beatings are put to shame; all the bowed down are enabled to stand erect, but also all the proud are brought to justice; and so all mortals are awakened to life and all sinners are washed clean.

For this kingdom we wait — but we do not just wait for it. For the One

71. From stanza 1 of the hymn "Allein Gott in der Höh sei Ehr" ("All Glory Be to God on High"), by N. Decius.

72. J. Calvin, *Auslegung des Propheten Daniel* (on 4:27) (Neukirchen-Vluyn: Neukirchener Verlag, 1938), p. 437. ET: *Commentaries on the Prophet Daniel,* vol. 1 (Edinburgh: Calvin Translation Society, 1852), p. 280.

who "will dwell with them" has already "dwelt among us" (John 1:14). The kingdom of God *has* already "come near" (Mark 1:15). This is shown in the manner in which Jesus lived his earthly life. It is shown in his *speaking,* for which the parables of the kingdom of God are typical. In them he not only gives vivid examples for an invisible idea, but in the parables the reality of the kingdom of God comes near in the present. It is shown in his *deeds,* for which his miracles are typical. Their point lies not in the miraculous breaking of natural laws, so that we would have to *believe* in the possibility of this. It lies rather in the kingdom of God's announcing itself in real physical help and rescue for those who suffer need. And this is shown in his resurrection from the dead, in the power of which "everything has become new" (2 Cor. 5:17). So we really do not wait for Saint Never Ever, unsure who or what or when, or if anyone will come at all. We wait for the *One who has come.*

But we *wait* for him, and the kingdom that has already come near in *him* is not yet here in any way except that it is promised to us more than ever. Why is the kingdom of God that has already come near, not here in any way except in the promise? Why is it not yet here so that instead of merely believing in it, we can see it, and have it manifest before all eyes? This enigma is linked with the puzzling, because unfounded, opposition to the kingdom of God. The theory of the "delay of the parousia," according to which the early church was mistaken in its expectation of the nearness of the kingdom of God (and instead of the kingdom, what came was merely "the church"), is too superficial. It does not take into account the opposition the kingdom of God comes up against, which pits itself against the kingdom and "holds it back" (cf. 2 Thess. 2:6-7). This opposition has, since the coming of Christ, neither right nor basis. It consists in the stubborn, abysmal *egoism,* without any foundation whatever, with which humans wall themselves off from the great healing togetherness of the kingdom of God and block its way to themselves. This is what humans all wrapped up in themselves do. They are always so filled with anxiety that they will not get enough that they also fear this is just what will happen in the togetherness of the kingdom. So they draw back from God and neighbor, unless these can be of service to themselves. This egoism can take various forms. It does not have to be only that of individualism. It can also take the form of a group egoism, which can also pass itself off as the establishment of an "empire" [*Reich*].

The most stubborn form of egoism, however, is its pious variation: salvation egoism, in which humans are content if only they are saved, even if the others are ruined in Hell. This egoistic opposition throws the shadow of suspicion on God that by presenting this great togetherness, God is engaged in mere wishful thinking, and so is standing all alone in a broad empty field. It is the suspicion that in such loneliness, God, in the final analysis, might also be nothing but an egoist. This sinister suspicion is apparently in a position to "delay" and "hold back" the public appearance of the kingdom of God. Yet it is not as if we have to jump to God's aid in order to clear God of this suspicion. At issue is only a suspicion without foundation; for in Jesus Christ the kingdom of God has already come near.

The nearness of the kingdom is confirmed by the fact that it is able to motivate people to link up with the petition of Jesus and to make the petition their own: "Your kingdom come." . . . "Destroy works of the devil, every power that raises itself against you" (Art. 123). However conscious they are of it, and however hesitantly they do it, and with however many slips backward, they are taking a step out of the egoism that opposes the kingdom of God. They let themselves be ruled "by your Word and Spirit," and instead of "raising" themselves "against" God, they exalt God (Luke 1:46) and obey God "more and more." They come *together* — to the *church,* and ask God to "support and increase the church" against "every power that raises itself against you." But in doing this they do not maintain a self-glorifying sacred society. This is shown in their freedom with respect to the questions: "What will *I* eat? What will *I* drink? And what will *I* wear?" They "strive first for the kingdom of God and his righteousness" and trust that "all these things will be given to you as well" (Matt. 6:31, 33; cf. Rom. 14:17). They then receive a widening of their horizon over and beyond their personal interests: a view for the distant and for the whole, for the stranger and for their "neighbor." They then understand that the reason the kingdom of God has not yet come in its fullness is not only and not primarily human resistance, but the patience of God, who wants us to become attached to "the good news of the kingdom" preached by Jesus (Matt. 4:23) and to give it to others. These persons who have made the crucial step of joining in Jesus' prayer for the kingdom also protest against "all ungodliness and wickedness of those who by their wickedness suppress the truth" (Rom. 1:18). At the same time they intervene on behalf of those who are deprived because of this wickedness, who do not know where to turn, or what they shall eat and drink, or clothe themselves with. In this opposition and intervention they will not be seen as victors, because with their crucial step of joining in Jesus' prayer they are taking part in God's cause, which is under heavy attack — through the suspicion spoken of earlier. Yes, in all this they will experience in earnest that it is "through many tribulations that we must enter the kingdom of God" (Acts 14:22), though they will not let themselves, on account of persecution, be misled by the logic of egoism, which calls for retaliatory hate.

3. *"Your will be done."* While the petition for the kingdom puts before us God's action for healing and wholeness, this petition is about the question of God's power. The question is not just about whether *God* has power. It is about what power is. We dare not presuppose a general concept of power and then ask who, according to the specifications of this concept, is the strongest. To understand God's power and will, we need to learn from the witness of holy scripture how God has actually used divine power and expressed the divine will. For in the Bible, the people who are praying would not know what they are praying for if God's will had not already been done, if the petition were not in effect this: let your will, which has already been done, be done anew and let it stand fast and prevail against what opposes it! God has shown the divine will and power by choosing "the fewest of all peoples" (Deut. 7:7ff.) to be God's people — as demonstration of God's great love for this people — and by choosing, in the midst of this people, a cross for the divine throne — as demonstration of the reconciliation of the world with God. "You know that the rulers of the Gentiles lord it over them and their great ones are tyrants over them," but "the Son of Man came not to be served but to serve, and to give his life a ransom for many" (Matt. 20:25, 28). This is a power entirely different from the kinds ordinarily exercised on earth. This is the power of *love* and of *reconciliation*. But it too is power. Yes, it claims to be the true power, which denies all other kinds of force opposing it the right to exist.

Yet this power meets a world in which *other* forms of power hold sway. They force the unique power of love into a shadow: the shadow of suspicion that it is pure *powerlessness.* Love's power may then be nice as decoration of a side chapel apart from the raw reality of what goes on in the world, but it achieves nothing at all against this reality. It cannot reach into this reality or change it — nor *should* it, add some all-too-clever theologians (in anticipatory obedience to this raw reality). The "will of God" in the third petition then plays out only in our hearts, or becomes a mere declaration of intent, without the strength and vitality to become actuality; God's *power* of love is then *mere* "fondness," without helping anybody. Those who one day get the feeling that this seems too little, and who now want no weakling as God, may then also correct the petition this way: now show yourself as the strong personality, with leadership qualities, who speaks a "word of power" with the ability to push it through forcefully. But with this, God's power is summarily put on a par with the powers of the world, and no longer qualifies as the power of love and reconciliation. This "God" can no longer save us from the feeling of our own powerlessness, in which we think we have to subject ourselves to what rules in the world — and in which we become pliable tools of these powers. And finally we come to believe that the more we do this without resisting, the more decent we are. This is called fatalism, belief in fortune. And this belief escalates in pious submission. In it people subject themselves to God as amenably as they ordinarily do in life toward what is stronger, because they fear that against it they will always get only the short end of the stick. Perhaps they subject themselves to God even more, because they consider God to be someone even stronger. So, as the saying goes: "Take care, but don't care too much, for it will turn out, after all, as God wills it." But in this way our "obedient" submission to God becomes practice for a compliant submissiveness toward everything else that exercises power on earth. And so God more than ever appears powerless in the face of everything else that has power, and toward our own feeling of being powerless against these powers.

In association with Jesus we can move out of this fatalism as soon as his petition comes close to our hearts: "Your will be done." For with this petition we distinguish between *God's* "will . . . alone" and all other wills that have their way in the world. With this we pray: Let not the will of those other powers be done — this must not and dare not happen any longer — "*your* will . . . alone is good"; let it be done (Art. 124). No, do not transform your power into that swagger, into the drive to outdo one another that marks those powers. Instead, let your completely different power, the power of love and of reconciliation, become visible "on earth." And let it be seen that it is not powerless in comparison with this swagger, but is able to undermine it and make it superfluous. And let us stop the nonsense of our fatal and fatalistic submissiveness by which we say to the power moves of earthly force, "we . . . surrender our own will and submit ourselves without grumbling to your will." And we can stop saying this only if we do not follow partly their and partly "your" will, but only "your will . . . alone."

It is not as though by praying this we lend power to God who appears powerless. God's love *has* strength and vitality. God's will is done already "in heaven," which is nothing else but the place where God's will is already done. And it is done in the service given by God's pure messengers, the "angels in heaven," whom we have seen where the message of God's gracious will meets us. It is not that those who pray this way strengthen God, but that they confess their faith in God's very different power, and share in it: the power of love. On this love they set their confidence, and no longer on those earthly forces. So they are really revolutionary. Yet their being revolutionary does not mean that instead of putting their trust in those forces, they now put their trust in their "own wills," in their own willfulness. Rather, it means that "all people," without retreating in pride or shame from the concrete place in which they find themselves, "fulfill their offices and callings as willingly and faithfully as the angels in heaven" (Art. 124). All kinds of things begin to change when humans commit everything to the end that not the will of some power figures, or our will in obedience to them, but "your will be done on earth as it is in heaven." By wanting to see this will be the one that counts in the world, they of course come under the shadow of the suspicion that the divine power of love is really powerlessness — and yet they unflinchingly confess their trust in the power of love. For this power, God's "power is made perfect in weakness," so that this holds true: "whenever I am weak, then I am strong" (2 Cor. 12:9-10).

4.3.3. Advocacy for Our Neighbors (Art. 125-29)

The second part of the prayer of Jesus relates to human, creaturely concerns. Three times the petitions speak of "our" needs. So this is not only about my private concerns. It is also about the concerns of all those, near and far, who live and move with us, who hunger and thirst, make mistakes, bleed and allow to bleed, suffer and sigh. Perhaps they cannot speak with us, or do not want to, for whatever reason. Perhaps they cannot, or do not want to, join us in speaking to God. But we can speak for them, be advocates *for* them — for all others. This is what the second part of the Lord's Prayer is about. Here the view expands into the horizontal, to fellow humans and fellow creatures. In view of them our prayer becomes intercession. Intercession is advocacy for others before God. And advocacy has its basis in intercession. In interceding advocacy, the community begins to resemble the ark of Noah, and in a kind of representative sampling the whole secular non-Christian world streams into the church. If anywhere, the Christian community makes itself responsible and liable right here for fellow humans, for the rest of creation.

There is also a false relation to our neighbors: that of perverse nearness, of *intrusiveness.* Here the neighbors exist only as the objects of my "good will," administered and spoken for by me. This does not necessarily result in making these objects passive. Sometimes the more persons feel themselves administered, the more egoistic they become in their thinking and action. This false relation is perverse above all on theological grounds. For with Christians it most likely results from their setting themselves on a par with Jesus. The oft-quoted statement of Luther that we in love become a Christ for others[73] is, at the least, open to misunderstanding. For it gives the impression that in loving acts only the others are dependent on Christ, and that they are the only ones who are dependent, since we are not dependent on them. Yet it is at least an open question whether the others are not more likely Christ for us than we for them (Matt. 25:40!). Yes, could not the impression arise that we would then also have to take the guilt of others on ourselves and that we could carry it? But actually, we have already loaded enough guilt on ourselves by our own doing and can only be glad when Christ carries this for us.

Against that idea we maintain that Jesus Christ, in a way that is completely irreplaceable and cannot be represented otherwise, "is our advocate [the advocate of all of us!] in the presence of his Father in heaven." It is not that he once was our advocate, but that he "ever" remains so (Art. 31, 49; cf. 1 John 2:1; Rom. 8:34). Let us hope that we are at least his disciples, and show that in following him, we too speak up on behalf of our neighbors! But we can do this only in a way that is not officious, because we know that we ourselves, no less than our neighbors, stand and fall with the intervention of "our advocate."

Another false relation to our neighbors is a perverse distance from them: *indifference* toward them. As distinct as this is from intrusiveness, it still does not have to be an opposite. If, in that intrusiveness, we treat others as objects of our good will, why should we not be able, just as we have sought them out as we pleased, likewise to let them drop? It can happen that the more people give without receiving, and so exhaust themselves, the more quickly they reach the point where they suddenly want to stop dealing with others, and to enjoy their lives only for themselves. Indifference means wanting to live life at a distance from others. "They don't mean anything to us" is a Swiss expression that characterizes relations with people who are not relatives. In earlier times people laughed about an African tribe in which the word for "human" is supposed to have applied exclusively to their own tribe. But in this laughter, people forgot the distressing ways by which in practice they operated exactly according to this way of

73. M. Luther, *WA* 7:35.

speaking. There is also the saying that people in trouble never want to lose their shirts. From this we can deduce that when widespread trouble arises and even reaches well-to-do people, it may well be revealed that the human problem is that none of us wants to lose our shirt. However, this indifference, which clings to us so closely, is put in question for those who do not distance themselves from Christ but follow him. We would have remained the self-seeking people we were as the old human beings if it were not that through him whom we follow, these people become our nearest neighbors — so that we would forget ourselves if we forgot them.

There is a third possibility beyond those of intrusiveness and indifference with regard to our neighbors: advocacy for them. This has its origin in our intercession for them before God, and it has its natural consequence in a stance of caring intervention for them. What gives the Christian community the right to do this? Is it not allowing itself an arbitrary transgression of boundaries, mixing into matters that really do not concern it? This would indeed be the case if the most decisive fact were not true: the God who lets divine matters be our concern, and thereby grants us the right to have a say, and who thus shows godly friendliness to humans — the same God, in the same friendliness to humans, lets *our* matters concern God so much that for God nothing human is foreign. In the Crucified One, God has intervened in a priestly way for us and has made our distorted and endangered cause God's own. And in the resurrection of Jesus Christ from the dead, God has shown that the human being so accepted belongs inseparably to God. Since God has done this in Jesus Christ, this Jesus is forever our advocate, our intercessor and caregiver. This means that he certainly does mix in our affairs. But it is a mixing carried on by God, which God does for our happiness and blessing. For what happens is that our affairs are no longer merely human and probably superfluous, earthly, relative, dispensable, empty things, but are meaningful for God. God takes them seriously as highly important. This divine mixing in our affairs we acknowledge and join with as we practice in our praying — and then also in corresponding caring action — the advocacy in which we say with Johann Andreas Cramer:

> For all who dwell on earth we pray as for ourselves, O God, each day.
> As Father, all to heart you press; give each what makes for
> blessedness.[74]

---

74. Stanza 1 of the hymn "Für alle Menschen beten wir" ("For All Who Dwell on Earth").

Let us now think about what makes for each one's blessedness as we look more closely at the last three petitions of Jesus' prayer. We note that these petitions correspond in order to the first three petitions of the prayer.

1. *"Give us this day our daily bread."* This means "provide for all our bodily needs" (Art. 125). Bread is here the embodiment of what is necessary, what humans need in order to be able to live and survive. How is it with daily bread "today"? Apparently humans have a panicky anxiety that they will not get what they need. For this reason they cannot get enough of heaping up what they think they need in order to live. They would like to get so much that they would have enough, and so not need to ask anymore. They are inclined to get so much that they no longer know what is really the essential that they need. They acquire so much that they think when they have heaped up more and more, it is always essential. They get so much that they are unable to see that what is being piled up is "more and more" endangering what they really need for living and surviving. It becomes so much that they are not able to become aware that their "more and more" takes away from others what they need to survive: they thus become poor. We will learn once more to pray honestly for "our" bread only when we see these poor before us and do not exclude them from what is needed for "us" to live. "Concretely, being poor means: to die of hunger, to be illiterate, to be exploited by others, and in all this not even to know that one is being exploited, yes not even to sense that one is a human being." "Poverty [ruins] . . . the dignity of the human being."[75] Poverty corresponds to the dishonoring of God's name in that it dishonors human beings, makes them nameless, and lets them sink into an anonymous mass of misery.

In no petition of the Lord's Prayer is it so obvious as in this one that we would not be praying authentically to God if we did not also *work* for what we pray for. In the petition, we show our awareness "that without your blessing neither our solicitude and our labor or your gifts can do us any good" (Art. 125). But we show this as those who with our worry and work tend to the provision of what we need for our physical life and survival. So the petition looks not only to daily bread, and that it will be given to us. It looks also to the world of work, and that its organization will suc-

---

75. G. Gutiérrez, *Theologie der Befreiung* (Munich/Mainz: Kaiser/Grünewald, 1973), chap. 2, n. 53, pp. 271, 273. ET: *A Theology of Liberation* (Maryknoll, NY: Orbis, 1973), pp. 288-89, 292.

ceed, so that by it people get what they need to live, so that no one does not get enough, and no one is without work and shelter. No one! For the very point of this petition is that it looks not only to "my" bread. It is about "our daily bread" and about its just distribution. It is about our not short-sightedly looking merely at today's use, but also at the possibilities for life "tomorrow." So in this petition we think not merely about ourselves.

Behind thanks for "my" daily bread stands a question mark, as long as many others are without daily bread, work, and shelter, and as long as we happily enjoy what is taken from others. Praying people "think of themselves last" — not because they are so selfless and modest, but because they would be very narrow-minded, and in that sense all too modest, if they thought only about themselves. They themselves do not get enough if others do not get enough. They cannot be egoists, not because they must be altruists, but because they can exist only in community with other people. They will be able to thank God rightly for daily bread only when it is consumed as "our" daily bread. So, not only is the poor person dependent on the rich for life's provisions, but also the rich are dependent on the poor — not because poverty is good, and not in order to keep the poor trapped in their poverty. The rich need the poor not least in order that by sharing with the poor and intervening for life's necessities for them, the rich themselves learn anew what they really need, freed from false cravings for empty delights.

But why do we need not only work, but also the petition for daily bread? We saw that it has to do with asking for "God's blessing" for our work and also for the means to live. But this is not just about support of our good efforts, let alone about a retroactive blessing of undertakings started without God. Rather, we pray in the conviction that "without your blessing" all our work would be in vain and that in "all our bodily needs" we would not be taken care of. Again, this is not merely about taking seriously in a general sense that we as finite beings are dependent on a "higher power." In view of the problem of life's necessities, it is about taking seriously the knowledge "that you are the only source of all good" (Art. 125). This says that our bodily concerns are not too material to have to do with God. They even have to do "in their source" with God. And this says at the same time that God is not too spiritual a being to have to do with our bodily needs. God has in fact "in their source" to do with them. God, who in the Son was "born in human likeness" (Phil. 2:7), knows — and knows concretely because of this birth — what we need. And God not only knows it; God makes it God's own concern. This is why the question of hunger, which is such a human question, is also a spiritual question. This is why the knowledge that humans do not live by bread alone, but by the word of God (Deut. 8:3; Matt. 4:4), includes taking an interest in what humans likewise need for their bodies. As surely as God has become human, this fourth petition is about nothing less than the humanity of humans, and therefore about their rising up out of being namelessly dishonored in poverty. It is no coincidence that Jesus describes the kingdom of God as a huge festive banquet.

Here the church has, sad to say, separated again and again what God in divine goodness has put together. The church has cared only for souls, while disgracefully leaving people in the lurch when it comes to their fight for "breadbasket matters." No wonder that a modern countermovement took these breadbasket matters seriously in such a way that it conversely wanted to leave heaven to "the clerics and the sparrows"![76] One could ask whether such bracketing of God out of these matters has not of necessity brought on that panicky anxiety — anxiety about not having enough, in which humans actually cannot get enough. Christianity can, however, take credible action against this damage only if it corrects the damage that it has itself caused — only if in the fourth petition it puts together what God, for the sake of the humanity of humans, has put together: "all our bodily needs" and God's own self as "the only source of all good."

2. *"Forgive us our debts, as we also have forgiven our debtors."* Here, in another context, Christ puts together something we are inclined to separate: God's forgiveness and our reconciling behavior in association with those who have offended us. What is at issue here? We said that in the last three petitions of Jesus' prayer we are called to advocacy for our neighbors. But does not our advocacy and intercession hit an insurmountable barrier where we come upon the kind of neighbors who are against us, and whom we therefore also have something against: the kind who are our "debtors"? We are looking here at the whole realm, covered with rage and tears, with pain and blood, of human opposition, of quarrels, of endless misunderstandings, of conflict and war, in our private and public relationships. Often enough one slips into this condition for minimal cause. But if you do not take to heart the wisdom of not letting the sun go down on your anger (Eph. 4:26), you can hardly get out of it later. Then one word leads to another. Then blow follows blow. Then, with half-truths, you look for people who will be on your side, in whose eyes you "can" no longer do wrong. Then you stand irreconcilably opposed.

76. H. Heine, *Werke*, vol. 2, p. 95. ET: *The Poems of Heine*, p. 329.

What makes a solution so hard here is our habit of always seeing the guilt predominantly on the other side, while being inclined to see our own side in a favorable light, to justify it and defend it against the other, even in the most hopeless case. (So that persons seem almost sick if they look for guilt within themselves!) As a rule it was, in our view, clearly the other side in which the evil began. And if we ourselves have barged in with severe corrective measures (because uncivil behavior calls for tough action), we think that we have only defended "our perfect right," always only waged a "just war." So we convince ourselves of having a good conscience, even when by this defense our relative guilt becomes ever more inextricably entanglement in guilt, when the other side is destroyed in the name of our "perfect right." Do we not have to say this: our standing up for our right dare not be won by making reconciliation with the other side impossible?! Otherwise our "perfect right" one day becomes the evil wrong, that of egoism, which we looked at in the second petition.

What are we to do in the situation of irreconcilability, in which persons and groups of persons stand opposed to one another? Pray! Not simply that God count me right! Not simply that God give me the strength to be reconcilable! In this very situation we are to speak the petition: "Forgive us *our* debts." This means praying that "for the sake of Christ's blood, do not charge to us miserable sinners our many transgressions, nor the evil which still always clings to us" (Art. 126). In this situation, the petition means the following:

1. It reverses our finger, which in the irreconcilable situation so eagerly points accusingly at others, and directs it first of all at ourselves. We then see above all "the evil which still always clings to us [*ourselves*]," and so know ourselves as wholly dependent on God's forgiveness. Genuine repentance is what we *ourselves* do, instead of requiring it of others. Those who do not know that they themselves live by mercy will not know it about anyone else.

2. We do not heal the damage, however, by throwing ourselves into a guilt complex. Such a complex is a twisted infatuation with one's own guilt. In it you must compulsively keep on interrupting yourself and must grovel in your faults, which "I can't forgive myself for." But we are not supposed to forgive them ourselves, or not to forgive them ourselves. When they are forgiven us, it is God who forgives.

3. This petition puts us in "solidarity with the enemy,"[77] who is per-

---

77. K. Barth, *Der Römerbrief* (Bern: Bäschlin, 1919), p. 373.

haps rightly opposed to us. But by including these persons so antagonistic to us in the petition for grace for "*us* miserable sinners," we already stand before God together with them and they stand together with us. So looking at those who are against me, and whom I am against, I can pray *for* them and intercede before God for them. I can step in only in behalf of those in relation to whom I do not sit on a high horse, but with whom I am in solidarity.

4. I acknowledge with this petition, and so trust, that it is *God* who is able to overcome this situation of irreconcilability. God is not our Reconciler in Jesus Christ in vain. Reconciliation with one another is inseparable from reconciliation with God. We would not believe in God as the Reconciler if we did not also want to let God be the Reconciler in our interpersonal relations.

5. God's reconciliation, however, does not have the form of grace instead of justice, but rather grace in justice. God's reconciliation does not suspend justice. It upholds it. It does not say that wrong is right. It condemns it as injustice and "those who must suffer violence, God protects in judgment."[78] We pray for God's just reconciliation in the fifth petition.

"We also find in ourselves this evidence of your grace, that it is our sincere intention to genuinely forgive our neighbors" (Art. 126). This does not mean that God forgives us on condition that we forgive. Nor does it mean merely that we should draw the consequence from God's forgiveness and therefore associate in a conciliatory way with "our neighbors." If in the fifth petition we opponents in guilt have appeared together before God, and if God has answered this petition in grace that includes me and the other "miserable sinners," then this grace is witnessed to in the intention given us to be conciliatory. Note carefully that the intention relates to the *guilt* in relations between people, and not to the differences between us and the others. Reconciliation is not being taken over into homogeneity, but "reconciled difference."[79] Again, the "intention," for those making the petition, means that they take the initiative. In the midst of the antagonism, and for the sake of easing it, they venture a first step, and probably a whole series of first steps, toward the other. Their initiative consists in the advantage given them of being awakened to step out of the vicious circle of irreconcilability. "Genuinely to forgive our neighbor" will in practice take various forms: it may be that you yield to the others; it may be that you settle with them on a

78. From stanza 4 of the hymn "Du meine Seele singe" ("Sing, My Soul"), by P. Gerhardt.
79. Johann a Lasco, acc. to J. R. Weeda, *Nach Gottes Wort reformierte Kirche*, Theologische Bücherei 23 (Munich: Kaiser, 1964), p. 98.

compromise, whether by quietly putting up with their strange ways or by explicitly drawing a formal end line that you do not come back to; or it may be that you come to the point of calling their wrong directly wrong. We will also need to ask God for the wisdom to know which form our forgiveness has to take in each particular case. But in all of this it must be clear that the forgiveness, whatever form it takes, is each time the expression of the intention "genuinely to *forgive* our neighbor."

The special difficulty of such reconciliation is pointed out by the recent distinction between "perpetrators and victims." There are actually situations of guilt in which one side is the guilty one and the other side is the one that is suffering. In this case it would be vexingly wrong for the guilty one to say: we are *all* sinners and *all* need forgiveness. This would mean that the victims have also themselves to blame for their fate, and so would make light of the guilt of the guilty and hurt their victims anew. Furthermore, it would brand every measure taken against the injustice they are suffering as itself an injustice. Reconciliation dare not be won through new injustice; otherwise it is not reconciliation. But even this difficult "case" is not let off by the fifth petition. For each side it will mean something particular. For the guilty, it will mean that they must persist in penitent praying for forgiveness for their guilt, knowing that they have no right to the reconciling hand of their victims. They have no such right, not even with the thought that one day enough penance will have been done, or that having taken care of the matter inwardly with God suffices. For the victims, the same petition will mean readiness to be led by God — not to give up claim to the right that is being violated, but to come to this insight: whatever I do and must do, I do not stand outside the clasp of divine reconciliation which encompasses both me and the doer of injustice. This clasp is not something that may perhaps become possible only after I have fought for my rights; even the fighting can take place only within the span of divine reconciliation.

3. *"Lead us not into temptation, but deliver us from the evil one."* We pray this because "we are so weak that we cannot stand by ourselves for one moment" (Art. 127). We humans are not only bad. We are also weak. And often where we consider people bad, and believe we must raise a protest against them, they are actually more weak than bad. So we owe them our advocacy because they are miserable, sick, victims of father or mother, prisoners of their conditions or their drives and addictions, puppets of what "people" think, "people" say, "people" do. Humans are less free than they are inclined to think. They are yoked in bonds of compulsions and obsessive ideas, mostly without its being clear who really is ruling over them. Whoever it is

must be vitally interested in keeping us as weak as possible, because that one's power stands literally on shaky ground. It depends on the servile, shaky weakness of many others, and their submitting to this power, supporting it, and putting up with it. And how much morality, how much religion consists basically only in instructions to adjust yourself to your weakness and powerlessness, to fit yourself into what is unavoidable. They want only to "strengthen" your resigning yourself to not being able to change anything in your whole situation. They want to "strengthen" your doing what you have to do anyway, with the least possible opposition. Perhaps such persons can content themselves because they are able to take care of a little garden on the side, or watch a talk show on TV. Maybe they sometimes assuage their feelings by secretly nursing a grudge against the one before whom they bow, by making "a fist in the pocket." One day they may even try a small uprising in which they replace a disliked X by a Y, so that they find their situation more bearable, without really having changed it.

Perhaps in no other petition as in this one is it so clear that we pray because God has "commanded us to ask" (Art. 118). For we weak ones, who are inclined to resign ourselves to our powerlessness, would not come upon the idea of praying urgently in this matter (once we have seen through our "early childhood fantasies of almightiness"). But since Christ puts this sixth petition in our mouth and commissions us to pray it after him, it dawns on us fully for the first time that our weakness and powerlessness, our bowing before those nameless powers and resigning ourselves to them, are not in order. By this petition Christ awakens us so that we rise up and take action against them. And in this petition there emerges before us in the mass of those nameless powers an apex that we can call by name. As God gives us the *divine* name so that we can call on God, so God gives us *this* name in order to renounce it: "the devil, the world, and our own sinfulness" (Art. 127). The devil is the concrete form in which evil encounters us as uncanny power. And it does so very dangerously, again and again in a different form and in such a way that it occurs to us not as evil, but as tempting, alluring, "a delight to the eyes" (Gen. 3:6). But its concrete form means at the same time that it includes within itself a total, closed system, built up consistently within itself (this is called "world"). This is a system that once we have fallen into it, will not let us go. And it is a system that, because of our being used to resigning ourselves to our powerlessness, we are able without inhibition to internalize (this is "our own sinfulness"). But in praying the sixth petition because God has commanded it, this internalizing begins to become questionable and to crumble. Then the three enemies become so outward for us that we can distance ourselves from them. With this we begin to attack the legitimacy of these very ones who "never stop attacking us"; yes, we rise up to "stand firm against" them (Art. 127). So we no longer put up with them, but find ourselves repelled by them.

In this petition we see clearly that we dare not keep in mind only "my" temptation and weakness, but always that of others as well. It is not only I who am attacked here; they are under attack too. In a given moment they may perhaps be even more so than I, and may be too weak to withstand all the pressure. When we pray this prayer, we pray for them and stand up for them, and see the pressure under which they stand. Therefore we do not accuse them, but understand the pressure as a heavy burden under which they struggle. So we put ourselves alongside them, together under their burden, and pray this way: "Lead us not into temptation, but deliver us from evil." In this way we are following, and will follow in what comes, the admonition: "Wake up and strengthen what remains and is on the point of death" (Rev. 3:2). In this way we begin to fulfill the "law of Christ" and to "[b]ear one another's burdens" (Gal. 6:2).

> If a weaker one should fall, the stronger one should give him aid; we seek to help and carry all. . . .[80]

For when we have prayed for them, we will also stand by them in a caring way, so that they do not fall farther, but get back on their feet, and take part in resisting as well. We need their participation in resistance for our own sakes too, and we need others to help as well, because we too, on the human plane, are not up to resisting that pressure alone.

"Only together are we strong" — or at least somewhat stronger. But this is not enough. Not only alone, but even together, we do not have the strength on our own to distance ourselves from those enemies and resist them. For such strength we ask God: "Preserve and strengthen us through the power of the Holy Spirit so that we may stand firm against them and not be defeated in this spiritual war until we gain the complete victory at last." Or in the words of G. Arnold:

> Thou of every bond the breaker . . .
> Look upon us in our chains, where we together with all creatures

---

80. From stanza 6 of the hymn "Kommt, Kinder, lasst uns gehen" ("Come, Children, Let Us Go"), by G. Tersteegen.

Cry and pray for your redemption . . .
Lord, demolish, break, destroy all deadly powers of tyranny,
Put them under righteous judgments: assure us of Thy victory . . .
Draw us into Thy true freedom, freedom in the Father's house . . .
Oh, the burden drives our pleading; all to Thee in hope we pray,
Show in grace the footsteps leading to the opened freedom way.
Grant that those at great cost ransomed, not by humans be
    enslaved . . .
Thou wilt not give up redeeming; let us not be lax today,
It will be as though we're dreaming when full freedom comes to stay.[81]

God has the power to hear this petition. As God is our God, who counts us worthy to have a say in divine matters, so we are also God's. "Through the power of the Holy Spirit" we are God's children, in whose journey, in whose misery and need God takes part. God has demonstrated that God is ours by humbling the divine self to us in the Son, to death on the cross. Then God has raised him from the dead and in him has lifted us into community with God, and so made us God's own people. In the Easter event, this is what God has presented to us: God's power, in which God does not lead us into temptation, but out of it; in which God does not make any pact with evil, but redeems us from it; in which God does not let "the devil, the world, and our own sinfulness" have sway, but spurns them, and so makes them "deadly enemies" (Art. 127). To be sure, they are not yet willing to admit defeat. But "he must win the battle."[82] God contends with these enemies *victoriously* — in a "spiritual war," one that we are in danger of losing and going down in (like Peter sinking into the sea), but that God now makes a *divine* concern, and that above all *God* leads. We are decidedly involved in this contest by praying that God will do this. *We* take part by setting our entire hope on God, in order to have "God, *my* stronghold" (Ps. 43:2, Jewish Study Bible; cf. 84:5). "The joy of the Lord is *your* strength" (Neh. 8:10). "Apart from me you can do nothing," says Jesus (John 15:5).

But in this way we *do take part* in this "spiritual struggle." In this way we, though weak, are not powerless, but rather "as dying, and see — we are alive" (2 Cor. 6:9). Since we "trust the Lord," we "find new strength," and "are strong like eagles soaring upward on wings," and we "walk and run

---

81. From the hymn with the title of the first line: "O Durchbrecher aller Bande."

82. From stanza 2 of the hymn "Ein' feste Burg ist unser Gott," by M. Luther. ET: "A Mighty Fortress Is Our God," in *LW* 53:285.

without getting tired" (Isa. 40:31). *God's* enemies become also *our* enemies. Because in lashing out at God they do not expel God, we do not have to "be defeated." Because God has spurned them, we too can issue them a refusal. Because God does not lead us into temptation, we can be sure in turning to God that despite all signs to the contrary God is leading us out of it. Because God "dominates the field," we too can be somewhat brave and can also stand some pressure. We do not have to let ourselves be pulled out of the fray easily. We can, though often stumbling and wounded, "stand firm against them . . . until we gain complete victory at last" (Art. 127). So we too are amazingly free: "whether . . . life or death or the present or the future — all belong to you, and you belong to Christ, and Christ belongs to God" (1 Cor. 3:22-23). So we too are *strong,* though we do not boast about our strength, as others do who show different kinds of strength. Our strength relates to and confesses itself to this: "for yours is the kingdom and the power and the glory forever." *This is why* we are so free that we have good courage: "because as our king having power over all things, you are both able and willing to give us all that is good." In the power of God's love, God will *and* can do it. For this reason, not our name, but "your holy name . . . may be glorified forever" (Art. 128).

What gives us confidence in the "spiritual war," what keeps us from dropping out and giving up, what lets us hold on and look up, is this: the world's throne is, praise God! not empty; and it is, double praise to God! occupied by none other than this God. God *reigns* — and *God* reigns: the "God with us." *God's* is the kingdom, the power, and the glory. God *alone* is to be praised. But God *does not want to be alone,* does not want to be without us, does not want to be without all creation. God does not want to let us go. God wants us to let go of what separates us from God. This truth is the eternal light. This is what shines on us and gives us light. This will one day shine fully into our hearts so that we see it clearly. And this truth is the "eternal gospel" (Rev. 14:6). This is surely so. This truth will one day surely let us join fully in affirming it, so that there is nothing left for us in all eternity but to praise God. Praise of God is the end of all the ways of God with us and with all creation. Even the community called out by God is not yet there. But it is on the way. It still cries "out of the depths . . . to you, O Lord" (Ps. 130:1). Yet it would not be the company of God's people if it would only sigh, if in the midst of all the sighing, struggling, and praying it would not already lift this song of praise. It has plenty of reason to do this. Praising God is already its calling.

Name Index

Adorno, Theodore, 123
Altner, Günter, 312n.49
Amery, Carl, 158
Anderson, Bernard, 113n.65
Anselm of Canterbury, 86, 95
Athanasius, 133
Augustine, Aurelius, 141, 224

Bach, Ulrich, 161
Barth, Karl, 3, 14, 15, 26, 41, 135, 213, 268
Ben-Chorin, Schalom, 132
Benedict of Nursia, 305n.43
Beza, Theodore, 13, 22, 24, 85, 86
Bizer, Ernst, 26n.41
Böll, Heinrich, 144
Bonhoeffer, 161, 173
Boquinius, Peter, 12
Brecht, Bertolt, 78, 310
Buber, Martin, 110, 121-24, 132, 274
Bullinger, Heinrich, 12, 13
Bultmann, Rudolf, 113

Calvin, John, 9, 12, 13, 17, 53, 66, 85, 125, 127-28, 131, 142, 148n.22, 157, 167, 178, 182, 192, 212, 233, 248, 250, 252, 280, 288, 290, 300, 308, 333
Camus, Albert, 315
Casimir, Johann, 18
Christoph, Duke of Württemberg, 17

Claudius, Matthias, 164
Cocteau, Jean, 6

Darwin, Charles, 139
Davidowicz, Lucy, 81n.43
Descartes, René, 156

Einstein, Albert, 139
Erasmus, Desiderius, 65-66
Erastus, Thomas, 13

Ferdinand I, Emperor, 15
Feuchtersleben, Ernst von, 49
Feuerbach, Ludwig, 2, 3
Frederick III, Prince, Palatinate Elector, 11, 18
Freud, Sigmund, 67

Gallus, Nicholas, 20
Gellert, Christian Friedrich, 154
Gerhardt, Paul, 187
Ginzel, Günther, 116
Goeters, Johann Friedrich Gerhard, 26
Goethe, Johann Wolfgang von, 34, 37, 66, 202
Gollwitzer, Helmut, 6, 124
Gutiérrez, Gustavo, 341n.75

Harnack, Adolf von, 87, 89-90, 113

Subject Index

animals, relation to God and to us, 156
Apostles' Creed, 138-257
atheism, 76, 169-71, 331
atonement, 116
    Anselm's doctrine of, 86-89, 94-99
    Luther and, 192
Augsburg Confession, 237-38, 244

baptism, 234-46
    doctrine of, 234, 243
    and faith, 237-38, 244-46
    and the Holy Spirit, 243
    of infants?, 243-46
    involves church membership, 234-24
    Reformation teaching on, 243-44
    sacrament of beginning membership
      in Christ, 241
Barmen Declaration, 61, 248, 256, 287,
    302
Bible. *See* scripture

Catechism, Luther's, 13, 17, 19, 60n.21
Catechism of Geneva, 13, 178
Christ. *See* Jesus Christ
Christmas, 178-80
Creator, 79-80, 138-50
    of body and soul together, 146
    continues to be precondition of our
      existence, 140-42

    of heaven and earth, 144-45
    love prior to creation, 147-49
    more than "original cause," 139
    of other creatures together with us,
      144
    out of nothing, 142-44
    precludes our presupposing God,
      141-42
    of reality different from God, 143-44
    of time, 141
church, 220-34
    body of Christ, 225-27
    bound with Israel, 228
    called out of world, 227-28
    calling of for mission in the world,
      228
    Christ as Head of, 222-25
    each member of Christ included in,
      236
    each member responsible part of,
      228-29
    ecumenical, 228
    as a fellowship of service, 226-27
    as a fellowship of sisters and broth-
      ers, 227
    and human differences, 230-33
    Jews and Gentiles in, 110-14, 231-32
    and kingdom of God, 220-21
    limits to fellowship, 227

Immanuel, 133, 168-71
incarnation of, 172-73, 178-80
Jew, 115-16, 179
King, 174-75
liberator, 52-53, 94-95, 100-108
Lord, 52-53, 57-60, 62, 100-101, 138,
    174, 204, 210
mediator, 23, 98-99, 102, 111-12
messiah, 111-16, 175-76, 188
names of, 174-75
obedience of, 106
our justification, 260
person and work inseparable, 172-75
Priest, 175
Prophet, 175
redeemer, 49-50, 68, 147
resurrection, 196-208
return, 207-8, 281
Savior, 39, 42-43, 52, 100, 146-48, 173,
    224, 278-80, 283
servant, 174-75
sinlessness of, 104-6
solidarity with sinners, 105-6, 186-87
Son of God, 172-73
teacher, 72
threefold office of, 172-78
two natures, 25-27
Way, 46-47
witnesses of resurrection of, 200-203
judgment, Calvin and, 280
justice, Calvin and, 333
justification, 258-66
    assurance of, 264-65
    completely sinner, yet completely
        righteous, 259-60
    does not lead to laziness, 264-66
    enables us to be free for others, 265-
        66
    frees me from trying to justify my-
        self, 261-62
    on ground of Christ's stepping in,
        259-60
    inability to justify myself, 263-64
    practical relevance, 261-66

Kingdom of God

conceptions of, 57-59
and Holy Spirit, 55-57
relation to church, 60-63
wideness, 58-60
Koran, 133

law of God
    dual purpose, 70, 86
    and gospel, 71-73
    inseparable from God's love, 72-73
    threefold use, 70-71
liberation, 94-95. *See also* deliverance
Lord's Prayer, 327-50
    for daily bread, 341-43
    forgiveness, 343-46
    hallowing God's name, 331-32
    help in temptation, 346-50
    seeking God's kingdom, 333-36
    two parts, 327-29
    yearning for God's will, 336-38
Lord's Supper, 246-56
    Christ's seal of fellowship with sin-
        ners, 251-52
    difference of Reformation from Ro-
        man Catholic teaching, 252-53
    importance of, 250
    meaning of, 250-51
    witness of Christ's grace and our
        thankful response, 253-54
love
    of enemies, 309
    and first table of Decalogue, 296-97
    for God, 296-307, 308
    misconceptions of, 309-10
    for neighbor, 307-19
    relation to love for self, 307-9
    and second table of Decalogue, 310

Mary, mother of Jesus, 178-80
monotheism, Calvin and, 131
moralism, 76, 256
Muslims, 125

National Socialism, 160
neighbor
    given by God, 308

love for, 307-19

pastoral care, 256
patience, 165-66
peace, 55, 63, 71-72, 312-14, 333
Pietism, 266
praise, 23, 24, 55-56, 284-85, 321-32, 323,
    350
prayer, 320-50
    act of maturity, 320-21
    belongs with work, 325
    carries out participation in three-
        fold office of Christ, 329
    confesses our neediness, 325-26
    heard by God, 321-22
    includes asking God to change
        things, 322-23
    most important expression of thank-
        fulness, 324-25
    recognizes our solidarity with others,
        326-27
    wanted by God, 323-24
providence, Calvin and, 157, 167

reconciliation, 26, 86-87, 125-27, 136-37,
    336-37, 343-46
redemption, 94-95
repentance, 269-73
    ongoing, 271-72
    opposition to, 269-70

sacraments. *See also* baptism; Lord's
    Supper
    action, rather than element, is sign,
        241
    belongs with proclamation of gospel,
        238
    Calvin and, 17, 250, 252
    and the cross, 242
    and Holy Spirit, 238-39
    relation to cross of Christ, 239-40
saints, 173
salvation
    from false bonds, 49-50
    to freedom in relationship, 43-47
    from self-centeredness, 40-43

limited to believers?, 235-36
    through the cross, 172-73, 178-81
sanctification, 209-10
    belongs with justification, 266
scripture
    Jesus as guide to use of, 6
    New Testament, 113, 115-16, 132-33,
        203-4, 290
    Old Testament, 109-14, 213, 268, 301-2
    relation of testaments, 109-18
    as witness, 5-6, 107-8
sin
    as bondage in alienation, 77-78, 94,
        142, 181
    as bondage to self, 78
    as bondage to things, 78-79
    doctrine of, 63-70, 73-87
    extent of, 187-90
    recognition of, 72-74
    redemption from, 190-95
    twofold form, 74-77
state, relation to church, 60-63
struggle of the soul, 194-95, 267-69

Ten Commandments
    First (no other gods), 298-300
    Second (no images), 300-303
    Third (honor God's name), 303-5
    Fourth (Sabbath), 305-7
    Fifth (honor parents), 311-12
    Sixth (reverence for life), 312-14
    Seventh (against adultery), 314-15
    Eighth (against stealing), 315-17
    Ninth (against false witness), 317-19
    Tenth (against coveting), 294-95
thankfulness, 164-65, 285-96
theodicy, 157-63, 179
theological instruction, Calvin and, 9
theology
    basic theme, 18-27
    of the cross, 182-95
    of liberation, 93
    method of thinking in, 3
    and natural science, 139-40, 144
    natural theology, 149-50
    object of, 1-2

oriented to Bible, 5-6
question and answer in, 2-3
self-criticism of, 170
task of, 1-9
time
 biblical concept of, 278-79
 future, 278-80
Trinity, 130-38, 171-72
 and grace, 135-36

Unitarian movement, 131

violence, 188, 312-13, 345

war, 313-14
women, Calvin and, 233
Word of God, incarnation of, 181
World War II, 295

Scripture Index